Language Management

Language policy is all about choices. If you are bilingual or plurilingual, you have to choose which language to use. Even if you speak only one language, you have choices of dialects and styles. Some of these choices are the result of *management*, reflecting conscious and explicit efforts by language managers to control the choices. This is the first book to present a specific theory of language management. Bernard Spolsky reviews current research on the family, religion, the workplace, the media, schools, legal and health institutions, the military, and government. Also discussed are language activists, international organizations, and human rights relative to language, and the book concludes with a review of language managers and management agencies. A model is developed that recognizes the complexity of language management, makes sense of the various forces involved, and clarifies why it is such a difficult enterprise.

BERNARD SPOLSKY is Professor Emeritus in the Department of English at Bar-Ilan University, Israel. His recent publications include *Language Policy* (Cambridge, 2004) and *Handbook of Educational Linguistics* (with Hult, eds., 2008).

Language Management

Bernard Spolsky

CAMBRIDGE
UNIVERSITY PRESS

CAMBRIDGE UNIVERSITY PRESS
Cambridge, New York, Melbourne, Madrid, Cape Town, Singapore,
São Paulo, Delhi

Cambridge University Press
The Edinburgh Building, Cambridge CB2 8RU, UK

Published in the United States of America by Cambridge University Press, New York

www.cambridge.org
Information on this title: www.cambridge.org/9780521735971

First published 2009

Printed in the United Kingdom at the University Press, Cambridge

A catalogue record for this publication is available from the British Library

Library of Congress Cataloguing in Publication data
Spolsky, Bernard.
   Language management / Bernard Spolsky.
      p.   cm.
   Includes bibliographical references and index.
   ISBN 978-0-521-51609-9 (hardback) – ISBN 978-0-521-73597-1 (pbk.)
   1. Language and languages–Variation.   2. Language
   policy.   3. Sociolinguistics.   I. Title.
   P120.V37S69 2009
   306.44'9–dc22   2008052012

ISBN 978-0-521-51609-9 hardback
ISBN 978-0-521-73597-1 paperback

For Ellen, with love, admiration, and gratitude

Contents

viii   Contents

Acknowledgements

The main purpose here is to acknowledge the contributions of my teachers, colleagues, and students to the writing of this book. Most of these will be clear in textual and bibliographical references, in particular the debt I owe to Joshua Fishman who has pioneered modern studies of language management and policy. It is also important to note the stated and unstated influence of colleagues with whom I have worked closely: Robert Cooper, Elana Shohamy, and Muhammad Amara in particular have played a considerable part in the development and shaping of my thinking. Strengthening the skepticism engendered by having my wife writing (E. Spolsky, 2001) in the next room, my doubts about inherent rights to try to control other people and their language have been further boosted by a summer reading Isaiah Berlin. Conversations with scholars and activists in the many countries I have been able to visit, thanks to a university policy that required me to retire from teaching while still able to write, have provided many examples of the complexity of language policy and attitudes to it. The three cases which I have been able to explore in detail (Israel, the Navajo Nation, and Māori regeneration) have encouraged me to see language in a fuller social and political context. And the conflicts, wars, diseases, starvation, slaughters, and environmental danger of the world in which I have lived have forced me to realize how small is the set of language problems that I have been able to work with.

Jerusalem, October 2006–February 2008

1 Towards a theory of language management

Language policy is all about choices. If you are bilingual or plurilingual, you have to choose which language to use. Even if you speak only one language, you have choices of dialects and styles. To understand the nature of this process, one needs an ecological model (Haugen 1987: 27) that will correlate social structures and situations with linguistic repertoires. Any speaker or writer is continually selecting features – sounds or spellings, lexical items, or grammatical patterns – which are significant markers of languages, dialects, styles, or other varieties of language, and which, bundled together, constitute recognized and labeled languages, like Navajo or English or Chinese, or more precisely, varieties of language like American English, or Midwestern English, or Cockney, or Indian English (Blommaert 2007), or what Blommaert (2008) refers to as "speech resources." One fundamental fact about named varieties is that they are socially or politically rather than linguistically determined. A dialect becomes a language when it is recognized as such: recently, the prime ministers of Romania and Moldova are reported to have argued (the former speaking in French and the latter in Russian) at an international congress over whether their two varieties were one language or two. The various Scandinavian languages are close enough for speakers of Norwegian to understand someone speaking Danish or Swedish (Delsing 2007; Doetjes 2007) but they consider them separate languages; the speakers of Chinese varieties cannot understand each other, but they all agree they speak Chinese. The differences between two varieties are critical, and because they are highly patterned, a listener notices them and tries to interpret them.

The goal of a theory of language policy is to account for the choices made by individual speakers on the basis of rule-governed patterns recognized by the speech community (or communities) of which they are members. Some of these choices are the result of *management*, reflecting conscious and explicit efforts by language managers to control the choices. My focus in this book is on this group, and my goal is to outline a theory that accounts for it.

The slow progress in the development of a theory of language management brings to light the difficulties faced by all social sciences in their endeavors to produce a satisfactory framework accounting for human behavior. In a recent essay Watts (2007: 489) explains:

Social phenomena involve the interactions of large (but still finite) numbers of heterogeneous entities, the behaviors of which unfold over time and manifest themselves on multiple scales. It is hard to understand, for example, why even a single organization behaves the way it does without considering (a) the individuals who work in it; (b) the other organizations with which it competes, cooperates and compares itself to; (c) the institutional and regulatory structures within which it operates; and (d) the interactions between all these components.

Watts suggests that the best way to capture this complexity is by using network analysis, but he recognizes the great difficulty in analyzing social networks which are not static, not unitary, and exist in a larger framework. Such analysis is currently beyond the state of the art in language policy too, but Watts' explanation does hint at the principal components that need to be taken into account: individuals, organizations, institutional and regulatory structures, and interaction. All of these will also be key elements in a theory of language policy and management. In this introductory chapter, I want to sketch a preliminary theoretical model. In the chapters that follow, I will apply this model to specific cases and data, which will lead in the course of the book to its modification and fine tuning.

The theory starts with a number of assumptions, which must themselves be open to testing and adaptation in the course of the exploration. The first assumption is that while language policy is intended to account for individual choices, it is, like other aspects of language, as Saussure (1931) pointed out, a social phenomenon, depending on the beliefs and consensual behaviors of members of a speech community.

What is a speech community? From its beginnings, sociolinguistics has avoided a precise answer to this fundamental question. Sociolinguists distinguished between a *language community* – all those who speak a specific variety of language – and a *speech community* – those who share a communication network, agreeing more or less on the appropriateness of the use of the multiple varieties used in that community. A language community as Hockett (1958) for instance used the term might be the English-speaking world, the complexity of which we realize since Kachru (1986) identified the many varieties which constitute World English, or the Francophone world (although *francophonie* is more a political than a linguistic concept), or at the other extreme, the last remaining speakers of a dying language. A speech community, on the other hand, may be a family, or a group of people who regularly use the same coffee shop, or an office, or a village, or a city, as Labov (1966) showed, or a region or a nation (Gumperz 1968).

Given this fuzziness, although I will regularly talk about speech communities, we need a more defined organizational unit. I will use the notion of *domain*, as introduced to sociolinguistics by Fishman (1972) in his classic study of the New Jersey barrio. Although he said that domains must be empirically defined for any specific community, Fishman laid down useful generalizations that I will adapt. First, a domain is named for a social space, such as home or family, school, neighborhood, church (or synagogue or mosque or other religious institution), workplace, public media, or governmental level (city, state, nation). In building a theory of language management, I will argue that each of these domains has its own policy, with some features managed internally and others under the influence of forces external to the domain. Language management in the family is partly under the control of family members, but its goals are regularly influenced by the outside community.

As defined by Fishman, a domain is distinguished by three characteristics: participants, location, and topic. The *participants* in a domain are characterized not as individuals but by their social roles and relationships. In the family domain, participants are labeled with kinship terms, like father, mother, brother, sister, aunt or uncle, grandfather or grandmother, or other appropriate roles such as maid or babysitter. In the school domain, the typical roles are teachers, pupils or students, or principals. In the workplace, they are bosses, employers, workers, employees, foremen, clients, and customers. In the government domain, they are legislators, bureaucrats, and citizens. Any individual of course may fill different roles in different domains, with conflicts sometimes obvious – how do I speak to my son at work if he is also my employer?

Secondly, a domain has a typical location – usually its name. Domains connect social and physical reality – people and places. Discomfort at the lack of congruity between participant and location – introducing my professor to my parents at home – signals the existence of norms. The physical aspects of the location are often relevant (a house only has space for a limited number of people, the countryside has fewer obvious places for signs than the city, the layout of a factory influences communication rules), but it is the social meaning and interpretation of the location that is most pertinent to language choice.

Fishman's third component is selection of topic – what it is appropriate to talk about in the domain. Gumperz (1976) has an illustration, showing how an employer and employee switch languages when they turn from business to social matters. In my model, this third component will be widened to include communicative function – what is the reason for speaking or writing.

Essentially I will be arguing that the regular language choices made by an individual are determined by his or her understanding of what is appropriate to the domain. Kymlicka and Patten (2003) recognize this when they distinguish between the internal usage of public institutions, the public services provided by these institutions, and private usage. My references to domains are admittedly imprecise (I haven't done the empirical work that Fishman suggested should be necessary), but they accord more or less with common practice. Nor do I attempt to consider all possible domains; most notably, I omit consideration of language management in adolescent groups or gangs.

A second assumption, presented in my earlier book (Spolsky 2004), is that language policy has three interrelated but independently describable components – practice, beliefs, and management. Language *practices* are the observable behaviors and choices – what people actually do. They are the linguistic features chosen, the variety of language used. They constitute policy to the extent that they are regular and predictable, and while studying them is made difficult by the observer's paradox that Labov (1972) identified – for an observer adds an extra participant and so modifies unobserved behavior – describing them is the task of a sociolinguistic study producing what Hymes (1974) called an ethnography of speaking. In one sense, this is the "real" policy although participants may be reluctant to admit it.

It is also critical to language management that language practices provide the linguistic context for anyone learning a language. Children's language acquisition depends in large measure on the language practices to which they are exposed. For example, immigrant parents are sometimes upset to find that their children do not know certain words in their heritage language, not realizing that they themselves regularly replace them in daily speech with words borrowed from the new language (Kopeliovich 2006).

The second important component of language policy is made up of *beliefs* about language, sometimes called an ideology. The beliefs that are most significant to language policy and management are the values or statuses assigned to named languages, varieties, and features. For instance, given the role played by language varieties in identification, the variety that I associate with my principal membership group – my nation, my educational class, my region, or my ethnic heritage – is likely to have the highest value for me, while some other varieties may be stigmatized. The status of a variant or variety derives from how many people use it and the importance of the users, and the social and economic benefits a speaker can expect by using it. Of course, beliefs are not practice: it may well be that I myself use stigmatized forms.

The third component of policy is language *management*, the explicit and observable effort by someone or some group that has or claims authority over the participants in the domain to modify their practices or beliefs. I use the term "management" rather than "planning" because I think it more precisely captures the nature of the phenomenon. Planning was the term used in the 1950s and 1960s in the post-war enthusiasm for correcting social problems; the subsequent failures of social and economic planning have discouraged its continued use. The two areas, health services and education, that still attempt centralized planning in western societies, continue to be problematic.

Nekvapil (2006), approving my use of the term "management" in Spolsky (2004), provides a useful explanation of the difference. The term language *planning* was developed in the 1960s for a process relevant to the modernization of developing countries gaining independence with the ending of colonialism. It was conceived of "as the concern of technical experts with efficient techniques at their disposal, as an objective process basically independent of ideology" (Nekvapil 2006: 92) and was modeled on the social and economic planning of the period. It was seen as "rational problem-solving," although it required approval of the political authorities of the state concerned. Over time, the greater complexity of language *engineering* (another term tried by some) was recognized, so that it would have to include "a broad range of different sociolinguistic situations at different levels of enlargement (from nation to firm), of a broad range of different interests and population groups (from women to refugees), under widely different communicative circumstances (of media, channels, information processing), and foremost, of the different ideological and real, global and local sociopolitical conditions" (Jernudd 1997: 136). This wider field was formally labeled "language management" by Jernudd (1987), freeing the term "language planning" to refer to the techniques of language-problem solving of the 1970s. To confuse the issue further, some scholars prefer "Language Policy and Planning," using the word "policy" as a synonym for "plan" and "planning" for the process of implementation. The difficulty is the ambiguity of the word "policy," for a language management decision *is* a policy.

For Neustupný, Jernudd, and Nekvapil, language management starts with the individual (they call this "simple language management"), while organized language management ranges from the micro (family) to the macro (nation-state) level. The most obvious form of organized language management is a law established by a nation-state (or other polity authorized to make laws) determining some aspect of official language use: for example, a requirement to use a specific language as language of instruction in schools or in business with government agencies. Another example is the decision of the Roman Catholic Church at Vatican II to change the centuries-old policy of requiring Latin for the mass. As with other aspects of language policy, management also applies to specific domains. In the family domain, efforts by immigrant parents to maintain their language constitute language management.

The theory assumes that each of these three components constitutes forces which help account for language choice. The language practices provide the models of language that help explain language learning and so establish the necessary conditions for language choice – language behavior is determined by proficiency; the beliefs explain the values that help account for individual choice; and the management may influence speakers to modify their practice or belief.

Each of these three components within (and, as we shall see, outside) the domain is relevant. Strongest of all in effect are language practices, for in their absence there is no available model and no proficiency. As no one in my home ever spoke Yiddish, I missed the early opportunity to learn it. The child brought up in a monolingual environment is denied the possibilities open to a bilingual. Proficiency in a language, whether spoken or written, sets a necessary limit for language choice, and provides a strong instrument for implicit language management.

The other two components are also crucial. My beliefs about the varieties of language from which I may choose, based on my perceptions of their use and users, help account for my management decisions: the different values assigned to standard languages and to heritage languages regularly explain decisions of parents as to what language to speak and encourage in the home, just as they explain government decisions on national language policy.

Management also accounts for many language choices, but it is not auto- matically successful. It presupposes a manager: the pressures produced by language practices and beliefs are different in that they may be authorless. Consider for example the argument as to whether the spread of English is the result of demographic and economic pressures, or the planned activity of an identifiable imperialist conspirator. As a rule, I will take the position that it is management only when we can identify the manager. I do not accept a simple argument of *cui bono*, the notion that because someone benefited from a development they must have brought about the situation. A number of scholars cite rhetorical statements in favor of a language as though they proved the existence of language managers, rather than the wishful thinking of politicians and language activists.

As a first step, the model I am building tries to account for language choices on the basis of internal forces, derived from language practices, language beliefs, and language management within the domain itself. But it regularly becomes clear that there are significant forces outside the domain. First, the fact that any individual is a participant in several levels of his or her community, that is to say, any individual has different roles in different domains – I am at once a parent, a neighbor, a congregant, an employer, and a citizen – means that I am familiar with the language practices and beliefs of a number of different domains, and may well have reason to favor the values of one domain when I am in another. The men from the Papua New Guinea village, who came home from working in the plantations and chose to speak Tok Pisin, provide an example (Kulick 1992); so did the Judeo-French speaking men who worked outside the Jewish community and brought into it the co-territorial Middle High German they needed as a prized ability, leading to the development of Yiddish (Weinreich 1980). Second, language management provides many examples of efforts to impose language practices on a lower domain, such as when an ethnic language revival movement or a school language policy tries to influence home as well as public behavior. This multilevel analysis helps explain some of the problems of centralized language management, which has to overcome practices, beliefs, and management at the lower levels. In our exploration of the significant domains, we will start with internal forces affecting a domain but also note obvious external pressures. Note also that these external forces are regularly extra-linguistic too: the New Guinea plantation system, the relations between gentiles and Jews limited to trade, the ethnic movements, the role of education, all affect language policy but are not linguistic. I am suspicious then of linguicentrism, the assumption that language is a central cause of human behavior.

The model entails a number of defined speech communities, social levels, and domains, ranging from the family through various social structures and institutions up to and including nation-states and supranational groupings, each of which has pressure for language choice provided by internal and external language practices, language belief systems and ideologies, and language management efforts. We will explore this model first at the fundamental level of the family or home, and move on up steadily to the national level and beyond. Of course, a domain is a generalization, made up from looking for common examples in many different cases. When I refer to the school domain, I am generalizing from a myriad of individual schools – the theory is not challenged by individual cases, but by its inability to account for the features of an individual case. We are working not with absolutes but with typicality conditions (Jackendoff 1983): a typical school has pupils and teachers, but schools in different societies vary in many ways.

This is an exciting and challenging time to attempt to write about language management, because we seem to be on the cusp of major changes. Three examples illustrate the dynamic complexity of the phenomenon. Ireland became independent at the beginning of the twentieth century on the shoulders of a language revival movement, but by the middle of the century, when it joined the European Community, it generously passed up on having Irish named as one of the official languages of the community. When, at the beginning of the twenty-first century, the European Community voted to expand by adding a dozen new countries each still insisting on its official language being used, nationalist sentiment was still alive enough for the Irish government to ask for Irish too to be added. The European Union agreed, and several million Euros were spent to translate official documents into the language and to provide interpreters for the few Irish officials and Members of the European Parliament who can use it comfortably. At the same time, the sociolinguistic reality has changed: few Irish politicians speak Irish fluently (and none do not know English), and Dublin is now a multilingual city, reported to have more speakers of Mandarin and of Polish than of Irish, so that its multilingualism makes the old bilingual problem seem outdated (Harris 2007).

The second example of what one might call divine irony concerns the Deaf. Slowly, Deaf communities in various countries are starting to achieve recognition for Sign language. It is recognized as a foreign language in many US state universities; it is an official language in New Zealand and a few other nations (South Africa is considering making it the twelfth constitutional language), and it is now widely accepted as a language for which civil authorities should be expected to provide interpreters. Just as this is happening, the cochlear implant is threatening to reduce the number of deaf individuals to a level which will not justify the services starting at last to be offered (Spencer and Marschak 2003).

The third example is provided by what Kymlicka and Patten (2003: 3) refer to as the "shock" of the sudden surge of ethnolinguistic conflict in eastern Europe. We shall see later (chapter 11) how western European organizations attempted to apply what they felt were agreed minimal standards to conflict areas in the Balkans, only to notice that language tensions have continued also to plague nations in the west (Belgium, Spain, Canada, Italy, the United States, and Switzerland).

There is then a critical time dimension to be taken into account, as sociolinguistic ecosystems change rapidly as a result of globalization, the contrary localization movement – the Long Tail (Anderson 2006) whereby in this world of mass culture, technological advances permit smaller and smaller groups to be served – the spread of English, the wealth of time or money that permits the retrieval of a moribund heritage language, and most critically, the massive demographic movements producing hugely complex multilingual urban areas (by 2008, the United Nations Population Fund reported on June 27, 2007, more than half of the world's population [about 3.1 billion people] will live in towns and cities). Between 1996 and 2006, the number of multilingual people in New Zealand increased by over 43 percent; in urban Auckland, over 25 percent were reported to be able to speak more than one language; and diversity of languages increased so that there are now significant numbers (over 20,000) of speakers of Mandarin, Korean, and Afrikaans. In 2007, a fifth of the children in the United States were reported to live with at least one foreign born parent; four out of five are American citizens; and nearly half speak English fluently and another language at home. It is no wonder that a theory of language management is taking so long to be developed or accepted, for the reality that it is expected to account for refuses to stand still. But as Fishman has remarked, the complexity of a phenomenon is not an excuse for not attempting to generalize about it.

A final point. This is a book about language management, and so focuses on language and linguistic issues. But it takes as a fundamental premise that it is not autonomous, but rather the reflex of the social, political, economic, religious, ideological, emotional context in which human life goes on. To talk, as some do, about language policy victimizing minorities ignores the fact that language differences account for only a tiny part of prejudice, injustice, and suffering.

2　Managing language in the family

Managing speech and linguistic communities

Students of language management commonly deal with the activities of the state or nation, perhaps considering it the sole "centering institution" (Silverstein 1998: 404) or, more cautiously, one of the most central of such institutions (Blommaert 2005: 396). Silverstein himself recognizes "local linguistic communities" to be groups of people "by degree evidencing allegiance to norms of denotational (aka 'referential,' 'propositional,' 'semantic') language usage" (1998: 402). He contrasts local communities with global processes such as formation of empires and nation-states, the growth of global economies and communication, and the emergence of diasporization of people with multiple cultural allegiances. Blommaert, in his study of language management in Tanzania, notes the inadequacies of state language planning when it came up against the forces at the local level, on the one hand of "transnational centering institutions" such as capitalism, democracy, and transnational ideas of prestige, and international educational models on the other. These supranational institutions assign values to the elements and clusters of elements that define language varieties, and so help account for the nature of language practice, language attitudes, and the motivation and effect of language management at the national level. Understanding the nation, then, requires recognizing forces that impinge on it from above and below. This is the goal of this book.

The many levels at which language policy occurs is a partial explanation of "unplanned language planning," a concept proposed by Baldauf (1994) and developed further by Kaplan (1997: 298) and by Eggington (2002) to account for what goes wrong in language policy. The first example that Eggington (2002: 4) cites is "a formal language plan" that does not take into account "existing unplanned language plans with the social ecosystem." For my own part, I would rather explain these as resulting from the fact that a higher socio-political level such as a central government producing plans or policies does not allow for policies that exist at other levels, such as the business world, the religious institution, the family, or supranational institutions.

Obvious examples are the problem created by the fact that Irish language management ignored the socio-economic reality of the Gaeltacht (Ó Riágain 1997), or that fifty years of Malaysian government efforts to establish Bahasa Melayu as a national language in official and educational domains did not prevent the continued spread of English in the Malaysian business world (Gill 2005). Williams (2008) insists wisely on a holistic approach to language policy; I have argued against what I call a linguicentric approach that fails to include the non-linguistic context. When I read about the political, economic, social, and health status of many African nations – the killings and starvation in Darfur and the Congo, the spread of HIV – I commonly wonder how we can try to concentrate on their failure to teach in local languages (Djité 2008).

In what follows, then, I shall be looking at domains (social or political levels or institutions) one by one, attempting to ascertain their language management activities and their results. Initially, I will explore an assumption that policy at this level can be studied as though it were autonomous, but I will inevitably be forced to recognize the complex interaction and virtual co-construction with other levels. For example, the family may be seen to reflect the ineffectiveness of more centralized management: witness the concern expressed about unwillingness to speak Māori in the family delaying the accomplishment of language revival (Te Puni Kokiri 2001, 2002). Or schoolteachers may complain about families that hamper their children's progress by continuing to speak the heritage language.

The individual and "simple management"

My definition of language management in Spolsky (2004) assumed a manager attempting to modify the language practices (or beliefs) of others. There is, however, an argument to be made for starting the process at the individual level, as in the theory of language management developed by Jernudd and Neustupný (1987). Language management for them starts when a speaker notes that his or her discourse deviates from the norm, however slippery that may be to define in a bilingual situation (Haugen 1987: 35ff.). "The starting point of language management theory is the identification of language problems by everyday speakers in the course of communication" (Nekvapil 2007). The individual speaker, noticing the inappropriateness or inadequacy of a choice he or she has made, may set out to self-correct. Immediate modification is equivalent to the speech accommodation within a specific discourse studied by Giles (1973) and many others since.

One illustration is the way an immigrant tries to avoid newly borrowed words when speaking to someone from the homeland, or the way someone self-corrects and self-censors when returning home from a period in the army or at an institution. Here is a journalistic account of the process written by a US Marine returning to civilian life:

It's been over three weeks since my last hair cut, and the urge to get it cut again is killing me . . . Less frequent haircuts have been just one small part of my adjustment to the civilian workforce. Changing my vocabulary has definitely been the largest adjustment. I was reading a tape measure at work a couple weeks ago and accidentally rattled off an incorrect number to my co-worker who was compiling the data into a table with a pencil. Needing to correct the error I quickly said, "As you were," which in the Marine Corps means, "Ignore what I just said; here comes a correction." Quickly realizing that phrase was only slightly clearer than speaking Arabic I back-tracked again and said "neg . . ." I got the first syllable of "negative" out of my mouth before I thought to myself, "What is wrong with you? First, you've never been taught to use the word 'negative.' Second, is it possible for you to speak like a normal human being for just a moment, or are you incapable of that?" Responding to my own criticism my next verbal utterance was "Damn it!" Now I was swearing, which I know isn't as acceptable at work as it was in the Marine Corps, so I was digging further yet into this self-induced black hole of vernacular. I said to myself "O.K. Just stop, take a breath, and recock . . . damn it! I did it again (recock)." At this point you're probably thinking, "He must have been lying in his previous blogs, because he's obviously got a lot of war-related mental issues." All of the above transpired within a couple seconds after which my co-worker asked, "What does that mean . . . what you just said?" In an interesting turn of events it seems my Marine Corps vocabulary is a curiosity to others as well as a personal cross to bear. Nobody seems to be bothered by my use of "check," "roger," or "out," although if I ever strung them together into "Check Roger out!" I would definitely get some strange looks. I have settled into keeping obvious and familiar words as part of my vocabulary, at least for the short-term. Some of them are more descriptive, and in my opinion, better. Take "roger" for instance. If I reply "O.K." to a question or statement, that could mean anything. If I reply, "roger" that means I understood what was said and what tasks it implies for me. Perhaps one day my neurons will link that thought to the phrase "O.K." – but probably not anytime soon. (Jeffrey D. Barnett, "Of (Marine) language," *New York Times*, June 26, 2007)

The individual self-correcting in discourse exemplifies simple management. Organized management is where the prospective manager notes the existence of language problems in a situation for which he is in some way responsible, evaluates the phenomenon, and may choose to plan for and implement an adjustment. Organized management differs from simple in that there is more than one participant (one party managing and the other managed), there is discourse about it (it is explicit), and "thought and ideology intervene" (Neustupný and Nekvapil 2003). A teacher correcting an Anglicism in the French spoken by a student in the class is an example. In much the same way, governments undertake organized management to deal with what they evaluate as negative language problems.

I find this model attractive because it requires that we focus attention on the initiator of the management and avoids the trap of concentrating on results without determining their causes. In other words, contrary to the traditional disinterest in agency – in the "actors" that Cooper (1989: 98) drew attention to – the question of who does the managing or planning is critical (Baldauf 1982).

Nekvapil (2006) criticized my earlier (Spolsky 2004) decision not to deal with the simple discourse-based management of a speaker's own usage. One reason I passed over this level was that one must either guess the implicit motivation of the surface behavior or carry out a post-event interview, as Nekvapil (2006) did, or rely on self-conscious accounts like the ex-Marine that I have just cited. Any self-correction in speech, or repetition or completing a sentence after a pause, or code-switching to work around an unknown word or phrase is *prima facie* implicit recognition of a language *problem*, and presumably a potential cause for remediation. But there are many complications. Berry and Williams (2004), for example, describe a classic situation: a British school recognizes the linguistic problems of its overseas students, and provides EFL courses to deal with them, but interviews later reveal that the students themselves recognized three overlapping sets of problems: linguistic, socio-cultural, and affective. One needs to set up either a theory of norms (how do I recognize my problems?) or adopt a more elaborated form of speech accommodation theory (Robinson and Giles 2001). Also, as one would expect in a Prague School approach, the concentration is on issues of language cultivation (how well can I perform in the standard variety?) rather than of choosing one variety over another, which is my main focus.

Adding recognition of inadequacies in one's own linguistic proficiency is then a useful if complicating step. It reminds us that organized management (a teacher's corrections, a government regulation, the academy proposal of an acceptable term) is only successful when it leads to changes in the language practices of the individuals who are targets of the management, so that evaluation (a rare activity in the field) must depend on changes in practices.

A word about the "micro/macro" level distinction, for there is fuzziness in the application of these terms. Kaplan and Baldauf (1997: 117) distinguished between the macro level, meaning national and above, and a micro level, meaning smaller organizations. They also use the term "meso" for intermediate levels like local government (Kaplan and Baldauf 1997). Mac Giolla Chríost (2006) uses "micro" for anything below the national level in Ireland, while Marriott (2006) distinguishes between university- or faculty-level planning which she calls "probably meso" and the provision of language support to individuals which she considers micro. All of these scholars agree on a range of situations, as I do, forming a continuum from individual to supranational, and agree the drawback of limiting concern to the national level. And all recognize that the tendency to deal only with the level of the nation-state produces a distorted picture of language policy and management. For these reasons, I start with the family.

Managing language in the family

Calvet (1998) in his book on "language wars" describes the family as a "battlefield." It certainly reveals some of the fundamental elements of management. When two people establish a regular relationship, one of the features governing their normal practices is the choice of a language variety. In many cases, although such cases are becoming less common with the increasing multilingualism of communities, both partners will have similar sociolinguistic backgrounds, with minor linguistic variations accounted for by demographic factors such as age, gender, and level of education. In the normal state of affairs, then, they are likely to speak to each other using much the same language and dialect, modifying their speech according to the stylistic situation and the presence or absence of other people. Again, in a normal situation, neither will wish to alter or manage the language practices of the other, although there will presumably be common cases of simple language management when a speaker notes that he was not heard or has difficulty expressing a notion. When there are systematic differences in their original varieties of speech, it is probable that over time they will influence each other, through *accommodation*, to move closer (Giles *et al.* 1973). For example, I now produce a flapped "d" in words like "butter," under the influence no doubt of my wife's dialect. As she never encouraged me to do this, this was not organized language management, but simply a normal effect of sociolinguistic environment on language practice.

But this suggests situations in which organized management might naturally occur. Assume that one partner has grown accustomed in school or the army to regular use of profanity; if the other partner has been brought up to dislike profane language, it may well be that he or she sets out to modify the partner's language by discouraging swearing. This is a basic example of organized language management: one member of the family speech community attempting to correct the language practice of another. A more extreme case is described in the following news story:

Jeddah, 2 December 2006 – An Egyptian woman filed for divorce from her husband, a doctor, because he would not speak English with her, the daily *Al-Ahram* reported yesterday. The woman, a graduate of the American University in Cairo and a translator by trade, said she wanted a divorce even though her husband was wealthy and generous.

The effort to control the language of other family members, especially children and especially to avoid obscenity and profanity is common, with success varying according to the nature of family relationships (Spolsky 2004: 17). An associated tendency, deriving from beliefs about language correctness and purism, is the efforts of parents to have their children speak in what they believe to be the standard or correct form of the language.

What gives *authority* to manage? Authority is perhaps a weaker word than its closest synonym, *power*. A textbook on business puts it like this: "**Authority** is the legitimate power of a supervisor to direct subordinates to take action within the scope of the supervisor's position." In introductory political science courses, authority is defined as rightful power (Brown 2003). How does this fit a theory of language management? I have somewhat begged the question by talking about the manager's belief that he or she has authority to modify some else's language beliefs and practices. If in fact the manager lacks that authority, the management will be unsuccessful. Following Berlin (2006), I might ask whether anyone has the right to control the language of others. It seems that success in language management is more likely in a totalitarian situation, where the power of the state is wielded indiscriminately, than in a liberal democracy. I will return to this troubling question from time to time; like the recognition of the significance of non-language factors, it tends to undermine the underlying premise of this book.

In marriages where the two partners each speak two different languages natively the issue is more complex. Exogamous marriage is required in some traditional societies, but linguistically mixed marriages have become even more common as a result of increased contact of populations caused by urbanization, migration, military occupation, tourism, trade, and study abroad. The resulting patterns are complex. Cheng (2003) traced five generations of her own family, three of whom had exogamous marriages. Her great-grandmother immigrated to Malaysia from Thailand and married a migrant from China; with no common language, the couple learned a pidgin variety of Malay to speak with each other and their neighbors. Their daughter married an Englishman, acquired Pidgin English, but spoke to her own children in Thai and Cantonese also. One of her daughters in turn married a migrant from China, a native speaker of Hakka, who had learnt Mandarin, English, and Malay. The couple spoke to each other in Cantonese, but used English with business clients.

Other things being equal, we might normally expect couples in a linguistically mixed marriage to establish a policy of continuing to speak to each other in the language that they first spoke. Spolsky and Cooper (1991) referred to this as the inertia condition: once we start speaking to someone in a certain language, it is easier and more natural to continue using the same language, and it may be uncomfortable to switch. In an informal survey of bilingual Israeli married couples, we found support for this. If a couple had met in an English-speaking environment, they continued to use English between themselves even when they had settled in Israel. If they had met in a Hebrew-speaking environment, such as in a Zionist youth movement in the Diaspora or in the Israeli army, they commonly used Hebrew to each other even when they shared another stronger language.

This brings us to the classic case, increasingly common, of language use decisions faced by couples moving from one country to another or moving from the countryside to a city. Perhaps couples are too small a unit, especially because there is no obvious internal authority, so consider a traditional nuclear family with children. The process here is language socialization, defined by Garrett (Garrett and Baquedano-Lopez 2002: 341) as the way that "younger children and other novices, through interactions with older and/or more experienced persons, acquire the knowledge and practices that are necessary for them to function as, and be regarded as, competent members of their communities." This definition is neutral as to management, allowing for non-directed as well as directed acquisition. It is organized management when the older persons consciously attempt to control the sociolinguistic environment by selecting a language to speak with each other or with the children, or give explicit instruction.

It is common for parents and caretakers to take for granted their authority to manage their children's language. Across cultures, caretakers have regularly been observed giving explicit instruction to children on what to say and how to speak (Ochs 1986). Basotho children are encouraged to speak and prompted for politeness (Demuth 1986): teaching a child how to talk is a major responsibility of mothers and other care givers. Among the Kwara'ae, three- to five-year-olds "undergo intensive instruction on how to speak and behave, with heavy dosages of imperatives, corrections, and explanations for behavior" (Watson-Gegeo and Gegeo 1986: 19). A few cultures seem not to accept responsibility for the language of children. Parents in a village in Papua New Guinea had such little interest in the speech of their children that they were surprised when Kulick (1992) told them their children were no longer using the village language but had switched to the Tok Pisin they themselves used only in code-switching. Traditionally, Samoan parents left speaking to children to their older siblings. Navajo parents that were interviewed said that it was up to their children to decide for themselves if they wanted monolingual or bilingual instruction (Spolsky 2002b); this reflected a fundamental Navajo disrespect for authority (Young 1978). However, it is commonly assumed that couples are responsible for the language of their children. King and Fogle (2006) asked a sample of well-educated, mainly professional bilingual couples living in the Washington DC metropolitan area, some English-oriented and some Spanish-oriented, how they arrived at their language policies. On the whole, the main explanation was their personal experience, but they did cite their reading and other people's experience. They all thought bilingualism was good and saw their task as good parents to be producing bilingual children. The 39th Annual Phi Delta Kappa/ Gallup Poll (http://www.pdkintl.org/kappan/kpollpdf.htm) found that the majority of respondents believed their children should spend more time in school learning about other nations; 85 percent agreed that learning a second language was very or somewhat important, and 70 percent that instruction should begin in elementary school.

In the nuclear family, the decisive choice in language policy is determining what language the child or children should speak. This decision, referred to technically as *natural intergenerational transmission* of the language, is considered by many to be the crucial factor in language maintenance (Fishman 1991b). In a pioneering essay by Stewart (1968), the feature of *vitality* was defined as speaking the language to one's offspring; in Fishman's (1970) perceptive reformulation, it was defined as *believing* that the language should be spoken to one's offspring. Vitality is the crucial characteristic of a living language. In language revival efforts, *revitalization* (Spolsky 1989) occurs only when this happens. Those who argue that Irish revival has been unsuccessful are referring particularly to the failure to restore natural inter-generational transmission, leaving the maintenance of the language to formal schooling (cf. Dorian 1987).

A key aspect of this policy is control of the home language environment. Even in the absence of explicit instruction, conscious control of the linguistic environment can be an effective method of managing the language social-ization of children. Lower-middle-class families in Antwerp avoided use of local dialect features when speaking to children to help them learn more standard speech which would prepare them for school (Houwer 2003). When both parents speak the same language, management becomes an issue only when they wish the child to speak another language. When both parents are plurilingual, however, a much wider choice opens up. William Mackey (personal communication) once told me how he and his wife arrived at their decision. Mackey is a native-born speaker of American English, his wife a native speaker of what linguists used to call Serbo-Croatian. Living in French-dominant Québec City, they felt confident that their children would pick up French without difficulty from the immediate environment: in fact, they reported that the children developed three varieties – Parisian French to play with the children of the French consul, educated Québec French for school, and *joual* (Québec French) for playing with their neighbors. Nor would English be a problem because of its dominance in North America. They decided therefore to share with the children their common proficiency in German. English-speaking friends of ours in Jerusalem hired a Russian speaker to look after their children who were growing up comfortably bilingual in English and Hebrew so as to add a third language. Recent newspaper stories speak of salaries of $60,000–$100,000 paid to Chinese nannies by New York parents who want their children to speak pure Mandarin.

One common practice for bilingual parents is to decide that each should speak their preferred language with the child. This follows the belief that young children will learn a language more easily if it is associated with a specific speaker. Some immigrant parents make a strong effort to continue to speak their heritage language with their children. Others, often with regrettable results, hope to help the children adapt more quickly to the new linguistic environment by speaking an inadequate and limited foreign version of the new language in the home.

The home language choice is influenced by the sociolinguistic ecology inside and outside the home and by the parents' beliefs about the best strategy. As long as there are only two adults and one child in the home, matters are fairly straightforward. One regular complication is the presence in the home of another significant person, perhaps a grandparent or member of an older generation, who is taking longer to acquire the new language or who is more committed to it. Sakamoto (2006) studied six Korean-American families in the New York metropolitan area, in each of which there was a young child and a grandparent: the parents rightly expected the grandparents to provide their child with access to the heritage language and culture. When I first came to Israel, I spent a weekend in the home of a classmate at the Hebrew ulpan where we were students. Her family was from Tunisia; her husband's parents spoke mainly Tunisian Arabic and very little French; her husband was fluent in Arabic, French, and Hebrew; and she knew little Arabic, was fluent in French, and was learning Hebrew. Their six-year-old son was learning Arabic from his grandparents, speaking Hebrew with his father, and French with his mother, except when they were at the school across the road from their house: his mother was a schoolteacher, and used only Hebrew there. This kind of switch of language when changing role and location is further support for the notion of domain. Variation according to interlocutor is common. Malays over the age of sixteen said they preferred to use Malay inside the family, only Malay when speaking to grandparents, most of the time when speaking to their parents, but with siblings they spoke in English and Malay equally (Burhanudeen 2003). Chinese-speaking immigrants in New Zealand switched to Chinese in order to include grandparents in conversations they were having with their children (Ng and He 2004).

The birth of additional children changes the home environment, as does the eldest child going to school. As soon as a child starts to come under the social and linguistic pressure of school and peers, he or she commonly brings the new language into the home, speaking it sometimes to the parents and regularly to siblings. Among Russian-speaking former Soviet immigrants to Israel, we regularly found children to be the source of Hebrew in the home (Dittmar et al. 2002). As a whole, the million Russian-speaking immigrants to Israel show strong loyalty to Russian language, literature, and culture; the adult generation maintains Russian as their preferred language for social interaction and culture, long after they have developed adequate proficiency in Hebrew to handle civic and professional activities. They also provide afternoon schooling in Russian for the children. Most of their children have nonetheless switched to Hebrew, and regularly respond to their parents' Russian by speaking Hebrew. With their bilingual peers, there is a good deal of code-switching (Donitsa-Schmidt 1999; Kopeliovich 2006).

As long as parents maintain authority, they can sometimes expect children to comply with the policies they favor. A great deal depends on the status of the parents and of the language. For instance, English-speaking parents in Israel are more successful in maintaining the language with their children than are speakers of other languages; this derives both from the status of English, its use in media (TV, computers, popular songs), and from the higher educational and economic level of English speakers. Thus, external domains enter the home by changing values assigned to language and varieties.

Parents or peers?

An important question is whether children are more influenced by their parents or by their peers. In terms of language management theory, one is asking about the relative strength of domain internal and external influences: parents belong to the family domain, but peers belong to the neighborhood or school domain.

Believing in the greater power of peers, Harris (1995) argued that the most effective technique for parents to manage the social attitudes (including attitude to language) of their children is to make sure they associate with peers with acceptable values. In other words, the selection of a neighborhood (and consequently of a school) is a critical aspect of family language management. The children living next door or down the road are virtual participants in the home domain.

There are other pressures for families to live in neighborhoods that share their values. First, urban housing patterns tend to cluster houses of a similar price together, creating homogeneity of income and wealth. Second, in some cultures, there is a strong tendency for extended families to live close to each other (Milroy 1980). Third, the selection of a neighborhood is influenced by the availability of valued institutions – religious institutions like schools or churches, synagogues, and mosques, social and sports clubs, or commercial enterprises selling heritage foods. Fourth, people migrating from a village or countryside to the city commonly seek to live close to family members or people from the same area. In this way, the neighborhood often mirrors the family domain in its language policy. In new suburban areas, homogeneity is common: in the city, ethnically or religiously marked boundaries develop. In such cases, the gap between the home domain and the neighborhood may well be small, but for many new immigrants, the neighborhood may represent a first connection with the outside world for children, as they play with neighbors who speak the dominant language and have already adopted the dominant values.

Harris (1998), arguing for the strength of peer pressure, cited in particular the speech of the children of immigrants in their parents' language, which was commonly marked by the same non-native accent their peers would have had if they learned the immigrant language. Once children start spending time outside the home, the external influence starts to dominate and determines a cluster of attitudes as well as language practices. In a study of immigrant former Soviet families in Israel, Kopeliovich (2006) found that some children appear to be more susceptible to internal influences and others to external influences: the one family in which she found strong Russian maintenance had only two children.

The interplay of internal and external influence is shown in a long-term case study of an English–French bilingual family in Louisiana (Caldas 2006). The mother was a native French-speaking Canadian and the father a native English-speaking American; the couple decided to learn each other's languages and to raise their three children in a predominantly French-speaking home, watching only French language TV. They spent summers in Québec in a totally French-speaking social environment. The twin girls were enrolled in a partial French immersion program in Louisiana; the son had one semester. The data for the study – the proportion of English and French words in random excerpts of tape recordings of family meals over several years – show considerable variation, with high correlation between the three children. The adults spoke more French than English, with the father's utterances dropping at times, but never below 75 percent. The children's use of French peaked at the beginning of the immersion program and during the summers spent in Québec. French decreased in the fall when they returned to Louisiana. The girls' use of French remained higher than the boy's. As the children grew into adolescence, pressure to conform to peers appeared to mount. During a school year in Louisiana, the boy virtually stopped using French at the table. When they were in Québec, his preference for French returned, and on one occasion he criticized the father for speaking English in public. Given that the children were equally fluent in both languages, it was the external environment rather than the parents' practices and desires that accounted for their changing language preferences.

In a longitudinal study of a community of immigrants to Israel from the former Soviet Union, Kopeliovich (2006) has clarified the seeming contradiction between Harris' urging of the major influence of the peer group and Fishman's insistence on the critical importance of the family decision, showing the contribution of each. Most adults in the community she studied expressed strong support for the maintenance of heritage Russian language and literature; almost all children developed dominance in Hebrew, maintaining varying levels of proficiency in Russian and various degrees of loyalty. Using a code-switching model based on Myers-Scotton (2002), Kopeliovich divided the children into three main groups: a small group of fluent Russian speakers, able to function effectively using Russian somewhat more marked for Hebrew influence than their parents'; a majority group showing attrition and interference in their Russian but capable of conducting a useful conversation; and a group of vestigial Russian speakers, virtually unable to take part in conversations. These classifications were dynamic rather than stable, and changing circumstances (leaving home for boarding school or the army, a visit to Russia) could modify them rapidly. A number of different factors helped account for individual proficiency. Those children who were born and started their education in Russia were more likely to be in the middle group than those who were born in Israel or came at a very early age. A conscious return to heritage values and special efforts to improve language ability, or a small closely-knit family committed to maintenance, were required to reach the top group. First-born children were more likely to maintain Russian than their younger siblings, although there was a widespread practice of speaking Russian to babies.

Noting the strength of these demographic variables, Kopeliovich asked whether there was room for explicit management policy to have any effect. Maintaining even a reasonable level of Russian knowledge and proficiency took a great deal of effort on the part of concerned parents faced with conflicting demands on time and emotional energy. Parents reported disappointment when their children rejected their efforts to provide books or other material in Russian or to arrange private Russian lessons. Less obtrusive indirect methods (reading books to the children for instance) proved to be more effective. Successful management also depended on neutralizing peer-group influence, either by working with the child alone or coming up with some activity that interested other members of the peer group. The usual pattern of adults speaking Russian and children, responding in Hebrew was inadequate to deal with difficult emotional issues. Much parental distress seems to have been the result of unrealistic goals: the children's Russian was commonly considered unsatisfactory because it included many Hebrew-influenced features that they had learnt directly from adult speakers. Evidence for the value of parental maintenance efforts came from the fact that in those families where the children showed the lowest level of proficiency, the parents had given up completely. To sum up, just as when swimming against a strong tide, it seems to take a serious effort to maintain a modest level of success.

Further evidence of the importance of cooperation between home and community comes from studies of East Asian immigrants in the United States

(Kondo-Brown 2006). Studying the home literacy practices of Chinese immigrant families, Li (2006) found that both parents and the ethnic community were influential, but that the success of their efforts at language maintenance was seriously damaged by lack of support from the school. Comparing a small number of fourth- and fifth-grade school children attending bilingual programs in the United States with a small group of Japanese children attending an English immersion program in Japan, Hayashi (2006) concluded that home, school, and community were all relevant to developing bilingualism. Stressing the importance of school and community, Chinen and Tucker (2006) noted the language effects of attending Saturday Japanese supplementary school on Japanese immigrant children in California.

As long as the home domain is closed, parents have the power to manage the language of their children, but once it becomes open to the outside pressures of peers and school, the family becomes the site of language conflict that reflects conflicts in the outside society, with children often rejecting their parents' language. Calvet gives examples of this process in Senegal, where children were shifting from the home language to dominant Wolof, in Mali, where they were moving from minority languages to the dominant Bamba, and in Niger, where they were adopting the dominant Zarma and Hausa; he found the same pattern in a small town in France where 27 out of 41 immigrant children were bilingual in French and their parents' language, while the rest claimed to speak French only, although in interviews they admitted they could speak to their parents in the immigrant language (1998: 74). Other studies have shown the development of code-switching and new merged varieties among adolescents, suggesting again the importance of peer pressure (Marongiu 2007).

Family as target

As mentioned earlier, the home domain is significant because it is the critical endpoint in many language management activities. The revival of Hebrew depended crucially on the replacement of traditional and temporary school teaching of the language by natural intergenerational transmission, showing the acceptance by target language speakers that they must pass the language on to their children. Similarly, the limitation (or failure) of a number of other language revival movements, such as Irish and Māori, is the unwillingness or inability of parents to speak the language with their children who have been learning it in school. In a survey of the state of the health of the Māori language, Te Puni Kokiri (2002) asked why parents were not speaking Māori with their children. The most common answer was their own feeling of inadequacy and a related fear of being laughed at by older native speakers. Presumably, the enthusiastic young Zionists who started to stumble in Hebrew, speaking with their more fluent children, did not have to worry about a critical older generation who would complain, as in the case of revived Māori, Irish, and Breton, about the way they were changing the language (Spolsky 2002a).

Is there any obvious manager inside the family? From anecdotal evidence, there is a wide range of possibilities. Either parent in a nuclear family or both may be committed to the decision on which language they will speak and which language their children will speak. There is evidence of various kinds of internal as well as external influences. In the development of Yiddish, a key factor was the introduction of German into Judeo-French-speaking communities and homes on the part of men with successful and status-giving external contacts (Weinreich 1980). In a Papua New Guinea village, men who had worked on plantations brought back Tok Pisin (Kulick 1992). In an Arab village in Israel, the major source of Hebrew lexicon in speech was a father employed outside the village (Spolsky and Amara 1986). In the case of Māori, service in the army in both world wars appears to have encouraged a commitment to shift to English (Benton 1981). Children going to school are an important source of the external language.

There is disagreement over the relative influence of fathers and mothers: it seems to depend on cultural patterns. There is debate over differences in the Islamic world between women who are restricted to the home and men who go out for work and leisure (Abu-Haidar 1989; Amara 1996). In many *Haredi* "ultra-orthodox Jewish" homes in Israel, women speak Hebrew with their children; when at the age of six or so the boys go away to *yeshiva*, they learn to speak Yiddish like their non-working fathers (Baumel 2002). I have heard of a family whose patriarch insisted on the use of Hebrew while the family lived in Morocco, and was equally insistent on the use of Arabic after they immigrated to Israel.

Methods of managing the home language ecology

Once they have made up their mind, family language managers have a choice of methods. Obviously, the first and most potent is the decision on what language to speak. In the many myths surrounding Eliezer ben Yehuda and his contribution to the revival of Hebrew (Fellman 1973), a common story refers to his refusal to permit any language other than Hebrew to be heard in his home. There was said to be a "dumb" aunt, dumb because she could not speak Hebrew and was not permitted to speak in the presence of the children. If the parents are fluent in the language they wish their children to hear, this strategy can work. In language revival situations, however, where the parents themselves are second language speakers, it can involve considerable strain. In New Zealand, a strong supporter of Māori language revival (professionally involved in teacher training and later in policy development) told me regretfully that he found it difficult to speak to his children after they were seven or eight years old, as he lacked the control of language to do this easily.

In actual practice, many homes offer a complex sociolinguistic environment, with more than one language used and regular code-switching. Wei (2005) notes that studies of code-switching now regularly invoke concepts like power, authority, prestige, and gender but he argues that code-switching should be looked at rather as a conversational activity. Following this approach, Williams (2005) analyzed a family dispute between a mother and daughter who switched regularly between Cantonese and English, changing roles as well as languages, with the adult daughter frequently taking on an advice-giving and parental role. In the outside community of Chinese Americans living in Detroit, older members prefer Chinese and the younger prefer English, but looking at discourse, Williams found that the two participants frequently used the interlocutor's preferred language in order to modify and restructure the family relationship.

The first management strategy is control of the home language environment. A second strategy is bringing a speaker of the target language into the household, such as a relative from the old country, or a servant from the new. Another approach is arranging for young children to play with other children selected for their language knowledge. A Samoan adolescent in New Zealand complained to me that her mother would not let her invite a friend to stay unless they both promised to speak only Samoan. Related to this is control of radio and television: permitting or banning its use in the home depending on its language. Similarly, access to computers may be restricted for language management reasons.

In order to strengthen their language management activities, parents may seek outside support. This includes the establishment of language-motivated playgroups (institutionalized in New Zealand Māori language revival efforts such as the *Kōhanga Reo*), the setting up of language-oriented independent schools (in New Zealand, the *Kura Kaupapa* movement), and various efforts to influence government and government-controlled institutions. Harris (1998), believing that external environment is more important than the home, even suggests that the main influence parents can have is by choosing an appropriate environment for their children, which might involve moving to a neighborhood where there is support for family language policy. Fishman (personal communication) was one of a number of Yiddish language activists who bought houses on the same street in New York in the hope that their families could reinforce each other's language management.

Those trying to control the sociolinguistic environment may attempt to be absolute ("don't ever let me hear you speaking that other language!") or be determined by presence of certain individuals ("you must speak that language when your grandmother is here!") or restricted to specific times, such as reading a story in the language to the children before they go to bed, or setting a language to be used at certain times. Some orthodox Jewish families used to expect Hebrew to be used at family meals on the Sabbath. Note that in these cases we have moved from implicit to explicit language management. These explicit instructions can be reinforced by various kinds of punishment when they are not followed.

As with other cases of language socialization (see for example Bernstein 1971), explicit instructions may be accompanied by reasoned explanations ("I want you to speak Russian because it is the more cultured language") or based on appeal to authority ("Your father wants you to speak Yiddish") or simply asserted ("Speak Māori or keep quiet!"). Lacking detailed studies, we can only guess at the circumstances in which these various strategies have been adopted and their relative success, although Kopeliovich (2006) found evidence that less direct approaches seemed to succeed.

Home language managers

Where there is explicit language management inside the home, we can assume that it is to be accounted for by some belief or ideology on the part of the manager that comes from outside. The most obvious cases are language activists – people actively involved in language revival movements who recognize that language reform starts in the home (see chapter 10). A second obvious case but in the opposite direction involves individuals encouraging members of the family to assimilate into a new culture. Among Māoris, there appear to have been three distinct approaches (Spolsky 2003a). A common non-Māori attitude, accepted also by many individuals of Māori descent, favors complete assimilation. A survey (Te Puni Kokiri 2002) found that 12 percent of non-Māoris interviewed believed that only English should be used in New Zealand. Among Māori, 12 percent were uninterested in Māori culture. The assimilationist view has no problem with the loss of the Māori language. They blame any conflict on a small group responsible for making Māori dissatisfied with their position in New Zealand society (Nairn and McCreanor 1991). A second non-Māori view, shared by many Māori, is that New Zealand identity can best be achieved by amalgamation of the peoples and the development of a single blended and merged population, with appropriate adoption of some aspects of Māori culture and language by the non-Māori majority (Ward 1995). Amalgamationists are likely to be neutral, using the language themselves but not objecting very strongly when their children start shifting. Among Māori, the survey (Te Puni Kokiri 2002) classified two-thirds of the respondents as "cultural developers," people who were willing to share Māori language and culture with all ethnic groups. The third view accepts that Māori and non-Māori can live side by side with equal rights but with distinct social and cultural institutions and languages. About one-fifth of the respondents in the survey (Te Puni Kokiri 2002) were categorized as "Māori only" respondents who held that Māori language and culture should be the exclusive domain of Māori. These separatists insist on the revitalization of Māori as the living language of the Māori community, ideally a Māori that reestablishes the appropriate dialect for each *iwi* "tribe." Although there are variations in degree of separatism, it is these separatists who have generally played important roles in the language revitalization movement and have been willing to establish schools where only Māori is spoken.

Ideological influences on the home

Studies of language loyalty provide evidence of the nature and strength of the beliefs that affect family language management. Because of their methodology using questionnaires, the studies give details of group rather than individual behavior, but it seems not unreasonable to interpret them in order to guess at the factors that influence language managers within the family. The shift from Ryukyuan to standard Japanese depended on increasing acceptance of Japanese ideology recognizing the standard language as the "emblem of national unity, modernity, progress and development." The Ryukyuan language activists have generally been unsuccessful in fighting this ideology (Heinrich 2004: 162). An ethnic or language revival movement and its ideology constitute an important external influence on the home domain.

The nation-state too may seek to modify the language behavior and beliefs of its citizens within their homes. Under traditional Chinese imperial rule, scholars and government officials in Taiwan shared a common language but interpreters were employed whenever it was necessary to speak to illiterate common people. Starting with the Japanese conquest, Taiwan suffered from the imposition of various state language ideologies. Japanese was dominant until 1945 (Sandel 2003). In 1945, the Nationalists brought with them Mandarin and the European view of "one language, one nation." Sandel interviewed twenty-five Taiwanese who were bilingual in Mandarin and Tai Gi, the earlier Chinese variety spoken there. Many of the older participants recalled being punished for speaking their home language. In spite of the changed atmosphere, many young children were growing up as monolingual Mandarin speakers, their parents who had suffered from the school policy having decided to teach their children Mandarin. Some now spoke the local language with their children. Others, living in the countryside where there was still contact with grandparents, assumed that children would learn both languages without active teaching. The urban parents considered exposure to Mandarin through television a handicap, while the rural parents saw it as an advantage.

It was the ideology of the Zionist pioneers that accounted for their willingness to encourage their children to switch from the Yiddish that they spoke to the revernacularized Hebrew that they had selected as a new language of identity (Spolsky 1991b). For many of them, the Zionism came first – they had left their homes in eastern Europe and come to Ottoman-controlled Palestine, taking up agricultural work in the new farming communities. Mandel (1993) suggests that Zionist ideology preceded Hebrew language revival for Ben-Yehuda as well. The pioneers' choice of a new language, first for their children and later for themselves, was a grassroots ideological rejection of languages which carried negative associations. As Zionists, they rejected the Russian that their more internationalist contemporaries at the end of the nineteenth century were choosing, the German that some of their scientifically inclined fellow-Jews were learning as they moved west for education, the Turkish of their new rulers, the Arabic spoken by the people they found living in Palestine, and the Yiddish associated either with the traditional *shtetl* "small town" or adopted by the Jewish non-territorial cultural nationalists. Given the chance to influence the schools in their small farming villages, they encouraged the teachers, knowledgeable in traditional literary and religious Hebrew, but lacking fluency in it, to teach in the language. With the grasp of literary Hebrew that most Jewish men had, and with the quite rich Hebrew lexicon in the daily Yiddish vocabulary of both men and women (Glinert 1987), these ideologically motivated families were eager for their children to start speaking the new language at home as well as at school.

Similar enthusiasm was apparent among other groups concerned with language revival, but in no other case was there the same willingness to bring the language into the home. Even stronger ideological commitment was to be found in the next generation of Zionist pioneers: the members of the Second Aliyah who at the beginning of the twentieth century formed the first kibbutzim. This group went even further in the radical changes that they made in their style of life. They virtually did away with the family domain. All property was communal and all members of the group shared equally in the proceeds of their labor. All were committed to Hebrew and agreed on a common principle that it must be used on all public occasions, a principle still in operation in many Israeli communities where a heritage language is spoken in private. By its nature, almost all aspects of life on the kibbutz were in fact public. There was no privacy in the dining room or in the shower room, or even, in early days, in the bedroom where there was a third person. Most importantly, all children lived in the children's house, which was by definition a public place in which only Hebrew could be spoken. Only when alone together might a couple use the native language in which they could achieve greater intimacy. Whatever language they might be speaking when alone, as soon as one of the children came into the room, the parents would switch to Hebrew.

We have moved beyond the nuclear family into the community to show how wider support might be achieved for language management. It is true that the shift to Hebrew was not the only motivation for the development of the kibbutz: the communal dining room and children's house were originally a matter of convenience rather than of ideology, releasing women for other work, but it illustrates the importance of controlling the linguistic environment. Parents convinced of the importance of maintaining or shifting to a specific language can find support in this way.

As Calvet (1998) showed, the reverse assimilationist ideology is commonly stronger. It is regularly supported by a strong belief that only by developing proficiency in the dominant external language can one achieve reasonable economic success. In the case of immigrant or minority languages, it is regularly the case that the speakers of these languages are severely handicapped until they can gain access to the workplace. In the gripping essays that accompany his stark photographs of life in the tenements of New York in the 1880s, Riis (1971: 113) regularly draws attention to the problem produced by immigrants not knowing English, "ground by poverty until their songs have died in curses upon their oppressors, hopelessly isolated and ignorant of our language and our laws." This reminds us again of the need to look beyond language issues.

Ideologies are ultimately expressions of moral judgment. Authority is defined as the expression of rightful power, but how does one determine what is right? Shweder (1990) has suggested that there are three distinct moral ethics. The first is an "ethic of autonomy," protecting the individual. The second is an "ethic of community," aiming to "protect the moral integrity of the various stations or roles that constitute a 'society' or a 'community,' where a 'society' or 'community' is conceived of as a corporate entity with an identity, standing, history, and reputation of its own." The third is an "ethic of divinity," with a goal to "protect the soul, the spirit, the spiritual aspects of the human agent and 'nature' from degradation" (Shweder *et al.* 1997: 138).

It is useful to explore the relevance of this view to language management. The first is clearly behind the "Leave your language alone" philosophy of the structural linguists, and challenges any attempt at managing other people's language. The second is the approach of organized groups, at whatever level, justifying management for the good of the group. And the third will be found to show up not just in the domain of religion, but in the common demand for purity of language (valued as purity of body) among many traditionalists.

A model of home language choice

Treating language policy and language management in the home as a matter of choice, it is possible to apply the model that we proposed for analyzing the language of signs (Spolsky and Cooper 1991). A fairly simple set of conditional rules accounts for most situations. The first rule is to choose a language that you know. If all members of the household are monolingual speakers of the same language, there is no choice unless one speaker is prepared to go and learn a second language or unless use is made of external sources (classes or schools or time spent in the old country – many Samoan parents in New Zealand send their English-speaking children to Samoa for the summer to learn the language). A related phenomenon is the unwise choice of a weaker language, with immigrant parents using the new language inadequately and so providing a limited and limiting model to their children.

Given that there is a choice, various possibilities emerge, and a decision among them will depend on value judgments. In a household that respects authority, there is likely to be accommodation to the desires of the person with most authority, who can become the language manager. In immigrant situations, the weak status of the first generation immigrant *vis-à-vis* the new society gives an opening to children to try to dominate language choice. Confirming or conflicting with the effect of personal status, the status of the languages themselves is relevant. The ideological status of each language usually reflects its status in the wider community. A standard or literary or religious language commonly has priority over an unwritten vernacular or dialect, at least in the minds of those to whom economic and social success is important. Similarly, a national or official language has greater appeal than a local one. Especially since the spread of the Franco-German notion of "one nation, one language," and when in the modern globalized society this is supported not just by external institutions but also by invasive media such as television and computers, the deck is well stacked.

The family then provides a first focus for the exploration of the nature of language management. While it is not inevitable, there will be many families in which the issue is salient: in which an attempt will be made to modify the language practices and beliefs of other members of the family. But the family is not a closed unit: its language practices and beliefs are open to the influence of peers, of school, of the environment, and of other outside forces. When these outside forces are in fact the language management activities of other parts of society (for example, of efforts by national government to develop the use of the national language), what happens inside the family becomes evidence of its effectiveness. We understandably want to judge the success of Māori or Irish language revival efforts by the number of homes in which people speak the language to each other, and especially to their children.

It seems reasonably obvious that internal factors play an important role: the relationships between family members, their respect for each other, and the authority that any one of them may gain. This accounts for some of the variation. In a study of Chinese-speaking immigrant families in Australia,

Tannenbaum (Tannenbaum and Howie 2002) found that children were more likely to use their parents' immigrant language when they believed their family to be cohesive but low in hierarchy. At the same time, many of the practices and beliefs within individual families can be accounted for by external language management.

The discussion of language management in the family or home domain has offered support for the model I am developing. It has revealed evidence of regular patterns of language practices, of beliefs and ideology, and of management activities. It has left open the relative influence of the various participants, suggesting that this will need to be empirically determined in various cultures. It has further confirmed the importance of external influences on the family domain: there are unlikely to be many cases where the family operates as a closed unit rather than as the focus for multiple external pressures. This provides an opportunity for reassessing the theory of language management in the light of what we have learned from the family.

First modification of the theory

Organized language management in the family domain begins when a family member with authority (normally a parent) decides to correct the unsatisfactory language performance or proficiency of another family member (commonly a child, but it may be a spouse or a newly arrived relative) and to persuade them to modify their language practices. This stems from a common belief that a parent has responsibility for the language competence of children and further depends on the values assigned to different languages or varieties or variants. These values in turn are derived most probably from experience outside the family domain, such as a sense of ethnic or other identity or a belief in pure language. As participants gain experience outside the family, they bring in new practices and beliefs. One such example is a peer group, the children they play with outside the home whose practices and beliefs have increasing influence as they become adolescents. Later, school will be another major influence. The domain-internal pressures are challenged by external pressures, making clear that while it is valuable to analyze domains separately, they are regularly open to influences of the wider sociolinguistic ecology. No man is an island, nor is a family a closed sociolinguistic unit.

3   Religious language policy

Introduction

In selecting the next domain to look at, there are a number of choices. The neighborhood makes sense: the languages one chooses to greet people in the street, the language choice in local stores (see chapter 5), street signs and other public examples of language (see chapter 6), the linguistic patterning of the peer-group or gang (Labov 1973), the neighborhood and extended family networks (Milroy 1980). I choose rather to look first at the domain of religious institutions and their language management, a field in which study has been ignored in the twentieth century secularization of western academic fields.

One of the most widely noted international language management actions of the twentieth century was the decision of the Second Vatican Council to conduct mass in the vernacular rather than in the traditional Latin. The fact that Arabic is so widely spoken today is partly accounted for by the insistence of Islam that all religious services be conducted in it. Hebrew was kept alive for nearly two millennia after people stopped speaking it as a vernacular language through its continued use as a language of prayer and religious learning. In much of Africa and in other parts of the world, the current sociolinguistic situation owes a great deal to arbitrary decisions by missionaries as to which local dialects to standardize for bible translation. All of these point to the central role that religion and religious institutions play in language management.

Religious institutions can be the focus of language conflict. One of the issues of dispute between Reform and Orthodox Judaism in the nineteenth and twentieth centuries was the language of prayer. The Vatican decision to use the vernacular opened the way to disagreement over which vernacular, but also led to a movement to maintain Latin. The new translation of mass into English, nearing completion in January 2008, was accompanied by theological and stylistic debate. Around the same time, Pope Benedict XVI signaled to bishops his support for congregations that wish to return to the Latin mass. At the end of 2006, a disagreement between Tamil and Kannada supporters in a parish in Jakkalli, an ancient city in Karnataka State (2,200 kilometers south of New Delhi) led to court actions and resulted in the police suspending religious services in the parish (*UCA News*, January 18, 2007).

Study of the interaction of language and religion is comparatively recent (Spolsky 2003b), and the study of religious language policy even more so. This chapter will therefore be exploratory, setting out to explore the language practices and beliefs that develop within the religious domain and asking how religious institutions and leaders claim and attempt to exercise the authority to modify the language practices and beliefs about language of their members and others. As with other kinds of language management, the processes involved may be stated explicitly as rules about language choice and use, or may be implicit in practice: a practice of conducting services in only one language, for example, sets a firm policy line.

In much of the world today, religion remains an important social force. From the point of view of language management, the religious institution is the first social structure outside the family that aims to influence language use. Western Europe may be moving out of a long period of secularization as it comes to grips with the fundamentalism of some of its new immigrants. Religion is no longer banned in the former Soviet Union. Most Arab countries are by definition Islamic: the same clause in their constitutions commonly declares Islam as the religion and Arabic as the national language. Nation-states which once separated church and state are again struggling with new religious movements or efforts to assert the authority of religion in matters of morality and of ethical choice. For many immigrants, the church, mosque, or synagogue remains the principal domain helping to preserve their heritage language.

It is important then to ask how religious institutions and leaders impinge, or attempt to impinge, on language practices and beliefs. In this chapter, I will first discuss the language policy, beliefs, and management efforts associated with some of the major religions, and then attempt to derive some general principles. Two questions might be asked: what help or hindrance can family language managers expect from religion and religious organizations, and what success might religious language managers expect to have in modifying the language practices and beliefs of their congregants? I will touch on, but not consider in detail, those areas where religion impinges on politics, or where governments expect to control the language of religious institutions.

As with the family domain, we must be cautious about over-generalization. Accepting Fishman's warning about the need to define domains empirically within each community (Fishman 1972), it is obviously blurring a great number of distinctions to speak about Judaism, Christianity, Islam, or any other religion, rather than concentrating on individual synagogues, churches, or mosques. At the same time, it is tempting to try to find some regular patterns.

Jewish language policy

I start with language policy and management in Judaism because I know it best and because it has a long recorded history, even if much of the history (like most historical sociolinguistics) is still open to controversy. As far as I can now recall, my own first introduction to the existence of other languages, growing up as I did in an observant Jewish home in apparently monolingual New Zealand, was the Hebrew used for prayers in our home and the one synagogue in the city. It was only later that I realized that this language could be used outside the religious domain, and that I learnt about the existence of other languages. With all the changes in Jewish sociolinguistics over three millennia, the use of Hebrew as a language of sacred text and for prayer has remained consistent, in spite of occasional changes.

While the details continue to be in dispute, the general picture of Jewish language use can be summed up as follows. Up until the Babylonian exile in the seventh century BCE, the common language in Judah was Hebrew, although a few diplomats and courtiers had learned Aramaic, which was the major imperial and trade language of the region. During the first exile, in Babylonia and in occupied Judah, growing societal multilingualism led to the beginning of Jewish plurilingualism. Shortly after the return seventy years later, it is claimed that it became necessary to accompany the public reading of Hebrew sacred texts by an Aramaic translation, a practice that continues in Yemenite synagogues today, even though knowledge of Aramaic is now rare. Over the next centuries, Aramaic became more than just a foreign imperial language and the customary language for legal contracts, but also the vernacular especially for those living in areas where there was a close association with Gentiles. To Hebrew and Aramaic was added Greek, the language first of settlers who established new cities in various parts of Palestine, and then of the Greek and Roman governments and their puppets. By the end of the millennium, at the time of Jesus and shortly before the destruction of the second Temple, Palestine appears to have been triglossic, with each of the three languages spoken dominantly in different parts of the country and the functional division, for Jews, between Aramaic as a vernacular, Greek for relations with government, and Hebrew for religious life (Spolsky 1983).

After their expulsion from Palestine, Jewish communities in their various exiles created a new multilingual pattern, developing a Jewish variety (Rabin 1981) based on a Gentile language for internal community functions (Judeo-Greek, Judeo-Aramaic, Judeo-French, Yiddish, Ladino, Judeo-Venetian, to name only a few), learned the local language for dealing with non-Jews (and how well they learned it depended on their acceptance in the local community), and maintained Hebrew to which had been conjoined Talmudic Aramaic as a language for religious activities (in particular, prayer and study) and, as time went on, for literacy. This pattern, with many minor variations and with regular changes of community and co-territorial languages as Jews were driven from one country to another or chose to emigrate for economic or safety reasons, continued more or less until the Enlightenment and emancipation that started in the eighteenth century in western Europe. The removal of some external barriers to civil freedom was accompanied by language changes too. In Germany, for instance, the opening of ghetto gates led some Jews to replace their Yiddish with standard German. At the same time, there were proposals to substitute German for religious uses of Hebrew. This modification continued after Jewish immigration to the United States, where many Jews switched to English for all three functions. At the same time, the successful revival of Hebrew in Israel led to the loss of earlier Jewish plurilingualism, as the revived Hebrew replaced immigrant languages, including most traditional Jewish languages (Spolsky and Shohamy 1999).

So much for the general picture. It remains to consider the specific effects of religion on these changing patterns, and ask about the extent of language management undertaken by and on behalf of Jewish religious institutions. Our first task is to clarify the notion and nature of Jewish religious authority. A pioneering study of the place of language choice in Jewish law by Glinert (1991) starts with an explanation of *Halakhah* "normative Jewish law." Like other religious legal systems, it covers not just civil and criminal matters but also relations between man and God, and claims its basis in "absolute and incontrovertible principles not subject to rational challenge." At the same time, it differs in that, due to an absent enforceable authority after the loss of political autonomy and of a centralized power, Jewish law is "a private matter between observant Jews and their conscience." Throughout the ages, there has been continuing study and discussions among observant Jews, for whom the learning of Jewish law is a religious duty, so that *Halakhah* has constantly been developing and growing. At any point in time, there are likely to be differences in detail within a broad canvas of consensus. In theory and practice, an observant Jew selects not just a congregation with whom to pray but also a rabbi whose rulings he or she will respect. There is no single central authority; while some rabbis may be more respected than others, each can only expect to bind his followers. In modern times, observant Jews remain a minority.

Glinert (1991) traces the varied opinions and changing rulings in *Halakhah* that deal with the choice of language for religious life. The Talmud records the rulings of the earlier periods. Generally, it prefers Hebrew for prayer, but allows exceptions. During the period of Greek and Roman rule, for example, it recognized the possibility of praying in Greek in certain circumstances. It was ambivalent about Aramaic, but agreed that certain prayers and certain documents (marriage and divorce contracts) could or should use Aramaic.

It was of two minds about learning Greek, at times banning it as a language of government and informers and at other times considering it an ornament for girls to learn and a permissable language for prayer.

Glinert (1991) notes that in the *Mishnah* (a major first compilation of Jewish law edited in the second century of the Common Era) specific details are given of what must be said in "The Holy Tongue" and what may be said in any language. The former includes some ritual texts used in certain ceremonies. He traces the debate as to whether the formula in the Jewish marriage ceremony should be in Hebrew or in a language that the participants understand, especially for women, who were not always expected to know Hebrew. Another matter for debate over the centuries was the use of "foreign formulas" as vows and oaths. In each case, the authorities that Glinert cites are rabbis whose contribution to the debate are recorded either in edited texts, such as the Talmud and the commentaries that accompany it, or in collections of *responsa*, in which individual rabbis during and following the middle ages answered specific questions that had been put to them. These named rabbis, whose statements form part of *Halakhah*, are the language managers within Jewish religion. As these first cases suggest, though, there is no uniformity over time or at any one time.

As a general rule, and with exceptions, the common pattern has been for Hebrew to be the normative choice for Jewish ritual and prayer. The regular weekly readings from the *Torah* "Five Books of Moses" and other scriptural readings that form part of regular services are normally in Hebrew. At one time, the practice developed to follow each sentence in Hebrew with a translation into Aramaic. Most of the prayers in public and private worship are also in Hebrew. One major exception is the *Kaddish* which marks certain divisions in the service and which has come to play a special role as the prayer for mourners (Wieselter 1998), which is in Aramaic. In the Diaspora, the prayer for the king or local head of state was commonly in the co-territorial language. A sermon (like most other religious teaching) is normally presented in the vernacular language of a congregation.

At various periods, some Jewish communities applied an early Vatican II approach, switching to the local vernacular. This seems to have happened in Alexandria at the time of Philo. It was also the approach taken by the Reform movement in Germany and later in the United States, but more recently, since the establishment of the State of Israel, more Hebrew seems to have moved into Reform worship.

In spite of the strong preference for Hebrew for ritual and public worship, there has generally been a willingness to accept the translation of sacred texts into the vernacular language of the community, and it has been assumed that the teaching of these texts, at whatever level, will be in the vernacular. Aramaic translations were developed for pragmatic purposes, but are now regularly studied for the interpretations of the sacred texts that they preserve. When the Bible was translated into Greek, contemporary Jewish authorities at first rejoiced in the miracle of seventy scholars apparently agreeing on a common version. Some centuries later, authorities were less happy at the effects of the translation – the opening up of the text to people without teachers, and the single interpretation enshrined in translation – and proclaimed a fast day on the anniversary of the translation. But generally, Judaism recognizes the value of translation in giving believers greater access to sacred texts, provided that the original text is preserved and recognized together with its traditional interpretations as the final authority.

The status granted to Hebrew as a language of sacred text and daily worship had one significant language management outcome: the need to make sure that children developed proficiency in Hebrew as well as in their home language. The Talmud said that as soon as a boy reached the age of five, his father should start to teach him Hebrew, evidence that by then Hebrew was not spoken in many homes. In practice, fathers joined together to set up schools in which their sons could be instructed, and at a later stage, the *Halakhah* stated that the Jews living in towns could require other Jews to support the school. The Leipzig *Mahzor* "prayer book" contains a picture of the ceremony at which young boys were introduced to reading by being given candy and letters coated with honey. In practice, the educational system seems to have been quite successful, leading to high standards of Jewish literacy in the middle ages. There were tiny medieval Jewish communities in which each head of household is known to have been the author of a learned study. Literacy of course permitted scattered Jewish traders to keep contact with their partners and families (Goitein 1967–93).

The revival of Hebrew by the Zionists at the end of the nineteenth century raised language policy questions for observant Jewish communities. Israeli Hebrew, like most revived languages, developed its own pronunciation, markedly different from the many different regional pronunciations of ritual Hebrew. Before the establishment of the State of Israel, most western Jewish communities continued to use their traditional Ashkenazi pronunciation, but slowly many of them were influenced to accept the modified Sephardic pronunciation that had become the norm in Israel. Ultra-orthodox communities resisted this change, continuing to use the various Yiddishized pronunciations that they brought with them from different parts of eastern Europe. One recent trend noticed in Israel has been for some younger observant Jews to attempt to recreate what they imagine to be their grandfathers' pronunciation for public worship.

One of the principal concerns of the *Haredi* "ultra-orthodox" Jewish communities, and in particular of the Hasidic sects among them, has been to maintain separation from the outside community. This is marked by living in more or less closed neighborhoods, by wearing distinctive black clothing, by strict interpretation and observance of dietary laws, and also by language practices. Fishman (1966) noted that the two groups in the United States most successful at preserving their heritage languages were the Amish and the Hasidim, each of whom shunned other aspects of the behavior and practices of their neighbors. Hasidic groups in the United States, the United Kingdom, and Belgium remain the most committed to the maintenance of Yiddish in the home. In Israel, while maintaining other aspects of communal separation, *Haredi* Jews have in the main moved to using Israeli Hebrew in the home, in place of Yiddish (Baumel 2002). Certain Hasidic sects, under the influence of their religious leaders, have been making a major effort to reverse this trend (Isaacs 1999). Yiddish is the language of instruction in schools for boys, with the result that male *yeshiva* graduates in the community are more fluent in Yiddish than in Hebrew. Women in these communities, however, commonly continue to speak Hebrew, so that some of the sects have now started to teach Yiddish as a language in schools for girls (Bogoch 1999).

Hebrew adopted an alphabetic writing system from the Canaanites in the twelfth or eleventh century BCE. In the ninth century, it started to be modified into what became Paleo-Hebrew script, but was later replaced by the square Aramaic script which continues to the present day. The older script was preserved for a while, and used for coinage by the Hasmoneans and to write the name of God in some Dead Sea Scrolls. The Talmud states a Halakhic requirement to use the square Aramaic script. The spelling system for biblical Hebrew texts was set by Masoretic scholars in the tenth century CE. Their language management activities paralleled efforts of Sanskrit and Islamic linguists and grammarians to maintain the accuracy and purity of sacred texts.

The decision to require the ritual reading of Jewish sacred texts in Hebrew led to a special kind of sacred literacy (Spolsky 1991a). The reading of the Bible in the synagogue must be done, the *Halakhah* lays down, from a text written by hand on a parchment or vellum scroll. A new scroll is prepared by a scribe who copies the text, letter by letter, from another scroll. If any mistake is found in a scroll, it may not be used for ritual purposes. The texts are written in square Hebrew letters, without punctuation or vowels. A synagogue reader must have learned the correct punctuation, vocalization, and cantillation of the text. He must also know when to replace a written word with another word laid down in the tradition. Thus, learning to read requires the moderation of a teacher. Traditionally, and this tradition is maintained in some Yemenite communities and a few others, any congregant called to the reading of the Torah was expected to be able to read for himself, but in more recent times, the task has been entrusted to a single trained reader.

This general statement of Jewish religious language policy provides the basis for understanding the policy of individual Jewish religious institutions.

In the smaller Jewish communities, where there is only one synagogue, a compromise has emerged between the vast choice of customary practices and beliefs that had developed over two millennia of exile. In larger communities, however, there is a strong tendency to establish a number of synagogues, temples (as Reform Jews call them), or *shtibels* (the tiny places of worship preferred by Hasidim), each of which is likely to vary according to the demographic makeup and community of origin of its congregants. Large establishment synagogues are likely to use the standard co-territorial vernacular for sermons and announcements; Reform temples often use the standard language for prayers too; shtibels will regularly use Yiddish as the accompanying language; and linguistically marked ethnic synagogues will use a heritage language such as North African Arabic or French, Yemenite, or English for any parts of the services that are not conducted in Hebrew.

Jewish religious language management then establishes language practices and propagates language beliefs that vary from the home and modify the language practices and beliefs of congregants and, especially, of their children. For observant homes, it sets a high value on proficiency in Hebrew, and a related acceptance of the normalcy of multilingualism.

Language management in Christianity

Founded by plurilinguals living in a multilingual society, and with a long tradition of active proselytizing throughout the world, Christianity has commonly been willing to translate its sacred texts into other languages. Peters (2003: Vol. II, Chapter 1) notes that there appear to have been two kinds of original Christian texts, one a collection of sayings and the other a narrative biography. It was the biography that became the Gospels of the early churches, which meant there was little problem in moving from the probably original Aramaic to the Greek of the New Testament. It does not seem to have been important to record the sayings of Jesus in the original language or languages. Early Christians thus seem not to have been concerned with a sacred language, and besides the Greek version, vernacular translations in Egyptian Coptic, Syrian Aramaic, Latin, and Slavic quickly appeared.

One of the three languages of trilingual Palestine, Greek had already played an important part in early Christianity even before the spread from Jerusalem to the Greek colonies and to Rome. Christianity became the official religion of the Roman Empire by the end of the fourth century. The Vulgate translation into Latin of the Bible in the fifth century by Jerome provided a text which gained almost sacred status during the middle ages. In the eleventh century, Christianity was organizationally divided between the western church, led by the pope in Rome, and the eastern church centered until 1453 in Constantinople. Latin became the language of the western church for all ritual purposes, maintaining this position until the Second Vatican Council (1962–1965) permitted the use of the vernacular in the liturgy. The authority of the Vulgate was affirmed at the Council of Trent (1545–1563), and a revised Clementine version of 1592 became the standard Bible text of the Roman Catholic Church.

On the other hand, the eastern Orthodox Church was linguistically pluralistic. With Syriac and Armenian traditions alongside Greek, it encouraged a Gothic translation in the fourth century and a Slavonic translation in the ninth (Sawyer 2001). Typical was the work of St. Stefan of Perm, the fourteenth-century Russian Orthodox bishop responsible for converting the Komi people and developing an alphabet for them (Ferguson 1968). Born round 1335, he studied in a monastery in Rostov, returning to his native Ustjug to work among the pagan Komi. He became the first bishop of Perm in 1383, by which time most Komi had been baptized into the Orthodox Church. Recognizing Komi opposition to the Russians who had settled and were starting to dominate the region, he used their previously unwritten language as the basis for his missionary work.

The western church in contrast maintained a strict language policy. The Spanish and Portuguese conquests of South America were partly conceived and operated as religious activities, with the goal and effect of conversion of the natives and the destruction of the autochthonous religions and languages. For the Roman Catholic Church, Latin was the language of ritual and the Latin translation of the Bible was the only approved version of sacred text. The catechism could, however, be taught in the vernacular.

In the sixteenth century, Christianity in western Europe underwent a major religious and linguistic change with the Protestant Reformation, which allowed direct access to the Bible by translation into the vernacular; Luther's translation of the New Testament in German appeared in 1522 and Tyndale's into English in 1526. This was not just a matter of providing new texts, but a radical case of language management. The Reformation also involved active iconoclasm: congregants who in the past had probably received most of their religious messages from icons and statues in the church were now expected to rely on written verbal texts. English churches during the reign of Henry VIII had their icons destroyed and were required to purchase English bibles for their still largely illiterate congregations (E. Spolsky 2007).

As the Protestant movement fragmented into small proselytizing sects, its missionaries started to spread ahead of or together with the soldiers and sailors who were establishing colonial empires for western nations. As Sugirtharajah (2005: 1) put it, the "Bible, beer, a gun and a printing press" became conjoined colonial artifacts. This process spread religion, colonial rule, and literacy, producing major changes in the sociolinguistic ecology of many parts of the world. As a general rule, Roman Catholic missionaries – no less colonialist than others, as witness the conquest of Latin America – were satisfied to learn the languages of their converts well enough to teach the catechism in it. Uncommitted to the sacred status of any language, the Protestant missionaries on the other hand set out to translate the Bible into some version of the local language. During the Reformation, many Protestants had been martyred for preaching and publishing books in the vernacular. As missionaries, they encouraged and contributed to the development of vernacular literacy.

Protestant missionaries played a major part both in the development of literacy in local vernaculars and at a later stage in the spread of the colonial and metropolitan languages. A good example is missionary work among the Polynesians in the South Pacific. In Samoa, New Zealand, and Tonga, English missionaries arriving at the beginning of the nineteenth century were rapidly successful both in converting the local people to their own version of Christianity and also in establishing strong vernacular literacy. Literacy was introduced into Tonga by the Wesleyan missionaries in 1829, when the first school was opened by Nathaniel Turner and William Cross, who set out to teach children and adults to read and write in the Tongan language (Latukefu 1974, 1980: 55). Reading and writing quickly became popular. In April, 1831, William Woon set up the first printing press in Tonga and published a school book of which 3000 copies were printed (Latukefu 1974, 1980: 57). Literacy in Tongan was firmly and quickly launched.

These missionaries had been sent to Tonga by the London Missionary Society which had as its fundamental principle, "our design is not to send Presbyterianism, Independency, Episcopacy, or any other form of Church Order and Government, about which there may be differences of opinion among serious persons, but the Glorious Gospel of the Blessed God to the Heathen" (Garrett 1982: 10). The translation of the Bible into the Tongan language was considered the first major task, which the missionaries began immediately in 1829. One of the most prolific of the translators was J. E. Moulton, who wrote, or translated with the help of his students, scores of books and pamphlets, including two volumes of world history, Milton's *Paradise Lost,* two volumes of *Pilgrim's Progress,* and a geography of the Holy Land (Spolsky *et al.* 1983).

Missionary activities in New Zealand led to the rapid spread of Māori vernacular literacy, so that by 1860, there was probably higher literacy among the indigenous Māori than among the English settlers who started to arrive in 1840. The Native schools taught in Māori and started to teach English and encourage bilingualism. Under colonial policy starting in 1867, however, the process was reversed, and serious Māori language loss started. In New Zealand, where the indigenous language appears to have been reasonably

homogeneous with minor dialect differences (Harlow 2007), the effect of
Bible translation was to standardize Māori. In other Pacific islands, there was
a more radical effect. In Fiji, the missionaries translated the Bible into the
Bau dialect, which as a result became the standard language still recognized
by the school system. For speakers of other dialects, the standard Fijian of
school is as distant from their home language as the standard Hindi of school
is from the many dialects actually spoken by Fijian Indians.

Fabian (1983) described the activities of missionaries in the Belgian
Congo. During the period from 1884 to 1904 of King Leopold II's independent state, the missions were under colonial control and the mission posts
were centers for agricultural, commercial, and industrial as well as religious
activities. In return for land, the missions were expected to run a system of
education as spelled out in the convention between the Vatican and the Congo
Independent State in 1906. The colonial charter issued in 1908 required that
French and Flemish be used for official documents but allowed the option of
teaching African languages in schools. For the next thirty years, the missionaries were active in producing a large number of the dictionaries and
grammar books subsidized in part by the colonial government. As in many
other colonies, the missionaries in the Congo became caught in the struggle
between two factions: indigenists who aimed to preserve African culture, and
assimilationists who argued for Europeanization.

For the missionaries, the principal task of education was to teach Christianity in the mother-tongue. Which mother-tongue, however, was a critical
question, and the missionaries generally adopted a hierarchical view, with the
idea that a small number of supraregional languages (with French at the top)
would best serve the needs of the colony. Four African languages were sin-
gled out: Kikongo, Lingala, Tshiluba, and Swahili. These languages were
managed by the colonial administration in consultation with the missionaries.
By 1948, Swahili had become the lingua franca of eastern Congo, a language
described and standardized in the grammar books prepared by missionaries.

Ranger (1989) believes that missionary policy resulted in ethnic conflicts
in Zimbabwe. In the Makoni administrative district, the three important
missions were the Anglicans, the Trappist/Mariannhill Catholic fathers, and
the American Methodist Episcopal church. Each of them conducted basic
linguistic research aiming to develop a written language which would be the
basis of conversion and education. The American Methodists assumed they
were reducing the common language of the Shona to a written form but in fact
they were creating a new dialect, Manyika. The Anglicans also took linguistic
work seriously, and set up their educational and missionary base near
Mutasa, so that their efforts, too, supported the status of Manyika, a term they
slowly started to use to refer to the people as well as the language. The
Catholics worked independently to establish a written language. There was

strong controversy among the missionaries, and a struggle for control between the Mariannhill fathers and the Jesuit group. By the 1930s, Ranger believes that Manyika identity, resulting largely from the work of the missionaries, was finally established. The next step was the drive towards a standard Shona, in which the mission churches shared. The Anglican Church now began to support the argument for a unified Shona language and an associated Shona identity. These two examples show the complex but important role played by missionaries and their language management activities in the changes in sociolinguistic ecology and the development of ethnic identities. Christian missionaries played a major role in language management, in choosing which variety became standard, and shaping the form of the standard variety.

Among the Navajo, the fact that only about a third of the people became Christian had important limiting effects. Here, too, there was a distinction between the Roman Catholic missionaries, who produced an early grammar book and dictionary, and the Protestants whose work in Bible translation had a major influence on the development of such vernacular literacy as came to exist. Again, as in the last two cases, the influence was strengthened by association with the colonial administration, or in this case, more specifically, the Bureau of Indian Affairs. The decision of the Bible translators to adopt the government orthography developed in the late 1930s by Bureau specialists was a critical factor in its acceptance (Young 1977). In the 1940s, those who were literate in Navajo could read the newspaper which was justifying the war effort, or the New Testament being printed by the American Bible Society. During the brief period of Navajo bilingual education in the 1960s, there seemed to be agreement between those working to maintain Navajo through using it in the schools and the Protestant churches. However, in many cases the opposition to the teaching of Navajo in schools came from the churches, which saw a danger that Navajo culture, meaning the traditional Navajo religion, would be taught (Spolsky 2002b).

The Protestant tradition of Bible translation was the basis of a very wide range of language management, for in most cases it required the development of written and standardized languages out of what previously had been loosely associated vernacular dialects. The British and Foreign Bible Society was founded in 1804 in London with the sole purpose of encouraging wide circulation of the Bible "without note or comment." The first foreign translation was the Gospel of St. John translated into Mohawk. In the first year at least one portion of the Bible had been translated into 67 languages; by now, there have been translations into over 2,000 languages. Societies have been formed in other countries. The American Bible Society was founded in 1816 and published its first translation into Delaware two years later. It supported work in India, China, and the Levant. Founded in 1934 as a summer training program, SIL International (formerly known as the Summer Institute of Linguistics) has trained linguists to engage in research and language development work. Over the years, SIL International has completed translations in 400 languages and is active in another 1,000. Over 450 translations of the New Testament and other scripture portions have been published. In the changing political climate, SIL researchers cooperate with national governments and with the speakers of endangered languages in developing literacy programs. SIL International defines itself as a "non-profit, scientific educational organization of Christian volunteers."

Religious language policy can play an important role in providing support for the maintenance of a heritage language. Earlier in this chapter, we described how Judaism, by preserving Hebrew as the language of ritual and adding an educational system to guarantee intergenerational continuity, effectively kept the language alive for nearly two millennia and provided a strong basis for its revival. Christian churches preserve the older form of languages (Old Church Slavonic, Gothic, and Latin). Vernacular church services and associated educational and social programs play a significant role in supporting family language policy in the encouragement of immigrant language maintenance. A key element in Diaspora churches (Polynesian churches in the United States, Australia, and New Zealand, and immigrant churches in the United States and Australia, for example) is that they tend to continue to conduct services in the immigrant vernacular. This is true of Tongan (Spolsky *et al.* 1983) and Samoan (Spolsky 1991c) churches in New Zealand, of ethnic churches in Australia (Woods 2002), and of Armenian churches in Jerusalem (Azarya 1984).

As may be expected, religious language management can intersect with political issues. The use of the national language in Protestant churches after the Reformation was clearly an expression of political policy. Weeks (2002) has studied one interesting example. In the nineteenth century, in what were then called the Northwest Provinces (nowadays Lithuania and Belarus), the Russian government felt itself threatened after the suppression of the Polish insurrection in 1863. Polonization was expressed in two ways: the spread of Roman Catholicism in competition with the Russian Orthodox Church, and the use of Polish in the sermon and other non-Latin parts of the ritual. The government's attempt to introduce Russian into the Roman Catholic services was part of its effort to combat Polish influence. A second example is Friesland, where the use of Frisian in church remains controversial (Zondag 1987). Friesland adopted Calvinism in the sixteenth century, at which time it started to use the official Dutch translation of the Bible in church, at home, and at school. A few ministers, supporters of Frisian nationalism, have managed to persuade the local consistory to permit the use of Frisian for hymns and sermons.

A Christian sect with its own language rules is Quakerism, also known as the Society of Friends, which was established in England in the middle of the seventeenth century. Quakers were expected to limit their speech, in worship as well as in normal life. Their worship meetings were marked by long silences, during which congregants weighed carefully anything they might say (Collins 2003). Like other Puritan sects, they encouraged "plain speech" which was intended to deny the hierarchical structure and ornamented style of Renaissance English. One marked grammatical feature was the use of the already archaic second person singular pronoun (*thou* and *thee* instead of *you*) although Birch (1995) reports that this is now rare both in Quaker homes and meeting-houses. Titles and honorifics were not used; clothing was plain; greetings were avoided. The pagan names for days of the week and the months of the year were replaced by numbers. While truth was insisted on, Quakers followed the biblical command not to swear an oath (Graves 2001).

Religious language management commonly concerns itself with the control and avoidance of certain kind of speech. Judaism forbade blasphemy, speaking evil of God. Christianity continued this and included speaking evil of sacred persons or objects. When Christianity became an official religion in the sixth century, blasphemy became a criminal offense under the code of Justinian I. After the Reformation in England, blasphemy was banned by common law and the ban was applied rigorously until the 1920s (Pickering 2001).

Both Christianity and Judaism have taken many institutional steps to manage the language of their congregants. This applies not only to the choice of language, but also to the form of expression. Jewish *Halakhah*, for example, includes a set of rules for euphemistic speech and another for avoiding slander. In Christianity, language rules come under the branch of the church concerned, determining whether an individual or defined body has authority. Religious language rules are most obviously applied to public speech events associated with worship within individual churches, but they also have serious implications for and effects on the language of homes and individuals. They are regularly associated with other domains, such as in the common alliances between missionaries and colonial governments, or when religion and ethnicity or religion and nationalism are blended.

Islamic language management

Islam was founded on principles and practices adapted from both Judaism and Christianity, and like them, its major development was in the Mediterranean area, so it can be considered a western religion like them, certainly in the pre-modern period (Peters 2003). In language policy, Islam broke from both its models in its continued insistence on the higher status of the particular variety of Classical Arabic in which the Qur'an was composed. The Qur'an, believed to be the actual word of God, may only be read or cited in Arabic (Mattock 2001). Peters (2003: 7) summarizes: "the consequence, then, is that the Qur'an contains the precise words of God, without human intervention or conditioning of any sort, that God had spoken, and Muhammad had heard and reported, Arabic speech." There are some Islamic authorities that do not permit translation.

Keeping the sacred texts pure was critical. Suleiman (2001) explains that the development of the Arabic linguistic tradition, starting at the end of the eighth century, was intended to deal with the phenomenon called *lahn* "solecism," the faulty speech of the new converts to Islam during the rapid spread of the religion and of Arabic. The phenomenon was noted not only in ordinary speech, but also in recitation of the Qur'an, where it represented "a dangerous interference in the effort to ascertain of the message of the Qur'an in its capacity as the revealed word of God *verbatim*" (Suleiman 2001: 327; original italics). One of the important tasks of Arabic grammar was as a pedagogical tool for teaching the language to non-Arab converts.

The spread of Arabic from the Arabian peninsula through the Middle East, North Africa, and Spain, was the result of religious and military conquest in the sixth and seventh centuries, the subjugation of Europe blocked finally at the battle of Poitiers in France in 733. The Umayyad Empire in the mid-eighth century already included Spain in the west and was starting to reach India in the east. By the fourteenth century, the borders had spread south along the African coast, through the Sahara and east into India; Turkey was included. By 1500, Spain had been reconquered by the Christians, but central Asia in the north and Malaya in the east had become part of the Muslim world. In the fifteenth century, the Ottoman Empire, having conquered Constantinople, included the Balkans, Crimea, Turkey, and Syria; later, it added Algeria and Egypt.

Linguistically, the spread of Arabic as a secular *lingua franca* was uneven; in the Middle East, it replaced Aramaic. The further regions – Persia, India, Turkey, the Berber areas of North Africa, the Sudan – continued to use other vernaculars, but Classical Arabic was the language of religion and of the high culture that developed in the period of the Golden Age of the Abbasid caliphs. In a few hundred years, Arabic replaced its predecessors – the South Arabian languages, Aramaic and their dialects, and even Coptic in Egypt. It did not, however, replace Turkish (an Altaic language) and while it dominated Persian (an Indo-European language) for a while, a revitalized version of Persian reemerged in the tenth century.

Islam continued to spread, south into Africa and east into south-east Asia, but it was often only the religious language and script that were adopted. Thus, there is a distinction between countries where Arabic is official – Algeria,

Egypt, Iraq, Israel, Jordan, Kuwait, Lebanon, Libya, Mauritania, Morocco, Oman, Saudi Arabia, Sudan, Syria, Tunisia, United Arab Emirates, Western Sahara, and Yemen, each with its distinct local varieties alongside the official Classical standard – and those where most Muslims speak a local language and have limited knowledge of Arabic for religious functions.

Mattock (2001) argues that Islam and Classical Arabic form a symbiosis, Arabic serving as the language of power for Muslims in the Middle East. For Muslims everywhere, Arabic remains a sacred language. Persians continued to speak their native language (Pahlavi) while writing in Arabic. Islam came to south-east Asia peacefully, spreading particularly in the island regions like Indonesia while the mainland generally remained Buddhist. It seems to have been introduced by traders (Kratz 2001). Malay, with borrowing from Arabic and Persian, became an important language of Islamicization. The 250 million Muslims in south Asia have accepted the sacred primacy of Arabic since the first communities were established. In many areas, Islam was spread by Persian-speakers, and Persian rather than Arabic was involved in late Muslim education, with Arabic for "ritual inculcation of a more or less mechanical recognition of Arabic sufficient for recitation of the Qur'an" (Shackle 2001: 63). The Qur'an was translated into Persian in 1737, and an Urdu translation was made in 1790; later there were translations into other south Asian languages. Beginning in the mid-eighteenth century, Persian was rapidly replaced as a major cultural language for south Asian Islam by Urdu. It maintains its place in Pakistan, but elsewhere has been replaced by other local languages. Islamic vocabulary in the local languages is marked by borrowings from Persian and Arabic.

While children in Arabic-speaking countries have to develop literacy in only one language, Muslim children in Pakistan and India must learn Arabic for religious purposes and another language for secular (Rahman 2006). Traditionally, children in Pakistan learned to read in Persian and in Arabic, with Arabic being taught in the madrasas. Under British rule, Arabic was restricted to religious use, and pupils learned to read the Qur'an but did not learn Arabic. Arabic is nowadays compulsory in schools in Pakistan; the medium of instruction is the official Urdu although only a minority speak it. While some Muslims oppose the teaching of English, most who can afford it want their children to learn it.

Sawyer (2006) discusses the effect of religion in spreading literacy. He comments on cases where religion has actively obstructed popular access to reading and writing. The first case he cites is the way that the Christian religious establishment in medieval Europe tried to prevent ordinary people from reading the Bible in the vernacular; he mentions the execution of Jan Hus and William Tyndale. In India too, the scripts in which Sanskrit and Hindi are written were considered divine and only to be used by trained personnel. In Persia, Zoroastrian priests taught that the sacred text (the Avesta) should not be written down: this, Sawyer said, was reported also to be characteristic of the Druids. He argued that the spread of Islam also had a negative effect on the vernacular. Muslim law forbade translating the Qur'an into the vernacular (the translations into medieval Persian and Ottoman Turkish were exceptions) and required the teaching of Arabic. Schoolchildren in Qur'an schools learn to read and write Arabic, to a certain extent, but not their mother-tongue. Arabic script was then used to write the various vernaculars. The effect of this policy, he argues, was to slow the development of literacy in those areas where Islam and the Arabic language were strongest. Illiteracy, according to current UNESCO statistics, continues to be higher in the Arab states, sub-Saharan Africa, and south and west Asia, than in east Asia or Latin America.

Maamouri (1998) emphasizes the relationship of Arabic diglossia in the Middle East and North Africa to formal education in the Arab region, which he considers to be characterized by growing inadequacy, questionable relevance, and an unacceptably low level of output. Arabic is important to these countries for identity. He cites various studies which show that literacy is acquired late. He points out that the Arabic language is "the chief instrument and vehicle of the sacred message of Islam" (Maamouri 1998: 19). Conversion meant accepting "an elementary form of Arabic literacy which allowed its users to achieve little more than going through the daily requirements of the creed" (Maamouri 1998: 20). Over time, a gap developed between the standardized Arabic of the Qur'an and the "corrupt" spoken language. The higher status afforded to the written language led to the current dichotomy and to diglossia (Ferguson 1959; Hudson 2002). Qur'anic literacy benefited a class of religious professionals but did not provide functional literacy for the people, which Maamouri sees as a major gap.

The first translation of the Qur'an, into Latin, was made by a Christian to be used in a project to convert Muslims. In the mid-fifteenth century, a translation was made into Spanish to be used in the education of the Moriscos, Muslims who had been converted to Christianity in northern Spain and could no longer read Arabic. Generally, however, Peters (2003) notes that Muslims have been reluctant to translate the Qur'an. Prayers must be recited only in Arabic. The exception is the Friday sermon, which may be given in the local vernacular in non-Arabic countries.

The linguistic effects of Islam have been strong. Where religious conversion and military conquest were combined, and in areas where the previous language was Aramaic, a new vernacular emerged, a local spoken variety of Arabic, but one that was held in contempt by the religious establishment with its fundamental commitment to the language of the Qur'an, the only language of prayer and learning. The battle over possible acceptance and standardization of the national vernaculars was fought in Egypt in the 1920s, and a combination of Pan-Arabism and Islam won out (Suleiman 2001; Suleiman 1996). There are those who believe that these language policy decisions help account for the failure of Islamic and Arabic countries to adjust to modernization.

As in the previous two sections, the approach in this has been to describe the general affect of Islamic language policy on the communities where it exists. We are talking then about religion as a force rather than attempting to describe specific examples of the religious domain. This approach implies a modification in the theory of language policy as it is being developed: it sets out to describe patterns that occur in many specific communities rather than in one. The religious speech community it deals with is larger than a single mosque and its worshipers, and the managers are more broadly defined than a single imam, but rather the result of generalizing the application of religious law.

Other religious language management

Hinduism is better considered as a "variety of religious traditions linked by Indian cultural history and to some extent by the use of the Sanskrit language" (Killingley 2001: 52). Its seeming similarity to the three major western religions is an artifact of its reinterpretation by western Orientalists, scholars, and missionaries (King 1999). The notion of Hinduism as a religion emerged in the nineteenth century: the 1955 British Hindu Marriage Act defines Hindu as anyone who is not Muslim, Christian, Parsee, or Jew, thus including Buddhists, Jains, and Sikhs. One of the results of this western view was to see Hinduism as a normative religion; another was to "textualize" it by concentrating attention on the Sanskrit texts of the Veda. The oral "popular" aspects of Indian religious tradition were ignored, and decried as not following the texts. This had major effects on the development of Indian literacy, providing "scribal communities and authoritative interpreters" that were essential for the efficient administration of colonial India. Elitist Brahman forms and traditions were stressed. The multiplicity of Indian religious traditions was thus standardized and unified, in a form consistent with western models. This development paralleled and was related to the growth of Hindu nationalism, which chose to stress the Sanskrit tradition.

Hindu remained an ethnic term until the nineteenth century, when it took on religious and nationalist meanings. In India, language choice often correlates with a religion: there are regions where Hindus speak Marathi, Muslims speak Urdu, and Jains Kannada. Hindu nationalism promoted Hindi as the modern language for all India, and Sanskrit as the language of scholarship. The oldest south Asian religious texts, forming the Veda, are in

Sanskrit. Beginning as early as 1500 BCE and composed over the next thousand years, the Hindu canon was not fixed. Sanskrit is the set language of ritual, and the texts, unwritten until the third century BCE, were transmitted orally from teacher to pupil. Because of the sacredness of the mantras, accurate transmission is required. Because of this, Vedic priests were trained in phonetics, grammar, etymologies, and meter. Sanskrit spread from ritual to scholarly use (Killingley 2001), and Sanskrit words were borrowed freely into Hindi. But the texts were regularly translated into other vernaculars, so that other languages (Kannada, Marathi, and English) were widely used. Outside India, Sanskrit is used in ritual (especially weddings and other lifecycle events), but English glosses and explanations are common.

Hinduism is an oral religion: traditional knowledge is passed orally, and in Brahmanic Hinduism, the Vedas, composed in Sanskrit, have formed the basic sacred texts (Lipner 2001: 295). Speech is in some traditions "conceived of as the expression of divine power" (Lipner 2001: 297). However, modern Hindus often use other religious texts, many in other modern Indian languages. Some Vedic hymns are used in major lifecycle rituals, though many participants do not understand them: women and lower-caste Hindus were forbidden to study the Vedas (Brockington 2001). Some of the verses of the Veda, called mantras, are believed to have special power and are used in worship; they must be used and heard only by initiates (Smith 2001).

In south Asia, Pandharipande (2006) argues, there is no longer a strict equation of religion and language. In the middle ages, content rather than form was accepted as the differentiating feature, and all languages were considered equally able to express the content. While the Classical languages (Sanskrit, Arabic, and Pali) remain connected with a single religion, other south Asian languages, including English, have begun to be used for the various religions.

Religion in the theory of language management

The exploration of the religious domain has shown the existence of pressure for language policy and of specific management policies applied by major religions. How should this be represented in the theory? First, it establishes the nature of practices for observant members of specific religions and their institutions, accounts for some of the values they and less observant members ascribe to varieties of language, and reveals the sources of some language management efforts that affect them. An observant Jew is expected to learn Hebrew, and an observant Muslim to acquire knowledge of Classical Arabic. A less observant Jew or Muslim might not set out to learn the language, but will probably believe that he should, and will be willing for his children to be taught it. Second, religious, ethnic, and heritage groups (the three often overlap) provide support for the maintenance of sacred and heritage languages. Third, religious institutions, each with its own internal policy structure – rabbis, priests, and imams passing on beliefs and practices to congregants – constitute an important external factor adding to the pressures on its members and on their families. Fourth, religion underlies also the expression of the religious ideology or "ethic of divinity" (Shweder *et al.* 1997); for believers, the choice of language is a matter of sacred tradition, which helps explain the strong reactions (akin to disgust) of some Catholics to the vernacularization of mass, of some Jews to the Reform use of German or English in prayer, and of Muslims to the potential impurities (*lahn*) in the Qur'an (Suleiman 2001). Religious belief and linguistic purity are closely related: linguistic cleanliness is next to godliness.

In translating these generalizations to any specific instance of the religious domain, it is necessary to take into account the communication requirements of the situation. The key participants in the religious domain are the divinity (to whom prayer is addressed and who is the accepted author of sacred texts), the congregants, and any intermediary minister. In different religions, there are different attitudes to maintaining a single language for sacred texts (communication from the divinity) and for prayers (communication from the congregation to the divinity). As a general rule, the minister is expected to be proficient in this special language, and when the congregants do not know it, he is expected to translate the sacred text or its message into a language that the congregants do know.

The minister's communication with congregants is in their own language. The case of the *Penitente* Brotherhood in New Mexico and Colorado is a good illustration. After Mexican independence in 1821, the Catholic Church withdrew the three existing missionary orders, replacing some of them with lay Mexican priests. In the absence of parish priests, many small communities established brotherhoods which included in their practices flagellation and reenactment of the Crucifixion. After the United States took over New Mexico in the middle of the century, the Spanish-speaking Mexican priests were replaced by French-speaking priests from Louisiana, leading to a breakdown in communication between priests and congregation; a campaign by the archbishop to abolish the brotherhood went unheeded, and the movement continued, finally being recognized by the church in the mid-twentieth century. In a small synagogue in a German town, the English-speaking rabbi told me that the German-speaking heads of the local community had discouraged his efforts to learn Russian, the language of former Soviet Jews who regularly attended services. Inability to communicate with congregants in their vernacular is a handicap for ministers. Recognizing this, Pope John XXIII cited his predecessor Pope Pius XII as saying that missionaries "must constantly keep before their mind's eyes their ultimate goal, which is to establish the Church firmly in other countries, and subsequently to entrust it to a local hierarchy, chosen from their own people" (Pope John XXIII 1959). Ideally, then, the priest, rabbi, imam, or minister is plurilingually proficient in the vernacular and the sacred language.

For congregants, the language demands are lower. They are assumed to be capable of memorizing or "reading" aloud prayers written in a language they do not understand: prayer books may then include translations alongside the text in the sacred language. Speaking to each other, congregants use their vernacular, adding perhaps identifying phrases from the sacred language.

Variations from these obvious patterns suggest the existence of forces external to the religious domain. For example, those ministers who attempt to conduct their services in Frisian rather than in the standard Dutch which has become the norm were clearly expressing strong activist language ideology (Zondag 1987). Lebanon also shows the strong influence of religion on language knowledge and use (Joseph 2006). Since the conquest in the seventh century, it has been essentially Arabic speaking, but during the Ottoman period, bilingualism started to emerge. Government officials of whatever religion were bilingual in Arabic and Turkish. Christians tended to be bilingual in Arabic and French (the language of their major western European protector), with Maronite Christians also maintaining Syriac as their liturgical language. Up to the end of World War One, anyone who knew French was likely to be Maronite or Roman Catholic, anyone who knew English to be an educated Orthodox Christian or Muslim. French-Arabic bilingualism continued to increase, especially among Christians. French declined after 1960, but in the recent unrest, is once again being claimed especially by Christians.

In Chapter 2, we explored language management within the home and family, asking what success a family language manager might expect to have in modifying the language practices and beliefs of other family members. In this chapter, we have been looking at religion and religious institutions, partly as a potential source of support for family language policy, and partly as an independent counterforce aiming to modify the language practices and beliefs of their congregants. We noted also the possibility of external influence on the domain, such as language activism, and sketched the communication requirements that set up the normal pattern for the domain. This latter feature suggests an interesting modification to the theory, implying that is not just participants but audiences that need to be taken into account. In a place of worship, the minister may use one language when addressing the divinity and another when addressing the congregation. In the same way, in the family, children regularly speak to their siblings in one language and to their parents in another.

An additional significant aspect of the religious domain is that the preservation or diffusion of a sacred language distinct from the vernacular involves providing translation as well as setting up schools and other institutions to make it possible for laymen to learn the language. Educational institutions originate with religious language management, as a method of assuring that priests and laity obtain proficiency in the sacred variety.

In particular, we have noted the impact of religious ideology (the ethic of divinity) on language management, and seen hints of the ways in which secularization may entail translation of this ethic to the nationalistic domain. Perhaps this explains why strongly religious groups like the Amish and the Hasidim were able to hold out against the secular forces of assimilation (Fishman 1966). Lilla (2007) cites Eric Voegelin as arguing in *The Political Religions* that after the Enlightenment, belief in God was replaced by belief in the new political orders like Marxism, fascism and nationalism; the ethic of divinity and the ethic of authority then were combined. Fishman (2002a) similarly shows how the contemporary status of Yiddish has been buoyed by the addition of sacred to political arguments. In the next chapter, we will move fully into the secular world, as we explore language in the workplace.

4   Language management in the workplace: managing business language

Domains and levels of language management

In this book, I have chosen to start with the smallest rather than the largest speech community. Chapter 2 dealt with the home and the family, which, while certainly "micro," turned out to be quite complex as a sociolinguistic ecology. If we were studying sociolinguistic ecologies, the logical next level might well have been the village or the urban neighborhood. This would also have made it possible to consider the effect of density of settlement on language policy, comparing the village with the city, and asking whether the city is indeed the root of all evil or the locus of solutions (Fishman 1999). I chose, however, to skip this level, for those with the authority to attempt to manage language practices are to be found in some governmental structure, such as a city or regional government which will be treated later. Instead, in Chapter 3, I dealt with a domain that is close to the family but distinct from it, religious organizations and institutions. Being part of an ecology means that there is complex interaction between domains, so that from time to time it was necessary to consider the effects of political and national policies. In the same way, while studying language management in the workplace we will need to make a somewhat artificial distinction by concentrating on language management activities that originate within the domain, and ignore in the meantime as much as possible the way government language management impinges on many workplaces. We will be looking at employers managing the language of their employees, and not dealing with government policy at the same level, such as the Chinese government's insistence on top management in securities firms passing an examination in Mandarin (*Bloomberg News*, July 13, 2007) or the Japanese proposal to require foreign residents to pass a Japanese exam (*Financial Times*, January 15, 2008).

It is also important to recall the distinction between management and the other two components of language policy: practices and beliefs. Management decisions are intended to modify practices and beliefs in the workplace, solving what appear to the participants to be communication problems.

Solutions will vary. Assume that the owner (the term that I will use for the person with the authority to make decisions, but clearly it could just as easily be a local foreman, middle management, or Central Office) wants the salespeople in the store to be able to greet customers in English rather than in the local vernacular. This might be handled in a number of different ways: by a local rule, by training employees in the desired practice, or by hiring employees known to be able to use English.

Workplace management decisions may be motivated by fairly obvious commercial aims, or they may be responses to more crucial threats to efficient operation. The crash of a Cypriot airliner in 2005 was blamed on "cockpit confusion" over a series of alarms, complicated by the fact that the experienced German pilot and his young inexperienced Cypriot co-pilot had no language in common other than English and had difficulty understanding each other's English (report in the *International Herald Tribune*, September 7, 2005). The owner of Helios airline would have been more than justified in demanding evidence of language ability from pilots as well as from cabin crew; the latter, according to a Helios statement of career opportunities on the web, are required to be fluent in English and Greek and to have a TOEFL score of 550 or a GCE English grade of C; confirming this, the application form for employment is in English.

There has been a recent attempt to analyze the language of work (Koester 2004) and a good number of studies of language practices in various workplaces. One early study dealt with language choice in Ethiopian markets. Cooper and Carpenter (1976) investigated a multilingual marketplace, expecting that they would find indications of the development and use of lingua francas to ease communication between buyers and sellers. What they found instead was evidence of a principle that sellers make an effort to learn the language of their potential customers. In New Mexico, the traders from Santo Domingo Pueblo were reputed to have plurilingual proficiency in the languages of the southwest. In the Old City of Jerusalem, Spolsky and Cooper (1991) found a similar phenomenon: the Arabic-speaking shopkeepers in the *shuk* had not only learned Hebrew and English but had also gained sufficient proficiency in the languages of tourists to be able to answer their questions or invite them into the store. To the extent that owners of businesses share the belief that sales improve when using the customer's language, we might expect to find them adopting a staffing policy that will permit this.

Evidence of this kind of management policy can be found in research on the economic incentives for learning a language. In a pioneering study of the spread of English (Fishman *et al.* 1977), Cooper and Seckbach (1977) gathered data on language qualifications listed in Israeli help-wanted advertisements. In the Friday editions of the three major Hebrew-language newspapers in the year 1973, they found that 17 percent of the 4,500 jobs advertised required English. The advertisements mentioning English most frequently were non-scientific and non-technical positions that required a university degree, and white-collar jobs such as office receptionist, switchboard operator, secretary, typist, bookkeeper, or clerk. Most of the advertisements asked for knowledge of Hebrew as well as English, reflecting the bilingualism of the Israeli Jewish economy.

The economic value of knowledge of the dominant language for immigrants has been demonstrated in a number of basic studies in Canada (Chiswick 1994), Australia (Chiswick and Miller 1995), Israel (Chiswick 1993) and elsewhere (Grin 1996). In a more recent study, Grin (2001) has started to look at the economic value of knowledge of English in Switzerland. The studies suggest, but of course do not establish, the existence of local management policies in hiring personnel with specific language skills.

The massive immigration of Russian-speakers to Israel in the 1990s set a major challenge to the Hebrew-English hegemony. The first sign of a break was the appearance of Russian-language advertisements in Hebrew language newspapers, published by banks offering their services to new immigrants who received government grants on arrival rather than being integrated (as earlier immigrants had been) into government hostels. Posters advertising banking services also appeared in Russian. Noting this, Glinert (1995) wondered if there was any government coordination or central policy behind the fact that many businesses and government offices started to hire bilingual clerks capable of dealing with Russian speakers. His study showed that in each case, the decision was in fact made locally. I observed a similar case at an Israeli university: the Dean of Students' office noticed that most of the new immigrant students were automatically going to the single student assistant who spoke Russian: when she left, she was immediately replaced by another assistant with similar skills. What this suggests is that language management is more likely to be local than central, challenging assumptions of centralized planning.

Workplace language rules

When I was in New Mexico, a friend once complained that the principal of the school where she was a senior teacher had placed a sign alongside the staffroom telephone reading "Only English may be spoken on this telephone." From time to time, newspaper stories draw attention to rules laid down by employers: some restaurant workers in the USA are forbidden to speak Spanish or Vietnamese in the presence of diners; some doctors and nurses in Israeli hospitals are forbidden to speak Russian in the presence of patients. In the United States, the Equal Employment Opportunity Commission sued the Salvation Army in 2006 for enforcing a rule requiring its sorters to speak only

English; the issue is being hotly debated in Congress and elsewhere. Reports of incidents like these where owners try to manage the non-work related conversation of employees are not common, but of course there may well be many more informal attempts that do not come to public attention.

There are also accounts of efforts to add language proficiency to the workforce, but here too success is not guaranteed. Training programs in the healthcare field for new immigrants to Canada focused on medical and general English language proficiency and nursing skills, but did not reflect the special communication requirements of institutions where there are many staff and patients who do not speak English (Duff et al. 2002). In a manufacturing company in Canada, Goldstein (1994) noted that Portuguese immigrant women resisted learning and using the official languages, English and French.

Because it caters to travelers, the hotel industry has potential language problems. Receptionists are usually prepared for this, but the housekeeping and cleaning staff are commonly low-paid immigrants. The Carleton hotels on the West Coast of the United States, a chain with a dozen hotels and restaurants that were advertised as boutique hotels for wealthy customers, tackled this by offering vocational English as a second language classes to its employees (Katz 2001). Senior management and desk staff were English-speakers; some mid-level managers were from the Philippines, able to communicate with upper management in English and with the cleaners in Spanish, Tagalog, Chinese, or English. When guests complained that the room cleaners did not know English, the management established a 're-engineering' program which included teaching English to housekeeping staff, hoping that it would lead to greater commitment. The program did result in increased interaction across the levels of staff and between workers and guests, but it did not result in greater job loyalty.

Language proficiency is a major problem in non-English-speaking countries that are attempting to develop international trade. Singapore changed its school language education policy relatively early in order to produce fluency in English in the general population. In Malaysia, the government has recently intervened in language education policy in the same direction, but earlier, its insistence on the use of the Bahasa Melayu as a medium of instruction in schools produced a problem in businesses where many executives with a good education were found to speak sub-varieties of Malaysian English in their international connections (Gill 1999). English is deeply entrenched in the Malaysian private-sector domains of corporate business and industry, banking and finance, although Chinese continues to dominate local Chinese business interactions (Nair-Venugopalk 2001).

Hong Kong workplaces are multilingual. Evans (1999) questioned 150 building workers studying at the Hong Kong Polytechnic; they reported that everyday oral communication in the workplace did not require English, but that workers needed to read faxes, letters, memoranda, and reports in English. After the ending of British rule, Evans and Green (2001) carried out another survey, this time of 1,500 professionals in public and private sectors. English was still the unmarked language for written communication in both sectors. Chinese professionals working for foreign companies needed more English than those working for local companies: larger businesses required more English than small ones. Cantonese remained the unmarked language for spoken communication, and English was generally spoken only when expatriates were present.

In South Africa, Hill and Zyl (2002) interviewed 58 engineers. At the management and inter-departmental level and for written communication, English was required. A good proportion of those interviewed believed, however, that spoken Afrikaans and indigenous African languages were important to "get the work done."

There are differences then according to mode, participant, and location, so that the workplace might well be divided into a number of separate domains. At the local level, two kinds of problem emerge: the need for workers to communicate with each other and with their bosses, and the need to communicate with customers. Solving these problems offers promise of greater efficiency in working and in sales, and so of greater profit, which one would expect to be the driving force in the workplace.

Global business

International business is not new. Archaeological studies have shown that trade crossed national and linguistic boundaries many centuries ago, and by the middle ages, many traders had to develop strategies for doing business multilingually. The field has continued to develop rapidly. In general, one would expect that businesses which have developed workable strategies have proved to be more competitive. However, many companies with potential international business have been slow to develop appropriate methods. Hagen (1999) investigated business communication in Europe and in the United Kingdom and found many firms that had not noticed any problem. A major survey commissioned by CILT, the National Centre for Languages, sent questionnaires to 2,500 international companies in ten different regions of the United Kingdom and found a surprisingly low level of plurilingual proficiency. Another study (InterAct International 2003a) looked at IT, telecoms, and call centers; only 40 percent said they used foreign languages regularly: the remainder used English or relied on local agents. Two thirds of the companies said they had employees with language skills among the technical and engineering staff. One in ten reported that they had a formal language strategy for dealing with non-English-speaking customers: a third of this group said they tried to respond in the customer's language. Fewer than one in five had invested resources in language training. In the science, engineering, and manufacturing technologies sector (InterAct International 2003b), just under 60 percent of the 780 international companies surveyed reported use of foreign languages regularly. The most common languages were French, German, Spanish, and Italian, with Japanese and Chinese following. The majority used local agents or externally hired translators and interpreters to deal with language barriers. Again, only 10 percent reported that they had a language strategy for overseas customers. One in ten used language proficiency as a criterion for hiring staff, and a quarter of the companies had invested in language training (generally part-time training). In the UK at least, it would appear that the profit motive is not enough to encourage active language management.

Feely and Harzing (2003) described the problems faced by Fiat in building an automobile, various components of which were produced in South America, South Africa, Poland, and Russia. Before they added the east European factories, Fiat had set up an elaborate communication system including e-mail, integrated stock systems, fax, and even desktop videoconferencing. However, because their logistics staff did not have appropriate linguistic versatility, they found it difficult to integrate the new factories into the system.

Bargiela-Chiappini *et al.* (2007) stress the continuing growth in the importance of English in Asian business organizations. In Japan, English-speaking employees are needed, especially at the senior levels. Non-English foreign firms are also adopting English, but Chinese is important. In Vietnam, success in a foreign joint-venture depends on language proficiency, but domestic business is entirely in Vietnamese. South Korea remains monolingual, with growing mixing of English in the speech of business people and a strong demand for English from parents of children. In Thailand, knowledge of English is a key to entry into the elite. Smalley (1994: 16) noted that until the 1960s, only members of the Thai elite were likely to know English, but its use by foreign businessmen and visitors and in international business has been spreading the language down. In Malaysia, English is becoming the normative choice for industry and commerce, but it is a localized variety rather than the standard language favored by the government. Hong Kong continues to use English as the language of business, but code-switching between English, Putonghua, and Cantonese is common. The chair of the Joint Business Forum in Sri Lanka blames the economic problems of his country on a number of factors: war, the failure to develop cheap energy, the electoral system, corruption and waste, the absence of law and order, the lack of leadership, and language policy – the failure to maintain the pre-Independence high standard of English (*The Sunday Times online*, Sri Lanka, June 24, 2007).

How many languages does a business need? The Integrated Product Service team in Windows International responsible for localization (which means seeing that Microsoft products are translatable into other languages and that their icons are not likely to give offense) aims to handle 80 different languages. Many global companies try to operate in major western and eastern European languages, Japanese, Chinese, Arabic, and if possible Malay, Urdu, Hindi, and Bengali. Making this more difficult, any system may be called on to fill every company function: finance, research and development, product engineering, logistics, sales, purchasing, human relations, and legal and public relations. The required level of linguistic proficiency will vary according to function: receptionists can manage with comparatively limited spoken skills, logistics clerks need to add written skills, engineers need to be able to communicate about technological matters with their peers and their managers, and international managers need a wide array of spoken and written skills.

Feely and Harzing (2003) summarize the various approaches that an international company may take, and discuss the strengths and weaknesses of each. One is to assume the existence of a *lingua franca*: many English-speaking companies simply take it for granted that its customers and partners know English. A second approach is called functional multilingualism, using those languages that happen to be available among staff. Here too, there will be many linguistic barriers to successful operations.

Another common approach is to use translators and interpreters hired from outside the firm. The Language Line was developed originally for the San Diego police force. It set up a large network of amateur interpreters available at any hour of the day or night by telephone to translate between a wide range of languages. The system works with initial contacts, but is likely soon to move into areas where the interpreter is severely limited in dealing with the specific technological needs of interaction.

Language training for staff is another approach (Feely and Harzing 2003). The Volkswagen Group was a pioneer in this field. Their employees are required to complete six stages of language training, each stage consisting of 90 hours of classroom tuition, supplemented by many more hours of self-study spread over a period of six to nine months. Employees spend at least three years in fairly intensive study before they are expected to be able to function effectively in the language they have learned.

Another solution chosen by some international companies is to select a single corporate language and then to focus recruitment and personnel training on that language. Among the major multilingual companies which have adopted such a strategy are Siemens, Electrolux, Daimler-Chrysler, and Olivetti. The approach is not simple: one large Finnish company was still writing minutes of its board meetings in Finnish several years after English had been designated as its corporate language. When Nestlé tried this, it led to a major breach between its English- and French-speaking staff. A Finnish elevator company that selected English had to deal with the fact that two thirds of its employees did not speak the language natively. French workers have protested that companies which make English the dominant workplace language are in breach of the Toubon law; General Electric Medical Systems was fined €500,000 for failing to translate company documents into French, and Europ Assistance was ordered to translate computer programs into French or face a €5000 a day fine (*Personnel Today*, September 25, 2007).

A cheaper but not necessarily effective approach adopted by some companies is to select certain linguistically qualified employees as "linguistic nodes" or communication gatekeepers (Feely and Harzing 2003). A study by Lester (1994) of Nestlé showed that "the easiest and cheapest way to approach the language problem is to hire people already possessing the required skills." There are two approaches to maintaining easy communication between headquarters and overseas branches and subsidiaries. The first is to send expatriates to manage overseas operations, providing them with interpreters unless or until they develop local language proficiency. This remains common among English-speaking and Japanese corporations. A basic decision for international businesses is whether to use parent or host country nationals as senior managers in their subsidiaries (Harzing 2001). A major reason to use local staff is their knowledge of the local market practices and culture. They are familiar with local conditions, much cheaper than expatriates, and do not have the same adjustment problems. A study of 100 different multinational corporations headquartered in Japan, the United States, and seven European countries with subsidiaries in twenty-two different countries (Harzing and Van Ruysseveldt 2004) found that three quarters of Japanese firms sent an expatriate to manage a subsidiary, but only a quarter of European firms did. Expatriates were least commonly sent to Scandinavia and most common in the Far East and Middle East. They were most often used by large multinational corporations and in situations where there was a high level of cultural distance between home and host country. The local employee was more likely to be used if the cost of living in the host country was higher than in the home country. Interestingly, language *per se* did not appear as a factor in the study. The reverse version of this approach is to "inpatriate" employees from overseas branches into head office. By the mid-1990s, Fiat had introduced French, Belgian, British, Spanish, and Lebanese managers into senior management positions. Royal Dutch Shell employed some thirty-eight different nationalities at its head office.

Another approach to international business is machine translation. In spite of half a century of research, computers continue to fail to produce satisfactory translations from one language to another. One working solution has been to develop a form of man–machine interaction called controlled language. The earliest approach to this was *Caterpillar Fundamental English*. Modeled on Basic English (Ogden 1932), it required translating documents into a restricted variety using a vocabulary of 850 words so that non-native English-speaking clients could read them (Allen 1999). Boeing and other airline industries continued this strategy, but the approach did not work. In the early 1990s, Caterpillar developed *Caterpillar Technical English*, a controlled language with a reduced vocabulary of 8,000 general terms, 50,000 technical terms, and a set number of constrained syntactic constructions that could be easily translated into ten languages (another 20,000 technical terms have been added). The translation is performed on the controlled text. Varieties of controlled English have been developed for the automobile industry and for financial businesses, and most recently for translation into simple Arabic to be used as part of technical training taking place in Iraq.

Nekvapil and Nekula (2006) made a detailed study of language management activities in the Czech subsidiary of a multinational company, applying the theory of language management developed by Jernudd and Neustupný (1987). In their model, it will be recalled, simple language management occurs when an individual speaker notes that his or her speech deviates from the norm. In organized management, a manager notes the existence of language problems in various situations in a workplace, evaluates the phenomenon, and may plan for and implement an adjustment. The company they studied was a subsidiary of the large German corporation Siemens, which has no single official corporate language, but allows local languages to be used in regional companies; headquarters publishes circulars in German and English. Individual divisions of the group are autonomous, and the automotive division decided in 2002 to make English its corporate language. Employees sent abroad are entitled to free lessons in the local language. There are 2,000 employees in the Czech subsidiary studied, some of whom are foreigners. The 1,500 blue-collar workers use Czech only; the 500 white-collar workers are expected to use Czech, German, or English. The foreign employees use German or English, which are also used in communication with headquarters and with foreign customers. But problems regularly arise: analysis of a conference call conducted in English showed regular self-correction. In follow-up interviews they discovered similar problems, to which the individual solution was attempts by the Czech employees to improve their foreign language proficiency through enrolling in language courses. The management set out to deal with these problems by requiring that all heads of manufacturing departments must learn a foreign language within three years. They provided language courses and also translating and interpreting services. English and German courses were offered to more than 200 employees. All foreign employees were enrolled in a Czech course, but results were limited. Meetings involving foreign employees were generally conducted in English, but Czech employees often used German. Translation and interpreting were common especially at the level of top management, provided not by specialists but by Czech employees proficient in English or German. An external firm was used to translate longer texts where style and accuracy were essential.

The important feature of this analysis and the model of language management it illustrates is to insist on the recognition of language problems at the micro (even individual) level, with efforts at solution taking place at that level and at various higher levels in the business hierarchy. Basically, the approach shows the advantage of assuming that the lowest level is indeed the individual who recognizes language problems and wishes to correct them. At higher levels, there is a wide range of choices, including the provision of language services and the encouragement of language learning. In non-English-speaking countries, where multilingualism is considered normal, this is likely to happen both in the workplace and in the school systems that prepare students for work. In English-speaking countries, where it is commonly assumed that other people need to learn English, such programs remain pioneering.

Language management at sea and in the air

Different workplaces produce different problems for language management. As a result of changes in the ethnic and linguistic makeup of their crews, cargo ships have faced new communication problems. In the past, there was a distinction between ships' officers – regularly speakers of a European language – and the lower ranked seamen and engine-room staff who were often of Asian background. It is now estimated that two thirds of ships' crews at all levels are of mixed nationality (Sampson and Zhao 2003). In the 1980s, a study of accidents at sea revealed that 90 percent of collisions and groundings and 75 percent of shipboard fires and explosions were the result of human error, increasing pressure to solve what was seen as a communication problem.

One solution was the development of a controlled language based on English for ship-to-shore communication. Developed by a retired ship's captain working with an applied linguist, *Seaspeak* (Weeks and Strevens 1984) had a controlled lexicon and syntax; the first word of each transmission labeled the speech act, for example, "information," "warning," or "command." There were set phrases for distress, urgency, and safety procedures, all intended for the voice communication that replaced Morse code. Seaspeak was neither suitable nor intended for shipboard communication. In an ethnographic study of multiethnic crews, Sampson and Zhao (2003) found that English was generally considered the most useful working language.

Resentment was reported when senior officers used their own language to speak to each other in the presence of junior officers who did not understand.

Similar problems have arisen in the sky. As a result of evidence suggesting that a number of accidents had resulted from miscommunication between pilots and ground controllers, the International Civil Aviation Organization (ICAO) developed a language management policy in 2002. It lays down that whenever possible, standardized phrases must be used in all situations for which they have been specified; otherwise "plain language" must be used. There has been a compromise over the choice of language: air–ground radio telephony must be conducted in English or in "the language normally used by the station on the ground," which need not be the language of the state, but can be a common language agreed upon regionally. However, all ground stations serving international airports and routes must be able to use English. The policy prescribes the language proficiency required of pilots and of air traffic controllers. In 2007, the ICAO published a policy on language proficiency testing.

Specific workplaces then have specialized communication needs, and their language management ideally will take functions and participants into account.

Advertising and signs

Language policy and management in the workplace can deal with internal communication, that is to say, communication between employers and employees, or between employees at the same or different levels of authority, or what we might call somewhat inaccurately external communication, namely communication between employees and clients, customers, or other firms. Advertising is a method of communicating with actual or potential customers. The choice of language for advertising is an important form of language management, and its study interacts in interesting ways with the study of the language of public signs, which may be seen as part of the establishment of linguistic landscape, a topic which will be covered in the next chapter.

The workplace in a theory of language management

Who manages the language of the workplace? In centrally controlled economies and Sovietized systems, it is not impossible for those responsible for management to ignore the pragmatic effects of needing to satisfy the shareholders on the one hand, and the customers on the other. This occurs when state-controlled language policy sets rules for workplaces, such as the many

Québec government interventions like one recently demanding that an "Irish pub" in Montreal offer service and menus in French. Otherwise, the profit motive (making the workplace as efficient and profitable as possible) and customer satisfaction are likely to influence the owner to develop a language policy that finds organized solutions to the simple communication problems that arise in regular operations. In practice, although there are increasing studies of the field (Harris and Bargiela-Chiappini 2003) and a continual advance in the provision of language services, there is still a long way to go. Perhaps one of the problems of language management in the workplace domain is the uncertainty of one class of participants: one can know (usually) who are the owners and the employees, but there can be uncertainty about the customers. The shopkeepers in the *shuk* easily see the value of proficiency in languages in order to attract tourists passing by as customers; the self-confident English-speaking factory owner might not guess at the possible foreign customers that might be attracted by appropriate language management.

Analyzing language management in the workplace has suggested some changes in the theory we are exploring. We saw the value of starting at the individual level (Nekvapil and Nekula 2006). Other studies show not just the need for efficient communication (already the dominant force at the simplest level) but its relation to profitability. There was, however, considerable evidence of inertia, of businesses which were slow to respond to the changing but unknown multilingualism of their potential customers. In particular, there was strong evidence that knowing English discourages learning other languages – if they all want English, why should we bother to learn their language? Is this simply an example of the smugness associated with speaking a large popular language? Or is it specific to English? Perhaps it is necessary to consider a specific language (or English) not just as the object, but also as a participant in a theory of language management? An easier answer is to suggest that the perceived value of a language (part of the belief system of the business domain) is a major force in driving management efforts to change language practices. As in other domains, beliefs may be as important as facts.

5   Managing public linguistic space

Public linguistic space

In our own homes, with some exceptions, members of a family expect to have control over linguistic space. If there are notes left by the telephone, we decide what language to write them in; we choose the books for the book-shelves and the newspapers to litter the living room; we select or veto a television channel; and as was discussed in chapter 2, we have our own way of influencing what languages should be spoken among family members and when. When we leave home and enter someone else's space, we recognize that the owner can decide on these matters. In churches, synagogues, and mosques, we acknowledge the authority of priests, rabbis, and imams. In commercial enterprises, while we are most likely to patronize those busi-nesses which make provision for our language preferences ("English spoken here"), we know that the owners of the business are generally in charge. Thus, we know and understand the rules for private and institutional space. In this chapter, I want to focus on public linguistic space – the language policy of areas of our mainly urban and generally built up or developed environment – the city streets and squares, roads and parks, railway and bus stations and stops – all places which are neither private nor institutional. Public linguistic space may include written material (public signs, newspapers and magazines, books), spoken content (announcements, radio, or television), or computers and the Internet. It may be biting off too big a chunk, but I think that it is worth exploring the way in which these various sub-domains share some common principles in the development and implementation of language management. Each has a similar pattern of participants: the owners not of the space but of the sign, the actual producers of the written or spoken linguistic material, the general public or some segment of it, and often an extra-domain authority (commonly some level of government) which has chosen to manage language choice in the domain. This is not always easy or possible: a US Federal judge issued an order to a web-name organization to cancel the URL address of a site that was broadcasting leaks of documents from a Zurich bank, revealing money laundering through its Cayman Islands branch; they did so, but within minutes the site was available on a Swedish web server (*CBS News*, February 20, 2008).

The space on which a sign is posted does have an owner; the signs in Times Square, worth $2,500,000 a year (Schaps 2007) or on New York telephone boxes (which, according to a *New York Times* report in August 2007, produce $62 million annually even though many of the pay phones no longer work) are commercially leased. This adds additional participants, the owner or lessee of the space on which the billboard is situated. But they are not usually concerned about the content or language of the sign. Signs share a public location – there are, with some obvious exceptions, no special permits needed to walk down the street or buy a newspaper or open a URL, although totalitarian systems (and democracies struggling to find a way to deal with terrorism) regularly try to control access.

There is another interesting fact that affects these domains, and that is the ambivalent effect of globalization. It is ambivalent because on the one hand public linguistic space is no longer entirely under local control – we have for a long time seen Coca-Cola posters in stores, international billboards lining highways, foreign television productions taking up many of the channels of cable television, and international editions of newspapers available both in print and on the Internet. Thus, the owner/originator need not be in our locality or even in our country. On the other hand, modern technology has produced what is called the "Long Tail" (Anderson 2004). As well as best-sellers and mass-appeal goods, which count print runs and audiences in the millions, there is room in the market again for items with quite small cir-culations – books like two of mine that are available through a "print on request" system, blogs that are written for a few readers, FM radio stations with very limited local appeal, sites like YouTube and Facebook that allow individual access to the Web. The interesting paradigm is the Internet, once assumed to be driving out small languages forever, and now recognized as available even to threatened indigenous languages (Danet and Herring 2007).

This chapter will start with written language and move on to other media. It will be clear that the domains overlap, and that control over them may well represent attempts by external participants (businesses, interest groups, governments) to influence language policy in a wider domain.

Public verbal signs

Early studies of public signage

Over the past thirty years or so, a number of scholars have been excited to discover or rediscover the riches revealed by a casual or systematic investi-gation of mainly urban public verbal signs. Labeled "linguistic landscape," the study of public multilingual signage is developing into a sub-field of sociolinguistics or language policy. A major topic of interest is the choice of language in public signs in bilingual or multilingual urban space (which is why cityscape might be preferable to landscape). Most studies of public signage have been in multilingual cities. Checking the effects of legal requirements in Québec, Monnier (1989) found that French signs were dominant. In a more recent paper, Bourhis and Landry (2002) report the changes in the *paysage linguistique* of the province of Québec as a result of the application of *Loi 104*.

The term *linguistic landscape* appears to have been first used by Landry and Bourhis (1997) in a paper reporting the perceptions of francophone high school students of the language of public signs in Canadian provinces. Landscape is of course a translation of *paysage* (Bourhis and Landry 2002). It was applied by Ben-Rafael and colleagues (2006) to their counts of signs in various Israeli communities. In their study, signs are observed and counted, rather than experienced as in Landry and Bourhis (1997), and the differences between Arab areas and non-Arab areas are noted, as well as the presumed effect of Hebrew hegemony and globalizing English on both.

But the topic has a longer history. Among the early studies in monolingual areas, Masai (1972) looked at Tokyo signs and drew attention to the growing presence of English. Tulp (1978) showed the predominance of French in officially bilingual Brussels; nearly twenty years later, Wenzel (1996) found a similar pattern with an increasing presence of English.

In a pioneering investigation of the spread of English led by Joshua Fishman (Fishman *et al.* 1977), Rosenbaum *et al.* (1977) included counts of the relative number of English and Hebrew signs observed in a Jerusalem street. These too were real counts of actual signs, and established the approach to a study of the sociolinguistic ecology of cities that has been one of the main methods of this field. They found a much higher proportion of English language or romanized script signs than might be expected from their observations of the language spoken on the street; this difference between written and oral language in the sociolinguistic ecology is general, and will be discussed below. Overall, a third of the signs used as much *Loazit* "romanized" script as Hebrew. There was a pattern in this use: grocery stores serving the local public used Hebrew only, but two thirds of the other stores which catered also to tourists used some romanized script. Private offices used romanized script more than did government offices. They interpret this in part as snob appeal, but also as a greater tolerance for foreign languages by the public than in the official government support of Hebrew hegemony.

My own interest in public signs dates from a visit to Jerusalem in 1979: it became the basis of a chapter in the description of the languages of the Old City of Jerusalem that Cooper (who had worked with Fishman) and I published (Spolsky and Cooper 1991). Three signs first piqued my curiosity. One was a sign above a stall in the market which read (only in English): "Names made in English, Hebrew or Arabic." There was an Arabic signature in a corner. The sign raised the intriguing question – who were these English readers who would want names written in other languages? And why wasn't the offer made to Hebrew and Arabic passersby? The second were a pair of street signs on opposite sides of a narrow pedestrian alley around the corner from where we were living. Each sign consisted of nine painted ceramic tiles, and was written in three languages. The Hebrew and Arabic were identical on both sides of the street, but on one side, the English read "Hamalakh Street" and on the other "El-Malak Street." In the first of these, the English was a transliteration of the Hebrew, and in the second, a transliteration of the Arabic. Closer examination revealed another major difference: the second sign consisted of nine tiles with a single frame, the texts each written over three tiles. In the first sign, the lower six tiles contained Arabic and the transliteration; a frame separated them from the top three tiles with Hebrew which had been added later. Fitting this to the historical context, the explanation seemed to be an original street sign in Arabic and English prepared during the period of Jordanian occupation of the Old City of Jerusalem (1948–1967). When the Jordanian Arab Legion conquered the Old City, all Jews living there were expelled, and no Jews were permitted to visit the holy sites for twenty years. Arabic street signs were put up, with English added for tourists. In 1967, the Old City came under Israeli rule, and was opened up again to the three major religions. A Hebrew line was added to existing Jordanian bilingual signs. New signs recognized not just a multilingual situation, but also, by placing the Hebrew on top, Israeli rule and associated Hebrew dominance. This interpretation was confirmed when we found some signs put up before 1948, during the period of the British Mandate, where English was the top language, with Arabic and Hebrew below.

These three intriguing signs set me off on a search for more, and the results are summarized in Spolsky and Cooper (1991). As well as describing other signs found in the Old City, we proposed a conditions model (Jackendoff 1983) explaining the choice of languages. The first condition, a necessary one, is to write a sign in a language you know. This rule explains why signs are not written in languages without a writing system (e.g., not written in colloquial Arabic but only in Classical Arabic, and why you see signs in India in only a few of its 2,000 languages) and accounts for the spelling errors common in signs written in foreign languages (especially menus in tourist restaurants). The second rule was suggested by the "Names made here" sign; it is a typical and graded condition named the "presumed reader's condition": prefer to write a sign in a language which can be read by the people you expect to read it. In a monolingual or monoliterate region, signs will be in the dominant language, but if there are foreign visitors (tourists for instance) or a literate minority whose language is recognized, bilingual signs may be common. Some signs may be intended only for foreigners and in their language; there was a sign in Greek in the Temple in Jerusalem saying that gentiles should not go past this point; the stone is now in an Istanbul museum. The third rule accounts for language choice on signs that assert ownership; it is also a typical condition, which we called the "symbolic value condition": prefer to write a sign in your own language or in a language with which you wish to be identified. This accounts for the order of languages on multilingual signs and for the prevalence of monolingual signs (e.g., in German or Turkish or Classical Arabic) on commemorative or building plaques. These three conditions, I believe, constitute the major part of a theory of language choice in public signage (Spolsky 2008).

Subsequently, we used this technique for studies of vernacular literacy in various parts of the world, comparing what I was learning about Navajo reluctance to adopt vernacular literacy while accepting literacy in English with the rapid acceptance of vernacular literacy that I had observed among the Māori and later found among other Polynesian peoples (Spolsky and Holm 1971, 1973). In New Zealand and Tonga (Spolsky *et al.* 1983), within a few months of contact with Christian missionaries in the early nineteenth century, many local people were reading and soon writing in their own language; among the Navajo, vernacular literacy was more or less limited to the choices of non-Navajo missionaries and schools systems (Spolsky 1981). In Tonga, we found not only the weekly newspaper but also small handwritten signs in shops and kiosks in Tongan; in the Navajo Nation, the only public written use of the Navajo language seemed to be in signs put up by the Anglo owners and managers of a supermarket, or by a few schools committed to bilingualism. The public signs in both these cases reflected the local literacy environment: Tonga was bilingual and biliterate – the local newspaper appeared in both languages, while the Navajo Nation at that time was orally bilingual (with most private and public oral events – home language use, Tribal Council meetings, local radio, tribal courts in Navajo) but its literacy was almost entirely in English (school language, minutes of Tribal Council meetings, weekly Tribal newspaper, court records). We found a slightly different pattern in bilingual Paraguay (Engelbrecht and Ortiz 1983). Spanish was the dominant language for most literacy functions, just as it was for schooling, for government, and for the city. However, there was symbolic use of Guarani – the spoken language of the countryside, of informal conversations everywhere, and of Paraguayan identity – in shop signs and in printed song lyrics.

Preliminary questions

Public signs have, as Landry (1997) noted, two major functions – to communicate, whether information ("Habad Street"), instruction ("No parking"), or persuasion ("Buy British," "Vote for Obama"), or to express a symbolic function – to declare ownership ("Presidential Palace," "First Methodist Church") or to mark linguistic dominance (to express power). In a multilingual (or more precisely, multiliterate) community, the second function may be added to the first by choice of language. Thus, writing a street sign in Hebrew, Arabic, or English in Jerusalem was a reflection of the political situation – the street signs from the British Mandate period where the English is on top, followed by the other officially recognized languages, Arabic and Hebrew in that order, and the signs from the period of Jordanian rule (1948–1967) with Arabic on top and English transcription, and contemporary Israeli signs with Hebrew on top, followed by Arabic and with the Hebrew translated or transliterated into English. The order of languages, like the language choice, becomes a claim of ownership: when the Israeli electric company took over the supply of electricity to the Old City from the Arabic company, the Danger signs switched the order of languages, with Hebrew moving to the top (Spolsky and Cooper 1991: 88).

From a language management perspective, public signs are the culmination of a process with several participants – the initiator or owner of the sign, the sign maker, and the reader. In a communicative sign, the owner (using a sign maker) is communicating with a presumed reader. In an ownership sign, the owner is communicating with anyone, reader or not. But there is also a significant fourth party, the implied "top" in the "top-down" model, and this is a language management authority, whether a national or local government or perhaps religious or ethnic authority, which sets a specific policy on language choice. Leclerc (1994) lists the many nations with laws controlling public signs. The best example is *Loi 101* in Québec, which required that the largest letters in public signs must be in French (Bourhis and Landry 2002); another is the Tokyo municipal policy on the use of English in street signs (Backhaus 2005). In Malaysia, the Minister of Culture, Arts, and Heritage, Rais Yatim, was reported as stating that fines of up to 1,000 ringgit (US$290) could be imposed for billboards and posters that display "mutated forms" of Bahasa Melayu – this was aimed specifically at the mixture of English called *Manglish* (*The Hindu*, June 10, 2007).

This raises the question of agency. The vast majority of studies of signs are based on observation, counting, and (nowadays thanks to small digital cameras) photographing actual finished signs, and not looking at the process by which that particular sign was produced. In the study on the Navajo Reservation, we asked about the initiation of each Navajo sign, and Backhaus has details of Tokyo municipal policy. Most studies, however, look only at results and then offer interpretations of why the sign maker chose a specific language. Was it government policy or the sign maker's interpretation that led to the language choice in the Old City? There was evidence of the absence of high level policy in the changes in two official signs in the Old City in Jerusalem in 1980; the Police Station dropped Arabic from its largest sign in the same year that the Post Office opposite added it. On the Navajo Reservation, the observers were often told that the initiator of a sign with Navajo was a non-Navajo, like the Anglo manager of a supermarket.

In fact, in one of the first studies that concentrate on authorship, Malinowski (2008) shows the complexity of the issue. He studied an area of Oakland, California, where about 10 percent of the signs observed included prominent use of Korean *hangul* script. Of a dozen owners who agreed to be interviewed, a third said they had bought the business with the sign already in place, and another third reported they had been influenced in various aspects of the sign (color, language, layout) by local sign-making companies. Some of the owners said that the purpose of including Korean was to encourage recognition of affinity; others agreed it was for non-readers of English; and others were unsure of what purpose it served (one had not even noticed the Korean and had to go outside to check). More studies like this that trace the decision back to the sign initiator will help us see how much management there is and who is responsible.

Another potential explanation of language choice in a sign must be the location of the initiator. With globalization, many signs in cities are international advertisements sometimes modified and localized but often simply reproductions of one used worldwide. These international signs should not be lumped together with the use of an international language like English within a local sign in Germany or Japan (where they constitute a special language of their own) or the equivalent use of a French or German word in an English advertisement. It is important to distinguish local from global signs – the existence rather than the language of the latter is what is most likely to be relevant. Of course, locally modified global signs (Coca-Cola advertisements in Hebrew or Arabic letters that imitate the appearance of the English original) show a willingness to accommodate to the reader while maintaining the cachet of the foreign or international origin.

Signs are very obvious in Japan. Following up on the study of Masai (1972), Lim (1996) found a much greater frequency of English as well as other languages in Tokyo (and similar high use in Seoul). In one of the first studies to benefit from digital cameras, Someya (2002) found that Kanji signs are dominant, but the Roman alphabet is strong. The latest study of Tokyo and its bilingual signs is Backhaus (2007). He provides a detailed case study of Tokyo, a city that the naïve foreigner, dazzled by the striking (and often electronic) display of three Japanese script types in public signs, at first assumes to be as monolingual as the huge crowds that threaten to overwhelm him as he emerges from an underground. It turns out that just as in many other large international cities, public signs reveal a complex but significant pattern of language choice. In Tokyo, Backhaus found that the language of some signs is "managed," the result of explicit decisions of central and local government agencies, rather than the result of local choices of the sign owner or maker. In this way, he made an important step to fit public signs into the study of language management.

The effect of advertising on the paysage linguistique

In this volume, my current aim is to account for the choice of language in public signage with a model similar to that used for language policy in general – a description of actual practice, an attempt to infer beliefs, and research into specific management decisions. The choice of language for advertising is an important form of language management. It is the second of the conditions proposed in Spolsky (1991b), "choose the language of your presumed or desired reader," that seems to be most relevant to advertising, although it can be argued that the choice of a language with certain associations (e.g., French for perfumes, Italian for foodstuffs) relates simultaneously to the third or symbolic condition. And the advertisements in Japan in a variety of English that no native speaker of English can understand is presumably a case of applying condition three in circumstances where condition one is not met, i.e., writing in English for symbolic reasons by people without proficiency. One of the advantages of the conditions model (Jackendoff 1983) is that it deals not with absolutes but with typicality and gradedness: all three rules can apply to a single sign, producing stronger or weaker interpretations.

To provide some kind of order to a large field, I make an initial distinction between advertisements under the control of the company or firm owning or producing the sign (including decisions in the case of international firms that affect national affiliates) and those influenced or governed (as nowadays in Québec and France and elsewhere) by national policies and laws. With this provision, we need to distinguish further between signs and advertisements inside the workplace, and those on the outside (especially on the building or shop front), and those physically separated (public posters for example). But there is an even earlier condition that needs to be considered: the expectation of the sign initiator that the potential clientele are in fact literate or interested in signs at all.

In principle, one would expect the normal case to be the communicative goal – a policy to advertise in the language of potential clients and customers. It is evident that this is not so when major enterprises come to realize the importance of the clients' language very late in the day. It was, for example newsworthy when at the end of March 2005 the large American retailer, Wal-Mart, announced a new advertising campaign in the United States that would present television, print, and radio advertisements in Cantonese, Mandarin, and Vietnamese, as though the speakers of these languages had just arrived. The company proudly asserted that the new advertisements would allow "Asian American consumers to see and hear firsthand what the Wal-Mart experience is all about – entirely in their own native languages." In the same month, the US National Association of Realtors published its first-ever Spanish-language television advertisements. Realtors having suddenly become aware that about 2 million Spanish-speakers would be buying homes in the next five years, their advertisements proclaimed the advantages of using a realtor in Spanish! This is another case of the slowness of English-speaking businesses to realize the value of accommodating to their potential customers.

Studying the communicative function of advertisement, Grin (1994) proposed a model to predict advertising choices in a bilingual or multilingual society. It showed the relation of sales to different language groups as the function of the level of advertising in each language, the language attitudes, the incomes, and an advertising response function. Indifference to language and the public can produce a monolingual commercial environment, and strong resistance among minority groups to the dominant language hegemony can increase the profitability of bilingual advertising.

Fieldwork carried out by Ladousa (2002) in the north Indian town, Banaras, supported this. The town is in a Hindi-speaking region, with the main local language being Bhojpurī. School advertising in the city uses various combinations of Hindi and English and various mixtures of the two writing systems, Devanagari and Roman. The state schools do not advertise. The private schools, however, have advertising posters all over the city, many of them making clear that they teach in English.

Many studies of multilingual advertisements have looked at the symbolic function of using a language other than the unmarked local language in an advertisement. Kelly-Holmes (2000: 67) argues that foreign languages are used in European advertising not for their communicative function, but for their symbolic value. She believes that "it is unimportant whether the advertisee understands the foreign words in an advertisement so long as it calls up the cultural stereotypes of the country with which the language is associated." Support for this is provided by Piller (2001) who collected 600 commercials broadcast on German television in February 1999 and more than 400 print advertisements that appeared in two national German newspapers during a two-week period at the end of 1999. She found that more than two thirds of the commercials included a language other than German. The main foreign language was English (70 percent of the foreign language commercials) but there were also examples in French (8 percent) and Italian (6 percent). The foreign items were not just words but phrases and discourse phenomena. There was no difference in the use of English slogans between

German companies and international ones. In another study, Piller (2003) traces the development of studies of multilingual advertising. Earlier studies had simply looked at the borrowing of individual lexical items as evidence of foreign influence, but starting with studies by Haarmann (1989) they have moved to discourse phenomena. Haarmann showed how Japanese advertisements used foreign languages to associate the product with stereotypes about speakers of the foreign language. Very commonly in Japan, product names were in a foreign language. Piller gave a number of other examples: American car names used French for connotations of fashion, elegance, and femininity; German commercials used French for feminine elegance and eroticism, and Italian for food. Often, the multilingualism produced a mock language. Takashi (1990) believes that loan words are used in Japanese to make the product seem more modern and sophisticated: they are generally targeted at younger audiences. Hyde (2002) argued that the English in mixed language signs in Japan were intended for Japanese speakers and not for tourists. In an empirical study of Dutch responses to foreign words in advertisements, considerable variation was found, but some of the regularly proposed associations (elegance for French, technical for German, beautiful for Spanish) did show up; only half of the associations were positive, and many were negative (especially German); but the number of positive associations made the advertisement more appealing (Hornikx *et al.* 2007). Irish, Kelly-Holmes (2007) suggested, is favored in the official sphere but clearly a minority language in the commercial: they therefore studied Irish advertisements in two Irish-language newspapers, finding use of the language while common in public service and official advertisements to be rare in commercial advertising, except those in traditional arts and crafts and the Irish language industry.

A large number of studies trace the spread of English into advertisements throughout the world. Griffin (2001) noted that English is commonly used in shop signs and billboards in Sofia. Griffin (2004) described the amount of English in Rome on storefronts, in shop windows, outside commercial and public buildings, in billboards and other street advertisements, and as graffiti. Schlick (2002) lists English words used in shop windows in Austria, Italy, and Slovenia. Friedrich (2002) analyzed the motivations for the incorporation of English into advertising and brand names in Brazil. Rajagopalan (2002) describes the backlash of linguistic chauvinism to the increasing use of English in advertisements and elsewhere in Brazil. Martin (2002a, 2002b) studied a sample of French television commercials that she collected during the summer of 2000; a third of them included some form of English, which she found somewhat astounding considering the 1994 Toubon Law restricting the use of English in the media.

It is not unreasonable to speculate that the mixture of languages is a result of growing globalization: contact with foreign languages has meant that other languages are more likely to be understood, and even if not understood, to carry symbolic associations that can be exploited by the sign maker. National language management agencies and language activists may object, and may be empowered by laws like *Loi 101* in Québec to try to correct the trend.

Public signs in a theory of language management

The study of verbal signs in public space has, over the past forty years, proved its worth as a tool exploring and characterizing the multiliterate ecology of cities. Handicapped by lack of agreement on a title (and even more by the growing use of the misleading term "landscape"), no clear consensus has yet developed on methodology or theory. Seen as a sub-field of language management, it provides a complementary view to that normally provided in analyses of spoken language use. Because of the quite different distributions of spoken and written language, and because it is easier to identify and count the language of signs than of conversations, it risks misinterpretation, recording the state of literacy rather than the status of spoken varieties. Not being easily open to the recognition of problems, with the initiator and the sign maker out of contact with the sign reader (or potential reader), it does not provide the feedback or monitoring that checks communicative effectiveness and encourages organized language management. It does, however, as a growing number of studies are showing, provide a valuable way to study language choice.

It is the symbolic function of public signs that provides the intriguing new perspective to a theory of language management. As Landry and Bourhis sagely recognized, the balance of languages in a multiliterate environment communicates the status of each language. It is for this reason that language activists (see Chapter 10) press for increased use of their favored language. Their study of *paysage linguistique* was as a backdrop to the francophone movement, and served for them as a measure of the success of radical language laws. Similarly, the Welsh language activists, the supporters of Arab language rights, the Māori language movement, and the Basque nationalists all made a point of calling for greater prominence for their language. Because of its salience, the choice of language on a public sign carries a high emotional value, helping signal territorial boundaries and proclaiming sovereignty.

Linguistic signs can be defaced (a negative choice) or produced unofficially (as graffiti), so permitting the unauthorized rebel to leave a mark on public space. We notice this frequently in the Old City: the semi-official trilingual signs often have a language painted over or chipped out, and pro-terrorist signs in Arabic or anti-Arab signs in Hebrew are regularly added to otherwise blank walls. Thus the language of public signs becomes an important record of the linguistic conflicts that Calvet (1990) highlights or of the changing sovereignty of multiliterate territory. Just as the language of advertising and the workplace showed the importance of the profit motive, so the language of public signs can reveal something about the changing power structure.

Graffiti provides an interesting counter-example to the patterns of official and business-produced public signage. It breaks the basic rule of appearing only with the approval of the owner of the space, for it appears at the whim of the writer and in direct disobedience to signs stating "Post no signs!" Often, it gives evidence of hasty production, as though the artist was watching for police. It does not usually have the formal frames defining public signs. Its messages too are transgressive (Pennycook 2008), proclaiming the presence of illegal organizations or posting anti-government slogans.

Visual space for private use

A related issue is public material produced for private use, such as newspapers and books. Here, the unmarked case is that such material is available in the standard written official language – English language newspapers in English-speaking countries, French language newspapers in francophone countries, Icelandic newspapers in Iceland (and an exceptionally prolific Icelandic book production): the interesting questions arise with the marked cases where a minority language or a non-standard variety is used.

Newspapers and magazines

Having a newspaper in your own language is clearly an important factor in maintaining the status and use of the language. In his Graded Intergenerational Disruption Scale, Fishman (1991b) does not mention newspapers specifically and refers to mass media at the two highest levels (stages two and three) where the chances of maintenance are strong. Stage five, however, just above the critical level of intergenerational informal oral transmission, includes literacy in the home, school, and community, which clearly relates to availability of newspapers.

In non-totalitarian states, the decision on the language of newspapers might be assumed to be dependent on commercial considerations and the existence of a readership prepared to buy the newspaper. In Fishman (1966), the chapter on the non-English and ethnic press used circulation figures as evidence of the strength of language maintenance in the United States. "No publications can indefinitely substitute the sentiment for substance. The ethnic press, therefore, must measure its success by the practical criteria of co-territorial American society" (Fishman *et al.* 1966: 72).

In multilingual India, Jeffrey (1997) described the increase in advertising support for Indian-language newspapers, mentioning specifically Hindi, Tamil, Malayalam, Telugu, and Gujarati, all of which seemed to be flourishing in spite of the continued spread of English newspapers on the one hand, and of television on the other. It will be noticed of course that all these named Indian languages are constitutionally official, but clearly in competition with English, the language that the constitution assumed was to last only a decade or so.

Guyot (2007: 36) believes that "the existence of newspapers and magazines dedicated to minority languages has almost always been left to the initiative of the linguistic groups themselves." Occasionally, the regional press in the majority language publishes articles in the local language, but he concludes that "for minority languages, the press can be considered as neglected media." But perhaps the view from Paris is limited. In France, the Minister of the Interior has the power to prohibit the "circulation, dissemination and sale of papers, periodical or non-periodical writings, written in a foreign language, or written in French but of foreign origin." In Israel, in contrast, there are currently eight daily newspapers published in the dominant language, Hebrew; two published in English as well as a local edition of the *International Herald Tribune*; four published in Russian; one each in French and German; and four Arabic newspapers that appear more than once a week. There is another score of national and local weekly papers, one in Arabic and the rest in Hebrew. All are privately owned. Most United Kingdom newspapers are in English, but there is a weekly newspaper published in Welsh and a plan to establish a daily; another daily appears in Polish. In the United States, there are at least nine newspapers still published in Spanish, and daily or weekly newspapers in Arabic, Chinese, Flemish, Japanese, Lithuanian, Russian, Urdu, Vietnamese, and Yiddish. As noted in Fishman (1966), the tendency for ethnic newspapers to switch from the ethnic language to English continues.

In the nineteenth century, Polynesian contact with European missionaries led to the rapid development of literacy which included the development of newspaper and periodical publication. Between 1842 and 1933, 34 separate periodicals appeared in New Zealand, 55 percent solely in Māori and 43 percent bilingual. In Tonga, there was a similar rapid development of literacy, and by 1980, the main newspaper on the islands was published weekly in Tongan (Spolsky *et al.* 1983). While most of the stories arrived in English, they were all translated into Tongan; an abbreviated edition was published in English for expatriates. After the 1980 cyclone and the success of a bilingual edition distributed throughout the growing Tongan Diaspora, the editor proposed to switch to a single bilingual edition; this was vetoed by the king, who understood the relevance of the Tongan newspaper to the maintenance of literacy and language.

In a totalitarian state, newspapers are under government control, and the decision on form (i.e., language choice) as well as content (censorship) is open to government management. Pre-state non-governmental language activist groups can also attempt to enforce control over newspapers. Shohamy (2007) cites a plan published in 1941 by the *Ha-mo'atza ha-merakezet le-hashlatat ha-'ivrit bayishuv* (Central Council for the Establishment of Hebrew in the Jewish Community of Palestine) aiming to require foreign language newspapers to become gradually bilingual – 50 percent Hebrew in the first year, 75 percent Hebrew in the second, and to cease publication in the third. The plan also noted that the owners of the German-language newspapers were resisting the plan. The ultimate ineffectiveness of this "plan" might be demonstrated by the figures given by Fishman and Fishman (1978: 212); whereas in 1940, there were ten non-Hebrew publications published in Israel, in 1960 there were 76, in spite of the reported refusal to supply newsprint for a Yiddish daily. Currently, newspapers are published in Israel in English, Arabic, French, Polish, Yiddish, Amharic, Farsi, Ladino, Romanian, Hungarian, Russian, and German, showing the futility of the effort to block non-Hebrew press.

In Singapore, the media are under government control, but privatization is developing. There are four major local newspapers, one for each of the four official languages: English, Mandarin, Malay, and Tamil. Circulation of the first three has increased, but there has been a decrease in the readership of the Tamil newspaper. A number of local tabloids have also developed, all in English, and written in simpler and more colloquial English than the major newspapers (Rappa and Wee 2006).

Canada has a long tradition of ethnic newspapers. The first ethnic newspaper was published in Halifax in 1788. Currently, newspapers appear in Arabic (3), Armenian, Bulgarian, Chinese (12), Croatian, Czech (2), Dutch (4), Estonian, Finnish (2), Gaelic, German (11), Greek (4), Hebrew, Hungarian (6), Icelandic, Italian (12), Japanese (2), Korean, Latvian, Lithuanian, Maltese, Persian, Polish (3), Portuguese (7), Punjabi, Russian (3), Serbian (3), Slovak, Slovenian, Spanish, Swedish, Ukrainian (5), Urdu (4), Vietnamese (1), and Yiddish (1); there are a dozen other ethnic papers which appear in English or French. In 1974, the Canadian Federal government started the Native Communication Program to support media services for the native peoples; the main support was for newspapers (Demay 1993). The program was canceled in 1991, and two newspapers ceased publication. Most are reported to be struggling for survival, finding it difficult to obtain advertising support, but eleven newspapers were still being published in 1993.

Avison and Meadows (2000) argue that print technology was the basis for the emerging aboriginal communications industry in both Canada and Australia. Its newspapers permitted Canadian and Australian aboriginals to develop their own public spheres, able to engage in public dialog. By 1985, with Federal funding, circulation for aboriginal newspapers had reached 46,000. With the end of Federal funding, seven regional aboriginal newspapers ceased publication. In Australia, aboriginal newspapers appeared in the mid-nineteenth century, but increased during the land rights protests of the late 1960s and 1970s. Some of the Australian aboriginal newspapers are supported by government advertising, but there has been no regular funding program.

The languages of newspapers then can offer a significant measure of the status and vitality of a minority language. Management depends on three major participants: owners to fund production, readers to pay subscriptions, and governments to support or ban publication.

Visual space: books

Traditionally, literacy is particularly associated with the book. In Chapter 3, we saw how decisions about the languages for sacred texts were important examples of language management. The willingness to translate the Bible into vernacular languages provided critically valuable status for the varieties selected, required extensive language cultivation to express biblical concepts, developed a new literary style for the variety, and became a focus of education in the variety and in literacy. Because of the centrality of books to schooling, the status of a variety without a literature is hard to maintain. Many vernacular literacies had to struggle against the classical language which dominated their school system. Many endangered languages find it hard to continue when they lack a written literature of their own. Many of the newly established national languages of the nineteenth century depended on the existence not just of an earlier literary tradition but also of a group of writers willing and able to produce and have published a high literature in the language. One of the problems faced by many language revival or maintenance programs is the increasing tendency of ethnic writers to prefer the standard language.

From sign to sound

Writing this inside the walls of the Old City of Jerusalem, I am generally spared the roar of traffic (apart from the occasional tractor collecting garbage) and the shouting of street vendors (for that I have to go to the vegetable and fruit market), but the silence is regularly filled by bells from the large number of Christian churches and the loudspeakers broadcasting taped calls and full services five times a day from the muezzins in the many mosques. In medieval England Europe, town criers (protected by English common law from interference) were long used to make official proclamations and pass on news. Occasionally, we hear announcements in public space: perhaps a police loudspeaker warning us of a suspicious object, or a store advertising a bargain sale. Management, if attempted, is likely to come under municipal regulations against noise pollution, often in the night hours, although Israeli towns have a customary discouragement of noise in the early afternoon. Nowadays, however, most public sound consists of electronic media.

Media: radio and television

Just as governments sometimes try to control public signs, they commonly interfere with the content of radio and television, and in particular have rules concerning indecency and obscene language. The presentation of nudity on television is one obvious target, but another is the use of obscene language. The US Federal Communication Commission (FCC) has regulations forbidding obscene language. In 2003, the FCC punished NBC for a vulgarity uttered by a singer during a live awards ceremony, and the recent Bush appointees to the Commission are reported to have set out to punish stations that permit "fleeting expletives." In June 2007, the United States Court of Appeal (Second Circuit in New York) overturned the Commission policy that utterance of certain words violated indecency rules, noting that such words are commonly used not for obscene purposes but out of excitement or frustration. They pointed out that the "top leaders of government" (specifically the President and Vice-President) had used the same language (*New York Times*, June 5, 2007).

Radio broadcasting in the United States began in 1909, and was brought under government regulation by the Wireless Act of 1912 which required radio stations to be licensed. In July, 1918, all non-government stations were shut down to prevent them from giving information to the enemy; the ban lasted one year. The number of stations increased and in 1932, a new kind of license called "limited commercial" was required, with stations required to share time on a single frequency. During the 1920s and 1930s, radio receivers became increasingly common in Europe and the United States, advertising was added, and networks were established. By 1958, it was estimated that there was a radio in virtually every American home and in two thirds of American passenger cars. A different approach was followed in the United Kingdom; licenses for radio reception and transmission were originally issued by the Post Office. When the British Broadcasting Corporation (BBC) was set up in 1922, it was decided to fund it by licenses to operate a radio receiver, and the system continued in operation until 1968 when combined radio and television licenses were first issued.

Minority access to radio and television

In the United States, the fact that radio receivers were so cheap meant that even the poorest groups, including immigrants, had access, and broadcasting in languages other than English was provided for linguistic minorities (Warshauer 1966). In 1956, there were over a thousand foreign language stations in the continental United States broadcasting an average of 5.4 hours per week; in 1960, there was an increase in the number of stations but a decrease in hours per week. Spanish accounted for two thirds of the broadcasting hours, followed by Slavic languages (about 10 percent). In Europe, minority language radio began in the 1940s and 1950s – Irish in 1945, Sámi in 1946, Welsh and Frisian in the 1950s, Breton in 1959 (Guyot 2007: 36). Television programs in minority languages began a few years later: Irish in 1960, Welsh in 1964, Breton in 1964, Basque in 1971, and Frisian in 1979.

During World War Two, fear of foreign language radio programs in the United States favoring the German and Italian governments led to a proposal to abolish foreign language radio stations and newspapers (Browne 2007). The US Office of War Information pressured radio stations to check the loyalty of broadcasters and develop programs supporting the US war effort. In Britain too, there was reported to be suspicion about the loyalty of Welsh language broadcasts. In 1942, the New Zealand Broadcasting Service added a five-minute weekly newscast in Māori reacting to the presence of Māori soldiers in the army (Browne 2007: 110).

Minority-owned and operated radio stations started to emerge in the United States after the war and increased in numbers in the 1970s. Low-power community radio stations also started and their numbers grew in the 1970s and 1980s; while they were not required to do so, most provided service for linguistic and ethnic minorities. But the provision of non-English television from public funds continues to raise debate: a decision to start a new Spanish language public television channel in Maryland is being challenged as favoring one out of many possible minorities (*Baltimore Sun*, May 26, 2007). In Europe, most radio broadcasting was done by government monopolies which provided very limited service to minority linguistic groups. In Canada, Australia, and New Zealand there was government support for ethnic minority broadcasting. In New Zealand, the 1989 Broadcasting Act provided for the development of two dozen Māori tribal radio stations; there are now also radio stations in other Polynesian languages (Browne 2007). In a report prepared for the New Zealand Treasury, Grin and Vaillancourt (1998, 1999) estimated how much it had cost to provide Welsh, Irish, and Basque television services. Subsequently in 2002, acceding to a long activist campaign, a Māori television service was established which survived a major hiring scandal and now offers several hours' daily programming in Māori and English – 90 percent of the programs are locally produced. Cormack (2007) points out that while there are good arguments in favor of providing media access for linguistic minorities, there is not yet clear evidence of its contribution to language maintenance.

In Sweden and Norway, pressure from non-Lutheran religious organizations led to the opening of community stations which became very popular with linguistic and ethnic minorities. In Britain, after a period of unlicensed broadcasting by minority groups, a number of low-power stations were permitted. In Germany, public radio stations provided short foreign-language broadcasts for the guest workers in the 1960s. Cable television now means that many ethnic minority groups have access to blocks of time. In France, with the ending of the public service broadcasting monopoly in 1981, a number of linguistic and ethnic minority groups started their own programs. In Spain, Catalan and Basque services developed after the granting of autonomy.

In Latin America, Roman Catholic-supported linguistic minority radio services developed at the community level and by the 1990s there were local radio stations using Native American languages. A number of African states also now have community radio services in local languages. The South African Broadcasting Corporation operates eight radio stations with programming in the official languages and two community radio stations in other local languages. Members of the National Assembly in Cameroon were assured by the Communications Minister that efforts were being made to maintain the level of broadcasting in the national languages on the CRTV Provincial Stations currently at between 20 and 40 percent; the difficulties were in finding qualified staff. They are supplemented, he said, by community radio stations (*Cameroon Tribune*, June 19, 2007).

Browne (2007) sums up: there was little if any support for minority language radio stations in the early days. World War Two created an increased demand for minority radio and television. By the 1960s, many groups had started to work for minority media. Most recently, the spread of cable and satellite broadcasting has offered new outlets; satellites for instance provide homeland services to linguistic diasporas.

Wales, Scotland, and Ireland furnish case studies of language policy activism in campaigns for linguistic minority television (Hourigan 2007). The Welsh Language Society began to campaign in 1966, arguing that the absence of Welsh language programs for Welsh-speaking children threatened the stability of the language. After the failure of a petition and of a march through Cardiff, the next stage involved "symbolic acts of damage" including the destruction of broadcasting equipment. A number of members of the Society refused to pay their radio and television license fees; some were charged and imprisoned. The government established committees to investigate the possibility of Welsh television, and before the 1979 elections, both Labour and the Conservatives promised to introduce legislation. The refusal of the new Prime Minister, Margaret Thatcher, to do this led to renewed protest including from groups of mothers and toddlers and protests by ordained ministers. The government finally gave in, and in 1982 set up the Welsh television service.

In Ireland, a committee of the language organization *Conrad na Gaeilge* felt it was having little influence in increasing the amount of Irish on the national broadcast service. Formal contacts with the Welsh society including a conference in 1975 encouraged them to step up the campaign and use similar tactics. A student leader climbed the broadcasting mast; members of the society picketed television studios and the General Post Office, petitions were submitted, and activists refused to pay their license fee. There was public criticism of the campaign, seen by some as related to the violence in the North. In 1985, the new president of the Society changed the ideological approach and combined it with a demand for a Bill of Rights for Irish speakers, which brought support from the Irish-medium school movement and from a group of Gaeltacht leaders. Under pressure, the government in 1987 allocated £500,000 to Irish language television. Over the next two years, there was a split between the Welsh-influenced activists and the Gaeltacht group, each of which had different goals. In 1990, an umbrella organization put together a compromise proposal, a model of national television service based in the Gaeltacht. The Irish government set up committees to report on its feasibility, and the new service began in 1996.

Hourigan (2007) believes that the campaign for Scots Gaelic broadcasting was influenced by the Welsh and the Irish campaigns. The Scots asked for the provision of Gaelic language television programs on the four existing channels. They could not claim the same political goals or argue for large numbers of speakers of Scots Gaelic. As a result, they accepted bilingualism, and supported a plan put forward by the Gaelic Television Fund asking for £10 million to provide 200 hours a year of Gaelic programming. Faced with a general election in which Scottish seats would be critical, the government accepted the proposal.

These are interesting cases of focused language activism (see Chapter 10 Influencing language management: language activist groups). There were signs, Hourigan (2007) believed, of fusion between the Welsh and the Irish campaigns, and some contact with Scots Gaelic, but no joint activities: each group had to develop its own strategy. The campaign ended in the mid-1990s with the establishment of the three services. The BBC Trust has now approved the corporation's plan to launch a £21 million a year digital Gaelic-language service. Co-funded by the Gaelic Media Service, the new offering for Scotland will be available via cable and satellite TV, and broadband radio (*Guardian*, January 28, 2008).

In the Spanish autonomous regions, the establishment of media was under the control of governments committed to linguistic normalization (Arana *et al.* 2007). The Basque language press in the autonomous region is almost as strong as the Spanish language press. However, there is much less Basque-language television. Spanish national television consists of five channels under the control of entrepreneurial groups. There are also two free channels, one in Basque and the other in Spanish. Of the five radio stations, one is in Basque, one bilingual, and three in Spanish. There is also a complex pattern of local radio and television. In television, there are two Basque channels, one political and one cultural. The Basque language channel tends to specialize in children's and sports programs. There are nearly fifty local television stations in the Basque country; sixteen have some programming in the Basque language but most broadcast in Spanish. There is hope that a new law will permit the autonomous communities to have more control over licensing and programs.

On the other side of the country, with autonomy the Catalonian Parliament passed a law in 1983 to create the Catalan Broadcasting Corporation, required to be responsible for promotion of Catalan language and culture (Piulais 2007). A Catalan radio channel was established at the same time. Before that, there had been relatively little use of Catalan in television and on the radio. In 1988, private television was introduced in Spain, and Catalonia launched a second channel mainly in Catalan. Catalan also became the normal language for use on municipal radio stations and local television stations. The 1998 Law of Linguistic Policy was aimed at linguistic normalization, that is to say, "the language normally used must be Catalan," and by 2002, 60 percent of the 187 radio stations were reported to use only Catalan, and one third to use it more than half the time. On their seven public service television stations, Catalan language programs occupy one third of the hours. However, private television is mainly in Spanish. The 1998 law also requires the use of Catalan in at least 25 percent of the songs presented on radio. However, Piulais (2007: 181) concedes that "the language remains secondary in state-wide media although it is dominant in local communication services." Clearly, authority to manage is not enough.

In South Africa, Du Plessis (2006) reports the development of the South African Broadcast Corporation's policy to implement the multilingualism called for in the constitution. Recently, there has been an increase in the centrality of English, a downscaling of Afrikaans, but an increased visibility for African languages, including daily television news bulletins and current affairs programs.

Media: telephones, cell phones, and call centers

Telephones carry the spoken word, but while in the early years calling was through a live operator, setting a language barrier for people who did not speak the standard language, direct dialing gradually took over. Of course, you need to know the language and script in which the telephone directory is printed. In some countries, long-distance operators (either live or increasingly computerized) now offer language choices, in the major varieties at least. Once connected, telephone conversations are presumed to be personal, although in the post-9/11 world, the growing use of wire taps adds an extra uninvited participant to two-way exchanges. A problem for these undercover listeners is to recognize the language being overheard in order to send it to the appropriate interpreter; the US National Security Agency is reported to have developed computerized programs to recognize danger words in a number of languages and to determine the language being used.

Businesses have a special concern with telephone calls, as many make their sales this way or provide follow-up service to customers. It soon becomes obvious that inability to speak a client's language leads to problems, so that providing answering services in a multilingual world requires plurilingual proficiency in the system. In Israel, for instance, computerized answering services now commonly offer a choice of Hebrew, Arabic, Russian, or English. A commercial enterprise, Language Line in California, offers a service to local firms – for a fee paid by the firm, customers have free access to interpreter services in Spanish, Mandarin, and other languages including Cantonese, Japanese, Korean, Russian, Tagalog, and Vietnamese. The interpreters are themselves connected by telephone to the service.

The proliferation and outsourcing of telephone services (ordering, handling billing complaints, advising how to use electronic devices, or how to install and debug software) has led to some interesting changes. As a result of outsourcing to countries where labor is cheaper, much telephone service for US and European businesses is provided in India, an additional motivation for Indians to learn English and to develop if they can appropriate dialectal proficiency.

Another example of the role of the telephone in language management is the growth of telephone translation businesses, which will be described later in Chapter 12.

The recent explosive multiplication of cell phones in much of the developed world has two interesting language management outcomes. One is the unexamined addition of an audience to private conversations in public places, recognized by regular announcements in concert halls and churches asking people to turn off their phones, and by the provision in some railway coaches of silent carriages. New language management rules are needed for new technology. The second is the interesting development of codes for SMS messages, often in romanized script even where that is not the norm; Lam (2007) reports code-switching between Chinese dialects among Chinese migrants.

Media: the Internet and e-mail

There was once a fear that the Internet would be a further nail in the coffin of language diversity, but quite the opposite seems to be occurring. Danet and Herring (2007) include chapters dealing specifically with Gulf Arabic, French, Greek, Japanese, Chinese, Catalan, Thai, Portuguese, Egyptian Arabic, Swiss, German, and Swedish, many of them dealing with code mixing and the development of ad hoc transcription systems. Web sites are increasingly multilingual: www.joelonsoftware.com offers translations in more than thirty languages.

Changes in technology have clearly had important effects on the potential for minority access to electronic media. When the government orthography for Navajo was developed (Young 1977), several decisions about the use of diacritics were made: the French acute accent for tone, the Czech reversed cedilla for nasalization, and the Polish barred "l." The Phoenix Indian School where printing was done at the time for the Bureau of Indian Affairs had to have appropriate typefaces prepared, but as far as I know the only typewriter that could handle Navajo was one built for Robert Young, responsible with William Morgan for the dictionary and newspaper published in the 1940s. When in the 1960s scholars started to input Navajo text to the computer, it was necessary to develop ad hoc conventions to handle these special problems. The first breakthrough came when special fonts could be added to the IBM typewriter ball, and a Navajo font ball was available in the 1970s. In the early days of computers then, it was assumed that development favored languages with easily available fonts. By the 1980s, however, it became relatively easy to create fonts in any language, removing the technical limitation on languages.

Cunliffe (2007) sees the Internet as both a threat and an opportunity for language diversity. He points out the diversity of media – websites, *Wikis*, blogs or Weblogs, chat rooms, bulletin boards, instant messaging, and videoconferencing – all of which work to establish communities. The Web was dominated by the US, and early developments were in English and other Romanized alphabets, but it is now wide open. Some 70 percent of websites are estimated to be in English. Access to computers is of course limited in many parts of the world, and perhaps 90 percent of languages are not represented. There are arguments against minority language use ("Other people won't understand you") and some cases of language banning. Moving a traditional language and its esoteric traditional knowledge to the Internet may be seen as a threat. Commercial arguments for minority languages are hard to make. But the potential is there: Cunliffe (2007: 107) concludes that "a real opportunity exists for those languages that have the resources and the determination to make the transition to the Internet." However, this remains speculation: the UNESCO Institute for Statistics (2005) presents a number of essays on the difficulty of measuring linguistic diversity on the Internet. There are no accurate figures of languages used on the Internet, and no surveys of users. But there are important developments taking place: Colloquial Arabic is now being written extensively (most commonly in Romanized or Hebrew letters) by young people in the Middle East.

While the Internet opens up the global market to companies (and more and more are adding translated web-pages according to the country of a customer), there are reports of continued apathy towards customers who are minorities. A study by a US market-research firm, Common Sense Advisory, in May 2007 found that only eighteen out of the 102 top online stores (including Target and Office Depot) offered any Spanish language content, and fewer than half of these could respond to customer enquiries in Spanish (*Business Week*, June 27, 2007). But there are signs of progress – a Swedish firm has now advertised a new service for firms with advertising portals. They will accept advertisements in any one of more than twenty languages and post it in any or all of the other languages. Technology and the profit motive work together to open up multilingual possibilities!

These last examples highlight the importance of language services like translation and interpreting to business as well as to the public sector.

Cultivating public language

One not uncommon form of simple language management is when a speaker corrects his (usually) or her use of bad language, such as an inappropriate obscenity or blasphemy (Spolsky 2004). As discussed there, this phenomenon involves organized language management too, such as the parental efforts to stop their children swearing, or the efforts of priests and ministers to prevent blasphemous language. I mentioned there also the existence of national, state, and municipal laws banning obscene language. In the middle of the twentieth century, there developed a concern about what has been labeled "political correctness" in language, the liberal campaign to prevent the use of racist or sexist language. By the 1960s, dictionaries were cautious in their listings of what had come to be considered insulting racist terms, and various publishers and professional associations had started to develop guidelines for avoiding racist or ethnic terms.

One campaign of relevance to our model was the effort to deal with sexist language, proclaimed in a paper by Lakoff (1973). Cooper (1989) described the struggle against androcentric pronouns (assuming that "he" includes "she") as one of the four cases of language management that he judged paradigmatic. Pauwels (1998) provided an account of the twenty-year grassroots feminist campaign for language reform, tracking the way that individuals, women's groups and collectives, and other ad hoc activist groups pressured governments, firms, and publishers to modify their usage. Cooper (1984) reported early effects of this campaign, which continues (Coates 2005; Lakoff and Bucholtz 2004). There has been resistance to similar campaigns in their respective countries on the part of the French and Spanish language academies.

Media in a theory of language management

Treating public space as a domain for language management has added to the complexity of the theory. Part of the problem is the number of different participants, whether managers or potential audiences. Managers can be not only the producers but also various levels of authorities wishing to control content and form, including governments aiming to enforce language policy. There is also considerable scope for activists, whether religious groups that are trying to keep the air waves and Internet pure, or minority language groups wishing to have access. Audiences (readers, listeners, or surfers) are equally varied, with the choice open to the producers to aim for a narrow or wide target. Technology allows for both a global and a local focus, making the issue even more complex. Calling public linguistic space a single domain may be theoretically interesting, but in practice, just as we need to look at individual families to see how management works, so we need to look at much smaller sub-domains.

A totalitarian state may try very hard to gain control of public space. The language activists using the power of the state in Québec and Catalonia can do a reasonable job of controlling the language of public signs, or the languages used in the media. But even China and Iran appear to be having difficulty in keeping the Internet under firm control. In democracies, governments set some fundamental guidelines in areas like obscenity: freedom of expression then becomes an issue. A split US Supreme Court decision held that a school principal in Alaska was not violating free speech when he punished a student for displaying a sign reading "Bong Hits 4 Jesus" at a school-sponsored function (*New York Times*, June 26, 2007). If they have a central language policy, governments can control through funding those media that meet their approval; but in practice, the media are open to the pressure of financial possibility and so of providing something that an audience (or a sponsor wishing access to an audience) is willing to pay for.

While signs form part of the outside environment – the neighborhood domain, one might say – the other media can and do penetrate home and the workplace. Newspapers and books, radio and television, and cell phones and computers all connect individuals wherever they may be to a virtually infinite domain, challenging the attempts to control communication provided only that the potential barrier of language difference is removed.

There may still remain remote areas of the world uninfluenced by public language – villages without signs or electricity, landscapes without billboards, islands without canned or packaged goods, jungles without radios – but increasingly, public linguistic space is being used as a means of communication, providing opportunities for those controlling the space – whether owners, advertisers, or governments – to invade it. Exploration of the domain calls then for an enriched theory of language management, but sets complex challenges for a workable methodology.

6   Language policy in schools

The language policy adopted by an educational system is without doubt one of the most powerful forces in language management. After religious institutions like churches, mosques, and synagogues, the school is the most likely to confirm or conflict with the pattern of home language use. In fact, most children find a serious gap between the language of their home (commonly a colloquial variety or dialect of the local language) and the language of school, most commonly aimed or claimed to be the national or official language. Many also find a gap between the home where they are encouraged to speak and the classroom where they are trained to keep quiet until called on.

This language gap is true not only of undeveloped third-world multilingual countries like Africa (Alexandre 1968; Brock-Utne and Hopson 2005), or of aboriginal minority groups like the Innu in Labrador (Burnaby and Philpott 2007), but of developed nations too. In Belgium, 40 percent of high school children reported such a gap, a result of the difference between the official Dutch and French taught in school and the dialectal varieties they speak at home (Aunger 1993). And of course with the rising level of migration worldwide, this home–school language gap is likely to increase rather than decrease.

The effect is enormous: first, when teacher and child do not understand each other's speech, teaching and learning are severely impeded. Second, a child whose home language is denied, ignored, or punished by the schoolteacher is persuaded of his or her deficiencies and of his or her parents' disadvantaged status.

The relationship between schooling and religion is close, both historically (most of western education began in church-controlled schools) and currently as in the religious schools conducted by fundamental Islam, Greek and Roman Catholicism, and Judaism. As a result, many educational systems were or are based on the central importance of teaching whatever language provides access to sacred texts – Classical Arabic, Greek, Latin, Hebrew and Aramaic, and Sanskrit. In the west, this was transformed initially into priority for classical languages – Greek and Latin – and then after secularization of the educational system, to priority for the language associated with the national identity. Fishman (2002a, 2002b) makes an important point when he notes the secularized holiness of national and ethnic languages; secular nation-states are able to claim the "ethic of divinity" for their programs to spread the national language.

Because teaching seems easier when there is a single approved "correct" answer to every question, and because of the commitment of schools to literacy which has come to assume a single correct writing system for each language, the consequent tendency towards standardization discourages any recognition of pluralism or plurilingualism in the school. Whereas the family as an institution may encourage the continuation of heritage language diversity ("You should speak the heritage language to Grandma, but may speak the standard language to me"), the school as an institution normally works towards uniformity and monolingualism in the approved variety associated with literacy. Multilingual schooling, able to reflect the linguistic diversity of its student body, remains rare, something in the words of the editors of a recent book (García *et al.* 2006), to be imagined, but rarely to be found. Monolingual education in the national official language is the unmarked case. A first level of conflict is persuading the educational establishment to consider the possible value of multilingualism.

Participants

Pupils

Schooling is by its very nature a domain committed to language management. The two principal participants are students whose language practices and beliefs are to be modified, and teachers charged with the process of modification.

Each of these two groups is complex and diverse. Students at all levels in the system vary on a number of critical dimensions: age, gender, ability level, motivation, for example. They differ also in the variety or varieties of language that they know and use and in their level of proficiency. The younger they are, the more likely their language pattern is to reflect the language pattern of their home. Their experience in the family domain, in the neighborhood, and elsewhere will have introduced them to various language practices, have developed in them beliefs about language and values they assign to the varieties, and exposed them to various attempts to modify their language practices and beliefs. Thus, schools are by no means dealing with a *tabula rasa*, for children come to school with established language proficiencies, behaviors, and values. Students also bring with them preferences for language policy, something seldom considered in developing school language policy (Barkhuizen *et al.* 2006). These pre-school practices and beliefs provide the basis on which school language management must build, whether the system recognizes it or not.

Individual schools may be linguistically homogeneous, when all the students come with roughly similar language backgrounds and proficiencies, or linguistically diverse, when the students come from different sections of a multilingual society. This obviously sets limiting factors for language management: in many African countries, the number of different languages spoken by the students is offered as the justification for not implementing a mother-tongue program, and even India, with its pluralist tradition, recognizes only a few of the 2,000 varieties said to exist there. Even where there is teaching in a local rather than international language, it is commonly not the home language of many of the pupils.

Teachers

The second group of participants in the school domain is the teaching staff. Again, teachers vary on such criteria as age, gender, training, experience, social status, and of course, language proficiency. Here too, there may be relative homogeneity or diversity. Cultural value ascribed by a community to its teachers also varies considerably. In ancient Rome, teachers were slaves; in some other traditional communities, they were priests. In many nations, teachers are underpaid and the profession is considered suitable for women until they marry or once their children have left home. The respect accorded to teachers varies according to the level at which they teach, with university teachers, for example, more highly regarded than elementary school teachers.

Like their pupils, teachers bring with them a set of beliefs about the value to be assigned to the languages and varieties used in their society. Commonly, their training will have predisposed them to believing in the essential worth of the school variety and the official language. Members of minority groups appear just as likely as majority members to agree to decisions to teach only in the dominant language, accepting widespread community beliefs about its value for national unity and individual economic success. On the other hand, ideologically committed supporters of language revival, whether in the Hebrew schools of the Jewish community of Ottoman and British Palestine, or in the *Model D* (Euskara as medium and Spanish as an additional language) Basque schools, or in the immersion-only *Kura Kaupapa Māori* of New Zealand, bring with them the zeal of radical language activists.

Teachers are no better than anyone else at distinguishing their own language practices from their beliefs. Arabic-speaking teachers report that they speak standard Arabic when in fact they tend to use a slightly standardized form of the local vernacular (Amara 1988). French teachers are positive they pronounce the /l/ in *il dit*. Teachers easily slip towards the creole end in a continuum. But a gap between teacher and student varieties can produce a serious strain.

The social, economic, and linguistic similarity or dissimilarity of teachers and students is a critical matter. When I first visited schools on the Navajo Reservation in the late 1960s, nearly all of the students were Navajo-speakers with limited if any exposure to English before they came to school, while over 90 percent of the teachers were English speakers with virtually no knowledge of Navajo (Spolsky 1970). This situation, not uncommon in developing societies or in communities with large numbers of immigrants, reflects the fact that teachers are commonly hired only from those who have successfully completed many more years of schooling than minority students can yet hope to aspire to. When teachers could be recruited at the end of primary school for a year or two of training, it was easy to find speakers of the vernacular; when they are expected to have completed tertiary level programs, the home–school language gap, the fact that teachers use a language which their students do not understand, is exacerbated. The first task in such situations is (or should be) establishing communication between students and teachers.

Other participants

There are other potentially significant participants in the school domain. The first among these are the professional administrators – principals and department heads in schools, provosts and deans and chairs in universities, owners and managers in private schools – who may be selected from the same group as the teachers, and who may be responsible to authorities outside the school for management of its educational and language policies. Given the definition of their roles, they may be expected to be further from the students and closer to the external administration, representing the powerful establishment outside. Often, they are brought in from other regions, or may be expatriates, with, as a result, markedly different language practices and beliefs.

A second significant group is the non-academic support staff – the bus drivers, secretaries, cleaners, and cooks, most likely to be local. In the Navajo schools in the 1960s, these were the only people on the staff who could speak Navajo and so communicate with the students and with their parents. Less educated than the teachers, their class and background mean that their language variety is closer to that of the students, but their lower status in the school hierarchy helps confirm the lower value of the variety. They serve, however, an important intermediary role between school (and teachers) and students (and community).

Where are the managers?

Each of these categories of participants brings significant language practices and beliefs to the school domain, but our key question is, what determines the language instructional policy of the school? Here, the variation is once again enormous, accounting for the difficulty of generalization. There are some schools where management is essentially internal, with the school staff (principal, teachers, and other relevant professionals) determining their own educational and linguistic goals and choosing their own appropriate method of achieving them.

More commonly, there is some individual or group external to the school with the authority to establish goals and methods. In some cases, this may be the parents of the students, working as members of an elected school board or through their financial power to influence school policy. In other cases, the school will be under the authority of a religious leader or religious organization, local or distant. In others, there may be a democratically elected school board with authority over several schools in the region. Sometimes, this authority is assigned to a local body such as a city council. In other cases, the authority is centralized and under the control of the central government, or in a federal system, of state or provincial governments. In colonial systems, authority was commonly maintained by the metropolitan home government.

Normally, authority over the school programs is divided among these various levels. Each arrangement is likely to have different effects on the establishment and implementation of school language programs. I will look at some of these later, but first try to establish the dimensions of school language management.

The self-managed school

One possibility is a self-managed school. In theory, this is rare for it ignores the need for parents to choose to send their children to the school and to contribute their share of the expenses. Imagine how such a school might make its curricular and linguistic decisions. Essentially, the choice of a language of instruction could be determined by the languages spoken by students and teachers, and the goals of the language education program could be driven by the teachers' and students' beliefs in the values of language varieties as established by their perception of the situation outside school. But in practice, self-managed schools depend on the financial support of parents or other local agencies, each of whom might add different beliefs and goals. Private schools then unless supported by trusts which leave all decisions to the staff will also have external participants.

There are interesting possibilities offered by the growth of what are called "virtual schools," which now provide online classes for half a million children in the US (*New York Times*, February 1, 2008), including 90,000 receiving their full education from 185 publicly financed elementary and middle schools. There is wide variation in the nature of these programs, some of which are funded entirely by tuition fees, and controversy over their status. I do not know of any that focus on serving the language management concerns of any specific group, but as the phenomenon develops, this may well happen.

The locally managed school

The contract schools on the Navajo Reservation in the 1970s were a good example of locally managed schools, and there is evidence of increasing numbers of such schools (LaRocque 2005). Rock Point Community School was under the control of a locally elected school board, all members of which spoke only Navajo – the Anglo principal always used an interpreter when meeting with them, not because he didn't understand Navajo, but to give them a feeling of independence. The school board was made up of parents and others from the local Navajo community, selected by the community and with full responsibility to hire and fire teachers and auxiliary staff and approve the curriculum (Holm and Holm 1990). The *Kura Kaupapa Māori*, like all schools in New Zealand now, each have locally elected boards, a proportion of whom are parents, with full responsibility for staff, curriculum, and physical plant.

But the independent Navajo schools needed to find their funding from the Federal government, who thus had control over their policy, and they were subject to the regulations of the relevant state education board. In Arizona, this meant that in the 1970s the school could establish its own language policy, and build a model bilingual curriculum (Rosier and Holm 1980), but by the 1990s, increasing pressure for state certification and examination requirements led to a major weakening of the Navajo language component (Holm and Holm 1995). In New Zealand, the legal designation of Māori as an official language made it possible for schools to negotiate agreements with the Minister of Education defining their curriculum as immersion in Māori. At the same time, they had to submit to the inspections of the Education Review Office (Education Review Office 1995).

When other participants have authority over the school's language policy, they need to be considered in the management model. The simplest case is where the school comes under the direct control of the parents. In a sense, school then becomes an extension of the home: when the home has complete control of language policy (for example, home-based schooling, or the hiring of tutors for their children by wealthy parents), the direction of language policy is under the direct control of the parents, who may choose to reinforce their normal home language or to add some highly valued variety (for example, the parents in New York reported to be hiring Mandarin-speaking nannies, or my friend in Jerusalem who selected a Russian-speaking housekeeper).

The transition from parent-controlled home schooling to a parent-controlled school is fairly simple, when a group of parents with similar educational ideologies and needs combine to establish a community school. There are many examples of this, each with its own characteristic pattern and language policy models. The Talmud states that fathers are responsible for teaching Hebrew to their children; the requirement presumably dates from a time when Aramaic or Greek was spoken in the home and natural intergenerational transmission of the heritage language could no longer be assumed. In a later development, the Talmud moved responsibility to the local Jewish community, requiring each member to contribute to the cost of hiring a teacher. In Ottoman Palestine in the Jewish villages, when a French philanthropist stopped paying for schooling conducted in his metropolitan language, the parents took over and encouraged the teachers to switch to newly revived Hebrew. Another example of parent- or community-controlled schooling is the development of Māori regeneration programs in New Zealand starting in the 1980s. While the first revival programs were focused on young adult university students, the more exciting and influential development was the beginning of *Kōhanga Reo*, pre-school language nests, parent-controlled and supported programs where Māori-speaking grandparents were expected to provide an immersion setting for the young children. It was the parents of the more effective and successful language nests who combined together with the teachers and a few community activists to begin the Māori philosophy schools, *Kura Kaupapa Māori*, which became the core of the regeneration program (Smith 1997).

The same kind of pattern is reported among the schools developed in the last 50 years or so in US Amish communities. There are about 200,000 Amish people in the US, and they conduct about 1,500 private schools, each more or less independent with considerable variation in their language policy. Depending on their ideological response to the challenges of modernization, various patterns of language policy are possible. Most use English as the language of instruction – English is needed for communication outside the community and for writing – but there is some teaching in the German dialect known as Pennsylvania Dutch (or Pennsylvania German), depending on the conservatism of the parents and the community. The schools also teach standard German, the language used in church and in the Bible. Generally, the Amish separate religious education – seen as the function of home and school – from schooling, a recent innovation in reaction to the consolidation of rural public schools in the 1950s and 1960s (Johnson-Weiner 2007). Indigenous Native American communities in Latin America are establishing locally controlled schools to give freedom in a curriculum that will help maintain traditional culture and language (López 2006).

Recognizing parents as significant participants in developing the language policy of schools helps account for many of the patterns. Where there are private systems alongside public, they commonly turn out to be under the control of or strongly influenced by parents. For example, Arab-medium state schools in Israel found it necessary to introduce the teaching of English much earlier than government policy permitted in order to compete with private schools, which were generally church-supported and so predisposed to teach an international language. Where there is language activism, it is often expressed in the development of parent- or community-controlled schools that favor a heritage or endangered language.

Externally managed schools

Another common pattern that was mentioned in Chapter 3 is where a school is under religious control. The added participant may be an individual religious leader – a missionary, a priest, a minister, an imam, a rabbi – or a religious community or a religious school system. Missionaries commonly establish schools alongside their other religious institutions, and their linguistic ideology – the acceptance of translating sacred texts into the vernacular or their commitment to the established language of the sacred text – has major influences on the school language pattern, and indeed on the later standardization of the variety they have chosen. In Ireland, much of the teaching of Irish takes place in Roman Catholic schools, although the originators of the revival movement were Protestants.

External control of the school may be local (with each community setting up its own local school board), city-wide, or regional; it may be under municipal, national, federal, or imperial government. To understand the complexity of US language education policy, it helps to realize that there are 15,000 school systems, each with its own curriculum. Each of these systems in turn comes under the direct or indirect control of the state government – the US constitution establishes education as a sphere for the states – but of course is further influenced by decisions of law courts on constitutional questions or by federal interventionist policies and federal funding. Thus, we are faced potentially with a large number of different levels, each of which holds different beliefs about language needs and values and each of which may turn out to have different strengths in setting and implementing language policy.

Conflicts among the levels are common. Parents may favor one language and teachers another; the principal may attempt to implement a policy that varies from the desires of higher and lower administrative levels; national governments may choose policies considered unsuitable in certain regions; state and federal governments may vary in approaches; religious groups may disagree with government policy. As an example, a group of parents in Chicago plan to keep their children home from the federally mandated tests in March which require new immigrants to take the same standardized tests as native speakers of English, and one Illinois school district (with 10,000 limited English speakers) plans to break the law and not administer the tests at all (*Daily Herald*, February 22, 2008).

Examination boards as language managers

There is great scope for variation because school teaching takes place in a closed room, difficult for outsiders to observe. This of course increases the power of teachers, so that complex systems of control (classroom visits, centrally controlled microphones and video cameras, or most commonly, externally administered tests and examinations) are felt to be needed.

Examination systems and the boards controlling them can become independent actors (Shohamy 2001; Spolsky 1995b). Many systems, emulating the Jesuit practices (de La Salle 1720) taken over by Jacobin secularizers, established examinations as a method of controlling the curriculum. The elaborate and powerful French and Chinese examination systems exercise great control over language as well as other parts of the curriculum (Suen and Yu 2006). The English system, where secondary school examinations were under the control of semi-independent university-based examination boards, depended on a strong consensus to maintain a common curriculum. The United States pattern is more diverse – in the 1920s examinations were published by private publishers under the influence of select universities, but the New York State Board of Regents conducted their own. In the current struggle for Federal control of education, the controversial No Child Left Behind Act is producing major effects on school language policy, especially by its failure to recognize any language other than English and by its misguided requirement that all pupils including new immigrants take the same examinations. He who manages high-stakes examinations also has a hand in managing languages. Many studies are starting to track these influences of external examinations in different countries (Bhattacharya *et al.* 2007; Wall 2005).

Patterns

All of this increases the number of participants who might function as managers of language education policy and whose beliefs need to be taken into account. Add to this the existence of activist groups – groups of parents or community members – attempting to influence the school or school authorities at any level, and one readily realizes the underlying structural explanation of the multiplicity of language education patterns that we find in practice.

Conflicting beliefs about language and education have been documented recently for Ireland. A survey conducted in 2000 revealed that half of Catholics in the Republic regarded the language as an essential element of their Irish identity, and most believed it should continue to be taught in schools. Protestants in the North were the opposite in almost all respects. Support for the language among Catholics in the North was weak (Ó Riágain 2007). Fieldwork among Irish speakers in the Gaeltacht, the region where the language is most strongly maintained, revealed a significant divergence of opinion as to how much Irish should be used with children at home and at school: the general opinion was that bilingualism rather than Irish monolingualism was the better goal (Ó hlfearnain 2007). Since the Good Friday Agreement, there has been renewed public debate on the place of Irish. In the Republic, there has been progress in the passage of the Official Languages Act, the appointment of an Official Languages Commissioner, and "official working language" status for Irish in the European Commission. There has also been an increase in the percentage of the population reporting some ability in Irish. There are, however, threats: an increasing demand for optionality and a decline in primary school teaching of Irish. In addition, the growth in the number of immigrants (7 percent in 2002 and 10 percent in 2006) has led to a demand for a basic reassessment of language education policy (Harris 2007).

The complexity of resulting school language patterns was captured by Mackey (1970) in his pioneering typology of bilingual education. Because of the great variation in the meaning and application of this term, and because of the great deal of political emotion that it engenders, I shall do my best to avoid using it without definition. It is probably safer to distinguish between single medium and dual medium instruction. The crucial dimensions of Mackey's typology were languages, year or level of instruction, amount of time allocated in the weekly schedule, medium, topic or subject. The broadest categories were single or dual medium curricula (using one or two languages of instruction) and transfer or transitional programs (starting in one language and gradually moving to another) or maintenance programs (starting in one and moving to two).

Using a language other than the mother tongue for instruction is usually referred to as *immersion* (Fortune and Tedick 2008). The notion is that the pupils, speakers of their home language, are immersed in the new language of school. In the original French immersion programs in Montreal (Genesee 1988), English-speaking children were immersed in French; in the *Kōhanga Reo* and *Kura Kaupapa Māori* programs, English-speaking Māori children are immersed in Māori (Nicholson 1990). Using only the official language with children who do not know it is sometimes called submersion. Immersion programs are *additive* when their goal is to produce bilinguals with academic proficiency in the home and in the official language, or *replacive* when the aim is to move students from one language to another.

The varieties of language in competition are commonly the various home varieties (vernaculars or dialects) and the official national language. In the

Arab world, for example, most people speak a local colloquial variety (Egyptian Arabic, Iraqi Arabic, Palestinian Arabic, Moroccan Arabic, for instance) but schools teach only Modern Standard Arabic, a variety based on the language of the Qur'an. In Belgium, schools teach standard Dutch or standard French rather than the dialectal varieties of each that people actually speak. In Haiti, schools teach French rather than the Creole that everybody uses. In both German- and French-speaking areas of Switzerland, schools teach High German rather than the Swiss German used in everyday life. These are the classic cases of diglossia (Ferguson 1959; Hudson 2002), but a similar situation occurs with standard language-vernacular or standard language-dialect opposition. In much of Africa, where schooling is exclusively in a European language (French or English or Portuguese), pupils speaking local languages are expected to pick it up (Djité 2008).

Local home varieties commonly do not have a written form, and school is the place to learn literacy, which means literacy in the standard written official language. Some school systems do distinguish between the language of instruction and the language in which school texts are written. East European Jewish schools in the nineteenth century conducted their teaching in Yiddish, but the texts were written in Hebrew and Aramaic. In many parts of the world, classes may be conducted in the local variety, but the only texts are written in English. This two-language approach is usually taken for granted or denied.

There are a number of possible junctures in the educational system chosen for a transition from a local variety to the school variety. One model, adopted in the British Empire after failures of the English-only program in nineteenth-century India, was to provide initial education in the vernacular with gradual transition to English-only no later than the beginning of high school. The number of years of vernacular instruction has varied, although a consensus from recent research in Africa and elsewhere suggests that six years is the minimum needed to achieve good educational results (Alidou et al. 2006). This is supported by the evidence from the Yoruba six-year primary project, which showed the improvement in educational results achieved by providing a full elementary school program in the Yoruba language (Bamgbose 2005). There continue, however, to be many systems which follow the French and Portuguese colonial models and that assert that education must be in the standard metropolitan language from the very beginning.

Mackey's model distinguished between the eventual goal of moving completely to the school language and of maintaining the home variety as well. It allowed for different amounts of time allocated to the two or three languages of instruction – there are for instance Jewish schools in Montreal that divide up the day between French, English, Hebrew, and Yiddish, and the "three-language formula" (a national language, a state language, and a local language) is one of India's common patterns (Khubchandani 1997).

The choice among these patterns depends on the goals or beliefs of whoever controls school language policy. One key issue is the decision on language of instruction.

Language of instruction

Educational evidence

The controversy over the educational value of initial instruction in the students' home language remains one of the most basic questions of language education policy. The position one takes depends partly on one's beliefs about the ability of children to learn language. One belief holds that it is just as easy for pre-adolescent children to pick up a new language as it is assumed to be for babies to acquire their first language. For some children, this appears to be true, but on average, the evidence of published research suggests strongly that the majority suffers educationally in such situations. Ever since Macnamara (1966), there has been published empirical evidence of the problem of teaching content in a student's weaker language. This has recently been confirmed in a number of studies in the US, Israel, Africa, and elsewhere. But this is an area, like belief in evolution or global warming, where empirical evidence seems not to convince (Revel 1988, 1991).

In the United States, starting in the 1960s, there was a period of fairly widespread acceptance of the need for initial instruction in a child's home language. However, a later campaign of political assault on bilingual education led to its being banned in several states. Realizing the difficulty faced by the US Federal government in trying to control education which is constitutionally a state concern, one of President Clinton's initiatives was to call a conference of state governors. The general approach that emerged and received bipartisan support when President Bush later presented the No Child Left Behind Act some years later was to set standards of achievement for schools, to be measured by state-authorized tests of student performance. The Federal government would then provide funds for those schools which showed improvement. A simple and appealing idea, the practice proved complex, and opposition to many of its features gradually emerged. Teachers complained that they were spending time preparing for the tests at the expense of untested subjects. There were serious questions raised about the reliability and validity of the tests. One major focus of criticism was the fact that immigrant and minority pupils were required to take the same tests as students who were proficient in English. There has been extensive public debate over the re-authorization of the Act focusing on the question of the effect of the NCLB on test scores. Regularly, the Secretary of Education or one of her spokespeople has claimed that data show improvement. Just as regularly, a scholarly opponent of the re-authorization analyzed the data and claimed that it either showed no improvement or considerably less than the number of NCLB added hours should have produced. The educational arguments are not simple, but there seems to be a consensus among scholars that there is no evidence from the research showing any important achievements from the application of the law. However, just as in the case of similar political debates about issues of scientific importance like global warming and birth control, there are those who will present contrary arguments, and the government seems able to turn it into a political controversy and ignore scientific findings. What this means in effect is that the development of language education policy regularly ignores the educational arguments. Thus, the final decision looks like depending on political lobbying rather than academic debate.

A survey (Garcia *et al.* 2008) tries to summarize the problem. In the United States, after considerable vacillation, the latest term for children suffering from the language gap is "English language learners"; they suggest a more healthy term would be "emergent bilinguals."

One of the most misunderstood issues in pre-K-12 education today is how to educate children who are not yet proficient in English...The central idea that will emerge from this review of research is that there is a growing dissonance between *research* on the education of emergent bilinguals and policy enacted to educate them. (Garcia *et al.* 2008: 8)

In the first part of the book, they show the inconsistency of data on this population between different definitions and different methods of data collection. In the second part, they track US policies to the group, showing the strengthening of the emphasis on English and standardized testing. In the third part, they summarize research evidence and relevant theory and show that the NCLB policy is dissonant with the research.

This is by no means the last battle over the policy, but as a result of strong opposition by educators and the public, in January 2008, after several months of Congressional deliberations, the proposed re-authorization had still not been voted on, and President Bush appeared resigned to its defeat. Policy, including school language policy, it seems, is politics and not science.

Developed languages

A second important consideration, after educational arguments for the best model of school language policy, is the state of the varieties of language involved. How well is each potential language of instruction developed? There is an obvious scale, ranging from an unwritten and unstandardized vernacular, dialect, creole, or pidgin to a standard or classical language

(Stewart 1968), the upper end implying the availability of a writing system (a critical feature in schooling which assumes literacy as a first goal) and of a dictionary and grammar (also demanded by school teachers) as well as of modern terminology. Fishman (2006) reiterates arguments against those linguists who, emphasizing universal features, claim that all languages are the same, by making clear the kinds of cultivation that are commonly needed for modernization.

This quickly becomes apparent if you visit schools beginning to use home languages for instruction. When we worked on developing elementary education in Navajo (Spolsky 1974), one of the big gaps that needed to be filled was lexicon for mathematics: Navajo had no simple way to label fractions, for instance. I also have vivid memories of watching a Māori first grade teacher discuss with her aunt, who was acting as language assistant, the school inspector, who was my escort, and the pupils in her class what Māori word to use for a new concept. It is this that sets the inevitable bridge between two kinds of language management: managing speakers, that Kloss (1969) labeled *status planning* and managing a language, that Kloss called *corpus planning*, but perhaps better labeled with the Prague School term *cultivation* (Prague School 1973). Fishman (2006) has argued that these two processes commonly share the same motivational dimensions, but there is an equally basic connection in that the assignment of a function to a variety regularly entails modifying it to fill that function, whether by developing a writing system, modernizing it, or adding new lexicon.

What this means is that school programs that want to use a local or home variety as language of instruction must be ready to incur the extra trouble and expense of a language cultivation component. One of the problems with implementing the South African constitutional recognition of nine languages alongside English and Afrikaans is the weak provision of resources for language development. The 1970s Navajo bilingual programs were supported by projects concerned with writing or reprinting material in Navajo. Māori education has been hampered by the absence of contemporary writing in the language, apart from material prepared for school use and translated government documents. Nineteenth-century European language maintenance and revival programs (including Hebrew) were fortunate that their leaders were often literary figures who had begun writing in the language. The low level of language cultivation can serve as a reason or excuse for not using home varieties in school.

This language cultivation factor plays an increasingly important role at more advanced levels of instruction. It is hard enough to develop appropriate terminology and materials for early elementary education, but by the secondary level, with more advanced courses especially in the sciences, the pressure becomes even stronger. This explains in part why North African

Arab nations are prepared to continue to use French at the secondary level even when they are active in Arabicization. Everywhere, there is pressure to use international languages for scientific subjects. At the tertiary level, the demands become even greater, so that many universities assume they need to use world languages (Ammon 2001). This was a key argument in the Malaysian switch back to English as language of instruction for science (Gill 2006). Even in systems like the Israeli, where almost all university teaching up to the highest level is conducted in Hebrew, it is expected that most reading in science and social sciences will need to be done in English (Kheimets and Epstein 2005).

Ideological arguments

But it will be rare for educational or linguistic considerations alone to determine school language policy. More commonly, schools reflect the ideological position of those who control them; they are by their nature conservative institutions expected to pass on established traditional values. Normally, their policy will be driven in part at least by the policy of the national government. The recent major changes from Bahasa Melayu to English in Malaysia and from Urdu to English in Pakistan for teaching science and mathematics, or the intention to provide six years initial instruction in the vernacular in South Africa, or the intention to restore English as medium of instruction in the Philippines, or the proposal of immersion education in English in Thailand were all announced as central government policy. Efforts to establish English-only programs and ban bilingual education have been focused on state governments in the US and in particular on those states with popular referenda. Language instruction in the school then is a key component in national language policy, and is recognized as a key stage in the Graded Intergenerational Disruption Scale that Fishman (1991b) proposed as a measure of the state of an endangered language.

The struggle over language of instruction in the southern Indian state of Karnataka (originally called Mysore but renamed in 1973) is an interesting example of the conflict of interests. Support for Kannada, spoken by about two thirds of the population and the basis for the recognition of the state in 1956 when the boundaries were based on linguistic demography, was stressed in a 1994 law making Kannada the compulsory language of instruction in all new primary schools. Many schools ignored this, choosing rather to teach in English, considered by parents to be better preparation for work in the software industry (the state leads India in exports in software). The enforcement of the Kannada-only regulation in 2007 – 800 schools were "de-recognized" for violating the government policy – led to a major dispute between the government and the Karnataka Unaided School Management Association, representing 1,100 primary schools that did not receive government aid. In June 2007, the High Court of Karnataka upheld the government policy and ordered all private schools to switch from English to Kannada (*Daily India*, June 25, 2007).

Efforts to introduce local languages do not always meet with parents' approval. Rajah-Carrim (2007) interviewed a group of Mauritians asking their opinion of the government proposal to introduce Kreol, the native language of about two thirds of the population into a school system that uses English as language of instruction and teaches in addition French and an ethnically related Oriental language (Arabic, Hindi, Mandarin, Marathi, Tamil, Telugu, or Urdu, offered as a substitute for Christian religious classes). While English is language of instruction from primary to tertiary levels, many teachers are reported to use French or Kreol in the classroom. Recently, a political movement has been calling for the sole use of Kreol. The interviews with a non-representative sample of various ethnic backgrounds found little support for the idea, most parents believing that international languages are more useful.

Dividing language functions

The language of instruction is an important component of language education policy, which may be further managed by changes in the proportion of the school week allocated to two (or more) languages in a multi-medium program. The allocation may be by subjects rather than time: mathematics and sciences are more likely to be taught in international and developed languages. Schools and policy-makers are often attracted to the idea of teaching science in English, avoiding the problems of terminological development when teaching in a local language. Assuming that target languages are easier to understand in less verbal subjects, Clyne (1986) recommended bolstering primary foreign language teaching in Australia by using the foreign language for subjects such as art, music, or physical education. In some models, the heritage language is maintained for teaching history or geography after the rest of the subjects are changed to the official language.

The allocation of the school day to different languages allows another set of possibilities. *Transitional* programs start with all teaching presented in the first language (in theory, the home language, but in multilingual areas it may not be the home language of all pupils), and slowly increase the amount of time allocated to the official language. In what are called *maintenance* programs, the endpoint will still maintain some time for the home language, perhaps once a day for enrichment or one or two subjects still taught in the home language. Where the home language is a relatively unsupported vernacular or minority language, it is likely to disappear from the curriculum once the prestige national or official or international language has taken over, though it may still be used surreptitiously by students or teachers; where it has a strong ethnic backing or a traditional literature, it may continue as a subject.

Teaching additional languages

In practice, any teaching in the students' home language may reasonably be categorized as enrichment, while the teaching of any other language can be categorized as second (or foreign) language teaching. This brings us to the second component of language education policy, the first being the choice of language of instruction and the second being the teaching of additional languages. *Additional* implies an additive approach, in contrast to the replacive approach of a monolingual immersion program in the official language or even a transitional program that pays no attention to the home language once the official language is considered to have been established. Again, which policy is adopted depends on the beliefs of the managers of the educational system, the community, and the ruling authority concerning the value of the varieties involved.

Commonly, absent pluralism, there is disdain or contempt for home varieties. This can be found in public rhetoric labeling the home variety as a dialect not worthy of attention in the school system. On the other hand, international and developed languages are granted much higher status; even when they are not chosen as languages of instruction, they regularly receive favored status in the school curriculum. The most obvious example nowadays is English, the first foreign language taught in most countries where it is not a first or second language. In some cases, it replaces official second languages, such as has been proposed in some Swiss cantons, and as in Israel where it is taught in state schools more seriously than the nominally official second language, Arabic.

The choice of language is one issue, but it is often compounded by the choice of a variety of language. In the Arab-speaking world, the school language is officially Classical or Standard Arabic and not the local national variety spoken at home. In Switzerland, French-speaking children learn High German and not the Swiss German used by their fellow-citizens in other cantons. In Singapore, it has been proposed to reduce emphasis on Literary Tamil and aim to teach Standard Spoken Tamil to encourage the maintenance of the language (Saravanan *et al.* 2007). As a general rule, schools teach the literary or written standard form of a language. Under the influence of language teaching ideologies like the Direct Method, Audio-Lingual Method, or the Communicative approach, they may add the spoken language, but usually as a small part of the curriculum.

Teaching foreign languages

The teaching of what is clearly labeled as a foreign language varies considerably. A first question is the choice of a variety or language. In much of the world, English is now the first foreign language, although in Asia there is pressure for Chinese, in countries with Romance languages pressure for Spanish or French, and in the former Soviet Union some inertia for Russian. The main forces here may be historical (former colonial status) or geographic (major regional languages) or increasingly, economic (major trading partner). Here again, various participants may have different beliefs or values. Strongly nationalist central governments are likely to stress the historical; parents are likely to be more influenced by their beliefs about the value of a language in getting a job or making economic progress; educational establishments are likely to defend the existing pattern, with its easily available materials and methods and teachers.

It is taking major efforts to replace traditional teaching of French in English-speaking countries by more relevant teaching of other European or Oriental or Middle Eastern languages. Lambert (1994: 54) commented on the traditional patterns in English-speaking countries: "In Britain and Ireland, the choice is overwhelmingly French, although Ireland in particular is trying to expand the study of German, and Australia is doing the same with the languages of the region they inhabit, Asia. In the United States, which like Britain or Ireland has no particular reason for choosing one language or another, we drift with no clear rationale, currently toward Spanish, with French and German somewhat in decline, and Japanese undergoing a minor, but I suspect short lived, boom." In Europe, and much of the rest of the world, most effort is expended on the teaching of English.

For educational systems, the decision on additional languages may be set at the top or left to individual schools. For some time now, the Council of Europe and the European Community have been attempting to persuade member nations to teach two additional languages, in order to add languages other than English. National language diffusion agencies (the British Council, the Alliance française, the Goethe Institute, the Japan Foundation) try to influence school systems in other countries to adopt their languages. The day we met with the Israeli Minister of Education in 1985 to discuss a draft language education policy, he received a telegram from the French ambassador in Paris on business reminding him of an agreement that Hebrew would be permitted to be taught in France as long as French was taught in some Israeli schools.

Once a language is selected, there is still a question about variety. Particularly with English, there used to be a debate in some countries as to whether to teach British or American English. German universities hired assistants from both England and the USA to offer conversation classes in the two varieties. Nowadays, the controversy is often widened to include other varieties of World English.

A second common debate concerns when to start teaching a foreign language. In European educational systems, for many years foreign languages were added to the curriculum only at the secondary level; more recently, the age of beginning foreign languages has been lowered (Bergentoft 1994). The debate usually turns on conflicting values and beliefs. Some people hold that the teaching of a foreign language should wait until the national language has been established firmly. This argument was expressed in 2007 by a new Japanese Minister of Education who argued also for other traditionalist ideas. A contrary argument cites the belief that younger learners are more efficient learners of a foreign language (Bongaerts *et al.* 1997), but the relation between age and ultimate attainment is very complex (Birdsong and Paik 2008). Older learners appear to do better, but this may be a result of the methods and materials available for younger learners and the absence of teachers trained to work with them.

In 2001, the Ministry of Education of the People's Republic of China mandated that students should start learning English as a compulsory subject in the third grade, rather than as formerly in the seventh grade. Five reasons were given for this decision: the increasing demand for English in China, the importance of English in an educational reform directed at technology, the expansion of English into an increasing number of regions since 1978, evidence of the value of an early start, and the support of the Vice Premier who wrote a book after his retirement calling for foreign language education. A number of problems quickly became apparent, especially the shortage of teachers and of teaching materials (Hu 2007).

In general, there has continued to be a tendency in Europe to set the compulsory starting age for foreign language learning earlier: it is now five in France and the Netherlands; six in Austria, Estonia, Sweden, Italy, Spain, Latvia, Croatia, Czech Republic, Poland, and Portugal; seven in England; and eight in Slovenia, Belgium, Greece, and German regions (Enever 2007). A similar sentiment has been expressed in other countries, including Israel and Thailand.

The results of language education policy

How well do schools teach languages? The answer is as complex as the reality it refers to. Western educational systems are generally assumed to do reasonably well imposing the standard language on their students, although the Moser report (Moser 1999) suggested that a fifth of the adult population of the United Kingdom were "functionally illiterate." The teaching of other languages is commonly reported to be even less successful in English-speaking countries and to vary considerably in others. The Council of Europe made a determined effort to assess the level of achievement in languages, producing as a result a very influential and valuable framework (Council of Europe 2001), with subsequent attempts to standardize measures. In other parts of the world, too, school systems achieve very mixed results, in part no doubt because the amount of time normally allocated in a school curriculum to additional language teaching is comparatively small.

How effective is school in reviving or maintaining languages that are endangered or show signs of loss? One key example is Ireland, where after the establishment of the Irish Free State in 1918, the government set out (contrary to the bilingual language maintenance program developed by the Gaelic League) to require the teaching of Irish in schools and its use in what was hoped to be a monolingual society. All evidence suggests comparative success in increasing knowledge of the language, but none showing increased language use. Fleming and Debski (2007) reported a study of six primary and secondary schools, two Irish-medium schools in the Gaeltacht, two Irish-medium schools in English-speaking areas, and two English-medium schools. Outside the Gaeltacht, virtually all students reported using English when speaking to friends outside of school – nearly half of the children in Irish-medium schools used Irish to friends in school. In the Gaeltacht schools, two thirds used English to friends both inside and outside of school; only 15 percent used Irish consistently to friends in school.

Given the strong political and social pressure that was soon to be entrenched in laws making French official, the St. Lambert experiments in immersion teaching of French (Lambert and Tucker 1972) and the immersion teaching of Māori (Spolsky 2003a) showed good results in increasing knowledge of the target language, as did the official school support for Catalan (Strubell 2001). Without school support, language maintenance is difficult, but it is not enough to lead to widespread use. Studies of some indigenous systems show some evidence that schools can help maintain endangered languages (Spolsky 2007).

The tools of language management in schools

To understand better the working of language management in schools, we will consider briefly some of the means that may be used. So far, we have dealt in some detail with curriculum, the design of the content of schooling, the choice of the language of instruction, and the age of starting.

Teachers as a tool of language management

The selection and training of teachers has an important effect on a school's language policy. Labov's work on hypercorrection (Labov 1966) demonstrated that the social group from whom teachers are commonly selected – upwardly mobile lower-middle-class females – are as a group particularly liable to accept establishment standards of accuracy and purism, reinforcing the standard language. Le Page (1968: 437) describes how unaware West Indian school teachers were of the differences between acceptable West Indian and standard English usage; younger teachers were "very unsure of their own command of the language" and in fact used a good deal of vernacular when teaching.

In the effort to assimilate non-English speaking communities and the schools they influenced in the nineteenth-century United States, Pennsylvania stopped training teachers in German in the 1860s, fifty years before they required all teaching to be in English (Lewis 1980: 144). In the Soviet Union, during the pluralistic period under Lenin in the 1920s, there was a high proportion of local teachers – in 1925, 80 percent of elementary school staff in the Armenian Republic were Armenian so that teaching in the language was possible (Lewis 1972: 71). Although teaching in the minority languages continued, it proved difficult to find teachers qualified to handle education in the non-Russian languages. Special programs were developed at Leningrad University to train students from the Northern nationalities otherwise not qualified for admission to the university, in order to support programs for teaching Russian to minority pupils (Lewis 1972: 137). In the late 1950s, the emphasis moved to training teachers of Russian as a second language (Lewis 1972: 199).

The kind of challenge faced in finding and training bilingual teachers may be demonstrated in the case of the Navajo Nation. In the late 1960s, when the US Bilingual Education Act provided support for such programs, schools like Rough Rock Demonstration School (McCarty 2002) and Rock Point Community School (Holm and Holm 1990), two of the pioneers, could find only a handful of Navajos who had completed high school and tertiary education programs and so were qualified to teach. During the 1970s, initiatives supported by various government programs and conducted by universities on the outskirts of the Reservation launched a scheme to train 1,000 Navajo teachers. As much as possible, the training took place at sites on the Reservation, the university professors driving or flying hundreds of miles to teach their classes, because it was feared that if the future teachers had to be brought to the university towns, they would lack the family support needed for those with children to study, and that after four years in the city, they might be reluctant to return to life on the Reservation. When Wayne Holm started the bilingual classes at Rock Point, he set up teamed pairs of teachers, a qualified Anglo to teach in English and a Navajo aide to teach in Navajo. After a few years, these aides had completed teacher training, so that Navajos were teaching in both languages (Rosier and Holm 1980).

Citing examples from Bolivia, where about half of school children speak Spanish, the official school medium, as a first or second language, and two thirds speak one of thirty-three indigenous groups, and from Mozambique, where no more than a quarter speak the sole official language Portuguese, the school medium, as a first, second, or foreign language, Benson (2004) describes the challenges faced by teachers in bilingual schooling. Salaries are low, living conditions difficult, and transportation infrequent, schools are poorly built, and attendance is poor. Teacher training is brief and inadequate, so that many teachers lack proficiency in the school language. In both countries, efforts are being made to develop bilingual programs, but few of the teachers have the training to deal with the social, pedagogical, linguistic, and communal aspects of the job.

Reflecting a naïve belief that only native speakers can teach their language, educational systems have often attempted to manage the shift to a school language by importing native-speaking teachers, whatever that might mean (Davies 2003). Phillipson (1992) argues that this belief was a major force in imposing colonialist language policies, serving also to lower the status of local languages. One of the most radical of these programs was the American colonial experiment in the Philippines, when teachers and textbooks were "imported by the shipload" (Prator 1968: 473). A similar approach was tried during American rule of Micronesia, but in American Samoa in the 1980s, a slightly more enlightened governor decided to put television sets in every classroom instead so that the influence of the few teachers fluent in English could be spread. The unanticipated consequence was that to bring electricity to the villages, roads had to be built, with the result that all the villages in the island were now in easy reach of Pago Pago, so that everyone could go to town and pick up English. A strong language diffusion program like that of France requires sending teachers to other countries: Ager (1999: 177) estimated that there were usually more than 20,000 French teachers recruited for teaching in former colonies, especially in Africa. The comparative figure for Britain was 6,000.

The training, qualifying, recruiting, and hiring of teachers thus becomes a key aspect of managing school language policy. Each of these aspects can be centralized, boosting central authority over language, or delegated or left to various levels, encouraging diversity.

Managing the admission of students

A powerful way to manage the language of a school is to set requirements for admission that exclude students without certain language proficiencies or encourage speakers of chosen varieties. In compulsory elementary education settings, if there are restrictions they are most commonly handled by setting geographical boundaries, the effect of which relies on the tendency of demographically defined groups (such as immigrants or religious communities) to gravitate to the same part of a city. In the United States, efforts to lessen school segregation involved modifying school boundaries and introducing the bussing of pupils to schools into other neighborhoods. Once a school (whether public or private) decides to establish criteria for admission, there is a natural tendency to attempt to select students academically, socially, and linguistically prepared to succeed in the school. Unless there is an established program to provide for assimilation of unqualified students, such as a special program to teach immigrants the school language, schools will be tempted to exclude those prospective students who are not already proficient in the school language.

The United Kingdom Department for Education and Skills' 2007 *School Admissions Code* comments that most schools have enough places for all children that apply, but where this is not the case, the local education body or the school governing body must set "over-subscription criteria" that are clear and objective. Schools with a program associated with a religious faith may ask about observance, but otherwise, interviews may not be used and schools may not ask about the first language of parents. Selective schools (such as grammar schools, which are a class of academic high schools) may use objective tests of ability (including subject ability) and aptitude, but comprehensive secondary schools may not select only the top performers.

In United States schools, Hillman (2006) identified three "admissions policy drivers." The first was a belief in the value of a common school for children of all social classes, religions, and races. Most children attend neighborhood schools, with ethnic and economic residential segregation affecting the makeup of schools. Since the 1960s, a second driver has been the effort to balance intake, expressed in diverse desegregation plans. Since 2007, plans that took race into account were ruled out by the US Supreme Court. More recently, the third driver has been for a choice and for differentiation of schools. Socio-economic background, race, and language barriers are recognized as having major effects on levels of achievement. Looking at some model cases, Hillman (2006) notes that the Cambridge MA system does not yet include language as a criterion to be considered in school assignment, but it is among the factors being monitored. On the other hand, the San Francisco United School District includes a pupil's English language proficiency and whether or not it is the primary home language as two of the six variables used in the monitoring of school intakes: English language proficiency is also one of four factors in weighting school funding.

In Sweden, language may not be taken into account in admission: "As The English School is grant maintained by the Swedish State, the school is bound to follow the regulations of the National Board of Education (*Skolverket*) regarding admissions. As such, expatriate and English speaking children may not be given preference. Nor will pupils be admitted with reference to ability and aptitude" (Admissions regulations of The English School, Gothenberg).

School admission was rigidly controlled as a method of enforcing French in Québec. *Loi 101*, the Charter of the French Language, provided that only children whose father and mother had been educated in English-language schools in Québec could be admitted to English language schools. This was intended to block the tendency of immigrants to choose English over French-medium schools (Bourhis 2001:112). Attendance at English schools dropped in 1995 to under half the 1976 figure, as a result of large numbers of anglophones who left the province as well as the policy preventing immigrants from attending such schools. The net out-migration of English-speaking university graduates between 1976 and 1986 reached 40 percent (Bourhis 2001: 121).

Punishment as language management

The provincial government of Québec managed to maintain French by limiting the teaching of English. Similar draconian policies were exemplified by the legal banning of Kurdish in Turkey and in the punishment of pupils heard speaking proscribed minority languages in schools enforcing efforts at replacement. McCarty (2002: 39–47) presents a series of accounts of Navajos dragged off (often by police) to boarding schools where they were forced to speak English, punished by Anglo teachers and Navajo matrons for using a word of Navajo, their mouths washed with yellow bar soap, or required to scrub the floor with a toothbrush. In Welsh schools, during the period when English was being enforced, anyone heard saying a word in the banned language was forced to wear a stick around his neck; whoever was left with it at the end of the day, having failed to pass it on to another pupil, was beaten with it. There were teachers in the Native Schools who punished pupils for speaking Māori as the shift to English was encouraged (Simon 1998). Stories like these are part of the folklore of school systems where language replacement was enforced. Two recent US incidents are reported by Dennis Baron on his Web log http://webtools.uiuc.edu/blog/view?topicId=1376): in September 2007 the St. Anne Catholic School in Wichita, Kansas, banned the use of Spanish in its playgrounds (there are 75 Spanish-speaking children in the school), and the following month, Robert Aumaugher, superintendent of the Esmeralda County Schools in Nevada advised parents that their children must not speak Spanish on the school bus (the American Civil Liberties Union on January 31, 2008 protested the rule which was later canceled).

Schooling in a theory of language management

In most societies, the school has become the primary agency of organized language management, setting out to remedy its students' perceived language inadequacies. From the day students arrive at school, they are open to continued pressure to modify their language practices and take on the varieties and variants chosen by the school language managers, whoever they may be. Two major conflicts are set up: the effort of the school to correct or suppress the language variety students bring from home ("Why don't you speak Hebrew with your daughter?" her teacher asked me when we moved to Israel, surprised at my insistence that I wanted her to maintain English as well), and the resistance of the peer group to adult values and variants ("Don't use that slang!" they are regularly admonished).

Complicating the model, the participants in the school domain vary greatly in authority, and the local language managers (the teachers) are themselves under a great deal of pressure from those in authority over them, whether within the domain or outside it. Because language management is such a central feature of schooling, it is a topic of debate and complaint among the general public and employers and language activists of all hues. Complaints are regularly expressed that grammar is no longer being taught properly, that children cannot spell anymore, that they can't write, and that a revived language has been changed irreversibly. As a result, even in a situation where language issues are not commonly debated, the failures of school and the latest generation of students are regularly protested in letters to newspapers and political speeches.

The school domain is probably the ultimate test of a theory of language management, because schools are there basically to manage the language of their students, because of the complexity of participants and management methods, and because of the difficulty of evaluating results.

7 Managing language in legal and health institutions

Safety and health

Legal and health institutions share a number of features that make it possible to consider them in a single chapter. Each has two distinct classes of participants: the professionals who control the domain and the lay public who come into contact with them. Even without other causes of language difficulty (such as the fact that lawyers, judges, police, doctors, and nurses are generally majority language speakers and their clients or patients come from all classes and usually include a high proportion of minority language speakers), the gap between professional and lay varieties of language is a critical issue. An early study of doctor–patient communication in Britain showed that it was not just foreign medical personnel who caused problems: most patients surveyed asked the nurse on the way out "What did he say?" Obviously, the lay/ professional difference is greatly exacerbated when it also encounters a language barrier. But communication is critical in these domains: a doctor must understand what a patient is feeling, a patient must understand what the doctor recommends or requires, and justice demands that police, judges, jury, witnesses, and accused all understand each other.

That at least is the view from the outside, but if it were shared by all those who control legal and health institutions, the domains would be self-regulating. Rather, they have acted (and in many cases still act) with less than full responsibility. Doctors show a tendency to ignore what their patients say – some sociolinguistic studies have reported that they tend to invent their own interpretations of the medical histories their patients give them – and when left alone, expect the patient's friends or children to interpret for those whose language they do not know. Judges and police use their greater power to ignore the need to communicate.

There have been exceptions. One outstanding example of police recognizing the need for interpreting services was the birth of the Language Line in San Diego. There, a pioneering policeman recruited volunteers to provide telephone interpreting to help police find out what was going on when they were called to situations where all of the participants were recent arrivals from south-east Asia. The system subsequently became commercial and was bought by AT&T.

There has also been growing recognition of the need for interpreters in law courts, but efficient remedies were slow to be found: there continue to be almost daily reports of trials delayed or abandoned and convictions overturned because of inadequate interpretation. Health services – doctors and hospitals – still tend mainly to rely on available amateur help. The pressure for change came from the outside, with growing concern especially in western countries for the rights of citizens who do not speak the official language. In this chapter we will commonly see that the effective language manager is outside the immediate domain, often a national government passing a law to implement a supranational statement of rights. The domain therefore presents a regular picture of external pressure for dealing with language problems.

The law courts

Public language management is regularly implemented by laws and regulations, but in this chapter we will focus on the management of language choice within the institutions directly associated with the law: the courts, the police, and the prisons. Communication is important in each of these, but to different degrees and in different ways. The task of a law court is to interpret and implement written laws, basically through structured debate among a set of professionals – the judges and lawyers – who establish the facts of the case by posing questions in defined forms to lay witnesses. These witnesses, professional though they may be in their own fields of expertise, are expected to answer in a way that satisfies legal professionals. Though professionals themselves, anthropologists find the rules of courtroom language and legal notions of evidence quite different from their own (Rosen 1977). Generally expected to be a silent observer, the accused prisoner constitutes an additional party to the speech event. There can also be a lay jury, expected to decide on facts as instructed, who constitute an involved audience.

The business of law courts consists of a series of verbal interactions, starting with a formal written indictment or list of charges presented verbally, followed by a long set of verbal interchanges that are usually recorded in writing to constitute the official record of the trial, and concluded by a judgment and a sentence. The recording adds an extra participant, the court recorder, who speaks only when invited by the judge to read back a portion of the transcript. Many courts now require tape recordings as well against which the transcript can be checked. There may also be an interpreter.

The authorized participants are professionals, with training and experience in the special rules of speech that apply, and they in turn provide guidance to the laymen who are to answer their questions in ways that they stipulate

("Answer yes or no!"). Obvious in the situation is the uneven power relationship, with the judge in overall charge (everyone must bow to his will), and the other professionals (the lawyers) able to dominate the witnesses and accused.

Which language is to be used in a court is generally laid down in the national constitution or by a law designating an official language. Changing the language of a court is a political issue. In western Europe, the change from Latin to the vernacular was a milestone in the development of national languages. It was considered an important step when the Tamil Nadu government decided in 2007 that Tamil as well as English could be used in the Madras High Court (*Zee News*, India, November 2007).

The potential unfairness of the power imbalance is greatly compounded when some parties lack proficiency in the language of the court. The general practice in systems where all the words uttered in court are recorded and transcribed to form a record that might be consulted on appeal to a higher court is that anything in another language must be translated into the official language, the resulting translation (right or wrong) constituting the official record. One lawyer told me of an incident that horrified him when he was just starting in practice many years ago. A New York judge (himself of Irish origin) carried on a discussion in Yiddish with a Jewish witness: none of this could be recorded. The US Supreme Court recently held that it was permissible to reject a potential member of the jury who was bilingual and who said that he would base his decision on his understanding of Spanish testimony and not on the interpreter's incorrect translation; a dissenting Justice suggested rather that he should have been told to report inaccuracies to the presiding judge. The issue has come up again in Florida, where the Florida Supreme Court ruled in August 2006 that jurors "cannot use their own knowledge of foreign languages to decide whether a courtroom translation is correct if all parties to a case agree on its accuracy." The Justice Minister of South Africa expressed regret that the law courts continued to be run in English and Afrikaans and supported the ANC position that the policy must be changed (*The Daily News*, June 13, 2007). The interpreter is an important additional participant in the court procedure. The other participants are at the mercy of the interpreter, whose ability to translate is generally unchallenged.

Civil rights

The provision of interpreters is not automatic, but depends on a growing acceptance of the civil rights of the accused. The notion that any accused person has the right to understand what he is being charged with and what is happening in the trial is now widely agreed, though implementation remains uneven. The US Bill of Rights (the first ten amendments to the US constitution ratified in 1791) established in Amendment VI the right of the accused "to be informed of the nature and cause of the accusation, to be confronted with the witnesses against him," both of which assume his ability to understand the language of the accusation and the witnesses. When it accepts this principle, a court's language policy is directly managed by decisions of an external agency, a constitution or a legislature, at the national or regional level. It may also be influenced by the policies of supranational bodies (see Chapter 11).

An early language management decision affecting law courts was the English Statute of Pleading 1362, itself written in French, which established the use of English rather than French, which most people did not understand, in all courts, but still required records to be kept in Latin. This was not so much asserting the right for anyone to understand their own trial, but a declaration by increasingly powerful English speakers of their own rights against those of their former Norman-speaking conquerors (Ormrod 2003). Showing how long it takes to change language practice, 300 years later, in 1650, Cromwell's Parliament adopted a statute "for turning the Books of the Law . . . into English." It was principally aimed at court proceedings but it included a requirement that "statutes . . . shall be in the English tongue." It was not liked by the legal profession and in 1660, after the Restoration, was repealed. A third attempt to change the language of the law to English was legislation passed in 1731 requiring that all court proceedings and statutes "shall be in the English tongue and language only, and not in Latin or French . . . and [court proceedings] shall be written in such a common and legible hand character, as the acts of parliament are usually engrossed in." All three statutes were aimed at making the law more understandable and accessible to the public. At least one English court continued to use French for its records until the middle of the nineteenth century.

Only in the twentieth century did arguments for civil rights lead to widespread provision of interpreters in courts. Article 14 of the International Covenant on Civil and Political Rights adopted by the United Nations General Assembly states:

In the determination of any criminal charge against him, everyone shall be entitled to the following minimum guarantees, in full equality:
  (a) to be informed promptly and in detail in a language which he understands of the nature and cause of the charge against him;
  (f) to have the free assistance of an interpreter if he cannot understand or speak the language used in court. (United Nations General Assembly Resolution 2200A (XXI) on December 16, 1966 which entered into force March 23, 1976).

Similar phraseology occurs in the constitutions of many former colonies becoming independent in the 1960s.

In the model I am exploring, the United Nations is a supranational domain, although the requirement that its implementation depends on acceptance by a nation-state makes it in fact a matter of national language management. Rights are supranational, derived from general principles, expressed by international bodies, but because the declarations and charters setting out these rights are treaties, they depend on ratification and implementation by sovereign nation-states.

The United States Congress in 1978 passed the Court Interpreters Act (PL-95–539; amended 1988), which based the right to interpreters on the fifth and sixth amendments to the US constitution and which called for certification and regulation of court interpreters in Federal courts. In 1979, there were 26,000 dockets requiring interpreters, and in 1988 there were 46,000 (Benmaman 1992). Influencing this development and similar developments in Europe was the success of interpretation in the widely reported Nuremberg Trials of Nazi leaders. The 1970s were also the beginning of a period of major civil rights activities, involving recognition of the rights of racial, religious, and ethnic minorities and the recognition of women's rights. During the same period, there was growing support in many countries for arguments about the relevance of language to human and civil rights (see pp. 214ff.).

Part of the campaign for recognition of language problems in courts has been a slew of reports of what happens in the absence of translation. When the accused cannot communicate with the court or understand the process, erroneous judgments are possible. In one much publicized case, a young woman from South America charged in the US with infanticide turned out to speak not Spanish but a Native American language for which no interpreter could be found. Following the acceptance of the principle, a number of cases in various US jurisdictions have been reversed because of faulty translation or the absence of translation. Other nations too have started to recognize the issue. In the United Arab Emirates, a court overturned the ten-year jail sentence given to a Ugandan woman charged with murdering her HIV-positive husband because of the absence of a legal translator: subsequently, the ruling was set aside and her jail sentence was confirmed (*Gulf News*, November 2006). In Australia, lawyers for five Japanese arrested at Melbourne airport in 1992 after customs discovered thirteen kilograms of heroin in their luggage claimed that poor interpretation during their interrogation and trials had given the mistaken impression that they were lying (*Asahi Herald*, February 2006). In New Jersey in 2001, a convicted murderer was granted a new trial because he had not been provided with sufficient translation services to understand the evidence against him. In 2005, a defendant was acquitted of a murder charge because the untrained and unqualified volunteer interpreter had not read the Miranda warnings clearly (*News Release Wire*, November 2005). In Libya, five nurses and a doctor were sentenced to death because of a translation error, in which the word "recombinant," which means a specific strain of HIV, was interpreted as "genetically modified," suggesting that it was man-made. In New Hampshire in January 2005, a man found guilty in 2002 of beating his infant daughter sought a new trial, claiming that he was confused by the interpreter during the trial and unable to follow what was being said. In July 2007, a US judge dismissed charges of rape when the failure to appoint an interpreter in a Liberian dialect had resulted in an unwarranted delay. Stories like these continue to appear daily in the world press, providing support for those who argue for the provision of court interpreters.

Legal systems engage in language management when they set the rules for language in the court. When US courts agreed that defendants must be advised of their right to remain silent and must also be allowed to consult a lawyer before being interrogated by police, courts were commonly required to adjudicate the ability of an individual defendant to understand the Miranda warning. The right to understand charges starts appearing in national con-stitutions after World War Two. The next step was a requirement to provide interpreters for all defendants, as well as to translate all evidence given in court into the official language. Some recent cases have dealt with the quality of interpretation, with judgments being overturned on appeal after comparing the recorded translation with an original tape of the witness giving evidence. The effect has been to add a new layer of adjunct professionals to the law court: interpreters have the same importance as stenographers or court recorders in establishing and preserving an accurate record of a procedure, and must be considered relevant participants in the domain.

In California, a Commission on Access to Justice reported in 2005 on the problems faced by residents who do not speak English. To remedy these problems, court interpreters are being trained and certified in a number of US states. In California, the Chief Justice expressed support for a plan to expand programs to train, test, and certify qualified interpreters for the more than 100 languages translated each year in California's courts (*Met News*, May 2005). In the United States, there is Federal court certification for interpreters of Haitian Creole, Navajo, and Spanish. In individual states the situation varies widely. Some (e.g., Washington, California, New Jersey) test interpreters in several languages; others have no certification at all. The Consortium for State Court Interpreter Certification has thirty-nine states as members. Tests are administered in fourteen languages, and in 2007, twenty states had cer-tification requirements. In the USA in the year 2004, the median wage for a court interpreter was $20.54 hourly and $42,720 annually. There were 18,000 employed, with a projected increase over the next ten years of 10–20 percent each year. In 2000, Federal courts paid US$305 per day to *per diem* inter-preters. Where the volume of work is greatest, courts tend to have full-time staff positions, almost all of them for Spanish-English.

In the US, this move to remedy linguistic problems in court depended on interpretations calling for civil rights based on the US constitution. The impact of the Civil Rights Act was further extended when in August 2000 President Clinton signed Executive Order 13166, entitled "Improving access to services for persons with limited English proficiency." Federal agencies and other organizations receiving Federal funding were required by the order to develop plans on how to provide necessary services to people who did not know English well enough (Brecht and Rivers 2005). Implementation of the program has been uneven but it is probably the major force protecting the civil rights of speakers of languages other than English (Spolsky 2006). The European Union has similar policies supporting the civil rights of speakers of minority languages, but leaves the definition of "minority language" to its original member states (Nic Shuibhne 2001).

Interpreters are used in courts in other countries too. In Japan, since 1970, and even more since the 1990s, there has been steady migration from many different countries. By 2000, 1.7 million foreign residents were registered with local governments (Taki 2005). Japanese law requires that only Japanese may be spoken during any investigation and public trial; this produces a language barrier noted both by civil rights campaigners and the legal institutions. To resolve the problems caused by witnesses who do not speak Japanese, the police increased its linguistic capability – in 2000 there were 3,400 police officers trained as interpreters and 5,300 external interpreters hired. The courts too began to hire interpreters, so that by 1997, interpreters were used in 85 percent of the public trials of non-Japanese speaking defendants. A further step has been to improve the quality of interpreting, adding professional training, recording interviews and cases, and moving the cost of interpreting to the public prosecutor.

Less common languages produce special problems. In Australia, the head of the Aboriginal Legal Service said many injustices have occurred in Western Australia's justice system because of a lack of accredited indigenous language interpreters (*The Melbourne Age*, November 16, 2005). A US district court judge ordered a new trial for a defendant convicted of arson whose interpreter spoke western Armenian while he spoke eastern Armenian (*Associated Press*, November 30, 2005). In Malaysia, the shortage of Tamil interpreters had been resolved but there were too few Chinese-dialect interpreters, with some lawyers bringing private interpreters to help in civil cases (*The New Straits Times*, June 6, 2005). In Colorado, a Guatemalan native on trial for rape spoke a dialect called Kanjobal. This language, according to Ethnologue (2005), has about 48,500 speakers in Guatemala and 10,000 refugees in Mexico, and an interpreter had to be flown in from Los Angeles (*The Greeley Tribune*, January 27, 2005). A case was reported in India in which ten members of the Koya tribe languished in jail without trial for two years for want of an interpreter (*The Telegraph*, Calcutta, November 29, 2006).

In those countries where interpreters are provided, the cost has risen rapidly. The cost of furnishing court interpreters to foreign nationals accused of committing crimes in Scotland has risen fourfold in the past three years (*The Scotsman*, January 4, 2008). In the United Kingdom, the grant of autonomy to Gaelic areas has involved new costs. In Wales, legislation put Welsh on an equal footing with English in public life including in the courts (Huws 2006). The Northern Ireland Office was reported to be concerned about the cost of implementing the Irish Language Act promised in the St. Andrews Agreement. The BBC estimated that the cost of translation and interpreting in Britain was over £100 million in 2006. In 2007, the Secretary of State for Communities and Local Government complained that the figure was too high and called for a review of the policy.

In 2004, court interpreting services in North Carolina went over budget by about $800,000, and many interpreters failed to become state certified. In a new policy, interpreters were to be contracted through the state and subject to uniform conditions of employment rather than contracting through courts in individual districts. Iowa paid courtroom interpreters more than $300,000 in 2006. In South Carolina, more than seven times the number of defendants needed an interpreter in 2000 than in 1985, a result of the growing drug trade. According to the Minnesota Court Administrator's Office, the total cost for interpreters was $3.3 million in 2007, a figure that has grown by nearly 40 percent during the past five years (*Winona Daily News*, February 4, 2008). The cost of hiring interpreters for court proceedings presents more challenges than just a monetary one. Both prosecutors and defense lawyers in Oklahoma pointed out that the language barrier increases both the time and cost of preparing and trying a case involving a defendant not fluent with the English language (*Muskogee Phoenix*, July 2006). Using interpreters slows down the court process, and when sign interpreters are provided, "to the pace of an infirm snail" (*The Nashua Telegraph*, May 2006). In this case, there was a sign interpreter screened from others to enable the defense attorney and the accused to confer.

The question of who should pay is starting to be raised. The *Irish Times* reported that the National Consultative Committee on Racism and Interculturalism had expressed concern at remarks from a district judge that foreign defendants should pay for their own interpreter services (*Irish Times*, May 2005). There is a growing resentment about the need to pay for interpreters – if only migrants would learn the official language (or stay in their own country), we would be spared the expense.

It is not enough to have an interpreter who can speak to a witness or defendant, but he or she needs sufficient training in legal language and procedures to be able to explain complex legal notions to an untrained layman on the one hand, and to provide some reasonable explanation of alien cultural behavior to the legal experts on the other. An Ontario Superior Court judge complained about the inadequacy and lack of qualifications of the interpreters available (*Globe and Mail*, November 18, 2005). In South Africa, the Justice Department's regional office in East London withheld the salaries of the only official Nigerian court interpreter for Port Elizabeth's courts, demanding that his foreign language qualification be verified by the Qualification Board in Pretoria (*Legalbrief.com*, March 2005). In the US, the growing number of non-English speakers appearing in court prompted the High Court in South Carolina to enact a code of professional conduct for all courtroom interpreters (*Charleston News*, May 2005).

More and more countries are now providing legal interpreters. In Sri Lanka, where Sinhala is the language of administration, the constitution maintains the right "to give information . . . with regard to the commission of an offence to a Police or peace officer in either Tamil or English." Article 135 of the 2003 Afghan draft constitution provided "a right to interpreter and speaking mother tongue in court." The Council of Europe in 2001 urged the Macedonian government to allow Albanians to use their own language in court. The 1995 Bolivian constitution provided for interpretation services in courts. Chinese law allows the use of Chinese or Tibetan in courts. The Georgian constitution allows for interpreters. The draft Iraqi constitution provided for the use of Arabic or Kurdish in courts. The Official Irish Act includes the right "of a person to be heard in and to use the Irish language in court proceedings." The Lithuanian constitution established that "in the Republic of Lithuania court trials shall be conducted in the State language" but also provides that "Persons who do not speak Lithuanian shall be guaranteed the right to participate in investigation and court proceedings through an interpreter."

But controversy continues: Romania has now determined that minority language speakers have the right to use their mother-tongue in court: a translator has to be guaranteed by the court requested and if all parties agree, the trial has to take place in the minority language concerned. However, the Hungarian minority has expressed concern that all documents connected with a trial must be written in Romanian (*Eurolang*). Russia and the Ukraine are currently disputing policy in the Ukraine. A court in eastern Ukraine ruled that a local government decision to grant special status to the Russian language was illegal (*Associated Press*, July 26, 2006). Banning the Russian language for Ukrainian legal procedures infringes upon the rights of almost 20 million Russian speakers living in the Ukraine, the Russian Foreign Ministry said in a statement published on its official website (*RIA Novosti*). In Macedonia too, the language for the legal domain remains a critical issue.

With the increasing complexity and number of languages to be found in major cities of the world, and taking into account the probability that new immigrants who do not know the local language are liable to be suspected of illegal activity, the pressure on the legal system continues to grow. The force behind language management in this case is threefold. The first is domain internal: pressure produced by demographic changes leading to a national sociolinguistic profile of increasing complexity, especially as a result of immigration. The other two are external: wider acceptance of the belief, expressed in international covenants, that persons accused of a crime have the right to understand the proceedings, and management decisions made by national or regional governments responding to civil rights concerns requiring the provision of interpreters. The failure of those within the domain to adjust to the communication needs produced by the growing multilingualism of most nations, and the consequent increase in the number of people with limited proficiency in the official language of the court have led to external pressure, partly in international recognition of civil rights and partly in national implementation of these rights.

The police

The same pressures have affected the police. The participants in this domain may be crudely characterized as cops, robbers, victims, and witnesses. One of the first problems faced by police in a multilingual situation is to determine the status of those people they find at the scene of a reported crime. If they are unable to communicate with them, how do they decide who is a victim, who a criminal, and who an innocent bystander and potential witness? In San Diego in the 1970s, with the beginning of immigration from Vietnam and Cambodia, it became increasingly difficult for police officers answering a call to the scene of a suspected crime to get a quick picture of who was said to be a victim and who was claimed to be the guilty party, because they did not understand what people were saying to them. As a result, they would simply arrest everyone in sight and take them to the police station to look for interpreters. A volunteer telephone interpreter system was set up, so that a preliminary investigation could be carried out on the spot. The resulting Language Line now serves businesses and the tourist industry more than the police, but it provided an additional answer to a critical problem in legal language management.

Provided originally for the police, telephone-mediated interpretation services soon spread to other domains. From the beginning, they were sought by relevant businesses in the private sector: an interpretation service avoided the cost of hiring multilingual telephone operators until practical experience could demonstrate the size of the demand for each language. The industry has grown, and several new firms offer similar services: "National Interpreting Service (NIS) is a wholly-owned subsidiary of the world's largest and fastest-growing provider of over-the-phone interpreting services. Established in 1984 and with clients in more than 20 countries, we currently process thousands of interpreting requests daily. Backed by the very latest call routing technology, our thousands of professional interpreters help millions of people each year to communicate across language and cultural barriers. NIS clients include hospitals, police forces and immigration services."

Police departments too have been worried by the increasing cost of providing interpreters in response to increasing multilingualism. South Korean police advise foreign suspects of their rights in thirteen languages, including English, Chinese, Japanese, Russian, Vietnamese, Thai, Indonesian, Mongolian, Uzbek, and Farsi. British police recorded a steep hike in its spending on language interpreters, mainly due to the large influx of immigrants to the country.

As a result, police now look for language proficiency in their staff: 470 of the New York Police Department's employees passed tests in more than forty-five languages including Arabic, Urdu, Hindi, Pashto, Farsi, Dari, and Punjabi; another 4,000 were waiting to be tested (*New York Times*, March 2, 2005). In Germany too, hiring police with plurilingual proficiency is becoming important: the Berlin police force wanted to fill 10 percent of the 200 new recruits they accept with members of ethnic minorities, particularly those who speak fluent Turkish, Arabic, Polish, Serbo-Croatian, and Russian. In the US, the Charlotte-Mecklenburg Police Department formed an International Unit in 2000 made up of six officers, all fluent in both English and Spanish and including skills in Vietnamese, Laotian, French, German, and Arabic (News 14 Carolina, January 15, 2005).

An increasing number of police in the US have been taking sign language classes: even under the best conditions, communication between a deaf person and an on-duty police officer can be difficult (*Intelligencer Journal*, Philadelphia, December 4, 2004). Members of the local deaf community requested that the Wichita Police Department hire state-certified sign language interpreters (*The Wichita Eagle*, November 16, 2005). In San Antonio, Texas, Deaf Link is an Internet-based interpreting service that provides communication access for the deaf and hard of hearing for the police department (*Officer*, Texas, May 17, 2006). There have been reports of the provision of sign language interpreters for the police in South Africa, and in Shanghai.

Even after someone has been convicted and sentenced to prison, language problems remain. In Britain, "failures in the prison and immigration services which led to the foreign prisoners' scandal have still not been eliminated, a watchdog has warned . . . Communication with foreign prisoners was difficult, with some officers reporting that a telephone translation service was too expensive to use" (Press Association report, September 2006).

The health institutions

I started the book I wrote on language policy (Spolsky 2004) with the case of a German hospital that refused a needed heart operation to an immigrant because she might not understand the post-operative instructions she would receive. One could easily fill a chapter or a book or even a multi-volume series with similar tales of the need for wise language management in the health domain – patients mistreated because no one could take an accurate medical history, misdiagnosis, the wrong doses of medicine given because the patient could not read the label or understand the doctor, young children used as interpreters in death-threatening patient–doctor interchanges, and confusion when foreign-trained medical personnel deal with local patients. Linda Armas who is chair of IMAGEN, the Executive Advisory Board on Latino Health, in Albuquerque NM said that "non-English-speaking patients' inability to communicate with health-care providers – even more than poverty, lack of insurance or lack of education – explains Latinos' higher rates of chronic disease and other health problems" (*The New Mexican*, February 5, 2006). Earlier that same week, a study estimated that "providing language-appropriate prescription labels could eliminate some of the medical errors responsible for 98,000 deaths each year in the United States" (February 2006 issue of the *Journal of Health Care for the Poor and Underserved*). It was estimated in 2007 that half of US pharmacies cannot provide adequate language services for their non-English speaking customers.

Tempting though such an approach might be, I will show restraint and try rather to sketch the dimensions of a working language management plan for medical and health services. Each medical system has its own role for patient–doctor communication. The Navajo medicine man performs a long verbal ceremony over patients who have been diagnosed as needing the particular treatment (Reichard 1963), with the patient simply required to respond at appropriate places. Western medicine assumes the taking of a medical history as the first step, followed by a physical examination accompanied by regular questioning ("Did it hurt when I pressed there?") and instruction ("Turn over on the other side and raise your arm!"). When the doctor has gathered enough information, she sends the patient for testing, and once the results are available, communicates a diagnosis to the patient.

Increasingly, health agencies and professionals have become aware of the problem in this system produced by language difficulties. The US Department of Health and Human Services in the Final Report on National Standards for Culturally and Linguistically Appropriate Services in Health Care (March

2001) states in Standard 4 that "health care organizations must offer and provide language assistance services, at no cost to each patient/consumer with limited English proficiency at all points of contact, in a timely manner during all hours of operation." In particular, there have been regular complaints about the misuse of child interpreters to enable doctors and nurses to communicate with non-English speaking immigrants.

But even a trained interpreter is not enough, unless he or she has training with specific groups and diseases. Hsu *et al.* (2006) studied a group of adult ethnic Chinese immigrants in the US who had had diabetes for at least one year (Asian Americans have a 50 percent greater risk of type 2 diabetes than Caucasian Americans). Those who preferred to speak English (they were US-born or had immigrated when young) scored significantly higher on a test of diabetes knowledge than those who preferred Chinese. All were then given a book on diabetes in Chinese and English; only the Chinese speakers showed improvement on a second test. It is not enough for the doctor to use an interpreter in the fifteen minutes that his health fund or insurance company allows him on average to spend with the patient; nurses and dietitians too need linguistic and cultural knowledge, and written material in the patient's language and based on knowledge of the patient's culture (e.g., dietary habits) is also necessary.

Effective health-care related language management depends on the nature of the demand, becoming increasingly complex with immigration. A US commercial over-the-phone interpretation service specializing in the health field now offers interpretations in 150 languages, 24 hours a day and 365 days a year. It claims to be able to link a health professional to an appropriate interpreter in less than 45 seconds and furnishes dual-handset phones so that both doctor and patient can talk to the interpreter, who is specially trained for medical interpreting. A flat rate is charged for all languages and all hours. The similar service operated by AT&T has different rates, averaging between $2 and $3 a minute. Some hospitals in Northern California are setting up video-based interpretations.

Naturally, the cost of these services quickly adds up – in December 2005, Denver Health reported it was spending more than $1 million to provide interpreting services in more than 160 languages. Representatives of managed care plans in California estimate that it will cost $15 million to provide qualified interpreters in place of the children commonly used.

In September 2006, the New York State Department of Health adopted regulations setting standards for hospitals and requiring them to provide skilled interpreters, translate important forms into common languages, and make sure that patients are treated rapidly in spite of language issues. The hospitals may use various means – bilingual hospital staff, interpreters, volunteers, and telephone language assistance lines. Family members may not be used. The medical chart must show the patient's preferred language. The regulations expect the hospital to provide interpreting within ten minutes in emergency settings and within twenty minutes in inpatient and outpatient settings.

As with the legal field, language management in health services has been initiated from outside the domain, with pressure from governments for civil and human rights, and (in the US in particular) threats of law suits and insurance claims for failure to communicate with patients. The pressure comes at a time when most nations have not found a satisfactory method to provide health services for citizens and legal and illegal immigrants. Providing qualified interpreters on a 24-hour basis for multiple languages calls for imaginative solutions in an area already under severe fiscal strain.

The legal and health domains in the model

What, we may now ask, are the changes to the theoretical model suggested by the legal and health domains? The major modification is no doubt the importance of external influence on management, on the one hand, and the changing nature of internal beliefs. In the United States, the influence of the civil rights movement was felt in congressional and presidential action, and the changing attitude to minority groups seems to have led to acceptance of the need to provide language services in the police, in courts, and in hospitals and doctors' clinics for those who do not speak English, particularly as instantiated in Executive Order 13166, the strongest current implementation of civil rights for language. In Europe, pressure in this direction was exerted by the ratification of the International Covenant on Civil and Political Rights. In addition, major changes in the sociolinguistic ecology and the development of multilingual populations almost universally produced a situation in which the efficient working of the legal and health services was seen to be severely threatened if some pragmatic solution to communication problems could not be found. There was thus both pragmatic and ideological pressure for language management.

The legal and health domains offer classic cases of organized language management: communication problems identified by participants and observers calling for resolution, and the widespread nature of the problem calling for national action and supranational concern. The solutions being developed are the result of complex interplay between the various participants inside and outside the domains, with the cost of implementation setting strong constraints on the possibility of achieving a utopian solution with efficient interpretation services available for all possible situations.

8   Managing military language

Communication needs in the military

By their very nature, armies, navies, air forces, and other military formations have special communication needs and problems, and as a result, need to develop language policies. At first examination, this might be expected to be a strictly pragmatic domain, with practical considerations ruling efficient decision-making, but here too there turn out to be external and symbolic forces.

As a rule, language management in the military depends on a number of definable parameters. First, there is the question of the organizational level: a different kind of management is needed at the level of the smallest fighting unit and at the level of the large combinations that armies form. We might perhaps loosely characterize these levels by the rank of the commander. The sergeant in a multilingual military formation needs to be able to communicate with the soldiers in his section and also with the officer commanding his company or regiment (I use these ranks and unit terms very loosely, understanding that they will vary for different armies at different times). Non-commissioned officers in multilingual armies generally serve much the same kind of function as foremen in factories, passing on orders received from their superiors in the official dominant language and using the vernacular to communicate with the rank-and-file soldiers. The *sergeant's problem*, then, might be characterized as the need to have soldiers speaking a common language and to understand the language used by their immediate commanders.

At the other end of the scale, the general or field marshal commanding a large army with units speaking different languages – for example, an army drawn from a coalition of nations – requires that the commanders of each unit either speak the common language or have qualified interpreters available. The typical *general's problem* may be characterized as the need to communicate with the commanders of subordinate units.

There are two other sets of communication needs common to military forces. The first is knowledge of the language of the enemy, basically for the purpose of obtaining intelligence. Let us call this the *spy's problem*. The second is knowledge of the language of civilians whose territory the army is fighting in: this we might call the *occupier's problem*.

The spy's problem is aggravated by a widespread belief that learning or knowing a language or a culture is strongly dependent on a positive attitude to speakers of that language and even on a desire to integrate into the culture. Following that view, there is a reason to suspect the loyalty of anyone who knows the enemy's language well. One does not need to be an *aficionado* of spy novels to recognize divided loyalties. Pragmatically, a high level of proficiency in a language often depends on a period of time living in the country where it is spoken, or being married to a speaker of the language. Their life histories make efficient speakers of foreign languages an object of suspicion to counter-intelligence agencies. Perhaps this helps account for the slowness with which US defense and intelligence and diplomatic agencies built up their Arabic- and Pashto-speaking staff. Most of the interpreters currently being used by the US Army in Iraq are civilian contract employees. A parallel problem was the US military decision not to use otherwise qualified homosexual interpreters, explainable as nervousness that they would be open to blackmail and so insecure.

The occupying army's problem is an economic one, because the two obvious solutions – to teach the soldiers the language of the occupied territory, or, as the Japanese did in Korea and the territories it conquered in World War Two, to insist on the conquered people learning their language – are both expensive and assume a long-term occupation, as in the case of Soviet domination of its conquests. During what is recognized as an occupation (as opposed to the colonialization that follows conquest), the situation is perhaps regarded as too short-term to warrant the investment required for long-term solutions.

In contrast to the situation in health and legal fields, we will find that most military language management is dependent on domain-internal decisions, with the advantage that in the military context, authority is clearly defined by rank. In the rest of this chapter, we explore some prototypical cases.

The Roman army and the sergeant's problem

Adams (2003), in a magisterial study of Roman bilingualism, devotes a chapter to language use in the army in Egypt. The Roman army was polyglot. In Egypt, there were Palmyrene soldiers (Palmyra was a city in Syria conquered by the Romans in the first century BCE) who were reluctant to lose their identity and added Palmyrene to bilingual inscriptions, the other language being Greek or Latin. Officers in foreign auxiliary units were expected to be bilingual in Latin and a vernacular language, but the soldiers themselves did not need to know Latin. There is evidence of the Romanization of the officer class. In the Byzantine army, some orders were given in Latin, but the army was Greek-speaking. A list of passwords in Egypt was written in Greek letters, but the words were Latin. More soldiers could write Greek than Latin.

Adams (2003: 599) does not believe that Latin was the official language of the army in Egypt. There were opportunities for soldiers to learn Latin, but the archives contained official letters and receipts in Greek as well as Latin. Rosters of soldiers appeared in Greek as well as Latin. Adams concluded that Greek could be used in the army in Egypt, but that Latin was the "super-high" language in the army. Even if Greek was the language of most soldiers present, stereotyped orders were given in Latin. Inscriptions and dedication to the emperor were written in Latin, symbolizing "the Romanness of the institution."

There were units that functioned entirely in Greek, and Latin was rarely obligatory. There is evidence of Germans, Palmyrenes, Thracians, Africans, and Celts learning Latin. In Egypt, this evidence is provided by Greek speakers whose literacy in Greek was not matched by the writing in Latin they were required to do as clerks. Similar evidence is provided in the errors in Latin made by Greek-literate civilians. In spite of the absence of any "explicit official policy" it was expected that Roman citizens, even if they were Greek speakers, should learn Latin. As a result, "the army was undoubtedly the most potent force during the Roman Empire behind the learning of Latin by speakers of Greek and vernacular languages, and behind the consequent spread of bilingualism" (Adams 2003: 761).

The sergeant's problem in other armies

One approach to the sergeant's problem is to put the onus on each individual soldier. This is the policy of the French Foreign Legion. French is the language of the Foreign Legion – all orders are given in French. Some language lessons are offered during basic training, but legionnaires are expected to learn the language, something that usually takes a year. The French Embassy advises prospective volunteers that knowledge of French is not necessary for enlistment as it will be acquired during the contract. The book of advice for recruits does, however, say that it is useful to arrive with some knowledge of French, and notes that those who come from Japan or China have the greatest difficulty. Until fluency is developed, it is necessary for soldiers and commanders to rely on informal interpreters.

The Israeli Defense Forces (IDF), on the other hand, took language teaching much more seriously, for both immediately after independence in 1948 and at various times since then, such as after the immigration of a million Russian speakers and 75,000 Jews from Ethiopia starting in the 1990s, a high proportion of its recruits have been new immigrants with little or no proficiency in Hebrew, the language in which all commands are given. Stories from the early days tell of the sergeant having to wait until his orders were translated into ten different languages! As a result, the IDF was quickly persuaded of the need for an Education Corps responsible among other things for basic Hebrew teaching. When I did my compulsory national service in the IDF in 1960, this program had been combined with a basic education program, the goal of which was for every soldier to complete the equivalent of elementary education in Hebrew by the end of his or her service. For some, this training was provided in intensive courses, and for others it was fitted in between regular recruit training and compulsory service. On entry, all the recruits were tested for Hebrew literacy, and passing the test was a requirement for advanced courses and promotion. The teachers were young women soldiers, high school graduates choosing to spend their two-year stint of compulsory service as teachers, and given fairly rudimentary training by training college lecturers doing reserve army duty. By 1960, there were also courses offered in the army at the secondary school level. In the Israeli case, the army solution to the sergeant's problem harmonized with the government policy of integration of immigrants.

A different kind of policy is possible when most soldiers in the unit speak the same language, as in the Roman army. In the Indian Army during British rule, British officers were expected to learn the language of their men, but the main burden of communication was borne by an intermediate group of Indian commissioned or non-commissioned officers, their ranks being given Indian names, such as *subedar* (captain), *jemadar* (lieutenant), *havildar* (sergeant), *naik* (corporal), or *sepoy* (private). They were expected to pass orders from the British officer to the Indian sepoys. By 1864, it was generally accepted that Hindustani (also known as Urdu, "camp" language) was the medium for the British Indian Army. There was some dispute as to whether to recognize the distinction between Hindi and Urdu: one senior official argued for using what he called the "common" language as a basis for all examinations of British officers, and saw no point in the effort that would be involved in having them learn two varieties as well as all the languages of the south (Ragila *et al.* 2001). There was in fact considerable debate in the British government over the specification of the language to be learnt and over the possibilities of standardization.

After independence, the British Indian Army was divided into three: one part became the Indian Army, a second part the army of Pakistan, and the third remained as the Brigade of Gurkhas in the British Army. Under recent policy, soldiers in the Brigade are offered English courses that "provide a strong foundation of professional and military-related vocabulary, which will be of direct relevance to the Gurkha soldier." The Gurkha Language Wing now offers English courses for Gurkha recruits and trained soldiers, and Nepali courses for British officers.

At this level, then, military language management is pragmatic and derived from domain-internal pressures for efficient communication.

Canada: making an army bilingual

Canadian military language policy is exceptional as the initiative came from outside the army. Language management in the last forty years in the Canadian armed forces has essentially been dominated by efforts to deal with the national English–French conflict by establishing workable and accepted bilingualism. In April 1966, the Canadian Prime Minister, Lester Pearson, made his historic statement of principle on bilingualism. Shortly after that, the chief of the Canadian Defense Staff set up a task force, the goal of which was to stem the loss of francophone military personnel by making sure they had the same career opportunities as anglophones (Letelier 1987).

In the fall of 1967, a Bilingual Secretariat was established in Canadian Army headquarters to put forward what should be done to implement a bilingual policy. The Secretariat prepared a number of recommendations. The first was to provide francophone schools for the children of military personnel, wherever they were serving. The second was to establish a French-language military trade training center in Québec. The third was to establish French-language units in the army, navy, and air force. These proposals were sent to the Defense Council at the end of 1967, but they were not unanimously accepted. They were subsequently sent to Cabinet, and while waiting for a decision, official French titles for various military units were chosen. In the meantime, opposition to many of the details in the proposal started to appear at various levels of command. In April, following a letter from the Prime Minister approving the general principles of the policy, the army issued its orders. It was made clear that for the "efficiency of operational communication" English would be used above the level of the unit and in all air force units even when the predominant language was French. In April 1968, a detailed program was approved. The armed forces were to be 28 percent bilingual (in Canada, a bilingual was a Canadian whose native language was French and had some mastery of English; in fact, the native English speaker who knew French was and remains an exception). Bilingual positions were to be designated, and language resources to be assessed. There were plans to provide French courses for francophones whose French-language skills needed honing. Courses for anglophones to learn French were to be offered as soon as possible. French would become the working language of some bases and units.

Letelier (1987), who led the bilingual unit, described the difficulty of implementing these programs. In the middle of 1968, he retired from the Canadian armed forces but, a year later (after some time in France improving his own language skills), he rejoined the army and in 1971 became Director General of Bilingualism and Biculturalism. The new directorate was responsible for terminology and translation services, planning research, and language training. In his new position, Letelier found serious problems with implementation, the key issue being the balance between francophones and anglophones in various branches and in various ranks. Another problem was how to make the officer training colleges bilingual. These problems were far from solved when Letelier retired; in fact, in 1977 the Commission on Bilingualism issued a highly critical report.

Bernier and Pariseau (1994) subtitle their account of language policy in the Canadian Armed Forces from 1969 to 1987 "Official Languages: National Defense's Response to the Federal Policy." They describe the difficulty of implementing a central management policy over a complex command structure with units scattered throughout Canada and overseas. In 1971, each command was required to appoint a coordinator for bilingualism and biculturalism with the rank of lieutenant-colonel. A study by the Commissioner of Official Languages in 1977 found that the duties of these coordinators were poorly defined, and a number of recommendations for improvement had not been fully implemented several years later: the situation was still problematic in 1987.

One of the main goals of the 1972 plan was to achieve proportional representation of francophones in the Canadian armed forces. This involved developing a complex policy for promotions, giving special consideration to language representation. In actual fact, there were only a small number of "deviations" based on language, but many officers felt they had been wrongly passed over for promotion. In 1987, the issue remained sensitive. The original plan proposed the creation of additional French-language units. There was dispute about which units to include. The 1972 plan had assumed that 50 percent of the francophones in the armed forces would serve in French-language units by 1990; by 1987, only 30 percent were in such units.

Starting in 1967, basic training was offered separately for anglophones and francophones. The next major problem was to establish technical and officer training in both languages. In the first phase, a course was to be offered for radio technicians with other trades to be added over the next ten years. A major difficulty was finding bilingual instructors. Gradually, and with constant problems, an increasing number of courses were made available in French, but by 1980, the program was in disarray, and francophones in training courses were at the mercy of their proficiency in English (Bernier and Pariseau 1994).

At the time of the Royal Commission on Bilingualism, bilingualism at the military colleges had been one-way, with francophones learning English. It was proposed to make the colleges bilingual. In 1969 it was requested that new staff be bilingual and efforts were made to increase bilingualism at the anglophone colleges. In the 1970s, there were increases in the proportion of francophone officer cadets, but mainly at the Collège militaire royal de Saint-Jean (CMR). Efforts began to recruit francophones into the Royal Military College Kingston (RMC) in 1976 and to offer as many courses as possible in French, with the hope of being bilingual in six years. By 1979, francophones made up a quarter of the student body, and a policy was instituted of using French and English alternatively each week for all meetings and parades. At the same time many courses continued to be offered only in English. Nonetheless, the 1980 *Official Languages Plan (Military)* optimistically assumed that the goal of making all three colleges effectively bilingual could be achieved, and while CMR achieved a 2:1 French–English ratio, the percentage of francophones at RMC remained lower than hoped, and the offerings in French remained limited.

Bernier and Pariseau (1994) describe the provision of translation services in the Canadian armed forces to meet the demand of the policy. The work was to be done by civilians, who would have to develop the military knowledge to be able to translate technical materials. Names of units and abbreviations needed translation too. A centralized translation unit was proposed, and the possibility of machine translation considered in the early 1970s. As time went on, a great deal of material was translated, but not enough to meet the needs of the French-language units. Efforts were made in the 1980s to catch up with the backlog and guarantee biliteracy; however, the diffusion of management led to inadequate supervision of the program. By 1987, orders and directives were being issued in both languages, but technical translation remained a serious problem.

These early difficulties were a sign that the policy was unlikely to work. It was not developed to meet the needs of the defense forces, but was imposed by the Prime Minister as part of government activities to deal with political pressure from the French-speaking minority and the threat of secession from Québec. It was resisted at various levels in the command structure and by units that saw bilingualism as unnecessary for their military mission, or indeed as impeding it. Two decades later, the failure of the policy appears to have been recognized, although official announcements still stress the importance of bilingualism. Only senior officers, from the rank of colonel and naval captain up, and senior non-commissioned officers need to be bilingual. These people are given priority in training. The general situation is that three quarters of the military are anglophones with a low level of bilingualism and the other quarter are francophones generally fluently bilingual and filling positions requiring knowledge of both languages.

The Canadian case provides support for the analysis that we are following, in that it reveals the great difficulty of managing language for reasons unconnected with the communication needs of the domain. True, the military is a hierarchical system and its commanders can be expected to pass on orders from the government, but when they do not see the relevance of these orders to their assigned tasks, it is not surprising to find them resisting. Why, one might ask, were the Israeli Defense Forces prepared to accept the immigrant absorption goals of the Israeli government and devote resources to teaching Hebrew? Surely it was because a monolingual army was seen as functionally valuable. In the same way, the Canadian defense forces were willing for francophones to become bilingual by learning English, but reluctant to work against the general ideological acceptance of English dominance in Canada.

US military language management in two world wars

In January 2005, the US Deputy Secretary of Defense signed a language management plan for the Department (US Department of Defense 2005). The preparation of the plan followed a decision to develop language capabilities in support of the 2004 Defense Strategy, with four overall goals: to create "foundational language and cultural expertise" in the military, to create "capacity surge of language and cultural resources" beyond these foundation capabilities, to establish a cadre of language specialists with professional reading, writing, listening, and speaking ability, and to establish a process to monitor the hiring and promotion of language professionals.

There had of course been earlier attempts to manage language policy in the US armed forces. During World War One, and even more during World War Two, front-line units made some use of Native American soldiers as code talkers. In World War Two, the armed forces also made use of recruits who spoke enemy languages natively. One such group consisted of German refugees sent to the Military Intelligence Training Camp at Camp Ritchie in Maryland, used after the invasion of Europe to interrogate prisoners of war. Second-generation Japanese-Americans (Nisei) mainly from Hawaii were also recruited into the US military, often from the internment camps to which they had been herded after the outbreak of war. They formed the 100th Battalion which served with distinction in the European zone. A significant number was also recruited by the War Office military intelligence division to be Japanese-language interpreters and translators. The first thirty-five were trained at the Presidio of San Francisco in time for the Guadalcanal campaign. The school was later moved to Minnesota and by the end of the war had trained 2,000 linguists. The Nisei linguists, MacNaughton (1994) reports, played a significant role in the Pacific campaign, serving both at the headquarters level and in tactical units.

During World War Two, the US Army was persuaded by Congressmen and senators to conduct a program to make use of college campuses for part of the training of soldiers: the Army Specialized Training Program (ASTP) included a well-publicized but ultimately ineffective project for giving language and area proficiency to recruits. The language and area studies section of the ASTP might well be considered another example, like the Canadian defense forces campaign for bilingualism, of the effect of attempts to drive the policy of a domain from outside. Recent re-evaluations of the ASTP Foreign Language and Area Studies program by Keefers (1988) and Cardozier (1993) suggest that the army believed the program was of little value, and felt it may have actually hurt the war effort by skimming off 150,000 highly qualified recruits from more useful employment. It did serve a useful function for the universities in making up for the wartime loss of students, and it did give the trainees a respite before they were sent, as most were, to regular infantry units where their language and other specially taught skills were not needed. But while many of the recruits benefited later from their language learning experience, the need for reinforcements in the final days of the European campaign meant that few or none were used by the army as linguists.

The exigencies of World War Two had exposed the major gap that had been left in American language teaching by the realistic if regrettable recommendation of the Modern Language Study a decade earlier in 1924–1928. Noting that most American university students studied a foreign language for only two years in classes that met only three hours a week, the authors of the study thought it wisest to reduce the goal of American foreign language teaching from the four skills that had been the aim of the earlier Direct method to the reading ability that could be achieved in this limited allocation of time (Coleman 1929). The result was that most universities dropped their earlier interest in teaching the spoken language. This pragmatic decision fitted in well with the melting pot philosophy that in the ethnocentrist and isolationist atmosphere of the United States after World War One had led to the closing of bilingual education programs that would have encouraged the maintenance of national linguistic resources. Thus, when in the early 1940s, the US armed forces started to gear up for a global war, their commanders quickly became aware of a shortage of recruits who could speak, understand, and read the large number of languages required for military purposes. Moreover, they found how inadequate was the ability of the current language teaching establishment to meet this demand and were challenged to develop a completely new approach.

The most effective answer was to make use of native speakers of the languages, including the German and Japanese recruits who were still considered enemy aliens. There were problems, in that there were questions about their loyalty on the one hand (what we call *the spy's dilemma* – if he knows the language so well, how can we trust him?), and on the other hand there were the prejudices faced by the Asian soldiers, especially in an army that was still segregated (MacNaughton 1994). In these circumstances, the Department of Defense was open to arguments presented in the main by Congressmen about the need to involve university and college campuses, emptied by the draft of their normal male students, in some aspect of the training of soldiers.

The effect of this domain-external pressure was the establishment of the Army Specialized Training Division, created on December 18, 1942. The program had three distinct parts. One was the training of engineers and the second was the training of medical personnel. The third entered the area of language management. This mission of the Division, under the direct command of Colonel Herman Beukema, was to produce soldiers with needed competence in all the languages and areas where the US armed forces could be reasonably expected to operate. By August 30, 1943, some nineteen different curricula had been established for language and area schools (Lind 1948).

The first Army Specialized Training Program language courses opened in April 1943, with 15,000 non-commissioned trainees in courses offered at fifty-five different colleges and universities. In the absence of language aptitude tests of the kind that were to be developed a decade later, the trainees had been selected on the basis of their performance on the Army General Classification test, their proficiency in foreign languages, and their having completed one year of college (Agard *et al.* 1944). The language teaching curriculum was based on that developed for the Intensive Language Program of the American Council of Learned Societies (ACLS). The ACLS program had started some two years before, with two grants from the Rockefeller Foundation of $50,000 each, and the goal of teaching "unusual" languages. It was directed by J Milton Cowan, secretary of the Linguistic Society of America. Reflecting not just practical needs but also the ideological revolt of American structural linguists against the overriding concern of their philological predecessors and rivals with the written text and the literary language, the objective of the ACLS curriculum was to develop control of the spoken and vernacular variety of the target language (Cowan and Graves 1944).

The army program endorsed the linguists' commitment to the specific goal of speaking the vernacular. In principle, any methodology was acceptable, provided that the teaching was "intensive," which meant providing the recruit students with about fifteen hours a week of direct classroom instruction. Myron (1944), a teacher in the program, in a talk he gave while the program was in full operation, was clear that "there is no such thing as the army method" but simply a directive insisting on emphasis on spoken fluency. Coming to the ASTP from more sheltered college teaching, Myron found his students to have generally poor attitudes to language learning (the high motivation ascribed by some to military discipline may also have been mythical), and described in some detail the modifications which he, as a traditional French teacher, had to make to fit the changed situation.

One immediate result of the wide publicity surrounding the program (Angiolillo 1947) was a controversy between the language teaching establishment and the linguists experienced in the army program. The immodest and modest reports of the success of the new approach led to a call for more careful evaluation. At a meeting of the Commission on Trends in Education of the Modern Language Association of America in November 1943, William Berrien (assistant director for humanities of the Rockefeller Foundation) passed on the suggestion of Elton Hocking of Northwestern University that a group of specialists should evaluate this new approach. With funds provided by the Rockefeller Foundation, an evaluation team began its work on February 16, 1944 but only just in time, for two days later, the War Department announced that by April 1, 1944, the Army Specialized Training Program would be suspended. Reinforcements for troops in Europe in preparation for the Normandy invasion had a higher priority than language specialists. Three of the field workers on the evaluation team had had some experience in ASTP programs; they spent two days preparing an outline of what they would look for. In the next six weeks, the six members of the project staff visited forty representative institutions across the country, saw 427 classes teaching sixteen different languages, met with program directors, teachers, and trainees, and talked to college and university administrators and faculty. Their report (Agard *et al.* 1944: 25) concluded modestly that for trainees for whom this was the first exposure to the target language, the results "while by no means miraculous, were definitely good, very satisfactory to the men in charge of the program, and very generally gratifying to the trainees themselves." Wherever the program was well conducted (and they made no attempt to specify how many of the institutions met this criterion), a "considerable percent" of the trainees developed ability to express themselves with fluency and a high level of ability to understand native speakers in normal conditions.

Apart from this belated interest in evaluation, there is little evidence of any attempt at a more general assessment of the results of the program. Agard and his colleagues (1944: 17) remarked on the absence of suitable tests of the spoken language. Most of the extensive debate, on one side or the other, depends on impressions and anecdotal evidence such as that recorded in Angiolillo (1947). The army experience also raised for the first time the challenge to educational administrators of showing that there was real value in clustering language teaching into intensive programs. It took years to move this idea into regular educational settings, such as in the immersion language programs that spread out from Montreal, although it became the model for military and government instruction.

One program was more successful: the program for teaching Japanese to navy personnel after the war slowly evolved into the Defense Language Institute which grew in time to be the major institution teaching foreign languages in the United States. Under effective military control (rather than the result of domain-external initiative) this was able to meet goals set by the Department of Defense, but it was weakened by the lack of a firm infrastructure for teaching languages in schools and the consequent need to spend time and effort and money on starting late.

US defense language policy in an age of global war

The shock of Sputnik drew US attention to the continuing weakness of the foreign language education system, and a group of Congressmen worked in 1958 to develop the National Defense Education Act (NDEA). After consultation with groups concerned with science and foreign languages, a program was developed to improve education in these areas (Clowse 1981). Language teaching was one emphasis in the National Defense Education Act, and an attempt was made to improve and increase foreign language teaching in the schools. Under the NDEA, a major effort began to introduce foreign language teachers to the new panacea, the Audio-Lingual Method, intensive programs for teaching Russian and other languages were supported at a number of universities, and fellowship support was provided for graduate study of languages and linguistics. By the end of the Cold War, the effect of the program was slight. Nonetheless, a few Congressmen and senators and the intelligence community in particular continued to call for a major effort to deal with the failures of state-administered education departments to meet a national need for foreign language proficiency.

One result of this initiative was the National Defense Education Program which funded the establishment of advanced level language programs at a number of American universities. Senator McClure (1983: 118) later confessed: "I invented that God-awful title: National Defense Education Act. If there are any words less compatible, really, intellectually, in terms of what is the purpose of education – it's not to defend the country, it is to defend the mind and develop the human spirit, not to build cannons and battleships. It was a horrible title, but it worked. It worked. How could you attack it?"

A second initiative followed:

The National Security Education Program (NSEP) was established by the David L. Boren National Security Education Act (NSEA), as amended, P.L. 102–183, codified at 50 U.S.C. 1901 *et seq*. It was signed into law by President George H. W. Bush on December 4, 1991. The NSEA mandated the Secretary of Defense to create the National Security Education Program (NSEP) to award: (1) scholarships to U.S. undergraduate students to study abroad in areas critical to U.S. national security; (2)

fellowships to U.S. graduate students to study languages and world regions critical to U.S. national security; and (3) grants to U.S. institutions of higher education to develop programs of study in and about countries, languages and international fields critical to national security and under-represented in U.S. study. Also mandated in the NSEA was the creation of the National Security Education Board (NSEB) to provide overall guidance for NSEP. (National Security Education Program, http://www.ndu. edu/nsep/index.cfm?pageID=168&type=page)

Of particular importance have been the flagship programs, whose goal is to produce graduate students with a professional level of proficiency in languages that are considered important by the defense establishment. A second initiative has been the establishment of the first university-associated research center in the humanities. The Center for Advanced Study of Language at the University of Maryland follows a model established in sciences and engineering to provide for advanced research in areas of interest to various branches of defense, but is severely handicapped in its efforts by the need to maintain secrecy and the difficulty of finding qualified researchers not contaminated by their foreign language knowledge and experience.

The next major step was the development of the Department of Defense language transformation roadmap (US Department of Defense 2005: 21). The roadmap established a plan for significant changes in military language policy. The underlying rationale was set out in the first paragraph: "Post 9/11 military operations reinforce the reality that the Department of Defense needs a significantly improved organic capability in emerging languages and dialects, a greater competence and regional areas skills in those languages and dialects, and the search capability to rapidly expand its language capabilities on short notice." Serious language-related intelligence failures in Afghanistan and Iraq called for rapid attention and remedy.

According to the plan, by the end of 2002, each military department, command, and defense agency was required to review its requirements for language professionals – interpreters, translators, crypto-linguists, interrogators, and area specialists. A year later, a review was conducted of the Foreign Language Center of the Defense Language Institute which revealed the need for raising the proficiency level of graduates. In May 2004, Senior Language Authorities were appointed in each of the major agencies making up the Department of Defense, and these officers formed a senior level steering committee for language.

The roadmap started with the assumption that the US would continue to be involved in conflict against enemies speaking "less-commonly taught" languages and that capability in these languages would be needed to maintain coalitions, establish regional stability, and conduct multinational missions in military and post-conflict operations. It assumed an increase in the range of "potential conflict zones" and of potential coalition partners.

The November 2006 Iraq Study Group Report highlighted the problem requiring resolution:

All of our efforts in Iraq, military and civilian, are handicapped by Americans' lack of language and cultural understanding. Our embassy of 1,000 [in Baghdad] has 33 Arabic speakers, just six of whom are at the level of fluency. (Iraq Study Group Report: http://8.7.97.203/isg.pdf)

It is important to clarify the distinction between institutional and national language policy. From the roadmap, it is clear that the underlying initiative for changes in military language management is ultimately the result of governmental *defense* policy. It is not, however, the result of US government *language* policy, but an interpretation, made within the Department of Defense, of the language implications of the non-language policy. The President and his supporters have initiated a policy that seems to guarantee military responses to the threats of international terrorism, but they have not established a national language policy.

Efforts by sections of government and a handful of Congressmen to do this have continued. In January 2006, the President launched the "National Security Language Initiative (NSLI), a plan to further strengthen national security and prosperity in the 21st century through education, especially in developing foreign language skills" (Press briefing). Like the NDEA, it proclaimed language as a defense (or in more up-to-date terminology, a security) issue, a result not just of governmental priorities but also a recognition of the constitutional responsibility of the Federal government for defense and inter-state commerce but not for education. A year later, with the change in political control of Congress, Senator Daniel Akaka held a hearing of his sub-committee on Government Operations to deal with the language question: the representative of the Department of Defense submitted a twenty-two page report of progress, including the K-16 model pipeline programs which start language teaching in kindergarten and lead ultimately to the university-level foreign language flagship programs. The representative of the Department of Education presented an eight-page report, dealing mainly with the NSLI programs. Senator Akaka is one of the sponsors of the National Foreign Languages Coordination bill, intended to provide Federal leadership and coordination in a field where policy has so far failed regularly. In May 2007, the Department of Defense announced the pilot implementation of the National Language Service Corps, a 1,000-member civilian organization managed by the Department of Defense consisting of volunteers to "provide diverse language services across a broad range of local, state and federal government departments and agencies." Initial recruiting was for "ten languages important to national security and welfare of the nation . . .: Hausa, Hindi, Indonesian, Mandarin Chinese, Russian, Somali, Swahili and Vietnamese."

At the same time, it must be noted that the funding of NSLI ($114 million, little of which is new money) is quite small, if one compares the cost of outsourced translation for Iraq and Afghanistan, for which one five-year contract was for $4.65 billion (*Associated Press*, April 12, 2007). In addition, the Defense Advanced Research Projects Agency (DARPA) is spending at least $22 million on research for handheld translation devices.

The military domain in a theory of language management

Analyzing these cases as domain-related management, one finds that the military domain has an advantage over others in its hierarchical structure. Once convinced of the need for language management, a military establishment can pass on orders to its lower echelons and start to achieve results. Resistance is much more difficult and unlikely than in less regulated domains, provided only that the motivation for the policy is seen as relevant to the military needs. In fact, there are examples where the military domain attempts to influence other spheres, such as the effort of the US Department of Defense to control foreign language education, or the call of the Taiwanese Army Commanding General Hu Chen-pu for improved English proficiency (*The China Post*, January 15, 2007), or the strong influence exerted by the Israel Defense Forces on the teaching of Arabic. But there are limitations, as in the constitutional difficulty that the US Federal government has in controlling education: the defense-related projects can add to but not modify the school curriculum. And when the initiative is not military but rather socio-political, as in the attempt of the Canadian government to persuade its defense forces to play a leading role in implementing a bilingual policy, and come from outside the military domain, the efforts are much less likely to succeed.

The military domain confirms the usefulness of the domain approach, and helps clarify the complications introduced when external forces attempt to influence a domain or a domain attempts to affect others. Because of its normal commitment to achieving results, an army is able to focus its resources and apply its in-built authority to language as well as its other goals. Of course, there is the normal inertia of large institutions, but management is potentially easier.

In the next chapter, we move to the domain of government, with its clearly defined authority, and finally look at the language management of the nation-state, once the only focus of language policy studies.

9 Local, regional, and national governments managing languages

Introduction

Studies of language policy, language planning, or language management have generally dealt with the activities of the nation-state. More recent books such as Kaplan and Baldauf (1997: 6) have drawn attention to the existence of a multitude of government and education agencies, quasi-government and non-governmental organizations, even if their emphasis is naturally and quite reasonably on the centralized political agency. Schiffman (1996: 2) too pointed out that a language policy can operate not only at the level of nation-state, but also at that of territorial divisions, and may differ at the municipal level, in educational institutions, at different levels of bureaucracy, and in non-governmental bodies. In his detailed studies, he included three nation-states (France, India, and the United States) and two territorial units (Tamilnadu and California). While Shohamy (2006) sees language policy as essentially the manifestation of hidden ideological agendas, her policy agents are identified as governments, educational bodies, the media, and other guardians of official language hegemony. In this chapter, we move inevitably to the level of government, a domain in which there is an obvious definition of authority, by which we mean rightfully exercised power. It is true that much of language management consists of attempts to persuade, but, as we saw with the military, the simplest situation is when the putative manager can reasonably expect that instructions will be followed; governments like commanders are assumed to have the power to enforce their decisions.

Authority was also found at the levels and in the domains that we have already considered. In traditional families, the authority of parents is taken for granted, although there are some exceptions to this rule, such as the Navajo belief that position does not grant authority (Young 1978), the common western middle-class liberal assumption that parents should persuade rather than command (Bernstein 1971), or the regular situation in immigrant families where rapidly assimilating children ignore or try to influence their parents. In religious institutions, the authority of religious leaders to determine language policy is also assumed, but while they might be able to control the language of prayer and of the sermon, they cannot guarantee that their congregants will understand that language, and so must either provide translations or develop an educational program to teach the sacred language. In business situations, it is the seller who is most constrained to adapt (Cooper and Carpenter 1976). In the workplace, unless the courts intervene, employers often attempt to require specific language use by their employees, most easily by hiring according to language skills or by setting up training programs. In the courts, judges for a long time had (and in many countries still have) unchallenged authority over language choice (and interpretation), but claims of human or civil rights now influence them or higher appeals courts demand the provision of qualified interpreters. Similarly, the once-absolute power of police to ignore the rights of speakers of other languages is now being challenged in democratic societies. School too tends to be a domain where pupils have little choice but to bow to the authority of their teachers. Of course, there are situations where students resist, and wise teachers are regularly prepared to use the students' language to explain what has not been understood in the official language. In other words, the need to maintain communication constrains the authority of teachers, as it does of businesses, media, police, courts, and doctors and medical staff. The domain approach enables us to distinguish cases of internal pressure from attempts of a higher level domain to modify language policy.

The level of government is the one at which authority is implicit but fundamental – the major participants in this domain are defined by authority as the rulers and the governed. Of course, as we shall see, there is a wide range in the absoluteness of this authority. In many political institutions, there is a hierarchy, ranging in theory from a constitution (with a court authorized to interpret it) through a central government (with different levels of authority assigned to or exercised by the executive power, the legislative, and the judicial) and delegated by constitution or law to regional or territorial governments and then to various forms of local government.

Government at its various levels has authority over its citizens, defined by territory or by sphere. For example, the United States constitution grants the Federal government responsibility for and authority over the spheres of defense and inter-state commerce, but maintains the authority of state governments over education and commerce within the state's territorial limit. Kidnapping becomes a Federal offense when the victim is transferred from the territory of one state to another; inter-state trade also gives the Federal government authority to interfere. The process of devolution in the United Kingdom is granting increasing authority to regional legislatures in Wales, Scotland, and Ireland, just as Spain granted a degree of autonomy to its regions. This ability to delegate authority often provides an attractive solution to problems of language status in a multilingual nation-state.

The organization of this chapter

This chapter will look at all levels of government, ranging from a nation-state to a local body, and ask about the particular kind of management decision or activity that occurs at this level. These activities are divided into a number of categories. The first is for the level concerned to pass on its authority for language management to a lower level of government: I will refer to this as *devolution*, and argue that *territoriality* is an approach commonly adopted by governments to respond to minority pressures for autonomy in certain spheres including language management, by passing authority for a defined territory to a regional government for that territory. Another kind of devolution is granting limited authority to a specific religious or ethnic community. The Ottoman millet system did this, recognizing the authority of Greek Orthodox, Armenian, Jewish, and Syrian Orthodox courts to judge their own members. Similarly, during the British Mandate of Palestine, the Jewish and Arab communities were required and authorized to conduct their own educational systems. The Archbishop of Canterbury roused a public outcry over his proposal that Britain offer a degree of autonomy to Muslim *Sharia* courts (*The Times*, February 11, 2008).

The second category consists of language management decisions concerning language status, that is to say decisions concerning the function or functions for which a language may (or should) be used. Functional allocation is often designated by a cover term such as *national* or *official*. Commonly, these terms are undefined, so that policy remains unclear. A regular topic for heated debate on language policy lists and elsewhere is whether England has an official language, or whether New Zealand has one other than the two defined by law (Māori and Sign). Sometimes the meaning of "official language" is specified precisely; for instance, the Māori Language Act 1987 gave the right to speak but not to be addressed in Māori in legal proceedings; it also established the Māori Language Commission. Four relevant functions commonly assumed to be included in the term are internal use by the government for meetings of elected bodies and for civil servants in their bureaucratic activities, use by civil servants in their relations with citizens and others (including prescriptions for civil servant language use in international relations), prescribed use by government and non-government agencies and institutions, such as schools, news and entertainment media, businesses, and prescribed use by citizens in other cases (including for example the long-time Turkish ban on the use of Kurdish, or Franco's efforts to suppress Basque and Catalan).

The third category of government language management involves cultivation of the language, which includes decisions such as spelling reform, or the establishment of agencies and institutions responsible for language modernization and standardization, such as language academies and terminology committees.

The full picture is obviously complex, but is simplified by the number of gaps in it. For example, about sixty nations do not have a constitution (the number of nation-states keeps changing, and constitutions keep on being adopted and amended), and many national constitutions do not have any reference to language in them. Similarly, a good number of governments (especially at lower levels) are singularly uninterested in language policy and management. Others, of course, take it very seriously, but the result is to bias the picture that we paint of government language activity. Essentially, we tend to notice and study the marked cases, losing sight perhaps of the general low level of concern for language issues among governments and citizens alike. Perhaps this lack of interest helps explain the ease with which a small group like the proponents of English Only in the United States has managed to impose its will on some local governments and on many states.

The pressure of a multilingual nation

If we start with the structural linguists' assumption that the unmarked case for governments at all levels is to leave language alone, the marked cases of government intervention are commonly produced by non-language-related pressures. One such pressure is produced by a multilingual sociolinguistic ecology (Calvet 1987), itself the result either of applying territorial authority to linguistically disparate regions, such as forming a single nation-state out of the linguistic complexity of Belgium, Switzerland, or India, or the movement of other-language speaking populations into the territory, as in the multilingual nations produced by immigration like the USA or Israel or more and more European countries. Conquest and colonization on the one hand and large-scale immigration on the other produce communication problems for a government, the solution of which calls for language management. Whether and how this pressure is responded to depends in part on internal activities of linguistic minorities (Williams 2008), or on an external encouragement of the recognition of the needs of these minorities. But language management, it seems, is more likely to be the result of widespread bilingualism or multilingualism, rather than an independent cause of these phenomena. Ironically, it is language revival movements like in New Zealand and Ireland that if successful would produce bilingual speech communities. And it appears to be in democracies that pressures for autonomy or even independence for minority groups are more likely to be felt. Non-democratic states are most able to resist minority demands.

The normal or unmarked pressure in the governmental domain is for monolingualism, providing for the most efficient communication, avoiding most communication problems, and asserting central power and unified identity. The communication goal fits the Jernudd and Neustupný (1987; Neustupný 1970) model most closely – language management as the solution of communication problems. The central power assertion underlies the interpretation by many scholars of language management such as Phillipson (1992) and Shohamy (2006). We have already noted three other independent pressures encouraging bilingualism or multilingualism. One is the pressure of religious institutions and ethnic groups to find a place for their sacred language in society. The second is the growing pressure of the globalized economy for the language proficiency needed to have access to international business. The third is the need for language proficiencies resulting from military activities and conquests.

In this chapter, we will trace the various activities of each of the levels of government, starting at the theoretically highest level, namely the constitutional, and working down to local governments.

Language management at the constitutional level

There are still nations without a constitution – England, New Zealand, Israel, for example – but most do have a constitutional document establishing the basic laws of the nation (Jones 2001). Among these, a significant group (some fifty-seven) does not mention a national or official language, but in eleven of these fifty-seven, there is a specific requirement that members of the legislature must know one or more specific languages (some of these are former British colonies). Because constitutions and nations are constantly being modified, the numbers in this section should be considered approximate.

Some of the nations without a constitutional clause do have a language law that defines their language policy or part of it (Leclerc 1994,1994–2007). Denmark and Iceland require foreign residents to learn Danish and Icelandic respectively. Luxembourg has a law naming Luxemburgish as the national language, but adds French and German as official languages. Mexico has a law requiring public announcements to be in correct Spanish. The Netherlands requires Dutch for administration, but grants some limited functions to Frisian. Norway requires documents to be in both Bokmäl and Nynorsk. Puerto Rico has a law making English and Spanish official. Sweden and New Zealand have laws giving status to minority languages – Sámi, Finnish, and Meänkieli in the former, and Māori and Sign Language in the latter. Attempts in the United States to establish English as an official language failed in 1991 and 1994, and similar attempts to drop Arabic as an official language have failed in Israel.

Of the 6,000 or so languages assumed in most counts (Grimes 2000), around 100 are recognized as official by national governments, either by constitution or basic law, or by some other government action. Where there is no constitutional language provision and no listed language law, I have used the listing of official languages in *Wikipedia* (Wikipedia Foundation), *The World Factbook* (Central Intelligence Agency 2007), or from various national government web-pages. Most nations (about ninety) are officially monolingual; about thirty are officially bilingual; and about ten are officially trilingual or multilingual. English is the most common official language (fifty-one nations include it in their list), but it occurs in constitutions as the sole official language only four times; in seventeen other nations, it is the only official language without a constitutional statement. This reflects the fact that the United Kingdom had no constitution and did not establish an official language by law; former British colonies typically followed a similar practice after independence. English is the constitutional second official language in twelve nations and second official language in another eleven nations without constitutional support, and a third official language in seven trilingual nations.

By contrast, Arabic is the sole constitutional official language in eighteen Islamic states, the constitutional second official language in two, including Israel which allows education in Arabic in Arabic schools and has recently established an Arabic language academy, and is recognized as an official language in one other state. Islamic states generally have a clause in the constitution stating that Islam is the state religion, Arabic the language, and adding the name of the capital. Their minority languages are never formally recognized.

French too tends to occur in monolingual isolation; former French colonies adopted it as the sole official language, so that eighteen nations list it as their monolingual choice (it also occurs in three bilingual nations formed as a result of the post-independence combination of British and French colonies).

The fourth most common official language is Spanish, adopted as the sole official language in seventeen nations, mainly the former Spanish colonies in Latin America which became independent in the early nineteenth century and showed little or no interest in their indigenous languages until the 1990s. German and Portuguese are official in six nations each. Another thirteen languages occur twice or three times; the rest occur in a single nation.

Just over half of national constitutions include one or more language clauses about national or official languages. Sixty-three countries name one official language; in addition, there are seven former Soviet republics that establish a single state language and another eight states with one official language and one or more national languages. The term *state* (used in former Soviet nations) appears to be equivalent to *official*. When there is a distinction between *official* and *national* languages, the second term seems to refer to indigenous languages of significance that have been granted symbolic recognition alongside the official status granted to former colonial languages.

Seventeen nations recognize two official languages, sometimes adding one or more national languages. There are three nations that recognize three national or official languages. One nation (South Africa) lists eleven official languages in its constitution. Belgium recognizes four languages as official in specific regions. Five nations claim to recognize all local languages as official.

If one assumes (as seems reasonable) that the constitutions without any mention of an official language represent cases like England and the United States where one language is dominant, we may conclude that the majority of nations function with a single official language, and that while changing demography and globalization may be leading to an increase in multilingualism, it has occurred too recently to be incorporated into national written constitutions. Changing a constitution is a major step: for many years, the English Only movement in the United States has been trying without effect to add a language clause to the US constitution, and the French constitution only added its language clause under the threat of the Maastricht agreement and the fear that English might become the official language of the European Community.

To say that a language is official is only a first step. Two questions follow immediately: what does "official" mean? And how (if at all) is the constitutional or legal provision implemented? Generally speaking, it is a safe guess that an official language is used for internal government functions, in legislative and bureaucratic oral and written activities (meetings of the legislature and the cabinet, records of these meetings including laws, oral and written communications among civil servants). Unless otherwise specified in legislation or regulations, it can be assumed that this is the language used by government to communicate with citizens, and that citizens will generally be expected to use it when communicating with government agencies. It is likely also to be the language used or required to be used as language of instruction in government-supported schools, and the language used in government mass media. If two or more languages are named as official, one would expect to find specific rules laying down differences in the use of the two languages, either territorially or by function.

Many constitutions, however, do include a clause or clauses establishing exceptions to the general rule, detailing provisions for communication with members of linguistic minorities in their language. We are moving here into the area of language-related human or civil rights, a topic that we consider in more detail when we look at supragovernmental institutions and international charters (see Chapter 11). At this stage, it might be useful to give some examples. The first is a fairly common constitutional provision requiring that an individual being investigated by the police or being charged in court should be able to understand the nature of the charges against him, as discussed in Chapter 7. Such clauses appear in some forty constitutions. Several of them are former British colonies; the group includes the Bahamas, Barbados, Dominica, Fiji, Kenya, Nigeria, the Seychelles, and Zimbabwe. Others are nations formerly under Soviet domination: Albania, Chechnya, Georgia, Lithuania, Romania, Slovakia, and Turkmenistan. There are similar clauses in the constitutions of China and Mongolia.

A second major area of special treatment consists of clauses detailing the rights of ethnic and linguistic minorities, sometimes open and sometimes specific. Former Soviet bloc countries that have maintained such clauses from the Leninist Soviet constitution are Armenia, Azerbaijan, Belarus, Bulgaria, Croatia, Georgia, Kazakhstan, Kyrgyzstan, Latvia, Macedonia, Poland, Russia, Serbia, Slovakia, Slovenia, the Ukraine, and Uzbekistan. These clauses also exist in the Austrian and Hungarian constitutions, added as part of the treaty provisions after World War One. Recognition of minority languages is starting to appear in more recent Latin American constitutions, such as Brazil, Colombia, Ecuador, El Salvador, and Panama. In Africa, it appears in the constitutions of Cameroon, both Congos, Gabon, Ethiopia, Namibia, South Africa, and Uganda. Norway has a clause recognizing Sámi, and Finland recognizes Sámi and Roma alongside Finnish and Swedish. In Asia, the nations with minority clauses are China, India, Indonesia, Mongolia, Nepal, Pakistan, and the Philippines.

Special treatment for minorities can be provided by other constitutional clauses. The United States does not mention language in its constitution or Bill of Rights, but the Federal government and the federal courts have regularly used civil rights as an argument for permitting private education in a language other than English or for providing access to civic services to people who do not speak English. In Europe, members of the European Union which have signed the European Charter for Regional or Minority Languages have been required to designate indigenous minority languages for a menu of specified treatments, and new candidate members have been required to provide similar support for non-indigenous languages, like Russian in the Baltic States and Roma.

The issue of implementation of these constitutionally or legally established rights is more complex. Within a nation-state, it depends on government funding, acceptance by civil servants, or decisions of courts. In Cameroon, for instance, more than a decade after the 1996 constitution proclaimed that the national indigenous languages should be promoted, Kouega (2007: 88) reports that no action has been taken for implementation. This is equally true of the nations which proclaim bilingualism or multilingualism in their constitutions or in their laws. This gap between law and practice provides full scope for the many detailed studies of language policy in monographs and academic journals.

The explanation of a specific language policy is often historical. Looking at the year when nations became independent, some obvious clusters emerge. The former Spanish and Portuguese colonies in Latin America that achieved independence in the early nineteenth century generally maintained Spanish or Portuguese as their official language, and only in the 1990s have they amended their constitutions to recognize the rights of those indigenous languages that have not yet been wiped out. The countries whose independence from the Ottoman Empire or the Austro-Hungarian Empire came at the conclusion of World War One generally adopted their territorial historical language, but were commonly constrained by treaty policy to recognize national minorities. Most of the British colonies which received independence in the late 1960s have continued without designating an official language, but some in Africa, where there is a strong indigenous language or where a French-speaking and an English-speaking colony have been combined, have chosen to be officially bilingual. In the Middle East, former British colonies or mandates have generally accepted the Islamic pattern of one religion and one language; Israel on independence continued listing Hebrew and Arabic but dropped English. In Asia, newly independent nations commonly chose their historical territorial language. Former French colonies in Africa, which also became independent in the 1960s, have continued with French as the sole official language: Madagascar, which made indigenous Malagasy official alongside French, and which added English in a 2007 referendum, is the exception. French territories in the Middle East and North Africa have switched officially to Arabic, although French continues to be used in North Africa for secondary and higher education and remains important, and those in Asia have reestablished their heritage languages. The breakup of the Soviet Union in 1991 freed the former Soviet republics to try to reestablish their heritage territorial languages alongside or in place of the previously dominant Russian, but those seeking admission to the European Union have been required to recognize minority languages including Russian. The breakup of Czechoslovakia and the former Yugoslavia has been accompanied by the choice or development of national territorial languages.

Center vs. periphery

The disputes and conflicts about language policy that attract most attention in news reports and in academic studies generally take place at the level of the national government. Indeed, serious efforts at language management started to emerge with the growth of the nation-state and with the use of language as a focus for the mobilization of national identity. There was early recognition of language differences – the Persian policy described in the biblical book of Esther of sending messages to the various parts of the empire in the local languages, the multilingual scribes of the Babylonian Empire, the language policy of the Roman army as it integrated multilingual forces, and the special status of sacred languages in the various religions. But the full force of national language identity started to emerge essentially with the Reformation and its acceptance of the vernacular, the printing press and its work to standardize national vernaculars for popular literacy, and the growth of national feelings associated with the territorial struggles of the sixteenth century. Reading Shakespeare, one notes the emergence of English pride and contempt for other nations and languages: witness the jokes at the expense of the Welsh and the French in the history plays. This was the period of the beginning of the anti-Welsh legislation in Britain, and the active encouragement of English over the Gaelic languages that had survived.

France probably provides the best example of organized efforts at centralization. As part of his campaign to ensure the power of the king, Cardinal Richelieu established the French Academy, intending to standardize the language on the model of Parisian French (Cooper 1989). During the early days of the French Revolution, the Jacobins were shocked to discover that only about 20 percent of the population knew and used French; they proclaimed that equality was only possible when everybody spoke French, and immediately started active policies intended to discourage and wipe out the many other varieties still spoken. Essentially, the approach that developed was to assume that French must be the language of any territory under French control: this policy was enforced both in metropolitan France and in the colonies. While the constitutional clause establishing the status of French was only added in 1992, fearing the danger to the language of the Maastricht Treaty and the growth of the European Community, all through the nineteenth and twentieth centuries there were continual efforts to guarantee centralization through monolingualism.

Spain too early on proclaimed the status and purity of Castilian, a continuation of the policies that began at the end of the fifteenth century with the mass expulsions and conversion of Muslims and Jews. In its colonies in the New World, the Spanish began an unmatched program to obliterate indigenous languages and to keep the Spanish language pure from Indian influence. In Spain itself, centralization was weakened under twentieth-century democratic rule but became a central feature of the Franco dictatorship which worked actively to suppress Catalan and Basque.

Germany was another major contributor to the development of the ideology of "one nation, one territory, and one language." Trying in the nineteenth century to unite a number of independent German-speaking states, Bismarck planned to bring German-speaking areas under central political control, a policy finally implemented in the middle of the twentieth century when Hitler took over Sudetenland and Austria. The Austro-Hungarian Empire had been multilingual: Germany was to be united by land, language, and blood. This accorded with and supported the German Romantic notions of nationalism (Fishman 1973).

Attracted by the one-nation, one-language ideology, the new nation-states formed during the nineteenth and twentieth centuries generally took on the task of selecting or inventing one distinguishing standard language. Norway is a good example, as it struggled to create a new national language that would differentiate it from its former subservience to Denmark and Danish. The only problem was how to form such a language out of the multiplicity of Norwegian dialects, and as Haugen (1966) demonstrated in the book that virtually founded the field of language planning study, came up with a strange working compromise: two distinct written varieties that all school children must learn, but continued respect for the local dialects that they brought with them to school.

Essentially, then, the most common tendency in the domain of the nation-state is centralization, monolingual hegemony based on a single national language, and rejection of any serious role for minority languages. This kind of policy goes beyond the simple language problem-solving defined by language planners in the 1960s (Fishman *et al.* 1968; Neustupný 1970); rather we have selection by national governments or some of their members of language as the mobilizing point for a campaign to establish centralized power.

This reflects two of the major functions of language: for communication and as a symbol for assertion of identity. It is of course not easy to separate the two. In the symbolic case, the goal is not to solve communication problems but to assert the power of the national official language as part of the process of centralized control. This becomes clearer if we look at another popular solution in the face of strong pressure from minorities and the periphery: that is territoriality, the effect of which is to split the domain into territorially distinct regions, each left free to develop its own symbolically satisfying monolingualism.

The territorial solution

Territorialism is often an obvious choice when there is multilingualism, for many new nation-states were founded by forming a federation of previously independent areas each with its own language variety. Switzerland, with its large number of semi-independent cantons, was, before the partition of India at independence, the best example of what is called the territorial solution to multilingualism (McRae 1975; Nelde *et al.* 1992). The Swiss Federal constitution recognizes the authority of the citizens of each canton to determine their own local policy in most spheres of government, including education and language. The popular belief that Switzerland is bilingual is simply wrong (Lüdi 2007): individual Swiss speak the language of their canton (German, French, Italian, or Romansch); speakers of the last two named languages generally also attain fluency in German; but for the French and German speakers, knowledge of the other major language is no more common than second language knowledge in European monolingual countries, and is also slowly being watered down by globalization and the growing demand for English (Harlow 2004; Stotz 2006). In the Swiss case, the division into quite small territorial units – the twenty-six cantons range in size from just under 40 to about 7,000 square km; the populations vary from 15,000 to 1,250,000 – and the historical basis – each was a sovereign state until federation in 1848 – made the solution easier to implement.

Belgium is another case of an attempt at a territorial solution to problems created by the existence of more than one Great Tradition (Fishman 1969) each with its own associated language. While in fact Belgium is divided into regions where various dialects of Flemish, French, and German are spoken, official policy ignores the dialects and recognizes three major standard languages – Dutch, French, and German (Covell 1993; Deprez 2000). One of the effects of this is that Belgium is a country where many school children report that they are taught in a language different from the one they speak at home. Historically French dominated, but Dutch, numerically and so under democracy politically stronger, slowly demanded and finally attained equality of treatment. The result is a territorial compromise, with regions designated for French, Dutch, or German to be official, either alone or in some towns with a special status for another language; only Brussels is legally (if not actually) bilingual in Dutch and French. There are indications that the territorial arrangement is not working; in September 2007, three months after a general election, a government had not been set up and there were increasing voices calling for independence for Flanders and full partition (*New York Times*, September 21, 2007).

There are other historical remnants of political unions or compromises. When Finland became independent from Swedish rule, it maintained a special status for both languages. Slowly, Finnish replaced Swedish as the language of education and government in most of the country, except in the southern coastal region where Swedish speakers were in a majority. Finns were expected to learn both languages at school (Lautomaa and Nuolijärvi 2002). The policy of reclassifying communes after each census means that the number of monolingual Swedish communes was reduced from thirty-two in 1922 to three in 2002; the increase in immigrant population also works to weaken the position of Swedish-speaking Finns (McRae 2007).

Still protected by fixed territorial unilingualism (McRae 2007) is Åland (details from http://www.aland.ax/alandinbrief/index.htm, published by the Åland government). This is a region of several thousand small islands, 65 of which are inhabited, currently with a population of 26,000. Originally Swedish, it was ceded to Russia after the 1808–1809 war and became part of the Grand Duchy of Finland. In 1917, with the breakup of the Russian empire, Finland declared independence, but declined to accept a claim from the population of Åland for reunification with Sweden, offering instead a form of limited autonomy. A compromise was worked out through the League of Nations in 1921 under which Finland retained sovereignty, an Act of Autonomy guaranteed the maintenance of Swedish language and culture and the establishment of a system of self-government, and Sweden was assured that the area would remain demilitarized and politically neutral. The Act has been revised. Under the Autonomy Act, Swedish is the only official language in Åland. This means, among other things, that Swedish is the language used by regional, municipal, and state authorities. Publications and documents sent by Finnish government agencies to Åland must be in Swedish. The language of instruction in publicly funded schools is Swedish. English is compulsory in schools, while Finnish, French, and German are optional. The "right of domicile," which means the right to vote and to own real estate, is granted to Finnish citizens with one of whose parents had the right. Immigrants may be granted the right after five years of residence, provided they can demonstrate adequate proficiency in Swedish. Francis Hult (personal communication) reports that this proficiency may be established in a number of different ways: a certificate from an employer, an interview, or a language test.

India is another major example of territorial compromise. The first step was the partition into two states, India and Pakistan, a decision based on the perceived differences of religion, and carried out at the cost of a million people murdered and twelve million "resettled," constituting one of the largest cases of "ethnic cleansing" in the twentieth century. This major demographic and political division was subsequently reflected in a language change, the separation of Hindustani into Hindi and Urdu. The modification of a once-common language into two distinct varieties represents a different kind of language management from the solution of communication problems dealt with in the Nekvapil (2008) model; while it has a partial motivation to produce unified communication in the newly established nation-state, its primary goal is to assert difference from the other territory. It is thus an example of the use of political power to establish symbolically valued hegemony.

India is highly multilingual: surveys in the 1880s listed 179 languages and 544 dialects: the 1961 census included 1,652 language names classified into about 200 languages. The 1948 constitution recognized eleven languages plus English as official, and tried to make the division into federal states correspond approximately with language divisions. Five states and two union territories have Hindi as their official language: the other eleven states each recognize one of the eleven major languages for various official purposes. The constitution stated that English would slowly be phased out, but partly to resist Hindi domination and particularly because of globalization, its status has continued to grow. Under British rule, three distinct educational patterns developed: in the larger urban centers, there were elite English-medium schools. In towns, there was a two-tier approach, with a local vernacular used for primary education and English for secondary and advanced education. In rural areas, where only primary education was offered, it was in a local vernacular. But complicating the Indian situation is the fact that all states have many minority languages, some quite large.

After independence, language management in India was driven by three competing views: recognition of the importance of indigenous languages, acceptance of the value of mother-tongue education, and the desire to establish a national language for political unity. Many educators wanted to restrict mother-tongue education to languages with a written tradition, but the linguistic minorities succeeded in spreading the notion that mother-tongue meant home language. The resulting compromise was the "three language formula." The home language was to be used in primary and lower secondary school, during which time Hindi was to be learnt and become the official medium and language of wider communication and national unity for all of India. English was to be kept for higher education and intellectual and international communication. The policy was interpreted differently in different states, some of which added Sanskrit or a fourth regional language. By the mid-1980s, only 67 of the 200 classified languages were actually being used in education, while English continued to spread, supported both by the resistance of non-Hindi speaking states to accepting Hindi as a national language and by the growing economic value of English as a global language. Perhaps it is the very complexity of the linguistic situation that has allowed multilingualism and democracy to continue together.

Pakistan, formally united by Urdu, later suffered further partition. At independence in 1947, Bengal was divided between India and Pakistan along religious lines. The first signs of friction in East Bengal (East Pakistan) were linguistic, and growing dissatisfaction led to an armed revolt, supported finally by India and leading to the establishment of independent Bangladesh, 100 million of whose 114 million population speak Bengali. Pakistan is left with 72 languages, with English listed on a government site as official and Urdu as national; however, the most widely spoken language is Sindhi.

The new territorialism: regional autonomy and devolution

In a number of nation-states, the growing power of regionally based minority language groups has been reflected in their seizing or being granted autonomy over language choice. Again, as with India, it is important to stress that the linguistic issues follow rather than lead the political, with language as a mobilizing force rather than a cause. Canada is a classic case. A combination historically of British and French colonies, Canada's dyadic nature was established after the defeat of the French. Québec, predominantly French-speaking, became bilingual as a result of English-speaking migration especially to Montreal. By the 1940s, the separate school systems guaranteed by the 1867 constitution helped maintain distinct French- and English-speaking communities. There was a small French Protestant sector and a small English Catholic sector alongside the major French-dominant Catholic sector and the English-dominant Protestant sector. It was the fact that new immigrants (many of them Catholics from Italy) were choosing the English schools that served as a warning to the francophones that their power and their language were threatened. Language and religion were closely intertwined. As the business world was largely controlled by English-speaking Protestants, it was the French Catholics who needed to become bilingual to fit into the wider Canadian and North American society. As we noted in the last chapter, a bilingual in Canada is still assumed to be a French speaker who has learned English.

During the 1960s, a "quiet revolution" took place in Québec marked by efforts to reform the provincial electoral system, to nationalize industry, and to modernize French-language tertiary education. Spared the secularization of the French Revolution, Roman Catholic education in Québec maintained the pre-revolutionary model, with the *Collège classique* preparing its graduates for law and the clergy at its apex, and leaving them unqualified for the North American business world. In the 1970 election, Québec nationalism started to show its strength, and laws were passed subsequently making French the official language of Québec. *Loi 101* made French the sole language of the provincial assembly and of the law courts. In education, only children whose father or mother had received English-medium elementary education in Québec could go to English-speaking schools, effectively blocking new immigrants from English education. Businesses were legally required to use only French for publicity. A government agency was established to enforce these rules (see p. 230). Threats to secede helped guarantee Canadian Federal acceptance of these policies, and although there continue to be efforts to develop national bilingualism, the main effects have been restricted territorially to Québec, where the French Catholics are now reported to be economically and socially as well as politically more successful than they were before 1970 (Ghosh 2004; Larrivée 2002). C. H. Williams (2008: 357) concludes that Québec has been successful in "widespread legitimization of the French language . . . within the public domain." But it is far from clear that it will be as successful in the private sector; additionally, the Federal response has been to substitute language recognition for recognition of Québec as a nation.

The ending of the Franco dictatorship in Spain was accompanied by the granting of limited autonomy to the major regions. The 1978 constitution granted a measure of self-government to the "historic" communities – the Basque country, Catalonia, Galicia, Navarre, and Andalusia – and a more limited variety of autonomy to another ten regions. The Basque country, Catalonia, and Galicia, which had been autonomous before Franco, were the first to take advantage of this devolution of authority. Catalonia was perhaps the greatest beneficiary. The Catalan language has a strong historical and literary basis, and was well enough established as a modern language to be granted co-official status by the Second Spanish Republic. This was reversed by Franco, who worked to suppress regional identities and political power; in addition, public use of the language was prohibited. Nonetheless, the large number of Spanish-speaking immigrants who moved into Catalonia for economic reasons continued to be dominated politically and economically by Catalan-speakers. When the region was granted autonomy in 1979, a program began to restore Catalan identity and power, focused also on a campaign intended to institutionalize the Catalan language, reestablish literacy among Catalan speakers, and develop active use of the language by Spanish-speakers. The law of "linguistic normalization" that was adopted in 1983 made the Catalan language equal with Spanish in all government domains, and established a Directorate General of Language Policy to implement the new policy. Spanish-speakers are still constitutionally protected, so that the normalization program has moved cautiously (Strubell 2001). A new agreement between Barcelona and Madrid negotiated in 2006 declared Catalan as the official language of Catalonia, but did not give Catalonia the right, which the Basque country and Navarre have, of collecting all taxes.

A second region of Spain granted autonomy is the Basque country, the region hardest hit by the Franco dictatorship. In 1982, the newly autonomous Basque government adopted a basic law which called for the standardization and normalization of the Basque language alongside Spanish. The challenge has proved difficult: most traditional use of Basque was oral, and natural intergenerational transmission of the language is mainly in the small towns and villages. Because of Franco's suppression, there was a shortage of teachers literate in Basque. In a report on policy, a senior official in the Sub-Ministry for Language Policy of the Basque Government (Mateo 2005) notes that Basque was recognized as an official language between 1936 and 1939, but prohibited until the Statute of Autonomy was passed in 1979. Activities since then have concentrated on language cultivation (a general dictionary, linguistic atlas, a grammar, a standard dictionary, a place name database and the terminology committee). But there have also been intensive efforts in the school system: in 2002, nearly half of school pupils were being taught in Basque with Spanish as a subject. However, Spanish continues to be "the dominant language in social relations among young people" (Mateo 2005: 13). In the academic year 2000/2001 nearly 40,000 adults learned Basque in 121 Basque language schools, but few reached the level of proficiency. There is TV and radio in Basque, but they face strong competition from stations in Spanish and other languages. The situation of Basque remains fragile.

In the autonomous community of Valencia, a struggle between Catalan and Castilian continues, with very slow progress for Catalan (Archilés and Marty 2001; Arroyo 2002; Casesnoves Ferrer and Sankoff 2003, 2004a, 2004b). A fourth significant community is Galicia, whose language with about three million speakers has now been recognized by the European Union alongside Catalan and Basque. Since autonomy, there has been constant pressure from Galician activists to establish the language. Initially, the Galician language and literature were required to be taught alongside Castilian language and literature, but in 1995 a new decree required the teaching of two other subjects in Galician, amounting to a third of the curriculum. The government claims that most state schools meet the standard, but it is not applied in private schools which are attended by 27 percent of children (Ramallo 2007). A new Plan of Linguistic Normalization recently passed by the Galician Parliament will raise the required percentage to 50 (*Eurolang*, February 9, 2005).

In each of these cases, then, the territorial partition has produced new polities which are struggling, often against heavy odds, to impose monolingual hegemony on a partly resistant population. Most recently, the United Kingdom too has adopted a policy of devolution which also provides territorial power to ethnic minorities and their languages. One of the longest debated and most bitterly contested devolution issues has been the proposal for Irish Home Rule, a topic that regularly concerned the British Parliament throughout the nineteenth century, which was partly solved by the establishment of the Irish Free State early in the twentieth century, but in the twenty-first still remains a major issue of contention for Northern Ireland. In the meantime, there has been the recent granting of a degree of local autonomy to Wales and Scotland. Historically, the Gaelic-speaking peripheral areas of the British Isles were at various stages independent kingdoms, and either conquered and colonized or incorporated by act of union (when James I took the British throne). Although recent DNA studies have shown very little genetic difference (Oppenheimer 2006; Sykes 2006), the notion of Scots, Irish, and Welsh national identity is well ingrained and forms the basis for strong cultural nationalism, which has finally been answered by devolution.

Especially in the Welsh case, this has led to increased efforts at local language management, in particular the increased recognition of the status of Welsh (Williams 2007). Whereas previously efforts to reestablish Welsh depended on non-governmental or sometimes local government activities, devolution has given the authority to the Welsh Parliament to attempt to provide official backing for language revival. In 1989, the United Kingdom government set up a quasi-non-governmental body, the Welsh Language Board, and took a number of steps to improve the position of Welsh, including the 1988 Education Reform Act which made Welsh a core subject in all schools. The 1993 Welsh Language Act made the board a non-departmental statutory organization with a major grant to work towards treating Welsh and English on an equal basis. Some forty local authorities developed language schemes, and others were asked by the board to do so. Grants were made to implement some of the schemes. On devolution in 1999, many of the functions previously carried out by the Welsh Office of the UK government passed to the National Assembly of Wales. Authority over the Welsh Language Board was taken by the Assembly, controlled by the Minister for Culture. One of the key questions, Williams points out, became responsibility for the implementation of language schemes. The success of local schemes depended, he argued, on cooperation between a local authority, its language offices, and the Welsh Language Board members and staff. Another critical area was the scheme developed by the Home Office, a UK government body with major influence on the daily life of UK citizens, including those in Wales. The Home Office scheme, approved in 2002 (having been submitted three years later than was requested) was also slow in implementation, as a result of reluctance of the senior civil service management team at the Home Office. Only a change of minister and pressure from police, fire, and ambulance services was able to change the situation. There are regular reports of areas of tension, such as sign-posting and the order of announcements in railway stations ("If you have to wait for the Welsh to finish, the train has often left," someone complained).

Williams (2008: 197) also describes how devolution made it possible for the Scottish Parliament to take on the "Herculean task in restoring Gaelic as a vibrant community language." Part of the problem is the competing claim of Scots, perceived by many to be simply a local dialect of English, and the poor state of Gaelic language maintenance. In 2006, the Parliament passed the Gaelic Act, dealing only with Scottish affairs (and lacking the wider scope that the Welsh Language Board had over UK bodies), and establishing the *Bòrd na Gàidhlig* to increase the speakers and status of the language. A National Plan is being worked on that will include statutory Language Schemes, and twenty-seven local bodies were required to submit such schemes.

In Northern Ireland, after decades of violence between the two competing religious groups, there are signs of a compromise being established. There is a language issue here too, with the claim for recognition of Gaelic on the one hand, and of Ulster-Scotch on the other. So far, the reluctance of the civil service and the post-devolution political stalemate have been blocking language policies. The Good Friday agreement led to the establishment of two all-Ireland bodies, the *Foras na Gaelige* and *Tha Boord o Ulstèr-Scotch*, but so far they lack statutory support.

The principal point here is that the granting of a degree of regional autonomy has permitted the effort to develop local management plans to implement language policies that are less likely to be accepted or implemented as part of national plans. The territorial principle relieves a central nation-state of the pressure of dealing with regional languages. But implementation depends on acceptance by significant participants, the bureaucrats who need to manage the details of language policy.

There remain questions about the success of this hope. In March 2007, the Committee of Ministers of the Council of Europe received a report from its Committee of Experts on the application of the European Charter for Regional or Minority Languages by the United Kingdom. The report, quite critical of the slowness of implementation of recommendations made in the first monitoring round three years ago, commented in particular on "a continuing insufficient coordination between the central government and the devolved administrations and regions" (Council of Europe 2007: 62).

Going further: the breakup of nation-states

Recent developments in the breakup of nations may perhaps be seen as devolution carried to its logical conclusion. The ending of colonial rule after World War Two was an obvious case, as authority was moved from European imperial governments to newly independent states. Political independence provided local national control of language as well as other policies, although as Phillipson (1992) and others complained, they were unable or unwilling to take full advantage of the new freedom.

The collapse of the Soviet Union is another such case. Soviet language policy, like the Russian imperial policy which preceded it, was centrally controlled, even under Lenin it allowed for the recognition of some minority languages as the fastest route to communism. This became even clearer when Stalin reversed Lenin's nationalities policy and began an intensive program of Russification that involved not just favoring the Russian language but also mass transfers of population to produce multilingual regions where Russian was the logical lingua franca (Lewis 1972). One of the early steps in the resistance that led to the Soviet breakdown was an effort to restore the position of territorial languages in the Baltic republics. After the comparatively bloodless breakdown, almost every new state chose to proclaim its new independence by asserting the equality or superiority of its local language, even when (as in the Ukraine) most of the members of government were more used to operating in Russian. Essentially, then, the linguistic result of local independence was a small Tower of Babel, with the assertion of the status of many different national languages.

Each of the newly independent nations has its own story, but the general pattern was first to proclaim the equality of the territorial language with Russian, then to work to raise its status even higher. In the Baltic republics, the presence of significant proportions of Russian speakers brought in from various parts of the Soviet Union had reduced the status and usefulness of Estonian, Latvian, and Lithuanian. Each country developed policies to restore its national territorial language so as to move power to the previously repressed group, only to meet with disapproval from the European Union, which did not make the distinction between local and immigrant minorities that it allowed to its original member states, and which did not grant to candidates for membership the privilege of determining which linguistic minorities to recognize.

Latvian had survived many centuries of foreign rule, and the nationalist movement that developed in the nineteenth century had to compete with German and Russian; from the 1870s, only Russian was permitted in government, schools, and courts. When Latvia became independent in 1918, Latvian was established as the primary language, but seven minority languages were recognized. By the end of the 1930s, most people could speak Latvian. When Latvia was conquered by the Soviet Union in 1940, many Latvians were deported or emigrated and were replaced by immigrants from Russia, the Ukraine, and Belarus. Under Soviet policy, Russian became dominant and by 1989, two thirds of Latvians and most others were said to be fluent in it. Even before independence, Latvian was declared the state language, but official functions were maintained for Russian. In 1991, the Republic of Latvia was set up and the position of the language was strengthened: the 1994 law required knowledge of Latvian for naturalization. Only 52 percent of the total population was ethnically Latvian. In 1989, 20 percent of ethnic Russians living in Latvia said they knew Latvian; by 1995 50 percent claimed Latvian (Druviete 1998; Hogan-Brun 2006). In Estonia, ethnic Estonians made up 62 percent of the population in the 1980s; in Lithuania, ethnic Lithuanians made up 80 percent. In Lithuania, the mother-tongue is permissible as language of instruction in "populous and compact communities of ethnic minorities." Note that this too is an application of the territorial principle. In Estonia, 60 percent of the curriculum must be taught in Estonian in secondary schools. In Latvia, it was planned to end municipality-financed minority-language education (Ozolins 2003; Tsilevich 2001).

There were similar developments in the former Soviet Muslim states (Landau and Kellner-Heinkele 2001). The granting of independence gave these new states an opportunity to manage their own language policy, although European Union policy requires that they recognize minority languages. Thus, the change of domain definition first allowed internal decision – the desire to join a supranational grouping allowed extra domain influence to be released.

The breakup of Czechoslovakia and Yugoslavia also produced similar linguistic diversification, usually following political and violent struggle and accompanied by "ethnic cleansing." Just as independence in India and the division from Pakistan had led to the splitting of Hindustani into Hindi and Urdu, so did the splitting of Czechoslovakia produce a renewal of separate identities for Czech and Slovak, while the Yugoslavian Serbo-Croatian established or reestablished Serbian, Croatian, and Montenegrin as distinct languages.

The Czech Republic, set up in 1993 with the breakup of the Soviet Union, restored a division that had been blurred when Czechoslovakia was created in 1918. In the interwar period, attempts were made to blend Czech and Slovak, mutually intelligible languages, into a national language. German and Polish minorities remain, reduced when 2.5 million German speakers were moved back to Germany after World War Two. The original 1993 constitution assumed a nation in which both Czech and Slovak would be used by their respective communities in their own regions, but it was soon decided to divide the state ethnolinguistically. The new Czech Republic has about 80 percent ethnic Czechs and includes Moravian, Slovak, Roma, Polish, and German minorities (Neustupný and Nekvapil 2003). In the new Slovak Republic, 86 percent of the population claim to be Slovak and 11 percent Magyar: Slovak is the official language but minority languages (Hungarian, Bulgarian, Croatian, Czech, German, Polish, Romanian, Ruthenian, and Ukrainian) may be used in any municipality where they constitute 20 percent of the population (Simon and Kontra 2000). In recommendations adopted in 2007, the Council of Ministers of the Council of Europe called on the Slovakian government to review the restrictions imposed by the State Language Act, especially on the right to use regional or minority languages in court, and to permit women to adopt or use family names in regional or minority languages. It also called for improvements in minority language education, especially in teacher training and in the provision of broadcast and print media in minority languages. Regional and minority languages were to be presented as an integral part of the cultural heritage of Slovakia both in the school curriculum and in the media. Romani language education was to be provided, a curriculum in the Romani language was to be developed, and the practice of enrolling Roma children in special education schools was to be abolished. In addition, Ruthenian language education was to be provided at all levels (Council of Europe 2007). Independence then may have solved the problem of Slovak, but it left minority language problems within the devolved nation; again, a domain-external participant has tried to counteract the tendency to monolingual national language hegemony

Under Tito, the Socialist Federal Republic of Yugoslavia was seen as a meeting place of three distinct civilizations: Western European Catholic, Byzantine-and-Slavic Orthodox, and Arabic-Turkish Islamic. Six nations were recognized: Serbs, Croats, Slovenes, Montenegrins, Macedonians, and Muslims. Each of these had a national home in one of the republics that made up the Federation. In addition, there were eight nationalities which had cultural and linguistic rights: Albanians, Hungarians, Roma, Italians, Ruthenians, Czechs, Slovaks, and Turks. A third group was made up of other nationalities and ethnic groups, including Austrians, Greeks, Jews, Germans, Poles, Russians, and Ukrainians. After the breakup of Yugoslavia, there lasted for a while some unions of former republics, but now six independent nation-states reflect essentially the ethnolinguistic pattern of the former Federation. They are Bosnia and Herzegovina (official languages are Bosnian, Croatian, and Serbian), Croatia (Croatian with some recognition of minority languages), Montenegro (the Ijekavian dialect of Serbian, called Montenegrin by some), Republic of Macedonia (Macedonian and recognition of Albanian), Serbia (Serbian written in Cyrillic, and some minority languages), Slovenia (Slovenian and also Hungarian and Italian in some municipalities), and finally Kosovo (Albanian, Serbian, and English are official) (Bugarski 2001).

The example of Yugoslavia shows clearly the strengths and weaknesses of the territorial solution. Breaking a multilingual nation-state into smaller units relieves some of the pressure by satisfying the aspirations of the larger minorities while producing nations which can attempt to unify around national languages. Even without the complications of immigration and globalization, however, it regularly leaves significant ethnolinguistic minorities in the new nation which require a solution. In the new states, we see the continuation of the territorial principle in provision for the recognition of minority languages in those municipalities or regions where they constitute a large enough group to warrant it. From a theoretical point of view, territorialism can be seen as an effort to simplify by redefining the extent of the domain. It has a chance of working when there is geographical concentration producing reasonably distinct language regions; it is further encouraged by historical earlier divisions that retain their ideological appeal. But it is important to avoid a linguicentric view: the territorial divisions are political, ethnic, or religious (or a combination); the linguistic reflex follows rather than causes the division.

Central government regulation of languages

Constitutions and other basic laws commonly establish the language policy of a nation-state, but they need implementation. Furthermore, as noted above, about half the nations in the world do not use a constitution for this purpose. In many cases, this probably means that the government is indifferent to or satisfied with the pattern of language practices.

There are other cases in which there will be intervention, to be traced in laws, regulations, and budgetary allocations. Leclerc (1994–2007) provides access to many national language laws. For Albania, he lists a number of laws from 1994 to 1996 dealing with school language policy; for Algeria, three laws concerning the status of Arabic and a 2005 regulation requiring that private schools as well as government schools use Arabic as language of instruction; for Andorra, a 1999 law making Catalan official; for Belgium, thirteen federal laws and proclamations concerning languages, and another ten language decrees and regulations issued by the French and Flemish communities; for Canada, twenty-nine Federal and provincial laws; for China, the 2001 law establishing Putonghua nationally; for Croatia, three 2000 laws on minority languages; for Denmark three recent laws concerning the teaching of Danish to foreign adults and bilingual children (a result presumably of the new concern about immigrants); for Spain, a dozen federal laws concerning language federally and in the autonomous communities, and another twenty laws on language from the communities themselves; for Estonia, four basic language laws and regulations; for the United States, the now defunct Bilingual Education Act, the No Child Left Behind Act of 2001, Executive Order 13166, and a collection of state laws including those establishing English as the official state language; for Finland, half a dozen laws on language including two on Sámi; for France, a collection of twenty-two laws and regulations; for Hungary, the basic language education law and some laws on minority languages; for Italy, a number of state and regional laws and regulations on language; for Latvia, the Basic Law establishing Latvian as the official language (the 1999 revision of the 1989 law) and a 2000 regulation permitting use of other languages for certain functions; for Lithuania, laws on the official language and ethnic minorities; for Malta, a 2003 Maltese Language Act establishing a National Language Council; for Moldova, the 1989 law making Moldova official and a 2001 law establishing rights of national minorities; for New Zealand, the Māori Language Act; for Poland, the 1999 law to protect the Polish language; for Romania, a 2004 law protecting purism in Romanian and a 2005 law protecting twenty recognized national minorities; for the United Kingdom, some recent laws and regulations concerning immigration and naturalization and recent language laws from Wales, Scotland, Northern Ireland, and the Isle of Man; for Russia, the post-Soviet language laws including the 2004 law proclaiming Russian the official language of the Federation; for Serbia, Slovakia, and Slovenia, laws establishing the official language and dealing with minority groups; for Sweden, two laws passed in 2000 dealing with Sámi, Finnish, and Meänkieli; for Switzerland, some federal laws on national languages and a large collection of laws and decrees from individual cantons; for Turkey, a 2003 regulation governing the teaching of languages and a 2004 regulation controlling languages used on radio and television; and for the Ukraine, the 1989 law making Ukrainian official and a 2004 law recognizing ten indigenous minorities. While not complete – the list does not yet include, for example, the 2007 New Zealand law making Sign Language official, or the 2007 Israeli law establishing an Arabic Language Academy – it does make it possible to draw some tentative conclusions about language laws.

National or federal laws are most commonly concerned with status, with the establishment of a national official language, or with granting limited status to minority languages. Regional (provincial or cantonal) governments commonly take advantage of territorial autonomy to pass laws raising the status of the regional variety. A good number of laws are concerned with language education policy, especially with the establishment of the school language of instruction. Occasionally, laws deal with language cultivation or with the establishment of agencies to carry out language policy. But again, it is important to note that language laws constitute marked cases; most nations, whatever their language policy, tend to establish it by practice and consensus rather than by specific acts of language management.

Spelling and language reform

While they are strictly speaking language cultivation or corpus planning, government efforts to change some aspect of a language (usually its writing system, orthography, or lexicon) often serve a political purpose and so cross the porous border into status planning. One of the best-known cases is Kemal Atatürk's major reform of Turkish. The 1908 program of the Young Turks was intended to purify the language by removing non-Turkish elements introduced under Islamic and Ottoman influence. When they came to power, they launched a major campaign in the late 1920s to switch the writing system from Perso-Arabic script to one based on Latin, and to purge the language of thousands of words of Persian and Arabic origin, replacing them by native words or by other foreign borrowings (especially from French). One unanticipated result was the continued gap between the spoken language and the language of intellectuals, and a need to translate classic Turkish texts into modern Turkish (Lewis 1999).

Another example is Norwegian, where two opposing ideologies of what the new language should look like led to the acceptance of two competing spelling systems.

Language reform is far from simple without the strength of a totalitarian state. In 1948, the Hebrew Language Council, forerunner of the Language Academy, published a set of draft proposals to reform the spelling system; twenty years later, the Academy accepted them, but neither the general public nor the newspapers have done so yet, so that Hebrew spell checkers offer three systems.

Political differences remain important: Taiwan does not accept the limited character reforms of the People's Republic; North and South Korea have distinct writing systems; Belarus is divided between *Tarashkevitsa* (based on a grammar published by Tarashkyevich in 1918) and the various reforms introduced under Soviet rule, condemned as Russification by its opponents (Brown 2005). Soviet language policy was applied to minorities, who from the 1940s until 1950 were required to spell all Russian words in Russian (Grenoble 2003: 53).

The struggle over Dutch spelling reform also lasted more than a century. The Dutch did not accept the Belgian reform of 1864; in 1954 and 1963 compromise proposals were published but led to major disputes, finally being accepted by the two governments only in 1994. German spelling became official at a national conference in 1901. In 1955, the education ministers of the *Länder* accepted the Duden reference publication as official for spelling and punctuation. In 1986, a joint commission from German-speaking countries proposed a handful of minor reforms, which were accepted by the education ministers of the *Länder* in 1996 and were to come into effect starting in 1998; public protest and legal action followed (Johnson 2002).

These and similar cases highlight one of the central problems in language management: that it is comparatively easy to establish policies, but far from simple to implement them.

Local government

We have dealt so far with national governments and with the devolved authority granted to states in a federal system or to autonomous communities. Local governments also occasionally make efforts to manage languages.

Wikipedia explains the complexity of the concept of local government:

In modern nations, local governments usually have fewer powers than national governments do. They usually have some power to raise taxes, though these may be limited by central legislation. In some countries local government is partly or wholly funded by subventions from central government taxation. The question of Municipal Autonomy – which powers the local government has, or should have, and why – is a key question of public administration and governance. The institutions of local government vary greatly between countries, and even where similar arrangements exist, the terminology often varies. Common names for local government entities include state, province, region, department, county, prefecture, district, city, township, town, borough, parish, municipality, shire and village. However all these names are often used informally in countries where they do not describe a legal local government entity.

In the United Kingdom, "over 20,000 elected councillors represent local communities and local people on the 410 local authorities of England and Wales. Employing over two million people, these local councils undertake an estimated 700 different functions" (www.local.gov.uk). In the US, there are fifty states, each with a governor and legislature: each of these states has local government bodies: New York State for instance has about sixty counties and a large number of city, borough, and village local government bodies.

Germany has sixteen *Länder*, each with its own legislature; within the *Länder*, there are 323 *Landkreise* and 116 *Kreisfreie Städte*, making 439 districts all together. Each district is governed by an elected council and an executive, chosen either by the council or directly, whose duties are comparable to those of a county executive in the United States, supervising local government administration. The *Landkreise* have primary administrative functions in specific areas, such as highways, hospitals, and public utilities. There were (as of March 1, 2006) 12,320 municipalities, which are the smallest administrative units in Germany. Cities are municipalities as well. *Gemeinden* (municipalities) are ruled by elected councils and a mayor, who is chosen either by the council or directly. *Gemeinden* have two major policy responsibilities. First, they administer programs authorized by the federal or *Land* government, such as youth, schools, public health, and social assistance. Second, the Basic Law guarantees *Gemeinden* "the right to regulate on their own responsibility all the affairs of the local community within the limits set by law." For instance, many municipalities develop the economic infrastructure of their communities. Local authorities foster cultural activities by supporting local artists, building arts centers, and having fairs. Local government also provides public utilities, such as gas and electricity, as well as public transportation.

In Australia, there are six states with legislatures and three territories. Local government in Australia is under the state government, and its functions are limited to "community facilities like libraries and parks, maintenance of local roads, planning, and local services like waste disposal."

In France, there are three levels: 22 *Régions* and four *Régions d'outre-mer* (Réunion, Martinique, Guadeloupe, and French Guiana), 96 *départements* and four *départements d'outre-mer* (Réunion, Guadeloupe, Martinique, and French Guiana), and 36,679 municipalities (in French: *Communes*).

Since the Meiji restoration, Japan has had a simple local government system. First, Japan is divided into 47 prefectures. Each prefecture comprises cities, villages, and towns. In Hokkaido, Nagasaki, and Okinawa, there are branches of the prefectural government sometimes referred to as "Subprefectures."

At the local level of government, language policy divides into three major spheres. The first is the choice of language for internal working: there can be a policy concerning the language to be used in legislative activities (parliaments at the national level, councils at the local level) and the language to be used in carrying out the internal business of the governmental unit – the language to be used by government employees. The second is the choice of language for communication with citizens within the territory controlled by the government. What language or languages are laws and regulations published in? What language is used for the announcement of policy? What languages can citizens use to address elected officials and bureaucrats? The third is the effort to manage the language of citizens. What languages are used and taught in school? What varieties of language are banned or punished? What varieties of language are encouraged? All levels of government necessarily have a policy dealing with the first two. The third kind of policy is most likely to occur at the national level, or where there is an effort to add to regional or territorial levels to modify national language policy. But it can occur at the local level too.

We start then with some examples of local government language management intended to illustrate these three kinds of policy. Our working assumption in the following will be that local governments will undertake language management to deal with local internal problems – if there is multilingualism, they must establish official or working languages for internal use and for providing services for citizens. Here, the main forces are likely to be pragmatic and communicative, reflecting the sociolinguistic ecology of the local area, but they can also be effects of beliefs about desirable outcomes, and ideologies being encouraged by local or external interest groups or agencies. Local government policy will also generally be subservient to regional or national policy, unless the demographic situation gives extra power to national minorities which reach a required percentage in a locality. Explicit attempts to modify the language practices of citizens are likely to depend on strong local ideology. Some individual cases should lead to refinement of these generalizations.

The US city of Nashville, in the state of Tennessee, was reported in September 2006 to be considering a proposal requiring that city agencies conduct their business in English; the proposal would also prohibit the city from offering services in any other language. This would appear to be a local manifestation of the English-Only campaign, which has so far failed at the Federal level but has had some success at state and local levels. It is in direct opposition to the Federal policy requiring agencies to provide access to services to limited-English citizens. The proposal passed, but was vetoed by the mayor. A similar change of mind was reported in a town in Nevada, where the newly elected Pahrump Town Board unanimously repealed an ordinance passed in November that made English the town's official language (*New York Times*, February 15, 2007). The American Civil Liberties Union of Nevada had threatened a lawsuit, but four members of the board, including the three who voted for the ordinance, left office in January.

A step towards tolerance of multilingualism was taken by the Waukee City Council in California in 2006 when it voted unanimously to approve a contract providing the city with over-the-phone translation services. Similarly, in 2007 the mayor of Seattle signed an executive order adopting a new citywide translation and interpretation policy to help people with limited English skills use city services. The policy, intended to improve the city's translation and interpretation services, calls for city assistance in translating important documents such as an explanation of city services; consent and complaint forms; notices of rights; and notices of free language assistance in a number of languages, including Spanish, Vietnamese, Cantonese, Mandarin, Somali, Tagalog, and Korean. Translation and interpretation services from the city will be free.

Working to implement its part of an uneven Canadian national bilingual policy, the City of Ottawa planned to designate 3,500 jobs officially bilingual by the end of May 2007. The *Ottawa Sun* reported that the bilingual designation will affect about 20 per cent of the 17,000 City of Ottawa employees. Those already in jobs deemed bilingual who don't speak, read, or write French would be safe. Once Ottawa's official bilingualism policy was in place, unilingual candidates would be expected to learn French for bilingual positions.

The issue of translation services became a major dispute in New York in 2006. More than 40 percent of the one million school students in New York lived in households where a language other than English was spoken. The city education department began to translate many school documents intended for parents into eight commonly spoken languages – Spanish, Chinese, Urdu, Russian, Bengali, Haitian Creole, Korean, and Arabic. In December 2005, the City Council passed a bill requiring public schools to increase translation services for parents. Because of the huge expense, and because the bill would violate the State Education Law, the Mayor vetoed the bill in January 2006. A month later, there was a demonstration organized on the steps of City Hall in support of the council action, and a compromise policy was negotiated between the Mayor and the council.

In the United Kingdom, Bristol City Council established a translation and interpreting service to make documents available and provide interpreters at council meetings. The council has established a register of 100 local translators and interpreters to provide service in twelve major immigrant languages, in all European languages, and in as many other languages as required. Similar local policies are providing translation as a normal part of the civic services provided by UK local government bodies, but a backlash has started to appear as a result primarily of the cost of these services. In June 2007, for example, the UK Communities Secretary Ruth Kelly was reported to be concerned at the cost (£25 million for local bodies, £31 million for courts, and £55 million for the National Health Service) of translators and interpreters: she argued that they had become "a crutch for foreigners and discouraged integration" (*The Sun*, June 11, 2007). She was also reported to object to translating road signs into Polish and to providing the Department of Health information service in Gujarati, Vietnamese, and Urdu for young mothers (*The Daily Mail*, June 18, 2007).

San Francisco, concerned about the quality of translations provided on its website, established a task force in September 2006 to make the translations more accurate. A similar attempt to improve the quality of translated signs was reported in Beijing, China, where an agency is working to standardize transportation signs in English. Shanghai was also concerned about translation and interpreting: it established a team of fifty professional sign language interpreters, set up a team of police officers to answer telephones in eight foreign languages, and was recruiting language professionals in those languages for the World Expo planned for 2010.

But more politically based policies also emerge at the city level. In Malmö, Sweden, two local politicians proposed banning foreign languages from the schools so that they could concentrate on teaching Swedish to their large number of immigrant students. In the Ukraine, a major dispute over the status of Russian emerged at local levels. The President insisted that Ukrainian should be the sole official language in the country, a plank of the 2004 "orange revolution" that brought him to power. Many local councils and regional administrations, such as the Sebastopol and Kharkov City Councils in the Russian-speaking east and south declared Russian a regional language.

The growth of immigration throughout the world has had a major effect on the demography and associated multilingualism of cities especially, for rural to urban migration is as important a factor as migration from one country to another. This pressure is especially recognized by city councils in the increasing demand for multilingual services. In those countries where education comes under the control of local government, the need for local action is especially strong. In pioneering studies of urban multilingualism in Europe, Extra and Yağmur (2004) provided detailed profiles of six major cities: Göteborg, Hamburg, The Hague, Brussels, Lyon, and Madrid. They showed the growing linguistic complexity of these cities, and highlighted the pressure that it put on the educational system. As a rule, there was very little teaching in the children's home or community language.

Most city governments are responsible for the street and traffic signs in the city. Signage is an important area of what some people call linguistic landscape (Gorter 2006) and in multilingual areas the choice and order of languages is a matter of considerable interest (Spolsky and Cooper 1991) (see p. 66ff.). With devolution, the Welsh government established a requirement that road signs should be written in both Welsh and English; before that, the presence of Welsh on signs depended on local government. In Israel, signs come under local municipalities, but two cases that came to court showed the issues involved. In Nazareth, the municipal government passed a regulation requiring that billboards be written in Hebrew alongside any other language, but agreed during a court case to permit a sign written only in Arabic advertising an apartment building in the Arabic-speaking area of the city. In Haifa, the municipality agreed during a court hearing to add Arabic to its signs written in Hebrew and English. Backhaus' (2007) study of multilingual signs in the city of Tokyo showed how the municipality established a policy of using English as well as Japanese on signs in areas where tourists are likely to be found. The rules are laid down in the *Tokyo manual about official signs* (Tokyo Metropolitan Government 1991), and then developed further in the *Guide for making the city writing easy to understand also to foreigners* (Tokyo Metropolitan Government 2003).

There are thus two main areas of language management at the local government level. The first concerns pragmatic decisions that need to be made because the locality is demographically multilingual or made multilingual by the desired presence of tourists speaking another language. These decisions will generally be governed by domain-internal considerations, although they may also be influenced by national policies. One obvious example is the modification of public signs and the provision of interpreting in a city chosen as the site for the Olympic Games. The second concerns possibly unimplementable symbolic decisions about language status taken by local governments which are more easily manipulated by activist groups than are higher levels. A good example was the way that some Welsh city councils pioneered the use of the language in street signs; another is the way that a handful of US city councils have adopted English-Only regulations.

Why is national policy so difficult?

The territorial principle emerged as a potential solution to the problem produced by the multilingualism of most nation-states. What would be the alternative? We saw in previous sections that even where nation-states are partitioned ethnolinguistically, significant linguistic minorities remain that must be accommodated. Of course, this happens in unitary states too. Looking at the effects of massive immigration on the United States, England, France, and even Ireland (there are said to be more speakers of Mandarin than of Irish in Dublin), one sees a constant replenishment of the section of the population which lacks proficiency in the official language. It is easy to propose a pragmatic solution – make provision for teaching the official language to those who do not know it, provide for their efficient access to the various civic services (police, medicine, law, employment, and education) while they are learning it, and make it possible for minority groups that wish to do so to pass their heritage languages to their children. When one looks at actual policies, the situation is quite different. Very few countries offer easy access to civic services in the languages of indigenous and migrant minorities. In the United States, this access is starting to be provided as a result of Executive Order 13166, but the process of providing interpreters for all languages spoken by recent immigrants is proving to be difficult and expensive. In the United Kingdom, the cost of providing interpreting services for the police is also leading to budgetary strains, and the government now proposes to stop funding for teaching English to migrants. Throughout the world, most children are forced to go to school in a new language: although empirical research continues to show the value of and need for bilingual schooling, it is rare. In spite of evidence of how much money they are losing as a result, many business firms are failing to provide multilingual service in the languages of their customers. Support for heritage language programs seems to depend on very strong pressure, and is banned or discouraged in many nation-states. There are nations that have multilingual policies, but in practice, most work towards the hegemony of the dominant national language.

At the level of the nation-state, language management then becomes extremely complex. Take each of the three sub-domains involved: the internal working of government bodies (legislative, bureaucratic, or judicial), the interaction of these bodies with citizens, and the attempts to manage language use by the population as a whole. As a general rule, legislators prefer to use the national official language for public sessions, although some countries allow for occasional interpreting into a recognized minority language. It is not uncommon to set proficiency in the national language as a qualification for election to public office. Civil servants in most countries conduct their internal business in a single language, usually the national official language but occasionally a former colonial or world language. To enforce a bilingual policy, one needs to encourage civil servants to be bilingual (as in Canada) or require all new recruits to be proficient in the two languages (as was to be the policy in Sri Lanka starting in July 2007). Citizens are generally expected to be sufficiently proficient in the national language to be able to read government documents, fill out official forms, and interact with civil servants (including police and health workers). In special cases, like the situation in Wales described above, efforts are occasionally made to accommodate citizens without the requisite language proficiency. Beyond that, and beyond setting school language policies, most governments leave private businesses and citizens to develop their own language policies. It is a marked case where a government sets out to make a major change in the language practices of its citizens – the teaching of Putonghua in Communist China, the long-time ban on indigenous languages in South America, or the efforts in former Soviet republics to correct the imposed dominance of Russian, to name a few obvious cases.

In an earlier book (Spolsky 2004), I suggested that language policy in an independent nation-state depended on four major factors: the sociolinguistic ecology (language practices) of the nation, a set of beliefs (language ideology) relating language to national identity, the effects of globalization (the pull towards international languages, especially English), and pressure for attention to the rights of indigenous or migrant linguistic minorities. Following suggestions of Lambert (1999) and Fishman (1971), I grouped nations according to the number of national languages and Great Traditions that they recognized as monolingual, dyadic or triadic, or mosaic (multilingual). We have already discussed in this chapter examples of the dyadic or triadic group, nations that recognize two or more Great Traditions with associated languages and that look for management solutions by partitioning linguistic space or by taking advantage of politically motivated territorial division. In any case, all evidence seems to support the notion that the main pressure in the national domain, when under control of central government, is for monolingualism.

Pressures for national monolingualism and multilingualism

Iceland is the exemplar of a monolingual nation: its population of 309,000 is reported to be monolingual in Icelandic, speaking it as a first language and using it as a "dominant language in all spheres of life" (Vikor 2000: 125). This strong monolingualism withstood 500 years of Danish colonial rule, but is again coming under pressure from globalization and English. Language management in Iceland now has two major prongs: cultivation intended to maintain the purity of Icelandic, and protectionist policies intended to work against the tide of English, which many Icelanders speak (Hilmarsson-Dunn 2006). Until recently, then, practice, beliefs, and management all coincided to maintain comfortable monolingualism, unaffected by school teaching of Danish and foreign languages. In the twenty-first century, this appears to be no longer enough, and in spite of efforts to provide software in Icelandic (Icelandic is supported in Windows XP), English is gradually invading technological, educational, and communication domains, and a rapid growth in immigration in the last few years is producing a visible number of foreign workers, especially in restaurants and bars.

A much more complex example of a monolingual nation-state is France, the paradigmatic case of strong ideology and language management. Since the efforts of Cardinal Richelieu in the seventeenth century to establish Parisian French as the unifying and only language for the territory under French rule, there has been continued centralizing and homogenizing pressure (Cooper 1989). The French Revolution reinforced this move, when the Jacobins seized power and called for a centralized and unified state supported by a common language. True, it took a century before primary education using French as language of instruction was free and compulsory, and another century before the French constitution was amended to make French the sole official language of the Republic. Regional languages were anathematized, and the French-only policy was enforced in conquered territory such as Alsace and in all French colonies. An elaborate set of bureaucratic institutions have been set up, starting with the French Academy in 1635, and now supplemented by more than a dozen language-related government agencies and committees responsible for maintaining the status and purity of the French language. All French civil servants are required to use official terminology and to use only French in international relations (Ager 1996).

Ideologically, then, France is monolingual, and virtually all management activities of the central government are directed to this end. The exceptions arise out of the somewhat reluctant compliance with European Union policies on minority languages. A number of regional languages, including Basque, Breton, Catalan, Occitan, and Corsican were permitted as school subjects for up to three hours a week, and since 1970, have counted towards the overall grade for the baccalaureate. The loss of these languages as home languages results from changing socio-economic conditions – industrialization, the growth of mass communication, and the breakdown of rural isolation (Bourdieu 2001; Strubell 2001). Assisted by these outside pressures, 250 years of language management were starting to have their effect, but needed to be bolstered by the 1994 Toubon law, which consolidated the hegemonic laws and regulations. French monolingualism remains under pressure, first from the external and internal competition of English globalization, secondly from the growing number of migrants, especially Arabic speakers who are firmly resisting integration, and more weakly, by some regional language activism.

Most nation-states with monolingual ideologies turn out on closer inspection to be under pressure. Most obvious and most often complained about is the threat of English in non-English speaking countries. But there are also commonly pressures from indigenous and migrant minorities, or from pre-independence colonial languages. On independence, many new nations proclaimed national monolingualism, on the principle of "one nation, one state, one language" in a language other than that introduced by the colonial power. This was as true of the nations that gained independence after the world wars as it was of those whose independence came during or at the end of the nineteenth century, and it remains true of the newly autonomous or independent polities that have arisen as a result of devolution in Spain and the United Kingdom, or the breakdown of the Soviet Union, Czechoslovakia, and Yugoslavia.

While most former French colonies have continued to use French for official and educational purposes, some did make efforts to choose their own national language. The North African Muslim polities which constitute the Maghreb have a common Great Tradition and a similar sociolinguistic history. The Islamic conquest of the ninth century imposed Arabic over the indigenous languages, but the autochthonous Berber varieties survive as spoken languages. French conquest in the nineteenth century led to the imposition of French for education and government. With independence in the 1960s, French colonists and Jews were expelled; and the new constitution proclaimed Arabic as the only official language. A campaign of Arabicization began, with varying levels of success: Algeria has been the most successful, while Tunisia and Morocco remain heavily francophone. There has been a new recognition of the large Berber-speaking minorities. Some African countries flirted with replacing French with African languages. After a short period of using mother-tongues in the 1970s, Guinea returned to French in the 1980s (Yerendé 2005). In Madagascar, too, French was restored as the school language of instruction in 1992, after twenty years of using Malagasy. In 2007, a referendum approved adding English as an official language. Elsewhere in Africa, former French colonies continue to keep French as the official language. In former French colonies in Asia, restoration of the native language has been more successful; in both Laos and Cambodia there is competition between French and English as a language for advanced education and international communication (Clayton 2006).

More common are nations which proclaim a single national official language in their constitution but also recognize the rights of linguistic minorities constitutionally. In many Latin American countries, Spanish or (in Brazil) Portuguese are constitutionally recognized as official languages and do indeed dominate public and official language use and education. Some protection has also recently been provided for minority languages, particularly the indigenous languages spoken by some 10 percent of the Latin American population. Many different languages are involved: only Uruguay is monolingual, and other countries have between 7 and 200 indigenous languages. Indigenous peoples are then in an inferior social and economic position and generally illiterate. In recent years, there have been programs starting up to support indigenous language maintenance.

Whether or not it has anything to do with the initial letter, India, Indonesia, and Israel (and Italy for that matter) shared a common ideologically based attempt to establish the monolingual hegemony of a national language. While the Indian constitution recognized its historical multilingualism and set out to find territorial solutions, the central hope of the Congress Party, frustrated by the resistance of other language groups and the spread of English, was to establish Hindi in this role. Italy, after unification, worked to establish standard Italian as an umbrella over the many local dialects, and is slowly driving them under. Israel worked to replace traditional Jewish multilingualism with revived, revitalized, revernacularized, and considerably modified Hebrew monolingualism, crushing in the process many heritage and minority languages.

Indonesia started with more than 400 languages, fifteen of which still had more than a million speakers in 1972 and chose in the early days of national revival one of its smaller languages, Malay, renamed Bahasa Indonesia, to be the "one language" in its "one nation, one land, one language" mobilizing formula. Indonesia was under Dutch rule from 1600 until the Japanese occupation in 1942. During this period, there was schooling for Dutch, Christian, and military children, but education for native children began only in the middle of the nineteenth century with a limited number of primary schools teaching mainly in regional languages but partly in Malay, a widely spoken lingua franca. In the twentieth century, primary schools for some native pupils were opened in Dutch. The decisive language management choice was made at the meeting in 1928 of the Indonesian Youth Congress, which selected Malay and named it Bahasa Indonesia as a national language (Alisjahbana 1976). There were various attempts to cultivate the language, but the breakthrough came during the Japanese occupation, when Dutch was banned, and Indonesian and Japanese were declared official languages. The Japanese permitted the cultivation of Indonesian and established an Indonesian Language Commission in October 1942 to develop terminology and write a grammar. Lists of terms were distributed to schools. After the end of the Japanese occupation, the new constitution declared Bahasa Indonesia to be the state language. For the next four years, the Dutch attempted to reconquer the former colony and set up regional states using regional languages, but Bahasa Indonesia was used by and became an emblem of resistance. The Republic was recognized as an independent state in 1949; in 1952 the government took over all Dutch-medium schools, since when all education is in Bahasa Indonesia. An intensive policy of standardization and modernization followed, including spelling reform and terminological development. An official standard grammar and dictionary was written and has been republished regularly. Bahasa Indonesia was extensively used in the mass media. Vernacular regional languages continued to be used for the first two years of primary school, reflecting the fact that a high proportion of the population still speak the vernacular as the first home language, and learn

Indonesian in school or in the community. Kaplan and Baldauf (2003: 99) conclude that the rise of Bahasa Indonesia to an effective and widely accepted national language is "a major political and linguistic triumph." At the same time, they list nine problems that were much the same as those listed in Rubin (1977): the need for continued cultivation and diffusion, the need for a standard variety in the light of regional varieties developing, functional differentiation between formal and informal, the teaching of English and other international languages, the need to support heritage languages, the need to enrich the literacy environment, the shortage of English texts for school, the need to upgrade teacher training, and the need to make English more relevant to students outside the major centers. Continued political instability and unfavorable economic conditions make it difficult for Indonesia to tackle these problems. While four fifths of the population understand Bahasa Indonesia, only a third uses it as their main language (Montolalu and Suryadinata 2007).

Japan and Thailand are two more examples of monolingual, single Great Tradition language policies starting to recognize the existence of underlying multilingualism. Japan has been essentially monoethnic for more than two millennia, but during this time its language has been exposed to outside influence, particularly from Chinese, for its vocabulary and part of its writing system (Kaplan and Baldauf 2003). With increased western contact towards the end of the nineteenth century, major language reforms during the Meiji period averted more extreme proposals including complete Romanization or even switching to English (Coulmas 1990). The Japanese constitution does not mention language, but it is simply taken for granted that all Japanese speak the language. During the nationalist period leading up to and including World War Two, Japanese was forcibly imposed on Korea and on Manchuria as well as on other conquered territories. More recently, there have been two breaches in the monolingual wall. One involves the recognition of the need to improve the teaching of English and other foreign languages. The second is the beginnings of the recognition of speakers of other languages inside Japan – Korean and other immigrants, foreign workers, and even indigenous minorities.

Thailand too is widely believed to be monolingual and to have a single Great Tradition, including a common religion, Buddhism. The reality is somewhat different, as Smalley (1994) made clear. There are in fact eighty different languages spoken in Thailand, many of them classifiable as varieties of Thai. Standard Thai is the official and national language, a symbol, along with the king and the Buddhist religion, of the nation. Few, however, speak it as a native language, but most learn it in school. For external contacts, English is the primary language – for international politics, advanced education overseas, international media, culture, and tourism. In practice,

Thailand is multilingual, but its ideology is clearly monolingual, as speakers of the other languages accept its hegemony. Only recently has there been a cautious suggestion that better recognition of the language of the Muslim Malay-speakers in the South might contribute to solving the current political unrest.

Given the continuance of nations, whether we like it or not, and the value of a national official language both as a mobilizing symbol of the nation and as an efficient method of communication, it is perhaps no wonder that the main pressure in modern nation-states of whatever kind is towards monolingualism. But there are counter-forces – activists who choose a different language as their object of desire, and supranational organizations without direct responsibility that are starting to argue for diversity and multilingualism. To better understand language management at the level of the nation-state, we need to look more carefully at the internal activists and the external supranational organizations.

10 Influencing language management: language activist groups

Entr'acte: the model to-date

Having taken a first look at the domain of the nation-state in the last chapter, this is perhaps an appropriate place to summarize the theoretical model that has emerged so far. First, I see organized language management as an attempt by some person or body with or claiming authority to modify the language practices or beliefs of a group of speakers. It is a political act, arising out of a belief that the present practices or beliefs are inadequate or undesirable and need modification. It assumes the existence of choice, whether of language, variety, or variable, and depends on the existence or perception of a significant conflict between two or more languages, varieties, or salient variables, such that a different choice can be expected to remedy the conflict.

Secondly, I have demonstrated, as Calvet (1998) argued, that one must study language management not just at the level of the nation-state, but at the various levels of the recognizable domains that make up human society, starting with the family and including religion, the neighborhood, the workplace, health and legal services, and the military, each of which functions as interrelated parts of the sociolinguistic ecosystem. Language management then encompasses, as Nekvapil (2006: 100) remarked, both "macroplanning" at the level of the state and "microplanning" in lower level institutions, and in fact the two dimensions interact. With this domain-centered approach, it is helpful to distinguish between management that derives from the action of participants within the domain (e.g., parents in the home, teachers in school, priests and ministers in religion) and management that clearly comes from outside (most commonly, government attempting to control language practices in the home, school, or church).

Thirdly, I argue that language management is a marked case, motivated either by communication breakdown or by non-linguistic concerns which provide the reasons and values for interference with the existing order. Communication failure drives the model of language management proposed by Jernudd and Neustupný (1987); the non-linguistic concern is most commonly the assertion of or search for power. Shohamy (2006: 44), in her eloquent denunciation of "hidden agendas," sees language policy as "the primary mechanism for organizing, managing and manipulating language behaviors" so that language has become "a tool for the manipulation of people and their behaviors, as it is used for a variety of political agendas in the battle of power, representation and voice." She is echoing the approach of Phillipson (1990, 1992) in his argument that the widespread international acceptance of English as a *lingua franca* is the result of linguistic imperialism, a variety of "linguicism" as proposed by Skutnabb-Kangas (1988), namely "ideologies, structures and practices which are used to the legitimate, effectuate and reproduce an unequal division of power and resources (both material and immaterial) between groups which are defined on the basis of language" (Phillipson 1990: 41). Phillipson in turn ascribed his recognition of the relevance of the power dimension in part to the work of Calvet (1974: 54) who had emphasized the power dimension in colonial language policy: "a dialect is never anything other than a defeated language, and a language is a dialect which has succeeded politically."

In a more recent book, Calvet (1998: 19) proposes that what he calls the war of languages has emerged from an ideological interpretation of the natural diversity which leads to multilingualism, commonly viewed as a curse. The Bible and the Qur'an agree that Babel was a punishment, leaving space for an ideological belief in the superiority of a single language. For Islam, it was of course Arabic. For the ancient Greeks who held a similar view, the world was divided between Greek speakers and barbarians. In the sixteenth century, Joachim du Bellay asserted the superiority of French over all other languages, taking part in the controversy between the French and the Germans as to whose language was closest to the pre-Babel language. There were seventeenth-century scholars who believed that the honor belonged in fact to Dutch, the Low German variety spoken by those who descended the other side of Mount Ararat and so did not have their language confused at Babel. By the late eighteenth century, Antoine Rivarol was asserting both the universality and superiority of the French language.

The opposite view, that multilingualism is not a curse but a blessing, is presented by Haugen (1987), and is the main theme of those who argue for trying to maintain language diversity. But it is seldom the position taken by nations and nationalists. Calvet (1998: 51) argues that multilingualism was dealt with by condemning other languages:

by converting differences into subordination, by considering the language of others as inferior (in general), even as a non-language (as with the Greeks), right from the beginning human beings have laid down the premises of a wall of languages which religious or secular ideologies have then continued. A quite theoretical war, certainly, but one which, as we shall see, developed in different directions and was taken up in less Platonic fashion by the machinery of state.

Language management or planning, then, according to Calvet, arises in the conflicts produced by multilingualism, itself the natural state of all societies, "a fate common to all" (1998: 66). It occurs at all levels, starting with the family unit – he provides data on family language choice in Senegal, Mali, and Niger. The family, he believes, reflects the language conflicts of the surrounding society, with prestige and dominance as the deciding factors. Markets are catalysts for the emergence of *lingua francas*, with prestige or hatred determining language use or avoidance (1998: 88). But while recognizing the possibility of management affecting larger or smaller social units, he argues that language policy, defined as the relationship between language and "social life as a whole, and more particularly between language and national life" is "linked to the state" (1998: 114).

For Calvet, the link of language to the nation-state sets up the typical situation of "warfare," as the state attempts one of a number of possible tasks: to manage the existing multilingualism, to cultivate a language so as to make it more suitable as a national symbol, to choose a unified writing system, and to cultivate by modernizing a national language. He gives an example from Ecuador of indigenous people seeking to preserve their identity through language maintenance. In each of these cases there is a strong political dimension, with language policy as an assertion of or search for power. Shohamy (2006: 25) goes even further: she argues that with the establishment of nation-states, language itself "turned from being a free communicative means of interaction into a closed and stagnated system. From the early nation-state period, language and culture have served as major tools of the state apparatus."

I suspect that the case is more complicated than this. Given the widespread variation in the sociolinguistic ecology of most social groupings, and the even greater variation in most nations, growing all the time as a result of globalization and migration, more and more national governments are being forced, however reluctantly, to face the need for language management. Ancient Persia, we read in the book of Esther, had a policy of communicating with its subject kingdoms and territories in their own languages, providing a corps of translators and interpreters to manage the business. With their monolingual view of the world, the Greeks assumed that everybody would learn their language. The spread of Aramaic in the ancient world and later of Arabic during Islamic conquests followed a similar view, one also adopted by the Spanish, French, and Portuguese in their colonial empires and initially by the British in India. The failure of the policy in India persuaded the British to reconsider the monolingual solution and to attempt rather a controlled multilingual policy, with a limited role for vernacular languages. The quandary was also faced by the new rulers of the Soviet Union after the Communist revolution. Lenin's solution was a strictly pragmatic one: he believed that recognizing national languages would make it possible to achieve communism faster than insisting that everyone use Russian. Stalin's reversal of this policy may well also have been pragmatic – he suspected that the failure of grain production in the Ukraine was the result of the autonomy that Lenin's policy granted. Later, however, Soviet language management was directed at achieving centralized power through symbolic mobilization around the Russian language.

I argue then that national language management aimed at dealing with the communication problems that result from multilingualism without wide enough plurilingual proficiency or a shared *lingua franca* inevitably starts with a domain-internal pragmatically motivated approach. It may well be compounded (as it was in the Soviet Union under Stalin and in post-Independence India) by an attempt to ensure symbolic monolingual hegemony driven by one ethnolinguistic group aiming to gain power in that way. This is not the same as the efforts to create new unifying national languages that were found in the new nations established in the nineteenth and early twentieth century or in the breakup of the colonial empires in the middle of the twentieth century or of the Soviet empire in its closing years. These too of course assume monolingualism as the ideal, the difference being in the choice of language. Similarly, I distinguish between essentially pragmatic efforts to modernize lexicon or reform writing systems and the nationalistically-driven Chinese policy of a single writing system, or the Russian insistence that Cyrillic be used for minority languages or any of the essentially puristic policies of lexical overhaul or modernization, such as in Turkey under Atatürk or in present-day Iceland or France. In other words, I do not automatically assume that national language policy is driven by the desire for power, but argue that in each case we need to find evidence of any major motivations besides the pragmatic.

To sum up, I believe that governments as well as putative language managers in other domains and at other levels are likely to have many different reasons for adopting language policies, as Ager (2001) demonstrates. The challenge is to show which sectors or members of government actually play a role in the language management process (see Chapter 12). We have few studies of this, unfortunately, and so are forced to speak about an undefined "they" who constitute "government."

However, we can do somewhat better when we survey another significant group of participants at the national level, those people or groups who attempt to influence national language policy by persuading the government to support one or more languages. We are looking here not at the formal language planning organizations established by national governments (Domínguez and López 1995; Rubin 1979) which will be looked at in Chapter 12, but at the voluntary associations formed in order to influence national language policies. These are operating in the national (or pre-national) domain, which has three classes of participants – the activists who are would-be managers, the other speakers of the target language (and of other languages) that they wish to enlist or persuade to join them, and the established authority they would like to take over the task of management. In this chapter, we will look at some cases of activism that have been described in the research literature.

Hebrew revitalization as a grassroots movement

I will start with the case of Hebrew, one that I have already written about in several places (Spolsky 1991b, 1995a, 1996; Spolsky and Shohamy 1999, 2001), and that is discussed in Shohamy (2006).

The main lines of development went like this. Eastern European Jews maintained the three-language sociolinguistic ecology that had emerged during the period of Roman conquest and later destruction of the Jewish state. Hebrew (or rather Hebrew-and-Aramaic) served as the language of sacred texts and prayer and for most literacy functions; a Jewish vernacular language (in eastern Europe, Yiddish, but there were many others) was the language of daily life within the community; and the appropriate co-territorial vernacular which was used for communication with the civic government and for business with the gentile community. Towards the end of the nineteenth century, each of these languages became preferred by a different sector of the Jewish population: the co-territorial vernacular by those in western Europe who wished and were permitted to assimilate, a revived Hebrew by the Zionists who supported the re-establishment of territorial nationalism which meant the return to Palestine, and Yiddish by the traditionalists who opposed change and by those who favored cultural non-territorial nationalism. There was an overlap between the two ideological nationalist movements, so that many of those who attended the decisive Tshernovits conference (Fishman 1991a; Glinert 1993) in 1908 were writing in both languages, and adopted a resolution claiming a role for Yiddish alongside Hebrew as "a" and not "the" Jewish language. Supporters of Hebrew were less tolerant and argued for the rejection of Yiddish as a Diaspora language.

But who were these supporters of Hebrew? First, there was a handful of ideologues and scholars, most prominent of whom was Eliezer Ben Yehuda, who saw mobilization around the Hebrew language as a natural continuation of his personal return to Zion. Ben Yehuda founded several language activist organizations. In 1883, he established in Palestine a secret organization called *Tehiat Yisrael* ("the revival of Israel") the purpose of which was to revive the language among Jews in Ottoman Palestine; members of the society were to speak to each other in Hebrew wherever they met. In 1888, he founded a second organization called *Safah Berurah* ("a pure language") to spread the speaking of Hebrew by adults. In 1890, he set up a four-member "language committee" (*Vaad Halashon*) intended to standardize the language. None of those groups lasted more than a year (Chomsky 1957: 234–239).

Second, there was a small group of Yiddish-speaking immigrants in a handful of farming villages who decided that their children should be taught in Hebrew. A pre-school program in Hebrew for four- and five-year-olds started in Rishon le-Zion in 1894. In 1896, three-year-olds were admitted. In 1898, all subjects were being taught in Hebrew in the school in Rishon le-Zion. A teacher was sent to Jerusalem to be trained as a teacher at the Evalina de Rothschild School, in English, and returned to open the first modern Hebrew kindergarten in 1898. More kindergartens were opened in the next few years.

The first formal organization established in support of this activism in 1895 was the Hebrew Teachers Association which adopted Hebrew as the language of instruction, using Sephardic pronunciation; Ashkenazi pronunciation was to be allowed in the first year and for prayer. The next meeting of the Association was not until 1903, convened by the visiting Russian Zionist leader Menahem Ussishkin, who was to move to Palestine after World War One. At this meeting, those present confirmed that Hebrew was to be the language of instruction and chose the direct method for teaching; also, they agreed to use Ashkenazi script and Sephardic pronunciation. Progress was slow, but by 1905 there were reports of children speaking Hebrew outside school and bringing it into the home.

Two important developments followed. The first was the strong commitment to Hebrew of the next wave of Zionist migrants, the founders of the *kibbutzim*, "communal settlements." For ideological and practical reasons, they changed their lives in a number of significant ways – they gave up private property and lived collectively, eating in communal dining rooms and raising their children in communal houses. They adopted a rule of speaking only Hebrew in public, which meant everywhere except in the privacy of the bedroom. The second development was the spread of schools using Hebrew to the cities with growing secular Jewish populations – Tel Aviv, Jerusalem, and Haifa. A major policy decision was made by the Labor movement in Palestine when in 1907 it voted to issue its official journal only in Hebrew, rather than in Yiddish as it had been.

The Hebrew teachers' organization played an important role in the "language war" of 1913. A German Jewish foundation, the *Hilfsverein der deutschen Juden*, whose goal was the advancement of Jews in technologically underdeveloped countries, had already opened a number of Hebrew-medium high schools in Palestine and now was planning to start a tertiary technical institution. The foundation announced in 1913 that the new institution would use German and not Hebrew as the language of instruction, on the grounds that the Hebrew language was incapable of handling scientific concepts. This idea was strongly opposed by teachers and pupils in the *Hilfsverein* schools, and their demonstrations persuaded the foundation to agree to the use of Hebrew in science subjects as soon as possible. In fact, the Technion did not open until ten years later, after the war, in 1924.

Under Ottoman rule, minority communities in Palestine were free to conduct their own educational system in whatever language they chose. A significant step in the establishment of Hebrew as an official language benefited from Zionist political activity in England. The fullest account of the "language war" appeared in a special supplement to the English Jewish weekly newspaper published in 1918, just as General Allenby and the British troops he led were marching into Jerusalem in pursuit of the retreating Ottoman army. This nineteen-page pamphlet (Cohen 1918) combines an account of the language conflict with the report of an incident in which the German consul, accompanied by a Turkish policeman, entered a Jerusalem Jewish school and forced the teachers to switch from Hebrew to German. At the same time, a Welsh Member of the British Parliament (a colonel whose young son had been killed while in Allenby's army in Egypt) asked the Minister of War about the situation in Jerusalem, and whether or not the British occupying forces had already interned the German language teachers found there. The minister replied that he had been told that Jews in Jerusalem spoke Hebrew, and that the army had been instructed to recognize Hebrew as one of the official languages alongside English and Arabic. This recognition of Hebrew was confirmed when the League of Nations awarded the mandate for Palestine to the United Kingdom and was formally included in the King's Order-in-Council of 1920. In 1948, the newly independent State of Israel was to keep this policy in effect, simply modifying it by canceling "any instruction in the law requiring the use of the English language." Behind these crucial events, the key figure was, I suspect, Chaim Weizmann. Weizmann, together with Ussishkin, had persuaded the 1913 Zionist Congress to support the establishment of the Hebrew University, and both of them had opposed the plans to use German in the proposed technological institute. During the war, Weizmann, who had become a British subject, was director of the British Admiralty laboratories, and his contacts with British politicians led to the issuing of the Balfour Declaration which promised support for the establishment of a Jewish National Home in Palestine. It seems reasonable to assume that the Zionist movement and Weizmann were pushing for recognition of Hebrew as an official language, so that political non-governmental activity was mobilized behind the revitalization of Hebrew.

The work of the Hebrew Language Council was interrupted during the war, as many members were deported to Damascus by the Turks and others left for America and Germany. They returned in 1920, and the Council started meeting twice a week in spite of the freezing cold weather, spending their time developing Hebrew terminology for business, carpentry, and kitchen utensils (Saulson 1979: 57). That same year, the presidents of the Council (Eliezer Ben Yehuda and David Yellin) wrote to the Zionist leadership asking for additional funds to support increased activities – the number of members was to be increased to twenty-three. In 1922, the committee, renamed the Hebrew Language College, wrote to the British High Commissioner explaining the importance of standardizing Hebrew and requesting that the College be consulted on the translation of all non-secret official documents (Saulson 1979: 62–5). The work of the College over the next two decades focused essentially on terminology development, a task that was passed to the Academy of the Hebrew Language which succeeded it after the establishment of the state in 1948.

Another grassroots organization of activists supporting the revitalization of Hebrew was the *Gedud l'meginei ha safa* ("Legion for the Protection of the Language"), led by Ussishkin and established in 1923. It conducted campaigns against the two principal enemies of Hebrew. Ussishkin, speaking at a conference of the Legion, attacked those Jews who used English to claim elite status. He was even more bitter in his complaints against those who used the Diaspora language, Yiddish, and the Legion was successful in blocking a proposal to establish a chair of Yiddish at the Hebrew University.

For the first fifty years, Hebrew language revival activities were the work of non-governmental grassroots activists, volunteer scholars, and Zionist political leaders, and depended on free acceptance by the minority Jewish community in British-controlled Palestine and by their educational and other institutions. The majority of Palestinian Jews accepted their views, the major exception being the small anti-Zionist ultra-Orthodox community for whom Hebrew was too sacred to be used for daily life.

As time went on, the Palestine Jewish community took on more of the characteristics of a resistance movement, especially after the publication by the British government of the White Paper threatening to close down Jewish emigration to Palestine, just at the time that the Nazi destruction of the European Jewish communities was getting under way. The *Vaad Leumi* ("National Council") of the community started to take on the appearance of an underground government in preparation. One major activity was the development of the *Hagana*, an underground army. Another, as Shohamy (2007) is now revealing, was a series of policy directives intended to establish the dominance of Hebrew within the minority Jewish population.

The Directive of the Central Council for the protection and encouragement of Hebrew in the Jewish community, issued in August 1939, set out an idealized program: Jews in Palestine must speak Hebrew and only Hebrew wherever they were; the Hebrew that they spoke must be pure; new immigrants must start to learn it immediately; all adults should be tested and hired only if they passed the test; all private names must be Hebraized; newspapers should be published only in Hebrew; only Hebrew dates should be used; and Hebrew courts should be established. A number of further idealized manifestoes were published in 1941 by the Central Council. Each town was to institute a Hebrew day; Hebrew "agents" were to be placed in all industries, professional organizations, factories, and hospitals; all non-Hebrew newspapers were to be banned; all street names were to be Hebraized; and foods were to be labeled in Hebrew. The similarities to the program adopted by the Québec government will be obvious. Another document issued just over a week later set out more plans that they hoped town mayors would adopt. They were to increase motivation for learning, spread slogans, demand that institutions appoint Hebrew language monitors, appoint Hebrew agents to monitor language use, establish action plans to transform all non-Hebrew newspapers to Hebrew, and close theaters that presented plays in languages other than Hebrew. A document two weeks later identified language violators, their violation, and the promised repair: a school which taught some courses in English, the failure to use Hebrew at rehearsals of the National Orchestra, the publication of a diet book not in Hebrew, bad Hebrew used by a café owner, and bilingual advertising for the opera.

Efforts were also made to persuade the British government to encourage the use of Hebrew signs. In Haifa, 128 signs were found that needed correction. Volunteers were sent to homes to count the number of people who could speak Hebrew. Basically, there was no legal authority to enforce any of these plans, but there was the moral weight of public opinion and even reports of violence against people using other languages in public.

If we accept a simple distinction between top-down (meaning governmental) (Kaplan and Baldauf 1997) and bottom-up (meaning grassroots) activity, then we would have to say that Hebrew language revival and revitalization depended on a bottom-up process until the establishment of the State at Independence in 1948. However, this description, sketchy as it is, suggests a much more complex picture. There were individual language activists like Eliezer Ben Yehuda and David Yellin who from time to time set up committees, organizations, and institutions to support and implement their ideas. There were political leaders like Chaim Weizmann and Menahem Ussishkin who worked alone or with existing or newly established organizations to persuade individuals or foreign governments to make Hebrew official and widely used. There were a number of different organizations which played significant roles in the process. One was the Language Council in its various manifestations, which developed from a tiny group of language enthusiasts into the foundation for a fully-fledged language academy. A second was the Hebrew teachers' union which provided the central support for those in the front line of teaching the new language. A third was the Legion for the Protection of the Language which for two decades appears to have been the principal propaganda agency and volunteer enforcer of language use. The fourth was the major organization of the Jewish minority in British Mandate Palestine, the *Vaad Leumi*, which appears to have encouraged Hebrew hegemony both by precept and example, and which established its own language enforcement agency. One of its final pre-state tasks was to plan language education policy for post-Mandate schools, deciding shortly before Independence that schools should teach in either Arabic or Hebrew, depending on the language of the locality.

Once the State of Israel was established, there was no single agency that took over the support of Hebrew, but it was left to various government agencies to continue the ideological struggle. The Ministry of Education and the army were two major implementers of the implicit hegemony of Hebrew, each making major efforts to teach the language to newcomers and to ensure that their institutions and divisions used the language. The Ministry of the Interior also worked with local councils and encouraged the adoption of Hebrew names.

While from time to time individuals attempted to modify national language policy (there have been several unsuccessful attempts to drop Arabic from the status of official language), I know of no voluntary group still working in this direction. However, in the last decade, an Arab Israeli civil rights organization, *Adalah*, has taken language issues to the courts, arguing for the use of Arabic on street and road signs and against a municipal policy banning monolingual Arabic billboards. They also played a role in persuading the government to establish an academy for the Arabic language. Similarly, there are no voluntary organizations working for the status of Yiddish or Ladino, but the government agreed a few years ago to set up and support institutions for each language, confirming in this way that Hebrew hegemony was no longer threatened by these Jewish languages.

Nationalist language activism

Those who assume that language planning and management occurs only at the level of the nation-state miss the richness of activities of grassroots organizations. Haugen's classic study of Norwegian (1966) shows this clearly. When Norway became independent in 1814, some language scholars argued for linguistic independence too. To start with, there was no agreement on what a Norwegian language should be like, but two scholars – Knud Knudsen (who published a grammar in 1856) and Ivar Aasen (who published a more radical grammar and dictionary in 1848) – put forward conflicting proposals, one based more on educated Oslo usage and one favoring folk dialects. Debate followed, intensified when the opposition leftist party supported the second approach, and when it took power in 1885, it established the policy which produced two competing varieties of Norwegian. For the next century, the conflict continued on the political level, with a compromise that recommended both and required schools to teach both. An organization supporting Nynorsk still exists. *Noregs Mållag* ("The Language Organization of Norway") claims 10,300 members in approximately 200 local groups. The first Nynorsk associations were formed as early as 1868. *Noregs Mållag* itself was formed in 1907 and its most recent triumph was in 2003 when it persuaded Microsoft to develop a Nynorsk version of Office for an estimated 400,000 users by threatening a school boycott.

In another Scandinavian nation, Danish patriotic societies developed in the decades around 1800, mainly in Copenhagen but elsewhere as well (Engelhardt 2007). They aimed at economic growth, popular education, and civil rights, but recognized the authority of the government. Danish national identity was often expressed as anti-German feeling – a third of the population of Copenhagen was German-speaking. The societies urged the incorporation of the Danish-speaking parts of Schleswig into the Danish state. Unlike the nineteenth-century nationalists, the patriotic societies considered patriotism to be a matter of attitude and did not mention descent, language, or national character; they had a low opinion of the peasantry, who were seen by nineteenth-century nationalists as the repository of national tradition. The patriotic societies disappeared after the defeat of Napoleon, and the nationalist movement replaced them.

Another classic pre-state language movement was the Gaelic League (*Conradh na Gaeilg*). Founded in Dublin in 1893 by Douglas Hyde, a Protestant, its principal aim was to maintain the speaking of Irish in Ireland. The specific goal, Ó Laoire (1996: 53) argues, was not to make Irish the language of the country at large but to keep it alive where it was still spoken, namely in the Gaeltacht in the West of Ireland. Other ideological leaders also agreed that Irish was not to replace English, but to be maintained in a state of societal bilingualism. The Gaelic league grew, but most of the support for its 593 branches came from middle income groups (MacNamara 1971). With the establishment of the Free State in 1922, the League's agenda was adopted by government, but transformed from societal bilingualism to Irish monolingualism, expressing the anti-English attitudes of the newly independent state. Ó Laoire (1996) and others have shown how this more radical program failed to achieve its aims, leading to compulsory learning of Irish in schools but not to its wider use, and turning out to be far from successful even in maintaining its use in the Gaeltacht (Ó Riágain 2001).

A more recent Celtic activist group is *Cymdeithas yr Iaith Gymraeg* ("The Welsh Language Society"), established in 1962 and said to be inspired by a radio lecture on the state of the language. The Society believes in non-violent direct action, and around a thousand people are reported to have been arrested and charged as a result of their campaigns. Their goals included making Welsh the official language in Wales, going beyond the 1993 Welsh Language Act which declared its equality with English, by making it apply to the private and voluntary sectors as well as government. They call for improvements in Welsh language medium education including major expansion at the tertiary level. Among the victories they claim are the use of bilingual road signs and the establishment of the Welsh language television channel.

The equivalent activist group in Scotland is *Comunn na Gàidhlig* ("The Gaelic Language Society"), a charitable society formed in 1984 at the initiative of the Scottish Office, an office of the United Kingdom government until 1999 when its functions were transferred to the Scottish Executive on the establishment of the Scottish Parliament. In 2003, the Scottish Executive in turn set up a quasi-non-governmental organization, *Bòrd na Gàidhlig*, intended to advise local authorities and to promote the language.

Parallel but supporting a different national language, the Scots Language Society and the Scots Language Centre are activist organizations whose goal is to encourage the use of the Scots language (*Lallans* or Lowland Scots) in Scotland.

The Cornish Language Fellowship (*Kowethas an Yeth Kernewek*) is an activist group promoting the revival of the Cornish language; the Fellowship elects most of the members of *Kesva an Taves Kernewek* ("The Cornish Language Board") which has adopted the standard for Revived Cornish developed by Ken George that is recognized by the majority of new speakers (estimated to be 300 in 2000).

Some of the better-known pre-state grassroots language movements started with a "First Congress" (Fishman 1993). The Flemish Movement developed in the Netherlands after independence in 1830 (Willemyns 1993). Initially, it consisted of a small number of intellectuals and language enthusiasts living mainly in Antwerp and Ghent. They were divided over three major issues: whether to maintain the split from Belgium, their attitude to the Roman Catholic Church, and their attitude to linguistic and cultural integration with the Northern Netherlands; they agreed on the need to fight the domination of French as *de facto* national language. One of their first goals was to achieve a standard orthography, and the system they proposed became official in 1844. In 1849, the *Nederduitsch Taelverbond* (a coordinating organization of Flemish literary and cultural societies) organized a Congress devoted to the advancement of Dutch language and literature. Most of the Dutch papers submitted were scholarly, while the Flemish presentations stressed political issues. The main practical decision was to develop a major dictionary.

In subsequent congresses, practical and political action was proposed; by the end of the century, political action became more serious. There were no congresses between the wars, but in 1949, the organization was reformed under the name *Nederlandse Taalunie* ("Dutch Linguistic Union").

In Israel and in Indonesia, Das Gupta (1977a: 181) points out, Hebrew and Bahasa Indonesia were the respective consensus choice of the nationalist revival. In India, on the other hand, competing language-related associations existed from the late nineteenth century and became "entrenched in a continuous tradition of competition and cooperation." In 1971, Das Gupta interviewed the top leadership of four Hindi associations. Most were over the age of 56, the normal age for retirement in India. More than half had postgraduate degrees, and only a quarter had not completed high school. All were high caste Hindus, generally with comparatively high incomes – two-thirds were either professionals or writers. Most of those that he interviewed were active also in non-language associations. The associations were conceived of as literary, cultural, or educational but not political. Most expressed the rationale for the association as the need to establish an indigenous language as the official language; they also stressed literary and linguistic objectives. The associations were reported to be democratic but the leadership in fact seemed to be drawn from a fairly small group. Most reported that the association they belonged to was "intensely faction-ridden," the divisions being based on personality rather than ideology. The majority believed that making Hindi the national language in place of English was the most important objective of the association; 40 percent thought that the choice of language of instruction and administration was important; a third emphasized language cultivation. Most believed that there were associations opposing Hindi, but with the exception of one Urdu association, they were seen to be regional in nature. Association activities included public meetings and the use of mass media. The members of the Association tended also to be members of the Congress party, whose support they sought. Members were generally dissatisfied with the official language planning agencies. Das Gupta (1977a) concludes that after statehood the weight moved from voluntary associations to bureaucratic agencies, more under the control of national than Hindi pressures.

One of the earliest Indian language associations was *Nagari Pracharini Sabha*, formed in 1893 by a small group of high school students in Varanisi (also known as Benares), a Hindu holy city in the North of India (Mehrotra 1993). Threatened by violence from supporters of Urdu, the meetings were held off-campus. It was agreed that members should use Nagari (Hindi) and work to promote it, establishing branches wherever possible. The organization was open only to males. At the time of its first congress in 1893 there were 12 people present, but by the end of the year there were 82 members, and a hundred years later, nearly 1,000. Emphasis was on the use of the Nagari script.

Mohanty (2002) reports on the establishment at Cuttack in 1867 of a society for the development of the Oriya language, *Utkala Bhassodipani Sabha*, which soon became involved in a bitter dispute with supporters of the Bengali language. The Lieutenant Governor of the Presidency of Bengal issued an order in favor of Oriya, but supporters of Bengali and especially the Calcutta School Book Society continued to resist. By 1871 the local schools in Orissa were using Oriya. Political disputes continued until 1936, when Orissa Province was recognized as a distinct unit. After independence, Orissa became a state with Oriya as its official language. Many of these Indian associations were started by high school students; the active members of the Legion for the Defense of the (Hebrew) Language were also high school students.

The Bangladeshi independence movement is said to stem from a May 21, 1952 student demonstration against the imposition of Urdu. The date May 21, *Ekushey* in Bangla, remains a red-letter day for the people of Bangladesh, and is celebrated in Bangladesh, independent since 1971, as International Mother Language Day.

In Indonesia too, several youth movements at high schools and junior teacher colleges were forerunners of the Indonesian nationalist movement (Moeliono 1993). Moeliono lists seven such movements from 1915 to 1925, in addition to an organization of Indonesian students in the Netherlands. They joined together to organize the first Indonesian Youth Congress in Batavia at the end of April 1926. At the Congress, an Indonesian was defined as any indigenous person from the Netherlands Indies. While no decision on a common language was made, Javanese and Malay were seen as the most suitable; it was suggested that the latter be renamed the Indonesian language, but a decision was postponed until the next Congress. In the meantime efforts were made to unify the organizations and to form a political party. Most of the leaders were in their twenties, and most members were still high school students when the Second Youth Congress took place at the end of October 1928, attended by about 750 people and observed by a contingent of armed Dutch police. After two days of debate, a resolution was passed calling for the adoption of Malay, renamed Bahasa Indonesia, as the "language of unity." The discussions were of course conducted in Dutch.

In South Africa, the *Genootskap van Regte Afrikaners* ("Fellowship of True Afrikaners") was founded in 1875 as a secret society by a small group of religious Afrikaners interested in an Afrikaans translation of the Bible (Holliday 1993). They published a weekly newspaper in Afrikaans. In 1890, the South African Language Union was set up to foster knowledge of the national language and national identity. In 1896, the first Language Congress for Afrikaans was attended by about 90 delegates. A proposal to prepare a bilingual English–Afrikaans dictionary was withdrawn because it might promote English; a committee was set up to prepare a monolingual Afrikaans dictionary and grammar. It was decided to start a monthly literary journal in Afrikaans. The Congress left decisions on Bible translation to the church, but said that Afrikaans must become the language of the church. It also believed that Afrikaans must become the medium of instruction, and called for the development of appropriate textbooks. Afrikaans was not at this stage supported by the intelligentsia, among whom Dutch was the preferred language. After the Anglo-Boer War (1899–1901), a number of local Afrikaans language associations were formed, and at a congress in Bloemfontein in 1909, the South African Academy for Language, Literature and Art was established. The Afrikaans movement combined religious, educational, and nationalist approaches.

The regeneration of Māori

The regeneration (Hohepa 2000) of Māori in New Zealand also began as a grassroots movement (Spolsky 2003a). In 1973 a radical Māori youth movement collected 30,000 signatures on a petition asking for a better Māori language policy. In the late 1970s, another movement for Māori self-sufficiency was active; both helped prepare the way for the government decision to establish the Waitangi Tribunal charged with determining remedies for the failure to implement the 1840 treaty. The Tribunal found that the treaty did require the government to protect the Māori language (Waitangi Tribunal 1986). As a result, the government brought to Parliament the Māori Language Act of 1987, which made the Māori language official and established a Māori Language Commission to promote the language.

In Māori education, too, there was a transition from grassroots to government. There were three contributing strands. *Te Ataarangi* was established in 1979 to promote a unique method of teaching the Māori language, based on the use of Cuisenaire rods (Gattegno 1976). The goals of the movement were to encourage the use of Māori and teach it to adults in the community. Its programs continue to be provided free of charge to participants. The program was created by Katarina Mataira and the late Ngoi Pewhairangi (Mataira 1980). In twenty years Te Ataarangi has trained more than 2,500 tutors and trainee tutors, and brought the language to more than 30,000 learners.

The second was the pre-school *Kōhanga reo* ("language nest") proposed originally at a conference of Māori language teachers in 1979, and endorsed at a large *hui* ("meeting") attended by elders a year later; the first two were opened two years later near Wellington, and by the end of the year there were about fifty similar programs throughout New Zealand. Each program, with twenty to forty pupils, was parent-controlled, meeting in church buildings, on tribal *marae* (a sacred area that is the center of tribal life), in empty school classrooms, or in private homes. The program was originally intended to pass language proficiency directly from Māori-speaking grandparents to their grandchildren (Benton 1989; King 2001). Funding for a National Trust was provided through the Ministry of Māori Affairs, but authority was moved to the Ministry of Education in 1990. The *whanau* ("family") of each individual Kōhanga Reo is chartered by the National Trust and licensed for early childhood education by the Ministry of Education. In 1994, there were over 800 Kōhanga Reo with over 14,000 children.

The third initiative, a development of the Kōhanga Reo movement expressing impatience with the provision of Māori-medium instruction in the regular school system, was the *Kura Kaupapa Māori* movement, when groups of parents established independent Māori philosophy schools. The first was opened in 1985, the second two years later. The 1989 Education Amendment Act made it possible to incorporate these schools within the state system; by 1997, there were fifty-four such schools, each governed by its locally elected school board and catering for nearly 4,000 pupils. The schools, while locally controlled and following an independent curriculum in providing Māori immersion, are now government-supported and monitored like other schools by the Education Review Office.

In New Zealand, then, Māori language regeneration was initiated and supported at the grassroots level both by organized special interest groups and by formally constituted school-governing organizations, the latter structure being partly integrated into the regular government-sponsored educational system, and the whole movement essentially supported by the decision of the Waitangi Tribunal and the passing of the Māori Language Act.

Language activism in Australia

In the 1980s, a rare combination of professional language scholars and grassroots minority language organizations was successful in stimulating Australian government interest in language policy, resulting in the production of a series of policy statements and an associated set of language management activities. These community ethnic groups, described in Clyne (2001), provided important support for the federal government accepting the multilingual program outlined in Lo Bianco (1987). Of particular significance were the ethnic schools, which Clyne (2001: 369) reports provided in 1997 for 90,000 pupils attending supplementary afternoon or weekend schools in 73 languages, including 22,000 in Chinese, 12,000 in Arabic, and 12,000 in Greek. There were also large numbers of non-government primary and secondary schools, a few of which taught ethnic heritage languages (Arabic, Hebrew, German, Yiddish, Greek, and Coptic are mentioned by Clyne). State schools also teach ethnic heritage languages. But, significantly, the National Policy of

Languages of 1987, the main result of which was the establishment of a number of university research centers, did not last, and was replaced by the more narrowly focused Australian Language and Literacy Policy of 1991, which stressed the teaching of English, and the National Asian Languages in Australian Schools Strategy of 1994, which emphasized the need to teach economically significant languages (Lo Bianco and Wickert 2001).

Language activism in the United States

The pioneering study of language loyalty in the United States (Fishman 1966) includes consideration of the large number of ethnic organizations which supported language maintenance among immigrant groups. The whole picture is obviously very complex, but certain generalizations are possible. As a rule, the established melting-pot philosophy meant that the leaders of immigrant groups generally became "the most effective propagandists for Americanization" as they persuaded their fellow immigrant "to put away his foreign ways, learn English, and become a citizen" (Fishman 1966: 366). The major exception was the provision of mother-tongue schools, especially among ethnic religious groups. As a general rule, the organizations provided support for maintenance for the first-generation immigrant, but switched to English for the second. Similarly, the ethnic press was gradually Anglicized.

Two groups are cited as being relatively successful in language maintenance. The first are those immigrants "who have maintained the greatest psychological, social, and cultural distance from the institutions, processes, and values of American core society" (Fishman *et al.* 1966: 396). The examples are nineteenth-century German-speaking fundamentalist sects like the Amish, and contemporary Hasidic sects. The second are those with continuing immigration, the outstanding case in the 1960s being Ukrainians with their parochial schools and ethnic mutual aid societies.

Since then of course the major continuing immigration has been Spanish-speakers. It was their support organizations that were able to take advantage of the civil-rights initiated Bilingual Education Act to develop in the 1970s a strong program of language maintenance in those parts of the country with the most intensive levels of immigration from Mexico, Puerto Rico, Cuba, and Latin America. Community organizations of newly arrived Asian immigrants and of other indigenous language groups (French- and Creole-speakers in Louisiana and the North East, and Native Americans in various parts of the country) also were able to use this initiative to sustain their efforts at reversing language shift.

A reverse thrust came from another grassroots language activist movement, English Only. When Samuel Ichiye Hayakawa was elected US Senator from California in 1976, he proposed an amendment to the US constitution which would make English the official language. His proposal was politely ignored. After he left the Senate in 1983 he founded an organization called US English, which now claims well over a million members and which was successful in 1996 in persuading the House of Representatives to approve a bill making English official. The bill lapsed when it did not receive approval in the Senate. The organization was more successful in lobbying at the state level, and English-only laws have been passed by about two dozen states, although their constitutional status is still in doubt. Two more organizations have been formed. English First, founded in 1986 and claiming 150,000 members, is actively lobbying in favor of English-only legislation and against Executive Order 13166 and various policies supporting bilingual education. A third organization, English for the Children, was set up in 1997 by a Californian businessman, Ron Unz, and successfully lobbied in California in 1998 for Proposition 227 that banned bilingual education in the state. It has conducted similar campaigns in other states. Ironic as it may seem, the most successful US language activist groups seem to be those working against Federal policies supporting multilingualism.

The volunteer stage

While many scholars in the field of language policy tend to stress what they call the "top-down" nature of the process, seeing national language policy as an effort to maintain the power of the central government and the elite which supports it, I have tried to sketch in this chapter the widespread existence of grassroots or bottom-up activist groups. While they lack the power to manage, they can be successful in supporting and spreading beliefs and ideologies which prepare the way for government management, and they can be successful in lobbying for legislation and other management decisions. The classical model was a nationalist organization favoring a particular language whose role was taken over by the state after national independence. Many associations then faded or disappeared once their language was firmly in place. Where language conflict continued to be salient through established or growing multilingualism, there was a place for activist organizations to continue or grow. Many of the organizations have had a much wider agenda than language alone, but language choice continues to be a useful issue for ethnic mobilization. These language activists, then, are significant participants in national language management.

Community language activism: indigenous and immigrant minorities

In this section, I propose to look at some cases of community language activism similar to those that have been described but more like the Māori case, where there is no anticipation of the minority ever becoming a majority, than the Hebrew and other nationalist cases where language activism was part of a movement towards autonomy and eventual independence. The distinction is not precise, but rather represents a gradient condition. There are two classes of minority groups with similar problems but likely to be met with different treatment, as is now especially marked in the European Community policy towards minorities. Again, the distinction is gradient rather than absolute: it is between minority groups classified as indigenous and those classified as immigrants.

Indigenous minorities are generally seen to be comparatively powerless and underprivileged groups which claim and are recognized to have been settled in the territory before the arrival of whatever constitutes the majority population group. Immigrant groups are similarly classified as those who arrived more recently than the majority. By these definitions, the Māoris in New Zealand claimed to be and are recognized as indigenous, while other Polynesians – Samoans and Tongans – are considered and treated as immigrants in New Zealand. However, to complicate the issue, the New Zealand Race Relations Commissioner Joris de Bres pointed out that three Polynesian polities, Cook Islands, Niue, and Tokelau, are considered legally as part of the "Realm of New Zealand" and their citizens are also New Zealand citizens; this, he argued, means that their languages are indigenous to New Zealand and that their languages have special status alongside Māori (Press release of speech by New Zealand Human Rights Commission, September 28, 2007). In Africa or in India, given the multiplicity of ethnic and linguistic groups and the complexity of demographic history, the distinction is less useful, but the so-called Tribal Groups in India (Ishtiaq 2000) probably would be seen as having similar status and demands for the special treatment given to minorities with a long history of discrimination within the territory. Similarly, refugees and other asylum seekers are sometimes accorded a more favorable treatment than other immigrants.

Let me clarify this by some examples. Take a traditional indigenous community in a country that has been colonized and settled by a new group. Before the coming of the English settlers, the Māori inhabitants of New Zealand lived in tribal areas, under the authority of their traditional chiefs, and speaking a common language with minor regional differences. In the early days of missionary contact, some of these chiefs encouraged the development of a writing system and the printing of bibles and other materials in Māori. To start with, schooling was also offered in Māori. In the 1860s, however, the size and speed of European settlement increased, and shortly after that, on the basis of government decisions that were supported by a proportion of Māori leaders, the native school system started to encourage and later insist on a move to English. Over the next half century, more and more Māoris left their tribal villages and moved to the cities. By the middle of the twentieth century, while the tribal organizations were still in place and the centrality of the village and the *marae* as the identifying anchor of tribal membership continued to be accepted, individual Māoris living in the city constituted rather an ethnic or racial group. Language maintenance was in some cases encouraged by Māori churches, but otherwise tended to depend on family ties and connections to the village.

Māori language regeneration was an ethnic movement rather than the expression of tribal government or community. Interestingly, the organization of Māori immersion schooling through the pre-school *Kōhanga reo* or the elementary school *Kura Kaupapa Māori* was the responsibility not of the tribes but of the extended family or *whanau* (Smith 1997). This produces a problem when a school wishes to conduct a formal greeting ceremony for a visitor, for the ceremony must be conducted by a chief of the local tribe, while the teachers and parents are commonly from elsewhere.

The story, however, does not stop here. Language was only one of the mobilizing forces for the Māori ethnic revival: the more central focus (as is common in indigenous peoples' claims) was on land resources. The Waitangi Tribunal (Māori: *Te Rōpū Whakamana i te Tiriti*) is a New Zealand permanent commission of inquiry established by an Act of Parliament in 1975, to make recommendations on the restoration of lands and resources to the Māori people or on the granting of appropriate reparations. The Treaty of Waitangi, which is the basic document, was signed in 1840 by a representative of Queen Victoria and by Māori tribal chiefs. It is therefore natural that the claims have been presented by and the awards paid to Māori tribes. One result has therefore been to reestablish the importance of the tribes and to encourage individual Māoris to claim membership. But only in the case of one tribe, in the South Island where there remain few if any speakers of Māori, have these funds so far been used for a program of language revival.

Some other cases of indigenous schooling

The recognition of the needs of forgotten minorities that accompanied the ethnic revival of the 1960s (Fishman *et al.* 1985) had important results for the Sámi, a people spread over Nordic nations, whose own efforts at regenesis started, Hirvonen (2008) reminds us, in the 1960s. The central feature of this was to mobilize the school to offer Sámi medium education, confirming that school-based reversing language shift activities can and do help. Not unlike the analogous case of Māori in New Zealand, schooling for Sámi was intended for Norwegianization. Only in 1959 did a new regulation permit the Sámi language in schools. Since then, there has been a slow but steady improvement in the legal status of the language, accompanying a series of political actions – the establishment of the Sámi Parliament in 1989, amendments to the Norwegian constitution, and the 1987 Sámi Language Act. In Sámi areas, pupils had the right to education in the language, and similar programs could be set up where there was demand from at least three pupils. The programs were supported by a Sámi curriculum, which also defined a Sámi school as an integral component of Norwegian education. Further reforms in 1998 added individual rights for Sámi children throughout Norway to study the language and for programs in municipalities wherever ten children asked for it. As a result, there has been a continued growth in the numbers of schools offering and pupils studying the language, many of whom are not Sámi. On the surface, then, there has been considerable progress. Looked at more closely, however, Hirvonen finds that there has not been a fundamental change in attitude, so that Sámi remains low in status in school as in society. Most of the programs are at best weak forms of bilingual education. There is no real commitment to language and culture but simply an external framework that awaits committed implementation.

South America provides other cases. The Spanish and Portuguese invaders worked harder and more successfully than almost any other conquering language group (except the Arabs in the Middle East and North Africa) to wipe out autochthonous languages, but while the Arabic-speaking states show little sign of regret, in Latin America there has been a reversal of attitude, with the rights of linguistic minorities starting to be recognized (Hornberger and King 2001). Perhaps it is too late, for the task of remedying centuries of policy is enormous. The numbers are high too. Indigenous peoples make up 10 percent of the region's population, but with major variation in intensity in the various countries, some seventeen of which are reported to be implementing some form of bilingual education, often limited to a few years of primary mother-tongue use and sometimes intended for (but not offered yet) throughout primary years. All the programs are in public education, sometimes in response to demands of indigenous peoples and often dependent on international agency support. The programs are regularly compensatory or remedial, but do also represent political victories for indigenous groups. But López (2008) identifies an unanticipated problem, not just opposition from the establishment, but questioning of the program by indigenous leaders and community. López notes that "reactions against this type of education have begun to emerge, from both the hegemonic and subaltern sectors of these multiethnic societies" (2008: 45). Here, the analogy with the Māori case is striking, producing the same ambivalence in both the "hegemonic" and official and "subaltern" or ethnic groups. This might explain why the South American programs have not yet made a major contribution to saving languages; at the same time, they have confirmed the value to indigenous and minority groups of language as a focus of ethnic and community mobilization.

An example is the schooling of a single group, the Hñähñö, whose 300,000 residents of the high central plateau make them the sixth largest indigenous group in Mexico, in the districts of Mexico City where a good number have been living for some decades (Recendiz 2008). Migration to the city has been one of the major features of twentieth-century demography, with consequent mixing of populations and loss of contact with the original land village where their rights of *tangata whenua* were established. In a sense, they have the worst of two statuses, the lower status of the immigrant and of the indigenous at one and the same time. Furthermore, as Rebolledo demonstrates, it is the poorer and weaker members who migrate to the city and cluster in ghettoized situations. Schooling and school are alien – poverty and culture conspire to discourage attendance. Rebolledo describes one small school that works to overcome this challenge but without any benefit of a bilingual program (for none of the teaching staff know the language).

Salvaging indigenous endangered languages

I had trouble with this section head: originally it was to be "Support for endangered language maintenance"; then I tried "Exploiting language loss." My ambivalence goes back to a colloquium at the meeting of the American Anthropological Association in Mexico City many years ago where a number of local scholars spoke on saving American Indian languages, and defined the task as making sure there were a dictionary and a grammar in the museum. At the time, I was just starting to learn the socio-economic reality of language maintenance and loss for the Navajo. Salvage archaeology is the recording of archaeological remains with a timetable set by the existence of engineering or building plans that will prevent future access. Salvage linguistics is collecting data for language description before the anticipated death of the last speaker. The "last speaker phenomenon" is at the same time a coup for an anthropological linguist whose grammar and dictionary can be expected to remain unchallenged and a tragedy for the people and for the scholar who has devoted many years to patient work with the last source of language knowledge.

Underlying both kinds of salvage is the assumption of uniqueness and the high value assigned to diversity. In spite of the search for linguistic universals, which preceded the work of Noam Chomsky but came to dominate the field under his influence, linguists accept that statements about language structure need to be modified to account for all known varieties. There was a period in the 1960s when American generative linguists seemed to be writing a universal grammar of their own English, but it was soon accepted again that any proposal must be tested against any and all languages. Just as a theoretical model of biology is expected to include all known varieties, so a theory of language must deal with all known language varieties. The sudden realization in the 1990s that languages were being lost at a rapid pace, suggesting that a good proportion of the world's 6,000 or so varieties would not last out the twenty-first century (Krauss 1991), led to a sense of urgency, indeed panic. Seeing that most of these languages are unwritten, all traces of them will disappear, taking with them the unique properties needed to be included in a grammar of the world's languages.

The arguments applied were taken from the movements concerned with the similar threat to biodiversity, the loss of plants and animals that has been recognized to result from human and natural conditions. As forests were cleared for farmland or cities, the flora and fauna of the area were decimated. In much the same way, the loss of small languages whose speakers move to larger ones as they migrate to the city or to another country, or as the city is opened up to them by road and media, is threatening a rapid loss of linguistic diversity.

This then can be seen as a special kind of challenge for language management, but very different from the issue of dealing with communication problems associated with multilingualism. In other sections, I deal with some of the solutions. In the next chapter, I will look at the development of international covenants that assert the natural right of any group of speakers to maintain their heritage, including their own heritage language. In the chapter on schools, I discussed the educational linguists who try to encourage and support school teaching in the heritage language that will make preservation of the language possible, and in the last section I mentioned some current cases of school-related programs. Here, I want to mention the pure salvage operations. They bring another participant into the domain of endangered indigenous languages: just as various tribal groups could once expect to have an ethnographer in residence recording and analyzing their customary way of life, so now there are efforts to see that endangered languages have a salvage linguist working to analyze and record the language before it becomes extinct.

While it is not guaranteed, the process may have valuable effects for the speakers of the language. Ideally, it will lead to the education of the speakers who work with the linguist; once called "informants" suggesting an inferior status, now increasingly they are collaborators in the work of studying the language, and often become teachers of it to others. Seeing their local way of speech recognized as a language, with books written in it, can help to raise self-respect of the speakers and encourage them to speak it with their children. Thus, while the motivation of the salvage linguist and the organizations and foundations that support them may be purely linguistic, with little regard for the speakers, the effects can be socially beneficial.

There are a number of centers working in this field: two of the most recent are *The Minority Languages and Cultures Program* at Indiana University

Bloomington and *The Living Tongues Institute for Endangered Languages* associated with the National Geographic Society. Others include *SIL International* (previously the Summer Institute of Linguistics), *The Language and Ecology Research Forum, Terralingua, Linguapax, The World Language Documentation Centre, Cultural Survival, Foundation for Endangered Languages, DiversCité Langues, The Endangered Language Fund, The International Clearing House for Endangered Languages, Gesellschaft für bedrohte Sprachen e.V.*, and *The Hans Rausing Endangered Languages Project* at SOAS (School of Oriental and African Studies), to list only those that deal with endangered languages as a whole. Each of these provides support for a number of linguists working with endangered languages.

Language activism in the theory of language management

Language activists are significant participants in language management. They constitute individuals and groups whose ideology is clearest in support of the maintenance or revival or spread of a threatened target language. Working at the grassroots level, they attempt to influence existing, former, or potential speakers of the language to continue its use and to persuade government to support their plans. Lacking authority, they depend on acceptance of their ideology by those they try to influence, though as we shall see in the next chapter, they are now commonly encouraged by supranational organizations and by the growing acceptance of views associated with language rights. They attempt to influence two groups – speakers of a language (or ethnic groups associated with the language), and governments who might undertake management favoring the language.

Laitin (2000) agrees with Gellner (1983) that in pre-modern times, most people did not worry about the language of official state business, which was considered a normal basic law like establishing uniform weights and measures. However, many people now believe language conflict to be incendiary, although there is no evidence supporting this belief. From an analysis of the MAR (Minorities at Risk) database, Laitin (2000: 532) found that "the greater the language differences between the language of the minority and dominant group, the *lower* is the probability of violence." Minority language grievances concerning the official language of the state or the medium of instruction were not associated with group violence, even when combined with racial differences or religious grievances. This he explained by the possibility of bureaucratic compromise, the way the state can make language commitments, and the difficulty that minority language activists have in taking collective action. He examined cases in India, where the central government was willing to make concessions to resolve conflict between Marathi and Gujarati in Bombay and between Nagas and Assamese in the Northeast. Similarly, in

Sri Lanka, the 1996 Tamil Language Acts helped limit the range of the civil war. Leaders of language groups can mobilize support for changing language policy, but the result is more likely to be bureaucratic dispute than violence.

Language activists, then, are potentially important participants in ethnic and in national language management; their linguicentrism enables them to concentrate their mobilizing efforts on a single goal, the status of a language. This means also that they can act as a safety valve for separatist pressures: it is cheaper to provide linguistic recognition and even autonomy than independence. Language activists interact with the supragovermental organizations which have become the main proponents of rights for linguistic minorities, to which we turn in the next chapter.

11   Managing languages at the supranational level

The supranational level or domain

The last chapter, concerned with ethnic and language activist organizations and individuals whose goal is to persuade bodies with authority, at whatever level of government, to undertake specific language management activities in favor of the language they support, was a continuation of the exploration of the national domain. These organizations try from time to time to manage the language choices of individual speakers or members of language-related ethnic groups, although it is not uncommon for the ideological goals of the activists to be somewhat ahead of the language proficiency of their members. There was also a not uncommon overlap with religious organizations. In this chapter, before we go on in the next to describe and analyze the organizations and bureaucratic structures charged with the implementation of government language policies, we move to a domain which in a sense constitutes a new level of authority, namely, the supranational organization. I wrote "in a sense" advisedly, for in spite of a widespread belief that twenty-first-century globalization marks the end of the power of the nation-state, devolution and partition of multilingual and multiethnic states into smaller ones constitutes a reaffirmation of the power of the nation-state, and supranational organizations regularly respect the sovereignty of the individual nations which constitute them. Commonly, international policies are expressed in treaties, declarations, or charters which only come into effect when ratified by a certain number of nations and which only bind those nations which ratify them.

As a result, supranational organizations do not so much have authority to set policy as they have the standing to influence nations to set policy. Just as the language activist groups described in the last chapter are participants within the national domain attempting to persuade government to develop a specific policy, so the international organizations might best be considered as activist groups outside the national group with a similar aim. However, supranational organizations do have authority over their own language practices and occasionally have authority over their members, thus constituting a distinct domain. This needs clarification.

206

Monolingual supranational organizations: language diffusion management

During the colonial years, imperial governments were responsible for educational policy and language management in the countries under their rule. Phillipson (1992) was one of the first to analyze these and later developments, especially in British Africa. Efforts to maintain metropolitan languages in former colonies and to encourage their spread to new territories did not stop with the breakup of colonial empires. There continue to be international organizations whose apparent *raison d'être* is language diffusion but whose goal appears to be rather the maintenance of associated power and influence.

The most striking case is France. When independence was granted to former French colonies after World War Two, the gap was partly filled by *Francophonie*, an international movement involving government and non-government elites in more than fifty countries where French was official or widely spoken (Weinstein 1989). More than a dozen French government agencies now share responsibility for these activities. The central institution is the *Organisation internationale de la francophonie*, with fifty-five state and government members. The 2005 Charter of the organization sees it as mobilized around the French language and "universal values" to promote cooperation between sovereign states. Every two years, the heads of states and governments meet and issue summary statements. While language is in the title, the real focus is political, economic, and cultural activity. In 2006, meeting in Bucharest, the organization stressed the importance of education, and surveyed the progress of conflicts in various parts of the world.

A similar model lies behind the recent establishment of the Lusaphone federation, *Comunidade dos Países de Língua Portugues* ("Community of Portuguese Language Countries") formed in 1996 by seven states: Portugal, Brazil, Angola, Cape Verde, Guinea-Bissau, Mozambique, and São Tomé and Principe; East Timor joined when it received independence from Indonesia in 2002. The federation recognizes national sovereignty and works for political and economic cooperation, suggesting that language in the title is rhetorical rather than a primary goal. Language promotion is the task of the *Instituto Internacional da Língua Portuguesa* ("International Institute for the Portuguese Language"), which is responsible for "the spread and popularity" of the language.

The Commonwealth of Nations, a voluntary organization of fifty-five nations that were formerly British colonies or associated with them, shares a common tradition and language, but individual members have their own language policy. The United States is not a member. It is not a political union, nor does the Queen of England or the British government exercise any power through it.

While there is an *Asociación de Academias de la Lengua Española* ("Association of Spanish Language Academies") which coordinates the activities of twenty-two separate national Spanish language academies, there is no similar political union. There are other language diffusion agencies – the British Council, for instance, and the Goethe Institute, but these are nationally established government or semi-government organizations and do not have the political characteristics of the French and Portuguese federations.

Internal policy at the supragovernmental level

League of Nations and United Nations

In studying international organizations, there is a critical distinction to be made between domain-internal policy – what language or languages is or should be used for internal legislative and bureaucratic activity – and the organization's efforts to influence the policy, language or otherwise, of its member states. The problem in the internal domain is much the same as in other organizations whether public or private: how to provide the efficiency of a monolingual operation while dealing with the multilingual background of the legislators and bureaucrats. International organizations, like nation-states, have a choice between a laissez-faire and a directed policy: "Most states require, as a minimum, that their public employees and officials be competent in some state or official language" (Kymlicka and Patten 2003). For an international organization, there is tension between the efficiency of a small number (ideally one) of working languages, and the symbolic claims of all member states.

During the eighteenth and nineteenth centuries, French, replacing Latin, was the language of diplomacy. Its monopoly was broken at the 1919 Paris Peace Conference, when US President Woodrow Wilson and British Prime Minister Lloyd George insisted on English as the second official language (Baigorri-Jalón 2000). Woodrow Wilson referred to the bilingual nature of the treaty being written when he defended his proposal seeking Congressional approval:

When I came back to this dear country in March, I brought the first draft, the provisional draft, of the Covenant of the League. I submitted it to the Foreign Relations Committee of the Senate of the United States, and I spent an evening discussing it with them. They made a number of suggestions. I carried every one of those suggestions to Paris, and every one of them was adopted. Now, apparently, they want me to go back to Paris and say, "We are much obliged to you, but we do not like the language." I suggested the other night that if they do not like that language there is another language in here. That page is English *[illustrating]*; this page is French *[illustrating]* – the same thing. If the English does not suit them, let them engage the interest of some French scholar and see if they like the French better. It is the same thing. It is done in perfect good faith. Nobody was trying to fool anybody else. This is the genuine work of honest men. (Baker and Dodd 1924 Vol. I: 40)

There was early discussion in the League about adding other languages – both Spanish and Italian were proposed in 1920 – but it was agreed to stick to English and French without actually excluding others. The 1924 Covenant of the League of Nations (http://www.yale.edu/lawweb/avalon/leagcov.htm) does not include any reference to official languages. There was also strong but fruitless support for a proposal to use an international language. Some argued for Esperanto, others for Ido, but neither proposal was accepted.

The international organizations set up as a result of the conference – the League of Nations, the International Labour Organization (ILO), and the Permanent Court of International Justice – all continued the English–French bilingual policy. The ILO currently has three working languages, English, French, and Spanish. The Permanent Court had two:

Official languages of the Court were French and English. The choice between these two languages was given to parties. Judgment was delivered in the language of the procedure, in the case of disagreement it was delivered in two languages, one of which was considered as authoritative. Upon the request from one of the parties the Court could have authorized another language rather than one of the official languages. In this case every submitted document should have had English or French translation attached to it. Oral proceeding was in one of the official languages and if parties have chosen a different language, translation from one to another and *vice versa* was made by the Registrar. The party that wanted to use an unofficial language was responsible for translation. (http://www.worldcourts.com/pcij/eng/procedure.htm)

In 1945, the Permanent Court was replaced by the International Court of Justice, established by the United Nations. The International Court continues the bilingual English–French policy.

These organizations used professional interpreters, at first for consecutive interpretation; by 1928, technological advances permitted an experiment with simultaneous interpretation at the 1928 ILO conference with seven languages. The first major test of simultaneous interpretation apart from this was the Nuremberg Tribunal established after World War Two to try Nazi war criminals: the judges were speakers of English, French, and Russian and most of the witnesses spoke German. Using new IBM equipment, simultaneous interpretation saved a great deal of time. The first meetings of the United Nations General Assembly used consecutive interpretation, with the result that a thirty-minute Russian speech required three hours to be translated into French and English. Using a team of interpreters from Nuremberg, simultaneous interpretation for the five official languages was tried and after initial objection to the effects of the technology, was adopted for the General Assembly and other bodies (Baigorri-Jalón 2000).

At its founding, the United Nations agreed to have five official languages: Chinese, English, French, Russian, and Spanish. The secretariat has two working languages, English and French. Arabic was added to the official languages in 1973. There continues to be controversy over the internal language policy: some believe only English should be official, while others argue for adding Hindi as the seventh official language. Spanish-speaking countries complained in 2001 that their status was not as high as that of English. English language documents follow British usage. When the People's Republic of China replaced the Republic of China in 1971, simplified Chinese characters were adopted in place of traditional characters.

Europe and the European Community: internal language policy

After World War Two, Europe was bifurcated by the Iron Curtain, on either side of which sat a politico-military alliance. Established in 1949 by the North Atlantic Treaty, NATO (the North Atlantic Treaty Organization) is an international military defense organization consisting originally of the United States, Canada, and nine western European nations. Others have since joined, including a number of former eastern bloc nations. The official and working languages of the organization are English and French, but NATO also publishes material in twenty-seven other languages. The counter-force during the Cold War was the Warsaw Pact, signed in 1955 in four languages: Russian, Czech, Polish, and German.

The European Union originated as a western European alliance with the goal of forming an economic union, but has developed wider functions and now incorporates eastern European nations. The European Economic Community (EEC) was founded in 1957 by the Treaty of Rome with seven members, but expanded to twenty-seven members and succeeded in 1996 by the European Union set up by the Treaty of Maastricht.

From its beginning, the European Union insisted on the internal use of all the official languages of its member nations. In 1995, France proposed reducing the number of working languages from eleven to five, but the European Parliament rejected the proposal. As a result, the provision of interpreting and translation services has always been a major portion of the budget. In 1999, at a conference to discuss internal language policy, additional problems were pointed out. Already, with only eleven official languages (Danish, Dutch, English, Finnish, French, German, Greek, Italian, Portuguese, Spanish, and Swedish) there were very few meeting rooms with sufficient space for interpretation booths. The planned expansion would more than double the number of languages. De Swaan (1999) argued that member states would not object to a more efficient arrangement, but only if their own language were included.

Current policy is that member states may write to the Union in any official language and expect to receive a response in the same language. Any communication from the Union to a state or to a citizen must be in the official language of the state. All official documents and regulations must be issued in all languages. Candidates for membership were required to translate all relevant Union documents and laws into the national language – some 70,000 pages of material. In 2002, the candidate nations – Bulgaria, Cyprus, the Czech Republic, Estonia, Hungary, Latvia, Lithuania, Malta, Poland, Romania, Slovakia, Slovenia, and Turkey – set up translation units with a staff of ten each. The Union provides full simultaneous translation for heads of governments in meetings of the full Union, scrambles to provide documentation translated into all the national languages for all working groups and committees, and provides more limited translation and interpretation services for these groups. In practice, however, the Union bureaucracy works in English, French, and sometimes German; reports suggest that committees conduct most of their business in English.

De Swaan (2001: 171–173) reported that French had been steadily losing ground to English. In 1991, 90 percent of job candidates were fluent in French, 70 percent in English, and only 16 percent in German. Two thirds of internal communication was in French and about a third in English, with the balance slowly moving. To handle this work, in 1989 the Union had 2,500 translators, 570 permanent interpreters, and 2,500 interpreters hired on temporary contracts. In 1999, interpretation costs came to €325 million, nearly a third of the internal budget. After enlargement, the cost is expected to be over €800 million. The European Court of Auditors complained in 2006 (Committee on Budgetary Control 2006) about wasted expenditure, such as translators booked but not used. It should be enough, they argue, to order languages according to the needs of members of a commission. There were still quality problems with the ten new languages, none of which had met their targets for recruitment of translators. In spite of these concerns, the report reaffirmed belief in the value of multilingualism as "one of the key features of the European Union."

Gazzola (2006) studied the policy as it applies specifically to the European Parliament. The decision on language policy is the responsibility of the Council; the language regime has been extended to additional languages whenever new members have joined, and in fact recently, Irish, which was not included in the original set, has been added. There is a distinction between official languages and working languages. The Parliament and the Council recognize all languages as both official and working, as does the Economic and Social Committee. The Commission has English, French, and German as working languages, as has the Court of Auditors. The Court of Justice has only French as a working language and the European Central Bank has only English.

Gazzola listed arguments in favor of maintaining full multilingual communication – the fact that community law applies to all nations, the need for democratic participation and the quality of all members, and the support given to linguistic and cultural diversity. Efficiency and cost work in favor of a reduction in multilingualism. She analyzed the seven possible language regimes proposed in 2001. These range from monolingualism through reduced multilingualism, controlled multilingualism, corrected full multilingualism to pure full multilingualism. She looked at the cost of each system and asked to what extent it allowed members of the European Parliament to speak and receive communication in their own language. Because some of the relevant factors were not yet known, such as the plurilingual proficiency of new members of the European Parliament, it would take some time to assess the cost of the various possible regimes. From her study of the European Parliament, Gazzola (2006) concluded that the member states of the European community would continue to be willing to pay the cost of maintaining the symbolic sovereignty represented by allowing the use of all official languages. The policy produces many strains – committee members are often personally more comfortable speaking in English or French than in their official language; committee meetings are said to open regularly with an apology for not yet having documentation available in all languages; some nations are under the strain to find qualified translators and interpreters; and the cost is open to easy public criticism. There was, for instance, strong criticism of the cost of providing thirty translators for Irish when no Irish representative is monolingual in that language and few speak it proficiently. But the demand for including Irish and the regional Spanish languages revealed the symbolic weight that the members attached to the internal language policy. It could be that in the course of time practical considerations will move the Union to increased use of one or a few working languages, so that the full panoply of languages will be restricted to ceremonial occasions. However, once the bureaucracy of translation and interpretation services is in place, normal inertia will probably tend to keep it there. Where once Geneva with the League of Nations was the world center of professional translators, Brussels has now taken on that role.

Internally, then, the participants (member states, their representatives, the bureaucrats, and citizens who need to communicate with the organization) set the parameters for language choice, either pragmatically (defined as depending on their proficiency) or symbolically, defined as status that accrues from using a language. Decisions reflect the beliefs of member states and their power.

Influence of international organizations on national foreign language teaching policy

When we turn to the external influence of international organizations, we need to distinguish between the pragmatic concerns of international organizations to make communication with and between their members more efficient, and the role that international organizations have taken in developing, disseminating, and even enforcing human and civil rights in the area of language policy. The first of these is most clearly illustrated by requirements set by the European Union for candidate members to make sure that officials (especially border and customs officials) and other professionals should be proficient in Union languages. This of course applied particularly to east Europe candidate nations whose officials were traditionally proficient in their own language and Russian and who were to be encouraged to add western European languages. This is a classic case of organized language management calling for language teaching to overcome communication problems.

But it affects not just officials but citizens. It is the basis for the interest taken by the Council of Europe and continued by the European Union in the teaching of foreign languages to citizens of member nations. The case is easy to make that such plurilingual proficiency, a term introduced by the Council (Council of Europe 2001; Scharer and North 1992), is a necessary basis for free trade and movement by the citizens of the member nations. Looking at the situation of language learning in Europe, as a result of globalization and the spread of English there is little need to argue for such a policy (except perhaps in the United Kingdom, with the reluctance of its citizenry to acquire other languages). The policy adopted, however, goes beyond a minimalist program by arguing for the need of teaching at least two other languages, in the hope that languages other than English will be added to the regular school program. The Council worked to standardize language teaching (Council of Europe 2001) and assessment (North 1992; North *et al.* 2003) in European countries and to encourage earlier beginning of such teaching (van Els 1993). It also developed schemes for educational visits to other member nations.

Going further, in 2001, the European Parliament adopted a resolution calling for the support of language diversity and language learning. The opening statement in the preamble sets the rhetorical tone: "all the European languages are equal in value and dignity and are an integral part of European culture and civilization." The first section of the resolution "reaffirms that the Member States and the Commission must take measures to enable all citizens to learn languages for purposes of communication as a basis for improved mutual understanding and tolerance, personal mobility and access to information in a multilingual and multicultural Europe." Subsequently, in 2003, the European Commission issued an Action Plan (Commission of the European Communities 2003) which proposed an €8.2 million budget for two years of work on forty agenda items. These include an early start on teaching "mother tongue plus two languages," lifelong learning, better language teaching and teacher training, and building language-friendly communities. No final evaluation report is yet available, but a 2004 progress report lists a number of positive developments in language teaching, noting at the same time the lack of interest in linguistic diversity – most national efforts seemed still to go into learning and teaching English: "The scene is clearly dominated by the steady increase of English as a second language at European and international level, while pupils, students, their families and even policy makers and authorities responsible for the educational systems do not always seem to fully appreciate the importance of teaching and learning additional foreign languages" (European Commission 2004: 15).

The Commission and its staff and committees are attempting to influence rather than simply represent the consensus of member nations and their citizens. National language plus English would achieve the pragmatic goal; national language plus two helps keep a place for other major European languages. These arguments for diversity perhaps help mask the language diffusion goals of France, Germany, and Spain, most likely to be the languages chosen after English. From time to time an "anything but English" rhetoric emerges, as claims are made for Esperanto as a suitable substitute (Phillipson 2003).

Human and civil rights and the role of supranational organizations

An important if relatively ineffective activity of the European Union is to encourage linguistic diversity, handicapped by the need to respect national sovereignty. Perhaps more important is its role as a proponent of human rights in general and specifically as they apply to language. I prefer to avoid the term "language rights" and to talk about human and civil rights relevant to language, to avoid the deification of language and the consequent disregard for speakers that sometimes follows from using this term. The connection is not obvious: one of the standard books on human rights (Donnelly 2003) has no mention of language in its index, and refers to rights of minorities as a comparatively recent development.

References to language in international treaties is not new, however: a 1516 treaty between France and the new Swiss state gave benefits to Swiss who spoke German; the 1815 Act of the Congress of Vienna permitted the use of Polish in some parts of the Austro-Hungarian Empire; and a treaty signed in 1881 protected the Turkish language in Greece (Varennes 1997). There was also protection of religious minorities in the Congress of Westphalia in 1648 and the treaty incorporating Roman Catholic communities into Sweden in 1660 (Ruiz Vieytez 2001). In the middle ages, the notion of linguistic minority was not relevant – peasants spoke local dialects, and the ruling class often intermarried and were plurilingual (Wright 2001). The church, using Latin as the sacred language and *lingua franca*, was international.

Linguistic nationalism started to appear during the Renaissance, as national borders developed and central governments promoted the status of their own chosen standard language. The Reformation, with its development of national churches, was paralleled by religious use of the national vernacular. Some treated every Christian language equally, but there was a growing tendency to prefer one national language over others, as in the *Ordonnance de Villers-Cottêret* favoring French in 1539 and the Act of Union of England and Wales in 1536 favoring English over Welsh. At the end of the nineteenth century, the French Jacobins and the German Romantic philosophers provided ideological support for the belief in the superiority of the national language. Any regional, ethnic, religious, or demographic group that used a different variety was a linguistic minority, membership of which was a cause for peripheralization, exclusion, or forced assimilation, tasks undertaken through compulsory education and universal military service.

In spite of and in opposition to this trend, arguments started to be heard and legislation developed that supported some kind of linguistic diversity. The main argument for recognition of the languages of powerless autochthonous groups was fairness. Deriving from a belief in the civil or human rights of all citizens, it led to legislation against discrimination and at a higher stage to the provision of equal rights. The preservation of linguistic diversity, modeled on arguments for biological diversity, appeared as a goal only quite recently (Grin 1995: 34).

A number of nineteenth-century European treaties included protection for ethnic and linguistic minorities: Serbian autonomy was recognized in the Treaty of Bucharest (1812) and Polish minorities were protected in treaties of the Congress of Vienna (1814–1815) and later (Ruiz Vieytez 2001). The peace talks leading to the Treaty of Versailles and the League of Nations at the end of World War One did award specific rights, including language, to selected minorities in the defeated enemy countries or in their former empires. Austria, Hungary, Bulgaria, and Turkey – the defeated powers – and the new nations carved out of them in Europe and the Middle East were required to agree that all citizens (except Kurds, who were ignored in all Middle East treaties) should be free to use any language in private, in religion, in business, in the press, or at public meetings. They should also be guaranteed access to the civil authorities. Interpretation and translation were to be provided in court proceedings when needed. In a town or district where there existed a sufficient proportion of citizens speaking a language other than the official language, primary education should be offered in the mother-tongue, but learning the official language could be made obligatory.

These treaty provisions were not always implemented. The Greek government ruled in 1925 that its Slav minorities were ethnically Greek, and launched a campaign of assimilation and population exchange (Poulton 1998). In Latvia, independent in 1918, recognition of minority languages was limited by the campaign to reestablish the status of Latvian which had been subordinated to German and Russian; some state elementary and secondary schools even offered education in seven languages (Druviete 1998).

While recognition of minority languages was limited to the territory of defeated enemy states and was not always effective, it did provide a set of models for the legal implementation of human and civil rights related to language. Other countries also provided constitutional protection for minority languages between the world wars: as Finland built up the status of Finnish, it maintained protection for Swedish; Ireland developed Irish alongside English; Belgium worked out a territorial compromise to protect French, Dutch, and German; and pre-Franco Spain recognized its regional languages.

Ironically, in the light of later developments, the nation that developed an exemplary policy of language rights for minorities was the Soviet Union. Under Lenin, the constitution proclaimed the right of "self-determination of all nations" that had been laid down in the 1896 International Socialist Congress of London (Lewis 1972: 72). The policy reflected Lenin's belief that the fastest practical way to teach literacy and socialism was through the ethnic languages; nationalism was a first step towards socialist internationalism. Many (but not all) national groups were told that their languages and their national and cultural institutions were "inviolable." In the 1920s, primary schools teaching in chosen national languages were established, and for the next ten years language minority rights were supported. Martin (2002) considers this to be the most ambitious affirmative action program that any nation had so far attempted. It even worked against Russian, as Russian children in the Ukraine were forced to attend Ukrainian medium schools, and Russian settlers in Turkestan and Kazakhstan were subordinated.

The growing Russian bitterness against the program came to a head during the collectivization of agriculture in the 1930s and the grain famine in December 1932. Stalin was upset by the resistance to collectivization in the Ukraine; he blamed it on the nationalism encouraged by the policy of indigenization (*korenizatsiia*). He began steps to reverse the policy: ethnic village Soviets were abolished, the teaching of the Russian language in schools was upgraded, ethnic units in the army were disbanded, and the national republics were required to follow the Soviet five-year plan. Initially, Martin (2002) argues, this was Sovietization conveniently using Russian as the *lingua franca.* While the Soviet constitution maintained its clauses on language rights, under Stalin there was a growing movement towards Russification. Later, the implementation of the policy became more brutal and violent. Rannut (1995) indeed saw the policy as simply a continuation of tsarist imperialist policies of Russification. He described how it affected his native Estonia: deportation of native Estonians, organized immigration of non-Estonians, required use of Russian in many domains, all showing the ease with which a totalitarian state can enforce language management. At the same time, he points out that there remained token support for the Estonian Academy of Science in its work of terminological development, paying lip service to the constitutional principle. Ozolins (1996) drew attention to the strong resentment that the Stalinist policy produced among speakers of the minority languages, sweeping under the surface ethnic and national tensions that reemerged after the collapse of the centralized totalitarian power.

During the 1920s, then, in western Europe and temporarily in eastern Europe too there started to be legal support, expressed partly in international treaties and partly in new constitutions, for the recognition of language among the human and civil rights of minority groups. In the United States too, the principle emerged as a corrective to the anti-foreigner actions taken after World War One. The key US statement of civil rights is in the fourteenth Amendment to the US constitution, passed in 1868 and laying down the principle of equal protection. In 1923, the US Supreme Court ruled in *Meyer vs. Nebraska* (262 US 390) that while the states could require that tax-supported schools use English as the medium of instruction, they did not have power to do this for private schools. In a second relevant ruling, the Supreme Court found in 1926 that a Philippine Bookkeeping Act that prohibited keeping accounts in languages other than English, Spanish, and Philippine dialects (the target was of course Chinese) violated the Philippine Bill of Rights that Congress had patterned after the US constitution. All of this was to receive more prominence after the end of World War Two.

Parenthetically, who has "language rights"?

Before we go on, it will be useful to set out some of the alternative meanings attributed to what are variously called "language rights," "linguistic rights," or what I prefer to call human (preferred by European organizations) or civil (preferred in the US) rights associated with language use and choice. There are three contrasting interpretations. The most widespread is that these are rights of individuals to choose to use (or learn, or teach) a specific variety of language. Which individuals varies: most commonly, citizens of the nation granting the rights, but more liberally, all individuals – including school children – within the nation. The second view, more controversial and only reluctantly held by sovereign nations and their governments, but strongly argued by language activists, is that these are collective rights given to a defined group of people, normally the speakers of a specific language or variety or the ethnic or heritage group associated with or that once spoke a specific language. The third position is that in some mystical way, the right or rights belong to an objectified labeled language (Blommaert 2001: 135), so that the government concerned is expected to make sure that there are speakers of the language and that they are forced or encouraged to use it. This last position is commonly taken by those who argue that language diversity should have the same status as biological diversity.

Kymlicka and Patten (2003: 30) note the distinction made between universal rights granted to everyone within a particular jurisdiction, and group-differentiated rights granted to members of a designated language group. They also comment on the distinction between individual and collective rights: an individual right can be claimed by any individual within the jurisdiction – an example might be the right of any person charged with a crime to have the charge explained in a language they understand. In contrast, a collective right is often triggered by some threshold level: for example, the language education policy put into effect with the establishment of the State of Israel in 1948 provided that the school language of instruction should match the majority language (Hebrew or Arabic) of the pupils; another example is that civic authorities in some European countries are expected to provide services in a language spoken by 20 percent of the local inhabitants.

One of the more difficult problems facing those who wish to understand the basis for rights to linguistic minorities is how to reconcile majority and minority concerns. This is the main focus of Williams (2008), who deals with recent developments in granting language status to minority groups in a number of democratic nations. He describes the tension between "commonality and fragmentation" (2008: 382) in European nations and in Canada, and presents as a possible solution "cosmopolitan democracy" as proposed by Held (2006), which assumes the granting of autonomy not just to spatial communities but also to overlapping "communities of fate." Indeed, as we have noticed, democracy and pluralism are not automatically in accord: minorities regularly call for autonomy or independence to have their own majority rights.

Wee (2007) is critical of arguments for linguistic human rights, arguing that it takes monolingualism in named languages as its basis, and ignores the growing plurilingualism of an increasingly mobile population and the development of what Gee (2001) labeled "social languages," fluid and often mixed varieties used by a group of people in a multilingual society, and depending on their environment. Only by developing a model that accounts for such varieties can one capture the essence of growing multilingualism. It is noteworthy that what starts out as an argument for multilingualism and diversity easily moves to an argument for the monolingual hegemony of formerly persecuted language.

International organizations on language rights

Successor to the hopes and prayers buried with the League of Nations, the United Nations Charter proclaimed in 1945 respect for human rights and fundamental freedoms, equality, and absence of discrimination. More specifically, the 1948 Universal Declaration of Human Rights included language in article 2/1 as a criterion that might not be used for discrimination.

Continuing its work under United Nations auspices, the International Labour Organization adopted in 1957 Convention number 107 "Concerning the Protection and Integration of Indigenous and other Tribal and Semi-Tribal Populations in Independent Countries." The important clauses were in article 23:

Article 23
   Children belonging to the populations concerned shall be taught to read and write in their mother tongue or, where this is not practicable, in the language most commonly used by the group to which they belong.
   Provision shall be made for a progressive transition from the mother tongue or the vernacular language to the national language or to one of the official languages of the country.
   Appropriate measures shall, as far as possible, be taken to preserve the mother tongue or the vernacular language.

The weakness in references to feasibility is obvious, as is the pragmatic provision that these people must learn the official language. The reference to "indigenous peoples" sets up a hierarchy commonly held. Speakers of the dominant language are assumed to need no protection, although members of the movements like English Only or for the use of simpler language in government documents would disagree. These policies are intended to protect minorities, defined not necessarily numerically but by lack of power (Paulston 1997). Among minorities, self-proclaimed indigenous groups defined as those living in the country before some arbitrarily determined date of conquest or colonization are assumed to have higher priority. Immigrants are considered not to need protection, arguably because they chose to move to a different country. Asylum seekers are presumably also considered immigrants.

Thirty years later, the International Labour Organization adopted an amended Convention (number 169) "Concerning Indigenous and Tribal Peoples in Independent Countries":

Article 28
   Children belonging to the peoples concerned shall, wherever practicable, be taught to read and write their own indigenous language or in the language most commonly

used by the group to which they belong. When this is not practicable, the competent authorities shall undertake consultations with these peoples with a view to the adoption of measures to achieve this objective.

Adequate measures shall be taken to ensure that these peoples have the opportunity to attain fluency in the national language or in one of the official languages of the country.

Measures shall be taken to preserve and promote the development and practice of the indigenous language of the peoples concerned.

This step, according to a brief history on the website of a non-governmental organization promoting the rights of indigenous peoples (Anonymous 2007), was a continuation of a campaign that had started in 1923, when a Haudenosaunee (Iroquois Confederacy of Six Nations) Indian was not permitted to present his case for autonomy to the League of Nations. At the United Nations, the campaign resumed in 1982 when the UNESCO Sub-Commission on the Promotion and Protection of Human Rights set up a Working Group on Indigenous Populations; over the next decade, the Working Group drafted a Declaration on the Rights of Indigenous Peoples, which was presented to the Commission on Human Rights in 1993. Two years later, a new Working Group in consultation with the representatives of various indigenous groups and various non-governmental organizations began work on a new declaration. A compromise document was submitted to the Human Rights Council in June 2006, which adopted it by a majority vote. When, however, it was sent to the Third Committee of the General Assembly in November 2006, the representative of Namibia, on behalf of the Group of African States, asked for the vote to be delayed for a year, and this was agreed to by the committee and the UN General Assembly. Finally, in September 2007 the General Assembly approved a non-binding Declaration of the Rights of Indigenous Peoples. In favor were the votes of 143 states; eleven abstained, and Australia, Canada, New Zealand, and the United States voted against. The African group agreed to support the resolution after it had been amended by adding provision that "nothing in the declaration may be . . . construed as authorizing or encouraging any action which would dismember or impair, totally or in part, the territorial integrity or political unity of sovereign and independent states." New Zealand said it voted against because it conflicted with New Zealand law and because it disadvantaged non-indigenous people. The declaration does not include a definition of "indigenous people." Moreover, its emphasis is clearly on land and political rights, with language only one of many issues to be dealt with.

As Lutz (2007) describes it, the problem is essentially collective as opposed to individual rights. Indigenous peoples, she says, want recognition as distinct groups able to pass on their traditions to their children. They want also a right of self-determination – autonomy rather than independence. They wish to govern themselves but also participate if they choose in the political and economic life of the nation. They want to be free from discrimination, which includes the right to give "free, prior, and informed consent" to any policies that affect them. They want their traditional lands, or reparations for what they have lost. Finally, they want to be free from logging, mining, or environmental planning, or any interference. A major problem for African nations (and presumably others too) is the definition of *indigenous*. Similar problems occurred, Lutz notes, with definitions of other politically weighted terms like *refugee* and *torture*. No agreed definition has been possible that includes all the groups who define themselves as indigenous, and different definitions are used in different countries. The relevant features of a definition will include self-identification as an ethnic group, experience of disruption or dislocation, long connection with a specific territory, and the desire for cultural distinctness. One of the major concerns of governments is likely to be the claims to land resources that have in the meantime been otherwise allocated. The chief activity of the Waitangi Tribunal in New Zealand has in fact been dealing with claims for lost land resources. In these circumstances, one can see why governments perceived claims to collective rights for indigenous peoples as a threat to sovereignty, and were reluctant to adopt the Declaration.

Kymlicka and Patten (2003: 32) note the absence of what they call a "normative theory of language rights." They consider two approaches. The first is "benign neglect," with a state refusing to recognize or support any language just as secular states do not support any particular religion. This might work when one is talking about private rights, but clearly produces serious problems with public institutions. A second is to argue for "linguistic human rights," but it turns out that existing human rights, such as in the Universal Declaration of Human Rights adopted by the United Nations in 1948, have quite limited reference to language issues. Freedom of speech, of the press, of association, and non-discrimination do not deal with such problems as the public funding of the schools of linguistic minorities, the choice of personal names, or the language of government interaction with citizens. In these areas, much more precise approaches need to be found to specific local problems, which are unlikely to be solved by universal statements. Confounding the issue are the two opposed views brought to language policy questions: the belief that the main goal of language policy is linguistic convergence in order to build national unity and social cohesion, and the contrasting belief that the main goal of language policy must be to maintain linguistic diversity (Kymlicka and Patten 2003). The tension continues, and one would be naïve to expect that many of the governments who voted for the Declaration will attempt to implement its provisions.

In fact, international organizations do not so much participate in national language management as they provide moral and rhetorical support for advocates within a nation: the non-binding charter on the rights of indigenous peoples sees itself as setting standards rather than establishing policy. This could help: there is for instance reason to believe that some parts of the US government were influenced by international concerns for civil rights during the period of civil rights activity in the 1960s and 1970s.

The European Community and language rights

Similar ambivalence can also be seen in the positions taken on rights by the European Union. In its internal workings the European Union has allowed each nation to use its own national language – the exceptions were Irish and Letzeburgesh, but the policy now includes Irish and some provision is being made for additional official languages such as Catalan and Basque for Spain. At this level, then, diversity means each member nation can have symbolic recognition of its own national language.

But the Union does also recognize limited rights for minority languages. Some support for selected minority, regional, or stateless languages is provided by the European Bureau for Lesser Used Languages, "a democratically governed Non-Governmental Organization (NGO) promoting languages and linguistic diversity." It is based on a network of *Member State Committees* (MSCs) in all the "old" fifteen European Union member states and many of the new member states that joined in May 2004. In addition, the European Parliament passed a number of resolutions in the 1980s calling for the protection of minority languages. These, and the European Charter for Regional or Minority Languages which was adopted by the Council of Europe in 1992, depend like other treaties on ratification by national governments. The Charter includes in its principles "the protection of the historical regional or minority languages of Europe," supporting "the right to use regional or minority language in private and public life," and stressing "the value of interculturalism and multilingualism," provided only that encouraging minority languages "should not be to the detriment of the official languages and the need to learn them." The Charter then left it to each original member state to determine which minorities were to be recognized and which of a number of possible rights were to be granted to each language. Excluded were dialects, a provision that permitted Sweden to deny an application for recognition by the speakers of Skanian, estimated to have one and a half million speakers. Sweden did recognize three regional or minority languages (Sámi, Tomedal Finnish, and Finnish) and two non-territorial (stateless) languages, Romani and Yiddish.

The Charter permits a member to designate languages as either territorial or non-territorial and requires them to state which of the provisions of the Charter they wish to apply to each language. In part II, there are a number of general provisions and in part III, detailed provisions concerning education at various levels, judicial arrangements, administrative and public services, media, cultural activities, economic and social life, and trans-frontier exchanges. A member must select thirty-five items from part III, including three concerning education and cultural activities, and at least one from each of the other headings. The possibilities of choice are large. In education, for instance, a member may decide to offer ("without prejudice to the teaching of the official language(s) of the State") pre-school education in the language, or "a substantial part" of pre-school education, or to offer pre-school education "at least to those pupils whose families so request and whose number is considered sufficient." If the state has "no direct competence" in pre-school education, it could offer to "favor and/or encourage" one of these provisions. The same pattern provides a choice of provisions for primary, secondary, technical and vocational, university, and other higher education and for adult and continuing education.

Twenty-two nations have by 2007 ratified the Charter – France claims that its constitution, amended in 1980 in preparation for Maastricht, does not permit ratification, and Ireland has not ratified. The members have designated between one and ten minority languages to which the provisions apply: Cyprus has selected Armenian, Denmark selected German, and Norway lists Sámi; Serbia lists Albanian, Bosnian, Bulgarian, Hungarian, Romani, Romanian, Rusyn, Slovakian, Ukrainian and Croatian. Still missing from the list of ratifiers were Belgium, Estonia, Georgia, Greece, Italy, Latvia, Lithuania, Moldova, Poland, Portugal, Romania, Russia, and Turkey, all countries with significant problems with linguistic minorities.

Nic Shuibhne (2001) believed that one could not expect much more from the European Union and the Council of Europe. The Council carefully nurtured support for the ideology of diversity and multilingualism. The Union then designed a system of language management that allowed the sovereign member states to decide how much of the ideology to apply to a select group of their own languages. Varennes (2001) concedes that individuals and minority groups cannot appeal against the form or the implementation of the Charter. In 1985, the European Court of Justice recognized the need to protect the language rights of individuals in the German-speaking municipality in Belgium, but noted that Dutch, French, and German were not classified as minority languages in Belgium.

There have been somewhat more effective if limited attempts to influence language management by the Organization for Security and Cooperation in Europe (OSCE), a security organization which sees its role as conflict prevention (Holt and Packer 2001). The fifty-six participating states agreed that human rights were a concern of the organization, and in 1992, a High Commissioner on National Minorities was appointed to seek "early resolution of ethnic tensions that might endanger peace, stability or friendly relations." Acting independently, the High Commissioner has made recommendations to a number of countries. In 1996, for example, he corresponded with Estonia on the use of language tests and the rights of non-citizens, protecting the Russian speakers against new regulations restoring Estonian. In general, the High Commissioner's recommendations have concerned the educational rights of national minorities, discrimination against Roma, the linguistic rights of national minorities, and the effective participation of national minorities in public life. Recent activities include the development of Armenian-language TV stations in Georgia, the distribution of Bosnian language books in Kosovo, and the training of ethnic Macedonians and ethnic Albanians as mountaineering guides. The High Commissioner presented detailed recommendations to Russia on Ukrainian education in the country, and to the Ukrainian government on Russian education there; to the government of Moldova on language policy; to the Romanian government on the multilingual policy and the place of Hungarian at Babes-Bolyai University; and to the government of Slovakia on various language laws. We have here an individual bureaucrat in an international organization who decided or was persuaded to take a pro-active position concerning language, gathered sympathetic advisers to his committees to support him in persuading his governing body that the steps he took accorded with the goals of the organization, and is now working to deal with specific targets for improving language policies.

Supranational organizations in a theory of language management

Globalization clearly does not yet mean world government; if we think of the world as a domain, it is clear that the various international organizations are very weak participants in its language management. International organizations need to solve their own internal language problems first, problems complicated by the tension between efficiency and respect for diversity. In the main, supranational organizations are able to support notions of human and civil rights, including rights relating to language, without being called on to implement them and face their practical consequences. They can formulate utopian policies without the responsibility to enforce them. Occasionally, they can become participants (such as when European Union courts make rulings on language issues in member states), but unless their charters are ratified and implemented by their otherwise sovereign members, their main influence is in spreading and supporting beliefs about diversity, multilingualism, and human or civil rights that can bolster the campaigns of language activists aiming to persuade their national governments. Thus, they influence beliefs and ideologies more than practices.

12　Language managers, language management agencies and academies, and their work

Agents and agency

The theory of language management that I am presenting insists on identifying agents, and is particularly opposed to what I perhaps a little unfairly dismiss as conspiratorial views of language policy. I have therefore attempted for each domain to explain which participants inside and outside constitute the "managers." I have, however, been somewhat lax in that I have not so far characterized precisely the nature of management. There are obviously several stages in the process: there are the efforts to influence the policy-makers, there is the initiation and formulation of policy, there is the implementation of the policy, and there may be the evaluation and subsequent revision of policy and its implementation. In simple language management (Neustupný and Nekvapil 2003), all of these steps are taken by the individual speaker, but in organized language management, how is it divided?

In the family, like the individual, the processes are likely to be combined. Few families have a family council at which a language policy is hammered out. The family member who tries to manage the language practices and beliefs of other members of the family is likely to be the implementer as well as the judge of the effectiveness of implementation. Parents who try to maintain heritage language see the effect of their efforts, and modify them. It is when we move to the level of more complex social and political organization that we expect to find the function of language management divided between the policy-makers – the writers of the constitution, the legislators, the law courts interpreting constitution and language law, the government ministers setting regulations and determining budgets – and the implementers of the policy – government agencies or ministries and their bureaucrats carrying out and evaluating the policy.

The division is partly artificial, as it will regularly be the case that implementers (agencies or bureaucrats) may independently attempt to develop a policy and certainly will attempt to persuade governments or legislators to adopt or modify a specific language policy. We must therefore expect overlap, and look behind policy statements to try to see who is the active agent involved. For example, the Organization for Security and Cooperation in Europe discussed in the last chapter demonstrates one common process. In 1992, the Organization appointed a High Commissioner on National Minorities to seek "early resolution of ethnic tensions that might endanger peace, stability or friendly relations." The High Commissioner saw language problems as a potential cause of ethnic tension, and with the advice of non-governmental organizations and language activists that he consulted, developed guidelines which he applied in studying language conflicts in some countries and making recommendations to their governments. In the cases that follow, we will need to watch for similar evidence of the division and overlap of policy-making and implementation.

In the organization of this chapter, it seems reasonable to follow the classic division of language policy into status planning, language cultivation, and language acquisition policy. This will also be the place to consider the management of multilingualism by the provision of language services.

Managers enforcing status

Prime place in the study of language management since Kloss (1966) has generally been given to the determination and implementation of policies relating to language status, namely the functions which the manager decides are required or permitted or appropriate for a specific language or variety or set of languages or varieties. In this chapter, I focus on the implementation of policy rather than on its determination, bearing in mind the possibility that implementers may also wish to determine policy. The question then becomes, in any particular political unit, who is it who carries out the will of the constitution writers or the governmental policy-making body (e.g., legislature or cabinet) in deciding what it means that a language is, for instance, *official*? It will be useful to distinguish between those agencies or individuals which are established specifically to deal with language management and those which include language management within the wider responsibilities of the agency.

Agencies that are not specifically linguistic in scope

Decisions on the meaning of the language provisions of the constitution and laws are part of the business of regular law courts. When an Israeli Arab human rights organization wished to challenge the policy of the Haifa municipality which put up street signs in Hebrew and English only, or to modify the policy of the Nazareth municipality which would not permit a billboard advertising apartments for sale with only Arabic on it, it went to court, arguing among other things that this was a breach of the Israeli law that set Hebrew and Arabic as official languages. In Israel, these matters go directly to the Supreme Court, which sets up smaller or larger tribunals depending on what it considers the seriousness of the case. Each country has its own organization of courts. In both these cases, the Israeli courts decided without considering the issue of an official language – in the first, they said it was reasonable to put Arabic on street signs in cities where Arabic speakers made up a good proportion of the population, as they do in Haifa, and in the second they held that it should be possible to advertise in any language. In a more recent case involving road signs, however, a court decision did cite the official policy requiring the addition of Arabic to road signs.

It should be noted that the courts were in fact modifying language management decisions that had already been made at other levels within the system. The street signs were prepared by sign makers following policy laid down by the Haifa city council, and it was the Nazareth city council that attempted to enforce its own regulation requiring the use of Hebrew on billboards. Similarly, it was an unidentified official in the Ministry of Transport who gave instructions to the sign makers as to the languages to be used on road signs.

Government agencies also enforce (or try to enforce) laws of purity. In Malaysia, the Minister of Culture, Arts, and Heritage, Rais Yatim, said that fines of up to 1,000 ringgit (US$290) could be imposed for billboards and posters that display "mutated forms" of Bahasa Malaysia – this was aimed specifically at the mixture of English called "Manglish" (*The Hindu*, June 10, 2007). In Iran, the President issued a decree in July 2006 ordering all government bodies and all newspapers to use words approved by the *Fahange-stan Zaban e Parsi* (Persian Academy) and avoid foreignisms.

One government agency which is massively involved in language management is of course a national Ministry of Education, or in a federal system when education is delegated by constitution to the state level, the state or provincial Department of Education, commonly authorized to decide on school language of instruction and on curricula, including decisions on teaching additional languages. Beyond this, regulations laid down for the qualification of teachers may directly or indirectly manage school language policy. For example, the decision of the US Bureau of Indian Affairs (responsible at the time for Native American schools) to follow the policy of the state in which their schools were located meant that Navajo schools had very few Navajo-speaking teachers in the 1970s; this followed from the application of an Arizona state policy requiring all teachers to have a college degree at a time when only a handful of Navajos were graduating from high school.

Another agency regularly involved in language management is the government agency responsible for radio and television broadcasting, which can determine which languages may be used. State radios are directly controlled.

Fishman and Fishman (1974) document the refusal of the Israeli Minister of Education (in charge of radio broadcasting at the time) to provide news broadcasts in Yiddish. Even where there is no direct control of the language of programs, US FTC regulations in the 1960s required that station logs must be kept in English, so that local Navajo FM announcers were required to write in English what they were saying in Navajo.

The important point here is that almost any government agency may in the course of its normal work implement language policy. The clerk in a government office who cannot or will not use any language except the official language, the government department which prints all its forms in one language, the hospital which has signs in only one language, all are language managers in that they are implementing (or not) a policy laid down for the domain. It is this very non-specialized abundance of decision points that leads many to see a conspiracy in hegemonic situations. Few seem to have the time or patience to track down who it was who decided the languages of a specific sign. In an early study of signs on a post office and a police station on opposite corners of a square in the Old City of Jerusalem, we noted two changes taking place in the same year (1980); the police station sign switched from Hebrew, Arabic, and English to Hebrew and English; and the post office sign switched from Hebrew and French to Hebrew, English, and Arabic, making clear that the decisions were internal to the departments and not evidence of government or national policy. In fact, my guess is that the sign writer had a lot of influence, following aesthetic rather than linguistic criteria. In another study on the Navajo Reservation, we did ask whenever we found one of the rare signs with Navajo as well as or instead of English; in each case, we were told it was a non-Navajo (a store manager or a school principal) who had made the decision. Thus, in the non-governmental domains as well, we regularly find managers and foremen and individual clerks and employees attempting to establish language policy in their own area of competence. As noted earlier, Malinowski (2008) found that many shop owners did not know the reason for their multilingual signs.

In a study of modifications of language policy in Israel as a result of immigration of a million Russian speakers in the early 1990s, Glinert (1995) showed in fact that most decisions appeared to have been made locally rather than centrally. Even when there is a national policy and even in the face of a linguistic hegemony, pragmatic considerations regularly established the importance of local demographic pressures.

Immigration and citizenship

There are two areas in which language management decisions are regularly made by non-specialized agencies of government, and these are the domains of immigration and citizenship. There are of course practical reasons to consider it desirable that the citizens of the modern nation-state are proficient in the official language or languages. It is not uncommon to find the award of citizenship or the right to vote (and in more extreme circumstances, the right to own land) made dependent on knowledge of the official language. In such cases, decisions on the language proficiency of the individual are likely to devolve to regular bureaucrats in the Ministry of the Interior or whatever agency is responsible to register citizens and voters.

Failing some specific legal provision such as the New York State's early twentieth-century requirement for literacy in English, intended to exclude illiterate Italians and Jews literate in Yiddish but not English from the voting register, the fact that the determination of citizenship is usually made at birth means that this policy affects mainly immigrants. In post-Soviet Baltic states, requiring proficiency in the territorial language as a method of reestablishing its status *vis-à-vis* previously dominant Russian became a major issue of dispute when the states were candidates for membership of the European Union, which applied the distinction between indigenous and immigrant languages only to the original members. In other cases, assessment of language proficiency is part of the procedure of admitting immigrants, so that immigration officers or frontier police are authorized to make language management decisions. The classic case in the literature is the Australian dictation test. Drawing on the results of two doctoral studies (Dutton 1998; Jones 1998), McNamara (2005) expands on Davies (1997) to explain the procedure followed. Customs officers were instructed by the Commonwealth Home and Territories Division to use the test "as an absolute bar to such a person's entry into Australia, or as a means of depriving him of the right to remain in the Commonwealth if he has landed" (McNamara 2005: 358). The officer was instructed to give the test in a language which the immigrant did not know. This idea of a language test for control of immigration was first introduced by the British government in Natal in the 1890s (Dutton 1998). In one of its latest developments, the British Prime Minister Gordon Brown announced in September 2007 that migrant workers will have to pass a test of English before they can enter Britain (*Guardian Weekly*, September 21, 2007). All skilled workers from outside the European Union will have to establish GCSE level (C1 on the CEF scale) English proficiency. Separate tests are already in force for migrants seeking citizenship or residence rights. An Australian-born professor of linguistics at the University of London was forced to take an English test in order to extend his work permit.

More recent versions of the use of language tests to control citizenship are reported for the determination of status as Ethnic Germans from the former Soviet Union: German embassy personnel in various former Soviet states were trained as testers and between 1996 and 2000 tested over 180,000 applicants for admission to Germany (McNamara 2005). Even more common over the past fifteen years or so have been efforts to use interviews and expert assessment to determine the country of origin of applicants for asylum as refugees (Eades *et al. 2003*; Reath 2004). This procedure appears be followed by a number of countries including Spain, Germany, the Netherlands, Belgium, the United Kingdom, Sweden, and Switzerland. Private companies in Sweden claim to be experts, but the procedure has been challenged by a number of linguists (Language and National Origin Group 2004).

To sum up, any government agency in a multilingual society can establish a *de facto* language management policy, which may or may not reflect official government policy. When the US Civil Rights Commission began studying the implementation of Executive Order 13166 that required all Federal agencies and all organizations receiving Federal funds to develop a policy for serving limited English speakers, observers were astounded to find how many agencies and organizations were affected. Similarly, the report to the New Zealand Cabinet on progress with Māori language policy reported on all branches of government and intended all non-governmental agencies to be similarly involved (Te Puni Kokiri 1998).

Specialized language agencies

There are agencies and individuals specifically authorized to manage language that constitute the "language police" for a specific domain. The term "language police" was, according to an article in *Wikipedia*, popularized in the American television program "Sixty minutes" describing the activities of the *Office québécois de la langue française* ("Québec Office of the French Language"). The agency was established in 1961 as the *Office de la langue française* in order to enforce the use of French in the province, and its scope was widened by the passage of *Loi 101*, also called the Charter of the French Language, in 1977. The new name was established in 2003 with the adoption of *Loi 104*.

The responsibility of the Office is defined as:

159. The Office is responsible for defining and conducting Québec policy on linguistic officialisation, terminology and the francization of the civil administration and enterprises. The Office is also responsible for ensuring compliance with this Act.

160. The Office shall monitor the linguistic situation in Québec and shall report thereon to the Minister at least every five years, especially as regards the use and status of the French language and the behavior and attitudes of the various linguistic groups.

161. The Office shall see to it that French is the normal and everyday language of work, communication, commerce and business in the civil administration and in enterprises. The Office may, among other things, take any appropriate measure to promote French. The Office shall help define and develop the francization programs provided for in this Act and monitor their application. (http://www.oqlf.gouv.qc.ca/english/charter/title3chapter2.html)

Working with a staff of 256 (including 152 professionals, headed by a deputy minister) in 2005 and a budget of over Can$18 million, the Office, together with parallel agencies, has been active in enforcing the province's language policies, albeit with regular conflicts with courts supporting freedom of expression. *Loi 101* gave power of enforcement, including setting fines, for non-observance of a requirement that commercial signs must be in French. There was objection, and the Supreme Court finally struck down the provision (*Ford v. Québec* (Attorney General), [1988] 2 S.C.R. 712). The amended law (*Loi 104*) requires that French be predominant on commercial signs. The Office acts on its own initiative or on the basis of complaints, most of which are resolved without legal action. Most complaints are about products imported without French labels. The Office publishes a "Guide to Cultural and Linguistic Norms of Québec," a thirty-six-page pamphlet which sets out regulations requiring accented letters (diacritics are required on both lower case and capital letters), organization names (only the first word needs to be capitalized unless it is a proper name), mail and e-mail addresses, telephone and fax numbers, units of measures (a comma needed for decimals, as 2,5 km), abbreviations for days and months (*L* is Monday, *janv* is January), time of day written on the 24-hour clock, money written with the symbol following (47 $ CA), the approved keyboard, how to set up Windows for Québec, and various standards for information technology.

The Office negotiates with businesses their compliance with the language regulations. A new business with over fifty employees has six months to register and then another six to analyze its language use and develop a plan to conduct its activities in French; it is usually allowed two to three years to complete "francization" of all its local activities (it may use other languages only if most of its business is outside Québec). Smaller firms are only required to use French in public signs, general notices, and communication with the public in Québec. This too is under the control of the Office, which stresses that 80 percent of the complaints that come to it are settled without legal action.

In establishing the Office, the Québec government chose a radical path to deal with a multilingual situation. Taking advantage of the degree of territorial autonomy (and testing its limits by adding a clause to *Loi 101* that overrode for some years Canadian constitutional rights to freedom of expression and equality), it gave the Office powers to enforce the use of French in public domains. Most other specialized language agencies, as we shall see, are set up not to enforce status but to deal with various aspects of language cultivation. The term "language police" is more likely to be used, as Ravitch (2003) uses it, to refer to censorship, whether of language or of content. A BBC news article (June 20, 2003) referred to lawyers' attempting to keep trademark brand names like Google and Xerox out of dictionaries and to prevent their generic use ("I googled the topic and xeroxed the article for you") as language police. Actually giving police powers to an agency – the power to fine or punish for using the wrong language – reminds one of schools where children are punished for use of their home language and of police enforcing municipal laws against obscenity.

A second nation that established a specialized agency to enforce language status is Estonia. To implement the 1989 Language Act, a State Language Board was set up, including in its departments a Language Inspectorate. Under the Ministry of Education, it was also responsible for adult language instruction and the training of language teachers. In 1998, the Language Board was merged into the Language Inspectorate, its management and organizational functions decreased and its supervisory role increased. In 2002, there were twenty-two positions in the Inspectorate, including fifteen inspectors. Its primary task is to see that the provisions of the Language Act are observed: it may issue warnings and impose fines. In February 2007, the Secretary-General of Amnesty International wrote to the Prime Minister of Estonia claiming that the Inspectorate was "repressive and punitive in nature" and "counter-productive in promoting social integration and social cohesion." This followed "the amendments of the Law on Language, introduced earlier this month and taking effect on 1 March this year which extend the powers of the Language Inspectorate to recommending dismissals of employees for insufficient Estonian language skills, making people who already have a language certificate re-sit a language exam and nullifying the language certificates of those who fail a re-sit of their language exam" (http://news.amnesty.org/index/ENGEUR510012007).

In Latvia too, a State Language Board has been set up to monitor the Language Act, and to certify Latvian proficiency of the Russian speakers who make up a large part of the population. The State Language Center is part of the Ministry of Justice, and its tasks include regulating compliance with state language laws (Poggeschi 2004).

The Commission of the Lithuanian Language (*Lietuvių kalbos komisija*) began in 1961 as The Language Commission, a non-governmental organization under the auspices of the Lithuanian Academy of Sciences, but is now a state-run institution, under the auspices of the Parliament of Lithuania. It is charged with the implementation of official language status. Commission decrees on linguistic issues are legally binding on all companies, agencies, institutions, and the media in Lithuania. Under the control of the Commission is the State Language Inspectorate which monitors how public and municipal institutions, agencies, companies, and other establishments throughout the Republic of Lithuania adhere to the provisions of the Law on State Language, the decrees adopted by the Commission, as well as other legislation requiring the use of the official language. Municipal authorities are in charge of supervising the use of the official language in their areas, acting through language officers who are employed by more than two thirds of the municipalities (http://www.vlkk.lt/commission/organisation-chart.htm).

Cases of language police are still rare. *Wikipedia* list seventy regulatory bodies responsible for standard languages, but this is a conservative count, as I discovered the existence of four "academies" in the state of Kannada, India: one for the state language Kannada and one each for Konkani, Tulu, and Kodava. But, as far as I can tell, the four in Québec and the Baltic states are the only specialized language agencies with legal authority to enforce the use of official languages. Of course, in many other cases other government bodies, especially education, carry out these functions. Generally, however, the main function of specialized language agencies is language cultivation, including the development of terminology and the encouragement of language purism.

Post-Independence India

India deserves a section of its own not only because of the complexity of the language situation before and after Independence, but also because of the multiplexity of language associations and government agencies involved in the early days of language planning. Exceptionally, there is also an early survey of both governmental and non-governmental agencies. Das Gupta (1977b) interviewed some thirty-six members of the most important Federal and state-level language planning agencies. At a Federal level, agencies existed within the ministries of Education, Home, and Law. Until 1971, the Central Hindi Directorate and the Commission of Scientific and Technical Terminology, later joined into one unit, had been responsible for the promotion and development of Hindi. There was also the Official Language Commission of the Ministry of Law and the Hindi Training Scheme of the Home Ministry. Within education, the Language Division coordinated a number of different agencies. The officials interviewed generally agreed that the most important function in planning was lexical elaboration for education, with codification of less importance. Few saw serious opposition to Hindi at the administrative level. Essentially, the agencies were under the control of their respective ministries and expected to implement government policy. They were small to start with, and lacked status and weight within the ministries. Their makeup was more bureaucratic than academic: their various boards were appointed from above and tended not to publicize their findings widely. They had little if any contact with media. There was little contact also with lower order educational associations, but some with "the higher echelons of the educational sector" (Das Gupta 1977b: 65). Supporters of Hindi working for the government were not expected to be involved in advocacy work, but it was surprising to find a lack of appreciation of the private associations which were active in this area. Summing up, Das Gupta (1977b: 77) writes: "what emerges from our interviews and other sources of evidence is a system of language planning that was politically conceived, bureaucratically conducted, organizationally dispersed, loosely co-ordinated and scarcely evaluated in terms of linguistic, economic and communicational criteria."

As part of a three-nation evaluation study, Das Gupta (1977a) reported on voluntary language associations in India, noting that his colleagues had not found significant activity in this area in Indonesia or Israel. In India, however, such organizations had been in existence since the late nineteenth century and had proliferated and become entrenched. For his survey, he interviewed sixty leaders from four prominent associations. They knew about the government agencies but not what they were doing. Most of them were disappointed with the work of the official language planning agencies.

Das Gupta (1977a) was not unnaturally disappointed at the lack of coordination between government and voluntary language planning organizations, but perhaps this is inevitable in a democracy: in totalitarian systems, like China and the Soviet Union, central planning is a reality; in democracies, only occasionally does one find the kind of uniting of language forces that Lo Bianco managed to achieve for a brief few years in Australia (Lo Bianco 1987).

What is particularly significant for a theory of language management is how few cases there are of regulatory bodies with legal authority over language choice. They are clearly the marked cases. More commonly, language policy is established not by legal fiat of political masters so much as by consensual language practices and beliefs. Because it is consensual, it is harder to pinpoint agency. Thus, the critics expressing concern about the power of a dominant language are forced to blame the historical development of an atmosphere in which linguistic minorities share majority beliefs.

Cultivating languages

Academies

Although the language academy is widely considered the major institution responsible for language cultivation and the maintenance of language purity, there has been surprisingly little study of the history and characteristics of national language academies. A major multi-volume *Encyclopedia of language and linguistics* has a single three-page article on the topic (Mugglestone 2006); a recent book by Fishman (2006) restating and supporting the arguments for corpus planning mentions three academies on two pages and devotes two pages to a photo of the *Académie française* and of the coat of the arms of the *Real Academia Española*; major libraries list proceedings of a single conference (Conference on National Language Academies and Their Mission 1986); and Saulson (1979) has published a collection of documents relating to the revival of Hebrew and the development of the Hebrew Language Academy. Fortunately, however, in the Internet age, these highly traditional institutions now have websites, and Google and *Wikipedia* provide relatively easy access, with all the discomfort one feels at citing these sources.

The first national language academies were founded in the Renaissance: the *Accademia del Crusca* in Florence in 1584, the *Académie française* in Paris in 1635, and the *Real Academia Española* in 1713. Each was concerned with standardizing and codifying the preferred traditional form of their respective languages. Carrying on the recognition of vernacular Italian as a language in its own right and not just a corrupt form of Latin, the *Accademia* published in 1612 a dictionary bearing its name that attempted to remedy the "degeneration" that had been produced by language change since the four-teenth century. The *Académie* too started work on its dictionary of French published in 1640 that recorded only *le bel usage* and that would contribute to establishing rules for the language and keeping it pure (Mugglestone 2006).

But, as Cooper (1989) brilliantly recognized, the motivation of Cardinal de Richelieu, realizing the value of a standardized national language for the unification of a centralized state, was political rather than linguistic when he persuaded a small private club of men interested in literature and language to form themselves into the *Académie*. He gave the new organization the task not just to purify the language but to develop it into a modern tool able to serve science and scholarship and so replace Latin in these roles (Cooper 1989: 10). In practice, the publication of its dictionary was the main activity of the *Académie* over the next three centuries: it also published a short grammar in the twentieth century. Because the dictionary left out words that the highly conservative members of the *Académie* did not approve of, its success was minimal; there has been no complete edition since 1935, although about half of the next edition has so far appeared in two volumes. Recently, the *Académie* has issued statements opposing the use of English loan words and the recognition of feminine forms of certain names of pro-fessions. It continues to define its first task as preserving the French language, but it now devotes most of its energy to act as a patron of the arts by awarding some eighty prizes each year. Members of the academy are appointed for life and selected on the basis of a distinguished literary career. They represent the establishment in literature, and are no more qualified in language manage-ment than the educated layman. In fact, this weakness in language manage-ment has meant that the French government has needed to set up more than a score of other agencies including terminology committees in each of the government ministries. The task of language diffusion has been given to a number of additional committees and agencies.

The work of establishing the monolingual hegemony of French was given not to the *Académie* but spread around a number of government departments. The earliest step was the absolute requirement of the use of French and only French as the language of instruction in schools, a policy initiated by the Jacobins during the French Revolution but the implementation of which was blocked for over half a century by the shortage of French-speaking teachers. Insistence on the use of French by civil servants (one aspect of which was to move them to other districts and so to dialects different from their home ones) in all their internal and external relationships was another important measure. International dealings are included: French civil servants are expected to use only French at international conferences and they are permitted to sign treaties only if the official version is in French. A long series of regulations and laws added to the process. For all its preeminence then, the *Académie française* has been more a symbol than an active language cultivation agency, but a stately emblem of the seriousness with which France considers its national language.

The third academy to be established was *Real Academia Española* in 1713, charged with preserving the purity of Castilian. It publishes dictionaries and grammars, and makes decisions about orthography. Recently, it ruled that only a handful of professions may have feminine forms, and strongly supported the generic masculine for pronouns (Paffey 2007). The dictionary is now available both in paperback and online. In spite of the growing cooperation with other parts of the Spanish-speaking world, there are complaints about the inherent conservatism of the Academy and its preference for Madrid regional variants.

Beginning in 1871, separate Spanish academies were established in Latin America, the first in Columbia; Ecuador, Mexico, and El Salvador followed, and more and more countries were added in the next hundred years. The most recent are Honduras (1940), Puerto Rico (1955), and finally USA (1973). In 1951, there was the first meeting of the *Asociación de Academias de la Lengua Española*. The *Real Academia Española* did not attend, but later joined the Permanent Commission and has been an active member since 1956. The members of the association have shared in developing the dictionary (since the 22nd edition in 2001), a new grammar in press in 2007, and an orthography (published in 1999 as the first joint project). The *Diccionario académico de americanismos* is in preparation, and projected to appear in 2010.

Spain is historically multilingual, as is recognized again since the granting of autonomy to the regions. Some of these languages have their own academies. *The Real Academia Galega* was established in 1906, and recognized by the Galician Autonomous Region in the 1980s. While Spanish is now dominant in Galicia, the Statute of the Autonomous Region of Galicia considers both Galician and Spanish as official languages (Ramallo 2007).

A rival organization, the *Associaçom Galega da Língua*, disagrees with the Academy on orthography; founded in 1980, it promotes an orthography with standardization based on Portuguese rather than on Castilian.

In the Catalan Autonomous Region, the principal language cultivation agency is the *Institut d'Estudis Catalans*, founded in 1918. The Philological Section of the Institute functions as a Catalan academy, working to set norms for the language. The Valencian Autonomous Region also recognizes Catalan as a second official language; it established its own academy in 1998, the *Acadèmia Valenciana de la Llengua*. In Valencia, too, there is evidence of a shift to Castilian (Gimeno-Menéndez and Gómez-Molina 2007). There is a dispute over the name of the variety spoken in Valencia: the present government considers it *Valencian*, but the Superior Court of the community held in 2007 that there is one Catalan language, as accepted by the Academy.

There are other academies in Spain. Aragón is also an autonomous region, and it is reported to have several thousand people who speak it as a second language. While it is not an official language, there is an Academy founded in 1986. In the autonomous region of Asturia, knowledge and use of Asturian is reported to be declining rapidly, but it is protected by the government and taught in schools. The *Academia de la Llingua Asturiana*, founded in 1920, has published a dictionary and grammar of the variety.

Euskaltzaindia is the Royal Academy of the Basque language, legally incorporated in 1919. It is responsible for both the promotion and the cultivation of the Basque language. As a major goal, it aims at the creation and acceptance of a standard variety that will unify the eight major dialects. The Academy is active in developing dictionaries, a prescriptive grammar, and a linguistic atlas. It recommends place names, encourages popular literature, and is working towards the development of standardized pronunciation. It has also started work on a social history of Basque. A new academy, the Institute of Euskara of Navarre is planned to be set up in 2009.

Commonly, academies grow out of non-governmental activist groups, as was described in Chapter 10 in the case of the Hebrew Language Academy and the Indian language associations described there. The pattern is repeated in the Indian state of Kannada, whose official language is also Kannada. *Kannada Saahithya Paishat* was formed as the result of a conference of editors, writers, and others held in Bangalore in 1915 with the aim of uniting Kannada speakers in several provinces, standardizing the writing system, finding a common textbook, publishing appropriate books, and developing scientific terminology. There are also organizations in Kannada supporting other languages: the *Kamataka Konkani Sahitya Academy* is working to develop the teaching of Konkani in schools. The *Karnataka Tulu Sahitya Academy* has a similar program, and like the *Kodava Academy*, is struggling for continued government support.

Not wanting to pre-empt the anticipated labors of a platoon of doctoral candidates needed to fill out the gap in the study of language academies, I will simply mention briefly a few more academies that round out this sketch.

Paschimbanga Bangla Akademi is the West Bengal Bangla Academy, founded in 1986. Older by some thirty years is the *Bangla Academy*, which is located in Bangladesh, and supported by the government.

The Chinese Communist Party and the government of the newly established People's Republic of China accepted in 1949 a literacy campaign and language reform as a central task. The Chinese Script Reform Association was founded that year, and replaced at the end of 1954 by the Committee for the Reform of the Chinese Written Language. In 1955, this committee organized a meeting on the simplification of Chinese characters and a second meeting on the definition of Putonghua. The following year, 2,236 characters were simplified. Putonghua was defined as being based on the vocabulary and grammar of Mandarin with the pronunciation of Beijing as a standard. The committee also issued a plan for a phonetic alphabet, *Hanyu Pinyin*. Between 1957 and 1964, political problems delayed further work, and the Cultural Revolution lasting until 1976 virtually froze the work of the committee. Towards the end of the period, a new draft scheme for simplification appeared, and was widely criticized. The committee was reorganized in 1980, and a revised list of simplified characters was finally withdrawn in 1986. The Committee was renamed "State Language Commission" and placed under the State Education Commission. It soon became clear that alphabetization had been abandoned and simplification was also to be delayed: the principal task became the promotion of Putonghua (Rohsenow 2004).

The efforts for the revitalization of the Cornish language are supported by *Kesva an Taves Kernewek* (Cornish Language Board), founded in 1967 and now governed by representatives of half a dozen groups. It has accepted as standard *Kernewek Kemmyn* (Common Cornish), a form developed by Ken George based on Unified Cornish using medieval sources and borrowings from Welsh and especially from Breton (George 2000). Ken George (personal communication) told me that when he was young, he went to Brittany to learn the language and married a woman from there with whom he spoke Breton. There is opposition to this decision from supporters of other varieties, focused in an organization called *Agan Tavas* ("Our Language") (Williams 1997).

The *Akademio de Esperanto* (the name was adopted in 1948) was founded in 1905 to regulate the language. A second artificial language that has a regulatory body is Ido, controlled by *Uniono por la Linguo Internaciona Ido* ("The Union for the International Language Ido").

Te Taura Whiri i te Reo Māori ("The Māori Language Commission") was set up in New Zealand under the Māori Language Act 1987 to promote the language. It is working on a monolingual dictionary. The first commissioner concentrated on cultivation, but his successors seem more concerned about increasing the number of speakers.

The official language of Uganda is English, but other languages are used in some elementary schools. The most widely spoken is Luganda, supported by the Luganda Society, a volunteer non-governmental organization. There is also the *Lusoga Language Authority* which is responsible for promoting a standard form of Lusoga.

Dutch in the Netherlands and elsewhere is supported by *Nederlandse Taalunie* ("Dutch Language Union"), founded in 1980 by the Netherlands and Belgium, with associate membership for Surinam. A reformed spelling system was issued in 1995 and a revision in 2005. This is reported to have been adopted in Belgium and by schools in the Netherlands, but the media there issued an alternative version in 2006. A second language academy in the Netherlands is the *Fryske Akademy*, founded to study and promote the interests of Friesland. Frisian now has limited official recognition, and the academy publishes the standard diction of Frisian.

The *YIVO Institute for Jewish Research* was founded in Vilna (then in Poland) in 1925 and moved to New York in 1940. It published the first edition of the *Modern English–Yiddish Yiddish–English Dictionary* in 1968. Four volumes (covering perhaps a third of the lexicon) of the *Groyser verterbukh fun der yidisher shprakh* ("Great dictionary of the Yiddish language") were published between 1961 and 1980, but work on it seems to have ended.

Fishman (2006) provides a theoretical consideration of the work of language cultivation organizations, but only mentions three briefly; he reprints an earlier paper (Fellman and Fishman 1977) describing the work of the Hebrew Language Academy terminology committees. He does not assess the effectiveness of the work of cultivation, something that has been largely ignored since the international study in which Fishman participated (Rubin *et al. 1977*) that studied the processes in India, Israel, Indonesia, and Sweden. His book constitutes rather a more moderately worded and more theoretically elaborated defense of corpus planning originally published as Fishman (1983), where he criticized linguists who believed with Hall (1950) that you should "leave your language alone" and lay people like the native-born Israelis who laugh at the Academy, or the Québec francophones who "gnash their teeth" at the objection to *STOP* signs, or the Yiddish speakers who "ridicule the gallons of ink (or is it blood?) spilled over" the spelling of the Yiddish word *fundestvegn* ("nevertheless"). Corpus planners, he argued, were faced with difficult decisions and need to make difficult compromises.

Fishman analyzes the principles accounting for the difficulties. There are, he argues, three distinct dimensions underlying the choices that language academies face in proposing lexicon. The first dimension is the choice between purism (generally meaning using existing words or coining new ones based on the existing language) as opposed to what he calls "folksiness" or "vernacularity," the acceptance of foreign words that appears to happen naturally if unchecked. As a general rule, the academies choose purity. The second dimension is a more extreme version of the first: supporters of uniqueness (keeping all borrowings out) as opposed to the westernization which seems to be affecting most languages as a result of globalization. The third dimension, although with more restricted application, is the opposing pull of classicization and "panification." Classicization is a choice for those languages with a Great Tradition associated with a literary language: classical Greek, biblical Hebrew, Latin, Old Church Slavonic, Sanskrit, classical Tamil, Classical Arabic, or classical Chinese. Each of these languages provides possible models for modernizing vernaculars. Sanskrit is seen as a model for Hindi; standard modern Arabic is strongly pulled to the classical; Hebrew has more or less freed itself from the claims of the biblical language. The second direction is panification, the attempt to develop a new language based on putative classical origins that will unite speakers of dissimilar but related languages. Pan-Germanism was one such movement, and Pan-Arabism was one of the principal arguments against developing and standardizing the local vernaculars. Fishman describes the efforts of the Slavic linguist Ljudivit Gaj in the early nineteenth century to persuade southern Slavs to develop a language based on Illyrian. More successful than this (or efforts to develop a pan-Dravidian or "Maphilindo" as a language uniting Malaysia, Indonesia, and the Philippines) has been the cross-border unification of Flemish and Dutch. The fourth dimension was already partly recognized and named by Kloss (1967), who distinguished between languages that were naturally different (*abstand*) and languages that were modified consciously to be different (*ausbau*). Fishman adds an *ausbau–einbau* dimension, the way in which Croatian and Serbian have been distanced from each other to disprove the Serbo-Croatian myth, or Hindi and Urdu have been built out of Hindustani by selecting Devanagari script and Sanskrit lexicon for the one or Perso-Arabic script and lexicon for the other. *Einbau* in Fishman's proposed usage refers to the tendency of stronger languages to pull weaker ones towards them, as when Yiddish is pulled towards German or Ladino towards Spanish.

Fishman argues that corpus planners must make choices on these four dimensions, the results perhaps clustering at a higher level towards independence (purity, uniqueness, classicism, *ausbau*) as opposed to interdependence. He seems to accept that the real world pressure is towards the latter cluster, but clearly admires the former, with its ideological support for independent smaller languages. Without this ideology, there would presumably be no language academies, organizations nourished by the love of their members for what is special about their own language.

Terminology committees

Terminology committees are commonly central activities of language academies and other language promotion agencies, as changes in language status force cultivation. They face, as Fishman (2006) shows, ideological as well as practical problems in developing new terminology in a language to handle the new concepts, techniques, and devices resulting from modernization and the inter-cultural contact of a globalizing world. Again, this is an area that calls for much more detailed study.

Presumably because it remains one of the few published descriptions of the actual workings of a terminology committee, Fellman and Fishman (1977) has been reprinted in Fishman (2006). Fellman described the work of two committees established by the Hebrew Language Academy, one on librarianship and the second on inorganic chemistry. The librarianship committee was set up to continue the work of a small group of librarians who had been developing Hebrew equivalents for the terms listed in the UNESCO Terminology of Librarianship. The Academy delegated a senior member to chair a joint committee consisting of three staff members and three representatives of the Librarians' Association. There had been an earlier committee on terminology for inorganic chemistry which published a list twenty years before, and the Academy appointed a new committee of eleven members (six from the Academy) to update the previous work. The librarianship committee met fifty times over a three-year period. It developed a preliminary translation of the listed terms and circulated it to librarians and members of the Academy for comments. A revised list was submitted to the General Meeting of the Academy. In a few cases, the Academy asked the committee to reconsider, and the final list was accepted, printed, and distributed to all Israeli public libraries. Government libraries were legally bound to accept the decisions. The inorganic chemistry list was reviewed by a General Committee on Terminology to avoid the problem of Academy members without expertise in the field trying to second-guess the process: approval by the Academy was considered *pro forma*.

The committees took on the extra task of trying to translate every term in the UNESCO lists. Generally, the librarianship committee took accepted usage into consideration, but occasionally "opted for perfection." The chemistry committee had difficulties with the preferences of older members for terms modeled on French patterns conflicting with the preference of younger members for terms based on English patterns. It also had problems in deciding whether to use international chemistry roots in creating Hebrew terms. The librarianship committee had difficulty with Swiss usages on the UNESCO list which did not coincide with French or German terms. Many individual terms of both lists took a great deal of time because of their various meanings in the original language. Meetings of the committees generally lasted three hours and covered fifty to sixty terms. Whenever there was no agreement, a split decision was reported. Staff members regularly reported on established Academy preferences. In chemistry, committee members tended to favor international terms while it was argued that Hebrew coinages would be easier for students. Summing up, Fellman and Fishman (1977: 94) noted that both committees were "constrained to pursue modernization within the general framework of an indigenous Great Tradition which frowns upon foreign language influences in language if not in behavior."

Terminology committees play a major part in language management but most of their work is done quietly in the background. Their efforts may be criticized by an occasional linguist or newspaper columnist, or ignored by most speakers of the language. Like dictionary makers, they provide a valuable service in their hope to modify the language of the general public.

Nomenclature and place names

The naming of places is a fascinating sub-field for language management. While generally we assume that nations should proclaim their own names and the names of their cities, there is a strong English preference to Anglicize country names (Holland, Burma, for instance) and city names (Marseilles, Calcutta). To deal with the resulting complexity, the United Nations established in the 1960s a regular Conference on the Standardization of Geographical Names. The Conference encourages each nation to set up its own national organization and publish its own gazetteer; at conferences, these national agencies report major changes and policies, help disseminate information about place names, and develop standards for Romanization and transliteration. Fifty-four nations were represented at the first conference in 1967 and ninety at the conference in 2007.

The list of delegates makes clear the diversity in national authority. Many nations were simply represented by their UN delegation. The Austrian delegate was from the Institute for the Lexicography of Austrian Dialects and Names of the Austrian Academy of Sciences; the Australian delegates came from the Committee for Geographical Names in Australia; the Belgian delegates were from Institut Géographique National; the Botswanan was from the Department of Surveys and Mapping; Canada was represented by several Federal agencies and Québec; the Chinese sent delegates from the China Institute of Toponymy and other agencies; Cyprus had a delegate from its Permanent Committee for the Standardization of Geographical Names; Estonia sent someone from the Place Names Board; France had delegates from the *Commission national de toponymie*; Iran had delegates from the

National Cartographic Center; Israel (which had just changed its Romanization system so that *Bene Beraq* is now *Bne Brak*) was represented by an Emeritus Professor of Cartography and Toponymy; Jordan sent delegates from the Royal Jordanian Geographic Centre; New Zealand was represented by the New Zealand Geographic Board; the Philippines sent several delegates including two from the National Mapping and Resource Information Authority; Russia was represented by the Federal Agency of Geodesy and Cartography; South Africa sent several delegates from the South African Geographical Names Council and other agencies; Thailand sent a delegate from the Royal Thai Survey Department of Supreme Command Headquarters, Ministry of Defense; the United Kingdom delegates were from the Permanent Committee on Geographical Names; the United States sent delegates from the Board on Geographic Names and other agencies; and there were also delegates from the Holy See and a Palestinian observer.

There has been a detailed study of one of these national committees. Hodges (2007) explains that in Australia, authority over place names was given to state governments in 1904 and that nomenclature advisory bodies appeared in 1916. The first was set up in South Australia during World War One to replace German names. Each state and territory followed its own pattern. In 1984, a central Committee for Geographical Names in Australasia was established, including the state agencies, other government departments, and the New Zealand Geographic Board; since 1993, it is a committee of the Intergovernmental Committee on Surveying and Planning. As well as standardization and the avoidance of overlapping, one task has been to reinstate indigenous names. Unnamed and newly discovered natural features are often given aboriginal names, and sometimes dual names are given. Some names considered offensive have been replaced.

Nomenclature then is an important sub-field of language management, with control and standardization developing at national governmental level with the encouragement of an international coordinating conference. The standardization is needed for efficient operation, so that it is appropriately the concern of professionals, but the decisions involved can have important symbolic weight and regularly lead to local controversy.

Language editors

Whereas once newspapers had copy editors and language editors with the task of making sure that their style preferences were observed and only "good" writing was permitted, the advent of the word processor, even with its automatic spelling checker that cannot distinguish correctly spelled errors and its strange grammar checkers, has meant that writers are left more on their own. This has even affected academic book and journal publishing, where authors are more and more expected to supply camera-ready copy. But there remain stylists and language editors and column writers who regularly check for inappropriate usage. *The New York Times*, for instance, has William Safire, whose column on June 10, 2007 dealt with the British usage "hots up," non-standard to his US ears. He was assured by the US managing editor of the British *Financial Times* where he spotted it that it was a longstanding Britishism (the *Oxford English Dictionary* cites a 1923 use) but more likely to be used in a headline than in the text. Safire went on to remark that the unrelated use of "hottie" as a sexually attractive person was probably a US term, a borrowing from black slang, permissible according to a source if it is no longer in style among black speakers.

While many publishers now ask for camera-ready copy, there is still plenty of work for in-house and freelance copy editors, as well as commercial firms which will edit written text for a fee. Copy editors enforce house styles ("do I need a comma before 'and' in a list?") and sexist language (Einar Haugen was surprised to find all the complaints a copy editor could make about his writing). They thus play a significant role as language managers, often being given the last word on what is printed.

Managers of language acquisition

Internally (language education)

At various levels, language management is concerned with language acquisition (Cooper's term for the third major activity). In the family, the language managers with most effect are those who determine the language to be spoken by children, but as children grow up, their work comes into conflict with peers outside the home, with religious and community leaders, and with the school. The school domain is of course the principal one in which efforts are made at "organized language management" or the teaching of new language variants or varieties. The various levels of government use the school as a principal medium for teaching languages to children, so that such issues as the decision on language of instruction and additional languages are a key activity of government. In the absence of specified language managers, however, this task falls to general educational managers – curriculum officers, school principals, education boards, ministers of education. Recognizing the gap, there is a pressure group in the US currently lobbying for a National Language Advisor, equivalent to the National Science Advisor, to coordinate federal language policy. As a first step, the US Department of Defense has designated senior language policy officers in each of its divisions, in a pioneering attempt to build a new group of professional language managers. There is no such officer in the Department of Education, nor do the state education departments make a similar effort to professionalize language management.

Externally (language diffusion)

In a number of larger nations, there have been formal efforts by the central government to establish agencies responsible for encouraging people outside the territory to acquire the national language. Commonly, these are semi-governmental agencies. The British Council was set up on private initiative but with some government support to teach English and English culture in order to counteract German and Italian cultural propaganda in 1934 (Phillipson 1994); it has survived various cuts in government budgets and the expectation that it pay for itself. In the United States, most such work was undertaken by private foundations (Carnegie, Ford, and Rockefeller) which supported overseas teaching programs and student exchanges, but they did not single out English teaching. The US Information Agency (a branch of the Department of State) includes the operation of overseas English teaching programs and officers, but only for a short time in the 1960s was it a priority of the agency. The principal French agencies for linguistic diffusion are part of the structure of *la francophonie*, a political and linguistic cluster of governmental organizations, institutions and committees responsible mainly for maintaining links with former French colonies (Kleineidam 1992). The French Ministry of Foreign Affairs provides support for several hundred schools abroad teaching French; there are over 100 French cultural institutes and centers and 900 or so local *Alliances françaises* receiving French government subventions for language and cultural programs. There was a German government fund supporting 900 overseas schools by 1914; under the Nazis, half a dozen organizations, including the *Goethe Institut*, handled linguistic and cultural propaganda (Ammon 1992). Post-war, these organizations were reestablished and in 1988 a small coordinating office was set up in the German Foreign Ministry. The private organizations like the *Goethe Institut* (with 149 institutes in 68 countries in 1989, and 142 in 81 countries plus 13 in Germany in 2007) receive heavy government funding on condition that they follow government directives on location and staffing. *El Instituto Cervantes* was established in 1990 and runs Spanish language and culture programs in more than 60 foreign cities (Sánchez and Duenas 2002). For Portuguese, the *Instituto Camões* has established language teaching centers in 23 countries and is planning half a dozen more (da Silva and Klein Gunnewick 1992). The Japan Foundation prepares language teaching materials and supports local Japanese teaching programs at schools and universities around the world (Hirataka 1992). These diffusion efforts focused on language are part of the efforts of former colonial powers to maintain some of the benefits of their lost empires.

Language services

First aid in language management

We turn finally to what help there is for cases where there has not been long-term language management. Even at the individual level, the speaker (and even more the writer) who recognizes a communication problem due to inadequate proficiency may call on a language service to help: the speaker commonly asks his or her interlocutor "How do you say this in your language?" or goes to a dictionary (or a computer) for help. Language services of various kinds – interpreters, translators, reference books, computerized translators – play a key role in first aid, dealing with immediate problems and providing shortcuts to relieve symptoms while waiting for longer-term management to be effective. The growing need to deal with multilingualism brought about by urbanization, immigration, and globalization has served to encourage the growth of language services, most of which have already been discussed in the domains which they serve. This final section then simply summarizes the main features of this phenomenon.

Translation services

Translators and interpreters are the first line of defense against the problems of multilingualism. The earliest empires depended on scribes trained to translate decrees into the language of conquered peoples. The Bible includes references to foreign ambassadors who had learned Hebrew, and repeats accounts of how the Persian king sent letters to each people in its own language. Tribes in multilingual areas depended on captives or foreign wives to make intercommunication with neighbors possible, and skill in other languages was a respected ability. Even at the family level, multilingual children can be valuable in helping family members deal with other-language servants and with the outside world. Once one moves outside the family domain, the need for translators and interpreters increases, reaching its highest point in international business and supranational institutions.

The problem is of course how long it takes to train an efficient translator and interpreter, and the enormous pressures produced in the modern multilingual world have been discussed a number of times in this book. Every day one can read accounts of problems associated with the absence of interpreters – accused rapists released because an interpreter couldn't be found, patients misdiagnosed and dying because the doctors relied on a child to interpret, bad intelligence resulting from shortage of diplomats and agents knowing the language of an enemy. And, as we have also noted, the high cost of providing qualified interpreters and translators produces an understandable backlash against those who argue for providing full civic services for those who have not yet learned the official language. The danger of interpreting for what is perceived as an occupying army has recently become clear; in Iraq, 60 interpreters working for the British forces have been killed, and 250 working for the US Army.

After listening to an account of translation problems of the European Union a few years ago, I rushed straight to the Internet to check up on the current state of machine translation. During the past fifty years, there has been ongoing research, regularly repeating the optimistic claims of the Georgetown experiment in 1954 which produced a program to translate sixty Russian sentences into English; just over ten years later, a report by a group of linguists (Pierce *et al.* 1966) raised serious doubts about the rate of progress. Research, however, has continued, and the problems of dealing with international terrorism have provided impetus for the expenditure of millions of dollars on new experimental approaches which continue to produce useful but far from perfect translations. The latest statement on the state of machine translation sees continued research but no promise of success: "After some 50 years of research, we can affirm that, barring an unexpected breakthrough, machines will not be able to compete with human translators in the foreseeable future. This refers not only to difficult material such as literary works, but also to all but the very simplest and repetitive texts (e.g. weather reports)" (Isabelle and Foster 2006: 405).

In the meantime, entrepreneurship has moved to fill a void; translation is offered by freelancing and employed experts, and computerized versions offer rough and ready help. Translation services are now big business.

Interpreters

Dispatchers have two options when an emergency call comes into a police station in San Joaquin County and the caller doesn't speak English. They can hope an on-duty staff member speaks the caller's language, or they can press a button and be connected automatically to a Thousand Oaks-based translation service. That auto-dial button is pressed often in San Joaquin County, where dozens of languages other than English are spoken. The third-party call goes from the dispatcher to NetworkOmni Multilingual Services, which provides over-the-phone interpretation assistance for businesses and government agencies. The company works with more than 2,500 linguists around the world and staffs language centers in North and South America. NetworkOmni won a three-year contract to interpret statewide emergency 911 calls in April 2005. (*Recordnet.com*, November 26, 2006)

The provision of interpreters and translation is now becoming a major industry. Just as private and commercial language teaching businesses have been quick to exploit the failures of regular educational systems to provide adequate service for the public, so too the rapidly growing demand for interpreters and translators has started to fill the gap recognized in legal, health, business, and military communication. Most major software firms offer some computerized translation, and research continues to provide portable interpreting devices able to actually provide the service in the form of the two-way wrist radio envisaged in the comic *Dick Tracy* in 1946: some such devices have been developed to provide limited interpretation for US soldiers in Iraq. The war in Iraq has shown how much money can be made by providing contract language services: in December 2006, Global Linguistic Solutions was reported to have won a $4.6 billion, five-year contract from the Department of Defense to provide language services to the US Army and other US government agencies in Iraq. The contract called for 6,000 local Arabic translators and up to 1,000 US staff trained in the regional languages.

In New Zealand, the Office of Ethnic Affairs funds a Language Line which provides online free interpreting in thirty-nine languages for the clients of some fifty or so government agencies; since 2003 when the service began, there have been over 100,000 interpreting sessions.

Language agencies and services in the theoretical model

Language agencies are active participants in language management, working essentially to solve long-term communication problems by changing participants or modifying the language. Language services, on the other hand, provide what computer programmers call a "work-around," a way to deal with an unsolved communication problem by providing a translator or interpreter. In some sense, successful language management will do away with the need for translation; in another, cheap and accurate translation will do away with the need for language management. But both complete solutions remain distant goals.

13　A theory of language management: postscript or prolegomena

Introduction

I set out in the first chapter to explore a theory of language management, intending to refine and modify my initial model to account as well as I could for the data that I have found that are relevant to attempts to control language policy, that is to say, to change other people's language practices or beliefs. In this final chapter, I will try to summarize briefly the theory that has survived this consideration. If this can be done in a short chapter, why not write an article rather than a book, my wife asks. I have two answers: first, I needed the space to present the data to support my final opinions, and second, I needed to go through the process of writing to arrive at them. As E. M. Forster wrote, I don't know what I think until I read what I say.

Simple language management: the accommodating individual

Individual speakers and groups of speakers have as a result of their experiences and dependent on their situations developed a complex set of language practices (choices among languages, varieties and variants) and language beliefs (values they assign to those languages, varieties, and variants). From time to time, they discover (or are informed of) a need to modify those practices or beliefs in order to be more effective in communicating with others. Also, from time to time, members of a defined group want some others to change the way they speak or to change the value they assign to languages, varieties, and variants, either to remedy what they perceive as problems in communication within the group or to assert or confirm their own image, status, and power.

To understand this process, it helps to look not just at complete speech communities, but at definable functional socio-political units within a community, which following Fishman (1972) I label domains. A domain is defined by the roles of its participants, its real or virtual locality, and its typical functions and topics. The members of a domain or speech network share values that they assign to recognizable languages, varieties, and variants, but individuals function within several domains, as they are members of more than one network.

When a speaker notes a communication problem in a discourse in which he or she is engaged, it is normal to try to correct the problem, either by repeating, or restating in other words, or in some circumstances by trying another language. This process, called accommodation (Giles *et al.* 1973) appears to be normal and unmarked: its absence is usually condemned or considered rude or pathological. Nekvapil (2006) called this *simple language management*, and considers it the basic level. To avoid similar problems in future, some individuals set about improving their proficiency in the appropriate variety or language by taking some action to learn it, from a book, a tape, or in a course.

In some domains, it is considered desirable and appropriate for certain participants to take responsibility to initiate such correction and learning. The most obvious examples are parents and caretakers in the family domain and teachers in the school domain, who are commonly assumed to have the authority as well as a duty to make it possible for their charges (children or students) to be more successful in their communication inside and outside the immediate domain.

Organized language management: the family domain

This process of correction is the basic functioning of organized language management in a nutshell. But of course, as we look closer, all sorts of interesting complications emerge. Start with the family domain. Assuming that the family nucleus consists only of two adults speaking the same variety and sharing the same beliefs about the values of that variety, children born into or adopted by that family will be exposed to their practices and will acquire their beliefs. But regularly (and increasingly, as a result of urbanization and migration), the family is more complex: the parents may be speakers (by birth or experience) of different varieties, and there may be other significant adults (grandparents, relatives, servants) in the household who speak a different variety. In such cases of multilingualism, we have the first indication of linguistic conflict (Calvet 1998), with a choice being needed between the varieties, and the first possibility for a more powerful participant to attempt to manage the language learning and practices of others. But, as a general rule, the decision and direction follow not only from the pragmatic needs of members of the domain, but also from beliefs coming from perceptions of practices in other domains. Put simply, there is commonly a conflict between values assigned to family tradition (including, for instance, membership in a religious or ethnic group) and values assigned to a language valued in a wider domain (the workplace, or school, or government, for instance).

It is the existence and influence of the other domains that helps account for the development of language policy within the family and helps predict the possible success of internal management. Family policy in turn serves as a significant measure of the effectiveness of wider domains (religious institutions, schools, businesses, ethnic groups, even national governments) in modifying the language practices and beliefs of their constituents, for it is there that natural intergenerational language transmission can be established.

The family/home domain provided a first unit for exploring organized language management, showing the relative strengths of participants and the significance of domain-external influences. As we explored other domains, the same pattern was repeated – a domain-internal relevance of pragmatic considerations related to efficient communication, and domain-external pressures attempting to modify the patterns. But each new domain added new features to the model.

The religious domain

In the religious domain, the critical element turned out to be an extra dominant participant, the divinity; the key question was in what language or variety was it appropriate to receive communication from the divinity (the language of the sacred texts) and to communicate with (pray to) the divinity. We saw variations in the approaches taken by different organized religions to this question: the openness of some (Judaism to a certain extent, eastern and Protestant Christianity, Hinduism, and Buddhism) to translation into the vernacular of sacred texts and the use of the vernacular for worship, and the insistence of others (Roman Catholicism from the Council of Trent until Vatican II and perhaps again; Islam; traditional Navajo medicine men) on using only a single sacred variety. Where a religion maintains the value of a sacred language, a normal consequence is the need either to provide translation into the vernacular or to establish an educational system to teach it to children, starting out in other words to add to and modify family internal management.

The workplace

The next domain studied was the workplace, where again the nature of the regular participants (bosses, workers, customers) sets the basic pattern. Bosses need to communicate with their employees, although often the bilingualism of an intermediate group (foremen, for instance) can provide mediation. Inside industry, it will normally be internal pragmatic considerations that apply, complicated increasingly nowadays in the case of international businesses and outsourcing that encourage firms to set up programs of translation and language teaching. The third set of participants, customers, would seem logically to establish a new level of need for language management, requiring a firm wishing to sell or provide a service to include in its workers an appropriate number with proficiency in the language of the customers. Some do this; others make use of available multilingual translation and interpretation services; while a good number appear to ignore the circumstances, presumably at some cost to their profits.

This is a point at which we need to note that effective language management (or in fact any language management at all) is not the normal unmarked case; there turn out to be many situations in which organizations (and nations too for that matter) would benefit from a language policy, but do not see it as of high enough priority to develop one. Thus, while one would assume that the workplace adds the profit motive as a force for language management, it does not always work. Nevertheless globalization does have an important influence on the workplace, in particular raising the value associated with international languages and especially with English. The result is felt all over, including in nations that are historically and traditionally under the influence of another world language like French, Russian, German or Spanish. Additionally, perceptions of the value of an international language and especially of English permeate other domains: in much of the world today, ambitious parents start their children learning English as early as possible, and select English medium schools for them.

Public linguistic space

We next looked at one aspect of the neighborhood, public linguistic space, divided into public signage (called by some linguistic landscape) and mass media. These two domains show significant evidence of the linguistic policy of the area, adding some further features to a theory of language management. While there are constraining methodological problems (signs reflect literacy rather than oral language use, providing a very biased picture of sociolinguistic reality, and their definition is fuzzy, raising questions about any interpretations of statistics), public signs in a multilingual area provide useful data on the historical and current status of the languages used. Because most studies look at products rather than processes, guesses about motivation are usually in doubt, but in some areas, clear evidence can be found of language management decisions by sign owners or by governments attempting to control and prescribe language choice. The languages of mass media, permitting conjecture about assumed audience, also provide further indications of language management.

The school domain

The school domain is critical in the development of language policy of a speech community. Left to the internal participants – teachers and students – language management should be straightforward: teachers (able to speak also the language of their students) should start with this and move them towards proficiency in this and whatever other variety or varieties the school considers a necessary part of the plurilingualism of an educated citizen. But it becomes much more complex, for teachers are themselves managed by school administrators, who come under authority of a myriad of external authorities, ranging from a school board of parents or local citizens through religious or political bodies at various levels, each of whom has different beliefs and sets different goals and constraints. Commonly, various qualification and hiring requirements mean that teachers do not know the language that their students bring from home (and often the students in a school or a class speak a number of different languages). The state of cultivation of these home languages also varies, making it difficult and expensive to modify them for school purposes even in those comparatively few systems that are willing to try to use home languages as languages of instruction. Both symbolic values and pragmatic constraints then mean that very many children are taught in official or international languages that they do not know, producing at the best a delay in their achievement. There is in fact a wide range of curricular choices in language education, and solid evidence supporting a preference for multi-lingual approaches, but the cases where this is tried turn out to be rare. The unmarked case is for school to use and encourage (if not demand) the national official language, producing a major gap between the language of the family and the school, and putting extra weight on the conflict in the home between varieties. The school domain is under strong external pressure: while schooling is conducted in a closed classroom where the teacher appears to be the manager, teachers' language beliefs and their consequent practices and management activities are largely controlled from outside, from some higher authority.

Courts, hospitals, and police stations

The health and legal systems also turn out to be domains where logic would seem to demand adequate provision for the multilingualism of their public participants. While one would assume that doctors recognize the need to communicate with their patients both in taking a medical history and in prescribing treatment, and that judges would expect accused persons to understand what they are charged with and what evidence is being given, this turns out not to be the norm: health professionals are generally content with using available translators (including the young bilingual children of their patients or cleaning staff), and police and legal professionals also seem to be willing to manage with minimal interpretation. Here again, the solution of the serious communication problems in these life-threatening situations has come from outside the domain, in the US through court decisions and Federal government regulations derived from civil rights, and in Europe and elsewhere from acceptance of human rights provisions. Under these circumstances, the legal and health systems are gradually (while resenting the cost) adding interpreters and translators as normal participants when dealing with patients, accused persons, and other non-professionals who are not proficient in the official language.

Military language management

Military units of various sizes and complexity have developed language management policies to handle the pragmatic needs of efficient operation. At the level of the smallest unit, some (like the French Foreign Legion) assume that foreign recruits will pick up the official army language quickly and that in the meantime, comrades will translate orders. Others (like the Israeli Defense Forces and the contemporary Gurkha Brigade of the British Army) provide language teaching for new recruits that do not know the army language. The Roman army kept speakers of other languages in their own ethnic units, requiring the officers of these units to know Latin in order to deal with their higher level commanders. Similarly, the Indian Army under British rule used an intermediate class of Indian officers able to pass orders from English-speaking officers. At higher levels, such as multinational military coalitions (e.g., NATO or the Warsaw Pact), officers are at least trained in the language of central command.

Armies face an additional language problem – the need to spy on or interrogate speakers of enemy languages. Partly this is solved by using native speakers of those languages (as with the Japanese- and German-speakers recruited in the US military during World War Two), in part by establishing language schools like the famous but unsuccessful ASTP or the less well known but effective Japanese language school that was the ancestor of the US Defense Language Institute (now reputed to be the largest teacher of foreign languages in the US), and most recently in Iraq, by contracting out to industry the supply of interpreters. Recognizing the continuing inadequacy of its policies in the area, the US Defense Department has recently adopted a long-range management plan intended to develop military multilingual proficiency. An interesting feature of this plan is the realization of the need to go beyond the military domain to achieve satisfactory results. Recognizing that learning a language is not efficiently handled in a few weeks or even months, the US has recently announced a National Security Language Initiative (NSLI), essentially (from our point of view) an effort by one branch of the Federal Government (Defense) to involve another (Education) in a domain constitutionally under the authority of state governments.

There are also examples of attempts of other domains to influence the military. The Hebrew teaching of the Israeli Defense Forces accords with the national consensus on immigrant absorption as well as the pragmatic needs of the army. The language training of the wartime Army Specialized Training Program was initiated by universities and their Congressional representatives to keep the colleges in business during a period of military conscription, and did not convince the military of its worth. The advanced language training programs offered, starting with the National Defense Education Act, were accepted with their funding by universities but did not persuade them to improve their language teaching or make it compulsory. It seems unlikely that the under-funded NSLI will have much better chance to break the lack of interest of the US educational establishment in language teaching.

One other example of extra-domain effort to use the military for language management was the Canadian program that aimed to make the armed forces an example of genuine bilingualism. While it contributed to the learning of English by francophones and produced some small progress in the roles of bilingual francophones, the resistance of the Canadian armed forces to this extra-domain intervention seems to have impeded any real success. Essentially, these military cases (and one would welcome more studies to test the tentative conclusions) seem to affirm the possibility of a powerful well-organized domain to carry out and modify its own language management.

Governments managing language

Earlier scholarship dealing with what Nekvapil (2006) thinks can still be labeled language *planning* was generally confined to the activities of the governments of newly independent nation-states. As this book has demonstrated, there is in fact a great deal of language management going on at other levels, starting with the individual and the family. Even at the government level, it is useful to apply a domain model, distinguishing levels of government from nation through autonomous region to local bodies, each with its own defined authority and sphere of influence.

The highest level is presumably the national constitution, depending commonly on interpretation by the courts and implementation by the government. Looking at constitutions revealed two generalizations that serve to correct linguicentrism, the tendency to assume language is central. The fact that many nations do not have a written constitution, and that many constitutions do not mention language, so that many nations do not have a central legal prescription of language status, showed that many nations do not have (or, more likely, do not recognize that they have) language problems. Consequently, clearly stated national language policies appear to be the marked case, depending on some especially manifest multilingualism or the action of some particularly successful activist group. Second, it is normally the case that language management derives from some social, political, economic, or religious motivation, depending on a decision of activists to use language for the mobilization of their claims to identity, recognition, or power. Territorialism as the solution of linguistic problems follows rather than drives political partition, and regularly (as in India and the Balkans) leads to producing rather than solving language diversity. It is difficult to find examples where language diversity was the motivating factor for partition, unless it be independent India, where after partition the division into states tried to set their boundaries to encompass a major common language (but at the same time ignored all the other Indian varieties).

That leads to another important generalization. The normal unmarked tendency of nation-states and their government is towards monolingualism, which serves the double purpose of more efficient communication and mobilization for a unified national identity. In comparatively few nations, multilingualism is recognized in the constitution (but seldom with the complete commitment of the Soviet constitution under Lenin) but implementation then turns out to be quite uneven: Hindi and English tend to dominate India and with the other constitutional languages to swamp all the minor varieties; English and Afrikaans struggle for pride of place in South Africa, and the other nine official languages get limited attention; Belgium and Switzerland divide up their polities into small regions, in each of which a single language is dominant; Israel tries to ignore the official status of Arabic; Arab states pay no attention to minority languages like Berber and Kurdish or even their own local colloquial varieties; Sri Lanka is far from satisfying its Tamil speakers; most African and Asian nations pay only lip service, if that, to their multilingualism. The pattern is demonstrated by activist movements like Irish: originally, the goal of the Gaelic League was strengthening Gaelic to produce bilingualism; then, with the establishment of the Irish Free State, the ideology hardened and the unrealizable and unrealized goal became monolingual hegemony; and now all that is left is an effort to maintain an endangered variety.

Newly independent nations (whether in the mid- or late-nineteenth century, in the breakup of colonial empires after the two world wars, or in the fragmentation of the Soviet Union, Czechoslovakia, and Yugoslavia) took advantage of autonomy to promote either their former territorial language (as in the Baltic states and the Caucasus) or to hasten to differentiate their previously fused language into distinct varieties that would match their new flags and frontiers. Nations have certainly not disappeared in the twenty-first century; in spite of globalization and the existence of supranational businesses and political unions, the pressure for symbolic identity controls their language policy, practices, beliefs, and management alike. Totalitarian governments seem to be able to keep linguistic minorities and other potential dissident groups under tight control; democracies struggle to prevent minorities from seceding into new states where they can become majorities.

Language management occurs at many levels of the modern state. Federal constitutions often leave education (and language) to the states, which are more open to recognizing and responding to regional concerns and to the pressures of activists unable to move national policy. Where there is complex multilingualism (and this generally occurs first at the city level), local bodies (city and town governments for instance) are likely to attempt language management in the areas of their competence – interaction with their citizens, education if under their control, and public signage.

Unfortunately, few studies enable us to see behind generalizations about government policy to identify the actual agents and agencies. We do not know enough about individual cases except rarely (e.g., Kemal Atatürk and his reform of Turkish, or Prime Minister Mahathir of Malaysia who reversed school language policy in 2002, or the changes in Soviet language policy that followed Stalin's accession to power) to be able to assign specific responsibility. This fuzziness of agency perhaps helps account for the tendency of some scholars to ascribe motives (a desire for power, for instance) to language policies that may well turn out to have been the result of complex compromises at various levels.

Finally, the fact that national language policies are built on top of sets of policies at lower levels and in different domains no doubt helps account for their common ineffectiveness: only a determined totalitarian state can enforce at all levels the sweeping changes in language practices and beliefs that some plans call for.

Activism and pursuit of minority rights

I concluded in the last section that language policy is only rarely a major concern of national governments, and that their management activities (apart from trying to deal with the communication problems engendered by widespread multilingualism) tend to be the result of using rhetoric about language to strengthen national unity. It is also, I suspect, the case that most language activism is part of a wider social, political, or religious movement seeking greater power, equality, autonomy, or independence. The legendary reviver of

Hebrew, Eliezer Ben Yehuda, was a Zionist before he became a language activist; the Māori language movement was part of a wider ethnic revival which focused on land rights and reparations; the Québec language program was the result of an independence movement being persuaded to renounce secession. But within these ethnic movements, the language activists are those who chose to focus their efforts on persuading their governments to support their efforts to enable or convince their fellow members to maintain or restore the use of their heritage language.

There can be language activists at all levels: members of the family who attempt to manage the language choices of others; religious leaders like Luther who provided translation into the vernacular of sacred texts; but the best-known cases are the various language minority organizations that set out to seek first recognition and then power for their language. Norway, Ottoman Palestine, Ireland, and India showed how grassroots organizations, often very small and with young members, conducted campaigns for their chosen language. Some were successful, and were then transformed into academies or language regulatory bodies. As a rule, these are the principal participants at the national level who take a largely linguicentric view of their task, the aspiring language managers who are most focused in their task.

Beyond the nation-state: organizations and rights

After the collapse of empires, there were some who believed that supranational coalitions like the United Nations or the European Union would take over regional or even world government. In fact, it now seems clear that these groupings can only work if they recognize the limitations of their powers and the need to accept national sovereignty. Nonetheless, their efforts at language management are significant.

By their makeup, supranational organizations are multilingual. Their first decision must therefore be how to manage the language in internal operations at both the law- or policy-making level and the bureaucratic administrative level. Secondly, they can enhance the possibility of communication between citizens of their members by a policy promoting foreign language teaching. There is a third significant sphere in which supranational organizations influence national language management, and this is in the development and promotion of statements and charters proclaiming human and civil rights relevant to language and language minorities. Because these supranational bodies lack authority over their members, their main participation in national language management has been in presenting rhetorical statements of international consensus, which are available to governments, and even more important to language activists, and helps account for the growing respect for linguistic diversity and the concerns of linguistic minorities.

Agencies for language management

The last chapter described specific governmental and non-governmental agencies responsible for carrying out language management. There turn out to be fewer designated language managers than one might assume, supporting the hypothesis that much language policy depends rather on language practices and consensual beliefs than on management. Most governments, it appears, prefer to leave language alone. There is a second kind of agency, concerned with not leaving language alone but cultivating it. While it is commonly assumed that this is the prime task of specialized language academies, it turns out that there are fewer academies than one might guess, and that those academies which have been studied (and the paucity of scholarship in this sphere is remarkable) keep busy mainly producing new terminology but with unknown effect. Finally, we sketched language services (translation and interpreting), the rapid recent expansion of which attests the slowness with which other more permanent language management activities achieve worthwhile results.

What sort of theory do we have?

I suggested in the title of this chapter that this might turn out to be the prolegomena to a theory of language management. My concern has been to account for the various data I have described by setting out a model which identifies the relevant factors and forces which help explain what I have observed. But can one go beyond an explanatory model and offer a theory that permits testable predictions?

Might one hope for a mathematical model that could be tested? The snag of course is the assumptions that are needed for such models. One approach that has recently stirred interest is the work of two scholars in a department of theoretical and applied mechanics, whose paper made it into the flagship science journal *Nature*. Abrams and Strogatz (2003) proposed a model to show the effect of the number of speakers and status (defined as social or economic opportunities) on language maintenance and loss. To build their model, they found it necessary to idealize languages as "fixed, and as competing with each other for speakers" and to assume "a highly connected population, with no spatial or social structure, in which all the speakers are monolingual." With all the fuzziness involved, they believed that "strategies such as policy-making, education and advertising" can increase a language's status and so "show stabilization of a bilingual fixed point." Might a more elaborate model and one closer to reality do a better job of prediction?

Casting doubt on this, there is good reason to believe that the sociolinguistic ecosystem may ultimately be chaotic and so unpredictable. Two papers find this outcome in other systems. Noting that "mathematical models predict that species interactions such as competition and predation can generate chaos," Beninca et al. (2008: 822) report on a long-term laboratory experiment with a complex plankton ecosystem under constant external conditions that produced "striking fluctuations over several orders of magnitude" and a chaotic result that limited predictability to no more than 15–30 days, "only slightly longer than the local weather forecast." Looking at a human system, May et al. (2008) describe the catastrophic systemic changes that affect global financial markets; can they be understood and managed? So far, the answer is clearly, no. Might not the sociolinguistic ecosystem be equally chaotic, open to unanticipated "butterfly effects"? Might efforts to control and manipulate parts of it be as unlikely to succeed as government efforts to control weather or markets?

Perhaps this is too pessimistic, but clearly language management requires a detailed understanding of multilingualism and social structure, as well as of multidimensional social and demographic space. We should be able to look at a specific situation, after a full study of its domains, and make relatively strong guesses about the likely short-term outcome of present or proposed language management plans. We can ask, for instance, whether the expansion of pre-school and elementary education programs in Māori will eventually lead to natural intergenerational language transmission or simply maintain language knowledge as schools maintain Irish and maintained Hebrew before it was revitalized in Ottoman Palestine. We can ask how long the European Union will be willing to pay the price of symbolic recognition of all its national languages. We can wonder when US Federal efforts will finally break the inertia of the educational establishment in second and foreign language teaching. We can ask when national educational systems will accept the UNESCO call for initial education in the vernacular. We can ask when European nations will accept the Union's reiterated proposals to teach a second foreign language. We can ask why Latin, in spite of its status, was driven out by lower status vernaculars even from protected domains, and how English will cope with all its new local varieties. In other words, we can use the domain model to focus our questions more precisely, and come up with hypotheses that need further testing, perhaps even mathematically. This, I hope, constitutes a useful step towards the development of a theory of language management.

But should we? Because so much of language management produces questionable results, apparently supporting monolingual hegemony and discouraging pluralism and multilingualism, is this not an area (like religious belief) better left to individual free choice? Does not the greater success of totalitarian states, willing to back language management policies with police enforcement and population transfer, than democracies wondering how to harmonize communicative efficiency with freedom and how to fit linguistic minorities into workable governments, suggest that the enterprise is basically undesirable? Qualms like these face modern scientists, whether in natural, physical, or social science. Was Babel such a bad thing? Jonathan Swift describes the plan for a universal language for Laputa, the scientific Utopia of *Gulliver's Travels,* in which words were replaced by things: "since words are only names for things, it would be more convenient for all men to carry about with them such things as were necessary to express a particular business they are to discourse on." This would "serve as a universal language, to be understood in all civilized nations, whose goods and utensils are generally of the same kind, or nearly resembling, so that their uses might easily be comprehended." This plan might have succeeded, Swift writes, if "the women, in conjunction with the vulgar and illiterate, had not threatened to raise a rebellion unless they might be allowed the liberty to speak with their tongues, after the manner of their forefathers."

We are left then with two basic questions: can language be managed? And if it can, should it be managed?

References

Abrams, Daniel M. and Strogatz, Steven H., 2003, Modelling the dynamics of language death. *Nature* 424: 900.

Abu-Haidar, Farida, 1989, Are Iraqi women more prestige conscious than men? Sex differentiation in Baghdadi Arabic. *Language in Society* 18(4): 471–481.

Adams, James Noel, 2003, *Bilingualism and the Latin language*, Cambridge: Cambridge University Press.

Agard, Frederick B., Clements, Robert J., Hendrix, William S. *et al.*, 1944, *A survey of language classes in the Army Specialized Training Program*, New York: Commission on Trends in Education [of the Modern Language Association of America].

Ager, Dennis E., 1996, *Language policy in Britain and France: The processes of policy*, London and New York: Cassell.

1999, *Identity, insecurity and image: France and language*, Clevedon, UK, Philadelphia, and Adelaide: Multilingual Matters Ltd.

2001, *Motivation in language planning and language policy*, Clevedon, UK and Buffalo, USA: Multilingual Matters Ltd.

Alexandre, Pierre, 1968, Some linguistic problems of nation-building in Negro Africa. In Joshua A. Fishman, Charles A. Ferguson, and Jyotirinda Das Gupta (eds.), *Language problems of developing nations* (pp. 119–127), New York: John Wiley & Sons.

Alidou, Hassana, Boly, Aliou, Brock-Utne, Birgit *et al.*, 2006, *Optimizing learning and education in Africa – the language factor: A stock-taking research on mother tongue and bilingual education in sub-Saharan Africa* (Working paper for ADEA Biennial Meeting), Libreville, Gabon: Association for Development of Education in Africa (ADEA).

Alisjahbana, Sutan Takadir, 1976, *Language planning for modernisation: The case of Indonesia and Malaysia*, The Hague: Mouton.

Allen, Jeff, 1999, Different kinds of controlled languages, *TC-Forum Magazine*, 1: 4–5.

Amara, Muhammad Hasan, 1988, Arabic diglossia: Conditions for learning the standard variety, *Aljadid* 12: 14–23.

1996, Gender differentiation in Palestinian Arabic, *Alrisala* 2: 197–205.

Ammon, Ulrich, 1992, The Federal Republic of Germany's policy of spreading German, *International Journal of the Sociology of Language* 95: 33–50.

2001 (ed.), *The dominance of English as a language of science: Effects on other languages and language communities*, Berlin and New York: Mouton de Gruyter.

262

Anderson, Chris, 2004, The long tail, *Wired*, October.

2006, *The long tail: Why the future of business is selling less of more*, New York: Hyperion.

Angiolillo, Paul F., 1947, *Armed forces' foreign language teaching: Critical evaluation and implications*, New York: S. F. Vanni.

Anonymous, 2007, A brief history of the declaration. *Cultural Survival Voices* 5.

Arana, Edorta, Azpillaga, Patxi, and Narbaiza, Beatriz, 2007, Linguistic normalisation and local television in the Basque country. In Mike Cormack and Niamh Hourigan (eds.), *Minority language media: Concepts, critiques and case studies* (pp. 151–167), Clevedon, UK: Multilingual Matters Ltd.

Archilés, F. and Marty, M., 2001, Ethnicity, region and the nation: Valencian identity and the Spanish nation-state, *Ethnic and Racial Studies* 24(5): 779–797.

Arroyo, Jose Luis Blas, 2002, The languages of the Valencian educational system: the results of two decades of language policy, *International Journal of Bilingual Education and Bilingualism* 5(6): 318–338.

Aunger, Edmund A., 1993, Regional, national and official languages in Belgium, *International Journal of the Sociology of Language* 104: 31–48.

Avison, Shannon and Meadows, Michael, 2000, Speaking and hearing: aboriginal newspapers and the public sphere in Canada and Australia, *Canadian Journal of Communication* 25(3).

Azarya, Victor, 1984, *The Armenian quarter of Jerusalem*, Berkeley: University of California Press.

Backhaus, Peter, 2005, Signs of multilingualism in Tokyo: A diachronic look at the linguistic landscape, *International Journal of the Sociology of language* 175/176: 103–121.

2007, *Linguistic landscapes: A comparative study of urban multilingualism in Tokyo*, Clevedon, UK: Multilingual Matters Ltd.

Baigorri-Jalón, Jesús, 2000, Bridging the language gap at the United Nations, *United Nations Chronicle* 37(1).

Baker, Ray S. and Dodd, William E., 1924 (eds.), *The public papers of Woodrow Wilson*, New York: Harper and Brothers.

Baldauf Jr., Richard B., 1982, The language situation in American Samoa: Planners, plans and planning, *Language Planning Newsletter* 8(1): 1–6.

1994, "Unplanned" language planning and policy. In William Grabe (ed.), *Annual review of applied linguistics* (Vol. 14, pp. 82–89), Cambridge: Cambridge University Press.

Bamgbose, Ayo, 2005, Mother-tongue education: Lessons from the Yoruba experience. In Birgit Brock-Utne and Rodney Kofu Hopson (eds.), *Languages of instruction for African emancipation: Focus on postcolonial contexts and considerations* (pp. 231–257), Cape Town, South Africa and Dar es Salaam, Tanzania: The Centre for Advanced Studies of African Society and Mkuki na Nyota Publishers.

Bargiela-Chiappini, Francesca, Chakorn, Ora-Ong, Lay, Grace Chew Chye *et al.*, 2007, Eastern voices: Enriching research on communication in business: a forum, *Discourse and Communication* 1(2): 131–152.

Barkhuizen, Gary, Knoch, Ute, and Starks, Donna, 2006, Language practices, preferences and policies: Contrasting views of Pakeha, Maori, Pasifika, and

Asian students, *Journal of Multilingual and Multicultural Development* 27(5): 375–391.

Baumel, Simeon D., 2002, Language policies of ethnic minorities as influenced by social, economic, religious and political concentrates: An examination of Israeli Haredim, unpublished Ph.D., Bar-Ilan University, Ramat-Gan, Israel.

Beninca, Elisa, Huisman, Jef, Heerkloss, Reinhard *et al.*, 2008, Chaos in a long-term experiment with a plankton community, *Nature* 451: 822–825.

Benmaman, Virginia, 1992, Legal interpreting as an emerging profession, *Modern Language Journal* 76(10): 445–449.

Ben-Rafael, Eliezer, Shohamy, Elana, Amara, Muhammad Hasan, and Trumper-Hecht, Nira, 2006, Linguistic landscape as symbolic construction of the public space: The case of Israel, *International Journal of Multilingualism* 3(1): 7–30.

Benson, Carol, 2004, Do we expect too much of bilingual teachers? Bilingual teaching in developing countries, *International Journal of Bilingual Education and Bilingualism* 7(2&3): 204–221.

Benton, Nena, 1989, Education, language decline and language revitalisation: The case of Maori in New Zealand, *Language and Education* 3(2): 65–82.

Benton, Richard A., 1981, *The flight of the Amokura: Oceanic languages and formal education in the Pacific*, Wellington: New Zealand Council for Educational Research.

Bergentoft, Rune, 1994, Foreign language instruction: a comparative perspective. In Richard D. Lambert (ed.), *Language planning around the world: contexts and systemic change* (pp. 17–46), Washington DC: National Foreign Language Center.

Berlin, Isaiah, 2006, *Political ideas in the Romantic Age: Their rise and influence on modern thought*, ed. Henry Hardy, Princeton and Oxford: Princeton University Press.

Bernier, Serge and Pariseau, Jean, 1994, *French Canadians and bilingualism in the Canadian armed forces* (Vol. II: *Official languages*), Ottawa: Ministry of Supply and Services.

Bernstein, Basil B., 1971, *Class, codes and control*, London, UK: Routledge & Kegan Paul.

Berry, Rita Shuk Yin and Williams, Marion, 2004, In at the deep end: Difficulties experienced by Hong Kong Chinese ESL learners at an independent school in the United Kingdom, *Journal of Language and Social Psychology* 23(1): 118–134.

Bhattacharya, Rimli, Gupta, Snehata, Jewitt, Carey *et al.*, 2007, The policy-practice nexus in English classrooms in Delhi, Johannesburg, and London: Teachers and the textual cycle, *TESOL Quarterly* 41(3): 465–487.

Birch, Barbara M., 1995, Quaker plain speech: A policy of linguistic divergence, *International Journal of the Sociology of Language* 116: 39–59.

Birdsong, David and Paik, Jee, 2008, Second language acquisition and ultimate attainment. In Bernard Spolsky and Francis M. Hult (eds.), *Handbook of educational linguistics* (pp. 424–436), Boston: Blackwell.

Blommaert, Jan, 2001, The Asmara Declaration as a sociolinguistic problem: Reflections on scholarship and linguistic rights. *Journal of Sociolinguistics* 5(1): 131–142.

2005, Situating language rights: English and Swahili in Tanzania revisited, *Journal of Sociolinguistics* 9(3): 390–417.

2007, Sociolinguistics and discourse analysis: Orders of indexicality and polycentricity, *Journal of Multicultural Discourse* 2(2): 115–130.

2008, Language, asylum, and the national order, paper presented to the Annual Meeting of the American Association of Applied Linguistics 2008, Washington DC.

Bogoch, Bryna, 1999, Gender, literacy and religiosity: Dimensions of Yiddish education in Israeli government-supported schools, *International Journal of the Sociology of Language* 138: 123–160.

Bongaerts, Theo, van Summeren, Chantal, Planken, Brigitte, and Schils, Erik, 1997, Age and ultimate attainment in the pronunciation of a foreign language, *Studies in Second Language Acquisition* 19(4): 447–465.

Bourdieu, Pierre, 2001, Uniting to better dominate, *Items & Issues* 2(3–4): 1–6.

Bourhis, Richard Y, 2001, Reversing language shift in Quebec. In Joshua A. Fishman (ed.), *Can threatened languages be saved?* (pp. 101–141), Clevedon, UK: Multilingual Matters Ltd.

Bourhis, Richard Y. and Landry, Rodrigue, 2002, La loi 101 et l'amènagement du paysage linguistique au Québec, *La Revue d'amènagement linguistique* (Special Issue): 107–121.

Brecht, Richard D. and Rivers, William P., 2005, Language needs analysis at the societal level. In Michael Long (ed.), *Second language needs analysis* (pp. 79–104), Cambridge: Cambridge University Press.

Brockington, John L., 2001, Hindu sacred texts. In J. F. A. Sawyer, J. M. Y. Simpson, and R. E. Asher (eds.), *Concise encyclopaedia of language and religion* (pp. 126–127), Amsterdam: Elsevier.

Brock-Utne, Birgit and Hopson, Rodney Kofu, 2005 (eds.), *Languages of instruction for African emancipation: Focus on postcolonial contexts and considerations*, Cape Town, South Africa and Dar es Salaam, Tanzania: The Centre for Advanced Studies of African Society and Mkuki na Nyota Publishers.

Brown, Donna Lee, 2003, Power versus authority, *BYU Magazine*, Winter.

Brown, N. Anthony, 2005, Language and identity in Belarus, *Language Policy* 4(3): 311–332.

Browne, Donald R., 2007, Speaking up: A brief history of minority languages and the electronic media worldwide. In Mike Cormack and Niamh Hourigan (eds.), *Minority language media: Concepts, critiques and case studies* (pp. 107–132), Clevedon, UK: Multilingual Matters Ltd.

Bugarski, Ranko, 2001, Language, nationalism, and war in Yugoslavia, *International Journal of the Sociology of Language* 151: 69–87.

Burhanudeen, Hafriza, 2003, Factors influencing the language choices of Malay Malaysians in the family, friendship and market domains, *Journal of Language and Linguistics* 2(2): 224–245.

Burnaby, Barbara and Philpott, David, 2007, Innu oral dominance meets schooling: New data on outcomes. *Journal of Multilingual and Multicultural Development* 28(4): 270–289.

Caldas, Stephen J., 2006, *Raising bilingual-biliterate children in monolingual cultures*, Clevedon, UK, Buffalo, and Toronto: Multilingual Matters Ltd.

Calvet, Louis-Jean, 1974, *Linguistique et colonialisme: petit traité de glottophagie*, Paris: Payot.

1987, *La guerre des langues: et les politiques linguistiques*, Paris: Payot.

1990, Des mots sur les murs: Une comparaison entre Paris et Dakar. In Robert Chaudenson (ed.), *Des langues et des villes (Actes du colloque international a Dakar, du 15 au 17 decembre 1990* (pp. 73–83), Paris: Agence de cooperation culturelle et technique.

1998, *Language wars and linguistic politics* (trans. Michel Petheram), Oxford: Oxford University Press.

Cardozier, V. R., 1993, *Colleges and universities in World War II*, Westport CT: Praeger.

Casesnoves Ferrer, Raquel and Sankoff, David, 2003, Identity as the primary determinant of language choice in Valencia, *Journal of Sociolinguistics* 7(1): 50–64.

2004a, Transmission, education and integration in projections of language shift in Valencia, *Language Policy* 3(2): 107–131.

2004b, The Valencian revival: Why usage lags behind competence, *Language in Society* 33: 1–31.

Central Intelligence Agency, 2007, *The World Factbook*, from https://www.cia.gov/cia/publications/factbook

Cheng, Karen Kow Yip, 2003, Language shift and language maintenance in mixed families: A case study of a Malaysian-Chinese family, *International Journal of the Sociology of Language* 161: 81–90.

Chinen, Kiyomi and Tucker, G. Richard, 2006, Heritage language development: Understanding the roles of ethnic identity, schooling and community. In Kimi Kondo-Brown (ed.), *Heritage language development: Focus on East Asian immigrants* (pp. 89–126), Amsterdam: John Benjamins.

Chiswick, Barry R., 1993, Hebrew language usage: Determinants and effects among immigrants in Israel, paper presented at the Conference on Immigrant Absorption, Technion, Haifa.

1994, Language and earnings among immigrants in Canada: A survey. In Sally Zerker (ed.), *Essays in Canadian social science* (pp. 247–264), Jerusalem: Magnes Press.

Chiswick, Barry R. and Miller, Paul R., 1995, Language and labor supply: The role of gender among immigrants in Australia, *Research in Economic Equality* 5: 153–189.

Chomsky, William, 1957, *Hebrew: The eternal language*, Philadelphia: The Jewish Publication Society of America.

Clayton, Thomas, 2006, *Language choice in a nation under transition: English language spread in Cambodia*, New York: Springer.

Clowse, Barbara Barksdale, 1981, *Brainpower for the Cold War: The Sputnik crisis and the national Defense Education Act of 1958*, Westbrook, CT: Greenwood Press.

Clyne, Michael, 1986, Primary school language programs and the second language acquisition process. In Michael Clyne (ed.), *An Early Start* (pp. 7–17), Melbourne: River Seine.

2001, Can the shift from immigrant languages be reversed in Australia? In Joshua A. Fishman (ed.), *Can threatened languages be saved?* (pp. 364–390), Clevedon, UK: Multilingual Matters Ltd.

Coates, Jennifer, 2005, *Women, men and language: A sociolinguistic account of gender differences in language* (3rd edn.), Harlow, UK: Longman.

Cohen, Israel, 1918, *The German attack on the Hebrew schools in Palestine*, London: Jewish Chronicle and Jewish World.

Coleman, Algernon, 1929, *The teaching of modern foreign languages in the United States*, New York: Macmillan Company.

Collins, Peter, 2003, Storying self and others: The construction of narrative identity, *Language and Politics* 2(2): 243–264.

Commission of the European Communities, 2003, *Promoting language learning and linguistic diversity: An action plan 2004–2006* (COM (2003) 449 Final), Brussels: Commission of the European Communities.

Committee on Budgetary Control, 2006, *Special report of the European Court of Auditors concerning translation expenditure incurred by the Commission, the Parliament and the Council*, Brussels: European Parliament.

Conference on National Language Academies and Their Mission, 1986, *International Symposium on National Language Academies and Global Demands on Language (April 25–26, 1986)*: Kentucky Foreign Language Conference.

Cooper, Robert L., 1984, The avoidance of androcentric generics, *International Journal of the Sociology of Language* 50: 5–20.

    1989, *Language planning and social change*, Cambridge: Cambridge University Press.

Cooper, Robert L. and Carpenter, S., 1976, Language in the market. In M. L. Bender, J. D. Bowen, R. L. Cooper, and C. A. Ferguson (eds.), *Language in Ethiopia*, London: Oxford University Press.

Cooper, Robert L. and Seckbach, Fern, 1977, Economic incentives for the learning of a language of wider communication: A case study. In Joshua A. Fishman, Robert L. Cooper, and Andrew W. Conrad (eds.), *The spread of English* (pp. 212–219), Rowley, MA: Newbury House Publishers.

Cormack, Mike, 2007, The media and language maintenance. In Mike Cormack and Niamh Hourigan (eds.), *Minority language media: Concepts, critiques and case studies* (pp. 52–68), Clevedon, UK: Multilingual Matters Ltd.

Coulmas, Florian, 1990, Language adaptation in Meiji Japan. In Brian Weinstein (ed.), *Language policy and political development* (pp. 69–86), Norwood, NJ: Ablex Publishing Company.

Council of Europe, 2001, *Common European framework of reference for languages: Learning, teaching, assessment*, Cambridge: Cambridge University Press.

    2007a, *Application of the Charter in Slovakia: Second monitoring round*, Strasbourg: European Charter for Regional or Minority Languages, Directorate of Co-operation for Local and Regional Democracy, Directorate General of Legal Affairs – DG I.

    2007b, *Application of the Charter in the United Kingdom: Second monitoring round*, Strasbourg: European Charter for Regional or Minority Languages, Directorate of Co-operation for Local and Regional Democracy, Directorate General of Legal Affairs – DG I.

Covell, Maureen, 1993, Political conflict and constitutional engineering in Belgium, *International Journal of the Sociology of Language* 104: 65–86.

Cowan, J Milton and Graves, Mortimer, 1944, A statement on intensive language instruction, *Hispania* 27: 65–66.

Cunliffe, Daniel, 2007, Minority languages and the Internet: new threats, new opportunities. In Mike Cormack and Niamh Hourigan (eds.), *Minority language media: Concepts, critiques and case studies* (pp. 133–150), Clevedon, UK: Multilingual Matters Ltd.

da Silva, Jaime F. and Klein Gunnewick, Lisanne, 1992, Portuguese and Brazilian efforts to spread Portuguese, *International Journal of the Sociology of language* 95: 71–92.

Danet, Brenda and Herring, Susan C., 2007 (eds.), *The multilingual Internet: Language, culture and communication online*, Oxford: Oxford University Press.

Das Gupta, Jyotirindra, 1977a, Language associations in India. In Joan Rubin, Björn H. Jernudd, Jyotirindra Das Gupta, Joshua A. Fishman, and Charles A. Ferguson (eds.), *Language planning processes* (pp. 181–194), The Hague: Mouton.

   1977b, Language planning in India: Authority and organization. In Joan Rubin, Björn H. Jernudd, Jyotirindra Das Gupta, Joshua A. Fishman, and Charles A. Ferguson (eds.), *Language planning processes* (pp. 57–78), The Hague: Mouton.

Davies, Alan, 1997, Australian immigrant gatekeeping through English Language Tests: How important is proficiency? In A. Huhta, V. Kohonon, L. Kurki-Suonio, and S. Luoma (eds.), *Current developments and alternatives in language assessment: Proceedings of LTRC 96* (pp. 71–84), Jyväskylä: Kopijyva Oy: University of Jyväskylä.

   2003, *The native speaker: Myth and reality*, Clevedon, UK, Buffalo, Toronto, and Sydney: Multilingual Matters Ltd.

de La Salle, Saint Jean-Baptiste, 1720, *Conduite des Ecoles chrétiennes*, Avignon: C. Chastanier.

de Swaan, Abram, 1999, The language constellation of the European Union, paper presented at the conference International Status and Use of National Languages in Europe: Contributions to a European Language Policy, Brussels.

   2001, *Words of the world: The global language system*, Cambridge, UK and Malden, MA: Polity Press and Blackwell Publishers.

Delsing, Lars-Olof, 2007, Scandinavian intercomprehension today. In Jan D. ten Thije and Ludger Zeevaert (eds.), *Receptive multilingualism: Linguistic analyses, language policies and didactic concepts* (pp. 231–246), Amsterdam and Philadephia: John Benjamins Publishing Company.

Demay, Joel, 1993, The persistence and creativity of Canadian aboriginal newspapers, *Canadian Journal of Communication* 18(1).

Demuth, Katherine, 1986, Prompting routines in the language socialization of Basotho children. In Bambi B. Schieffelin and Elinor Ochs (eds.), *Language socialization across cultures* (pp. 51–79), Cambridge: Cambridge University Press.

Deprez, Kas, 2000, Belgium: From a unitary to a federalist state. In Kas Deprez and Theo Du Plessis (eds.), *Multilingualism and government: Belgium, Luxembourg, Switzerland, Former Yugoslavia, and South Africa* (pp. 17–29), Pretoria, South Africa: Van Schaik Publishers.

Dittmar, Norbert, Spolsky, Bernard, and Walters, Joel, 2002, *Convergence and divergence in second language acquisition and use: An examination of immigrant identities in Germany and Israel* (Final scientific report. Contract No. G-0500–157.04/96 GIF), Ramat-Gan and Berlin: Bar-Ilan University and Free University.

Djité, Paulin G., 2008, *The sociolinguistics of development in Africa*, Clevedon, UK, Buffalo, and Toronto: Multilingual Matters Ltd.

Doetjes, Gerke, 2007, Understanding differences in inter-Scandinavian language understanding. In Jan D. ten Thije and Ludger Zeevaert (eds.), *Receptive multilingualism: Linguistic analyses, language policies and didactic concepts* (pp. 217–230), Amsterdam and Philadephia: John Benjamins Publishing Company.

Domínguez, Francesc and López, Núria, 1995, *Sociolinguistic and language planning organizations*, Amsterdam and Philadelphia: John Benjamins Publishing Company.

Donitsa-Schmidt, Smadar, 1999, Language maintenance or shift: Determinants of language choice among Soviet immigrants in Israel, unpublished Ph.D. dissertation, University of Toronto, Toronto.

Donnelly, Jack, 2003, *Universal human rights in theory and practice* (2nd edn.), Ithaca, NY and London: Cornell University Press.

Dorian, Nancy, 1987, The value of language maintenance efforts which are unlikely to succeed, *International Journal of the Sociology of Language* 68: 57–67.

Druviete, Ina, 1998, Republic of Latvia. In Christina Bratt Paulston and Donald Peckham (eds.), *Linguistic minorities in Central and East Europe* (pp. 160–183), Clevedon, UK and Philadelphia: Multilingual Matters Ltd.

Du Plessis, Theo, 2006, Implementing multilingual language policy at the SABC since 1994, *Acta Academica Supplement* 2: 45–75.

Duff, Patricia, Wong, Ping, and Early, Margaret, 2002, Learning language for work and life: The linguistic socialisation of immigrant Canadians seeking careers in healthcare, *Modern Language Journal* 86(3): 397–422.

Dutton, David, 1998, Strangers and citizens: The boundaries of Australian citizenship 1901–1973, unpublished Ph.D. thesis, University of Melbourne, Melbourne.

Eades, Diana, Fraser, Helen, Siegel, Jeff, McNamara, Tim, and Baker, Brett, 2003, Linguistic identification in the determination of nationality: A preliminary report, *Language Policy* 2(2): 179–199.

Education Review Office, 1995, *Kura Kaupapa Maori* (No. 10), Wellington: Education Review Office.

Eggington, William, 2002, Unplanned language planning. In Robert B. Kaplan (ed.), *The Oxford handbook of applied linguistics* (pp. 404–415), Oxford: Oxford University Press.

Enever, Janet, 2007, Yet another early-start languages policy in Europe: Poland this time! *Current Issues in Language Planning* 8(2): 208–221.

Engelbrecht, Guillermina and Ortiz, Leroy, 1983, Guarani literacy in Paraguay, *International Journal of the Sociology of Language* 42: 53–68.

Engelhardt, Juliane, 2007, Patriotism, nationalism and modernity: The patriotic societies in the Danish conglomerate state, 1769–1814, *Nations and Nationalism* 13(2): 205–223.

European Commission, 2004, *Implementation of the Education and Training 2010 work programme: Working group languages* (Progress report), Brussels: European Commission.

Evans, Stephen, 1999, The English language needs of building services practitioners in Hong Kong, *Asian Journal of English Language Teaching* 9: 41–57.

Evans, Stephen and Green, Christopher, 2001, Language in post-colonial Hong Kong: The roles of English and Chinese in the public and private sectors, *English World-wide* 22(2): 247–268.

Extra, Guus and Yağmur, Kutlay, 2004 (eds.), *Urban multilingualism in Europe: Immigrant minority languages at home and school*, Clevedon, UK: Multilingual Matters Ltd.

Fabian, Johannes, 1983, Missions and the colonisation of African languages: Developments in the former Belgian Congo, *Canadian Journal of African Studies* 17(2): 165–187.

Feely, Alan J. and Harzing, Anne-Will, 2003, Language management in multinational companies, *Cross-cultural Management: An International Journal* 10(2): 37–52.

Fellman, Jack, 1973, *The revival of a classical tongue: Eliezer Ben Yehuda and the modern Hebrew language*, The Hague: Mouton.

    1977, The Hebrew Academy: Orientation and operation. In Joan Rubin, Björn H. Jernudd, Jyotirindra Das Gupta, Joshua A. Fishman, and Charles A. Ferguson (eds.), *Language planning processes* (pp. 97–109), The Hague: Mouton Publishers.

Fellman, Jack and Fishman, Joshua A., 1977, Language planning in Israel: Solving terminological problems. In Joan Rubin, Björn H. Jernudd, Jyotirindra Das Gupta, Joshua A. Fishman, and Charles A. Ferguson (eds.), *Language planning processes* (pp. 79–96), The Hague: Mouton.

Ferguson, Charles A., 1959, Diglossia. *Word* 15: 325–340.

    1968, St. Stefan of Perm and applied linguistics. In Joshua A. Fishman, Charles A. Ferguson, and Jyotirindra Das Gupta (eds.), *Language problems of developing nations* (pp. 253–265), New York: Wiley.

Fishman, Joshua A., 1966 (ed.), *Language loyalty in the United States: The maintenance and perpetuation of non-English mother tongues by American ethnic and religious groups*, The Hague: Mouton.

    1969, National languages and languages of wider communication in the developing nations, *Anthropological Linguistics* 11: 111–135.

    1970, *Sociolinguistics: A brief introduction*, Rowley, MA: Newbury House.

    1971, National languages and languages of wider communication. In W. H. Whitely (ed.), *Language use and social change* (pp. 25–56), London: Oxford University Press for the International African Institute.

    1972, Domains and the relationship between micro- and macrosociolinguistics. In John J. Gumperz and Dell Hymes (eds.), *Directions in sociolinguistics* (pp. 435–453), New York: Holt Rinehart and Winston.

    1973, *Language and nationalism: Two integrative essays*, Rowley, MA: Newbury House Publishers.

    1983, Modeling rationales in corpus planning: Modernity and tradition in images of the good. In Juan Cobarrubias and Joshua A. Fishman (eds.), *Progress in language planning: International perspectives* (pp. 107–118), The Hague: Mouton.

    1991a, The Hebraist response to the Tschernovits conference. In Alan S. Kaye (ed.), *Semitic studies in honor of Wolf Leslau on the occasion of his eighty-fifth birthday* (pp. 437–448), Wiesbaden: Otto Harrassowitz.

    1991b, *Reversing language shift: Theoretical and empirical foundations of assistance to threatened languages*, Clevedon, UK: Multilingual Matters Ltd.

    1993 (ed.), *The earliest stage of language planning: The "First Congress" phenomenon*, Berlin: Mouton de Gruyter.

1999, The city as the root of all evil: A brief history of ideas about cities for educators of urban minorities, and for the "maiden voyage" of their journal. *Educators for Urban Minorities* 1(1): 45–50.

2002a, The holiness of Yiddish: Who says Yiddish is holy and why? *Language Policy* 1(2): 123–141.

2002b, "Holy languages" in the context of societal bilingualism. In Li Wei, Jean-Marc Dewaele, and Alex Housen (eds.), *Opportunities and challenges of bilingualism* (pp. 15–24), Berlin: Mouton de Gruyter.

2006, *Do not leave your language alone: The hidden status agendas within corpus planning in language policy*, Mahwah, NJ: Lawrence Erlbaum Associates Publishers.

Fishman, Joshua A. and Fishman, David E., 1974, Yiddish in Israel: A case-study of efforts to revise a monocentric language policy, *International Journal of the Sociology of Language* 1: 126–146.

1978, Yiddish in Israel: A case study of efforts to revise a monocentric language policy. In Joshua A. Fishman (ed.), *Advances in the study of societal monolingualism* (pp. 185–262), The Hague: Mouton.

Fishman, Joshua A., Cooper, Robert L., and Conrad, A. W., 1977, *The spread of English: The sociology of English as an additional language*, Rowley, MA: Newbury House.

Fishman, Joshua A., Ferguson, Charles A., and Das Gupta, Jyotirinda, 1968, *Language problems of developing nations*, New York: Wiley.

Fishman, Joshua A., Gertner, M. H., Lowy, E. G., and Milan, W. G., 1985, *The rise and fall of the ethnic revival: Perspectives on language and ethnicity*, Berlin: Mouton de Gruyter.

Fishman, Joshua A., Hayden, Robert G., and Warshauer, Mary E., 1966, The non-English and the ethnic group press, 1910–1960. In Joshua A. Fishman (ed.), *Language loyalty in the United States: The maintenance and perpetuation of non-English mother tongues by American ethnic and religious groups* (pp. 51–74), The Hague: Mouton.

Fleming, Aisling and Debski, Robert, 2007, The use of Irish in networked communications: A study of schoolchildren in different language settings, *Journal of Multilingual and Multicultural Development* 28(2): 85–101.

Fortune, Tara Williams and Tedick, Diane J., 2008 (eds.), *Pathways to multilingualism: Evolving perspectives on immersion education*, Clevedon, UK, Buffalo, and Toronto: Multilingual Matters Ltd.

Friedrich, Patricia, 2002, English in advertising and brand naming: Sociolinguistic considerations and the case of Brazil, *English Today* 18(3): 21–28.

García, Ofelia, Kleifgen, Jo Anne, and Falchi, Lorraine, 2008, *From English language learners to emergent bilinguals*, New York: Teachers College, Columbia.

García, Ofelia, Skutnabb-Kangas, Tove, and Torres-Guzmán, Maria E., 2006 (eds.), *Imagining multilingual schools*, Clevedon, UK, Buffalo, and Toronto: Multilingual Matters Limited.

Garrett, J., 1982, *To live among the stars*, Geneva and Suva: World Council of Churches and University of the South Pacific.

Garrett, Paul B. and Baquedano-Lopez, Patricia, 2002, Language socialisation: Reproduction and continuity, transformation and change, *Annual Review of Anthropology* 31(1): 339–361.

Gattegno, Caleb, 1976, *The common sense of teaching foreign languages*, New York: Educational Solutions.

Gazzola, Michele, 2006, Managing multilingualism in the European Union: Language policy evaluation for the European Parliament, *Language Policy* 5(4): 393–417.

Gee, James P., 2001, Educational linguistics. In Mark Aranoff and Janie Rees-Miller (eds.), *The handbook of linguistics* (pp. 647–663), Oxford: Blackwell.

Gellner, Ernest, 1983, *Nations and nationalism*, Ithaca, NY: Cornell University Press.

Genesee, Fred, 1988, The Canadian second language immersion program. In Christina Bratt Paulston (ed.), *International handbook of bilingualism and bilingual education* (pp. 163–184), New York: Greenwood Press.

George, Ken, 2000, *Gerlyver Kernewek kemmyn: English–Cornish, Cornish–English dictionary* (2nd edn.), Cornwall: Kesva an Taves Kernewek.

Ghosh, Ratna, 2004, Public education and multicultural policy in Canada: The special case of Quebec. *International Review of Education* 50(5–6): 543–566.

Giles, Howard, Taylor, Donald M., and Bourhis, Richard, 1973, Towards a theory of interpersonal accommodation through language: Some Canadian data, *Language in Society* 2(2): 177–192.

Gill, Saran Kaur, 1999, Standards and emerging linguistic realities in the Malaysian workplace, *World Englishes* 18(2): 215–231.

2005, Language policy in Malaysia: Reversing direction, *Language Policy* 4(3).

2006, Change in language policy in Malaysia: The reality of implementation in public universities, *Current Issues in Language Planning* 7(1): 82–94.

Gimeno-Menéndez, Francisco and Gómez-Molina, José Ramón, 2007, Spanish and Catalan in the community of Valencia, *International Journal of the Sociology of language* 184: 95–108.

Glinert, Lewis, 1987, Hebrew-Yiddish diglossia: Type and stereotype implications of the language of Ganzfried's *Kitzur, International Journal of the Sociology of Language* 67: 39–56.

1991, Language choice and the Halakhic speech act. In Robert L. Cooper and B. Spolsky (eds.), *The influence of language on culture and thought: Essays in honor of Joshua A. Fishman's sixty-fifth birthday* (pp. 157–182), Berlin: Mouton de Gruyter.

1993, The first congress for Hebrew, or when is a congress not a congress? In Joshua A. Fishman (ed.), *The earliest stage of language planning: The "First Congress" phenomenon* (pp. 85–115), Berlin: Mouton de Gruyter.

1995, Inside the language planner's head: Tactical responses to new immigrants, *Journal of Multilingual and Multicultural Development* 16(5): 351–371.

Goitein, S. D., 1967–93, *A Mediterranean society: The Jewish communities of the Arab world as portrayed in the documents of the Cairo Geniza*, Berkeley: University of California Press.

Goldstein, Tara, 1994, Bilingual life and language choice on the production floor, *Multilingua* 13(1/2): 213–244.

Gorter, Durk, 2006 (ed.), *Linguistic landscape: A new approach to multilingualism*, Clevedon, UK: Multilingual Matters Ltd.

Graves, M. P., 2001, Quakerism. In John F. A. Sawyer and J. M. Y. Simpson (eds.), *Concise encyclopedia of language and religion* (pp. 83–84), Amsterdam, New York, Oxford, Shannon, Singapore, and Tokyo: Elsevier.

Grenoble, Lenore A., 2003, *Soviet language policy*, Dordrecht: Kluwer Academic Publishers.

Griffin, Jeffrey L., 2001, Global English invades Bulgaria, *English Today* 17(4): 54–60.

2004, The presence of written English on the streets of Rome, *English Today* 20(2): 3–8.

Grimes, Barbara A., 2000 (ed.), *Ethnologue: Languages of the world* (14th edn.), Dallas, TX: SIL International.

Grin, François, 1994, The bilingual advertising decision, *Journal of Multilingual and Multicultural Development* 15(2–3): 269–292.

1995, Combining immigrant and autochthonous language rights: A territorial approach to multilingualism. In Robert Phillipson, Mart Rannut, and Tove Skutnabb-Kangas (eds.), *Linguistic human rights: Overcoming linguistic discrimination* (pp. 31–49), Berlin and New York: Mouton de Gruyter.

1996, The economics of language: survey, assessment and prospects, *International Journal of the Sociology of Language* 121: 17–44.

2001, English an economic value: Facts and fallacies, *World Englishes* 20(1): 65–78.

Grin, François and Vaillancourt, François, 1998, *Language revitalization policy: Theoretical framework, policy experience, and application to Te Reo Maori* (Treasury Working Paper No. 98/6), Wellington: New Zealand Treasury.

1999, *The cost-effectiveness evaluation of minority language policies: Case studies on Wales, Ireland, the Basque Country*, Flensburg, Germany: European Centre for Minority Isssues.

Gumperz, John J., 1968, The speech community. In David L. Sills (ed.), *International Encyclopedia of the Social Sciences* (Vol. IX, pp. 381–386), New York: Macmillan Company.

1976, Social network and language shift. In J. Cook Gumperz and John J. Gumperz (eds.), *Papers on language and context: Working paper no. 46*, Berkeley: Language Behavior Research Laboratory, University of California.

Guyot, Jacques, 2007, Minority language media and the public sphere. In Mike Cormack and Niamh Hourigan (eds.), *Minority language media: Concepts, critiques and case studies* (pp. 34–51), Clevedon, UK: Multilingual Matters Ltd.

Haarmann, Harald, 1989, *Symbolic values of foreign language use: From the Japanese case to a general sociolinguistic perspective*, Berlin: Mouton de Gruyter.

Hagen, Stephen, 1999, *Business communication across the borders: A study of language used and practices in European companies*, London: Languages National Training Organisation.

Hall, Robert A., 1950, *Leave your language alone!*, Ithaca, NY: Cornell University Press.

Harlow, Ray, 2004, Switzerland. In Phillip Strazny (ed.), *Encyclopedia of linguistics*. London: Taylor & Francis.

2007, *Māori: A linguistic introduction*, Cambridge: Cambridge University Press.

Harris, John, 2007, Bilingual education and bilingualism in Ireland North and South, *International Journal of Bilingual Education and Bilingualism* 10(4): 359–368.

Harris, Judith Rich, 1995, Where is the child's environment? A group socialization theory of development. *Psychological Review* 102: 458–489.

1998, *The nurture assumption: Why children turn out the way they do*, New York: Free Press.

Harris, Sandra and Bargiela-Chiappini, Francesca, 2003, Business as a site of language contact, *Annual Review of Applied linguistics* 23: 155–169.

Harzing, Anne-Will, 2001, Who's in charge? An empirical study of executive staffing practices in foreign subsidiaries, *Human Resource Management* 40(2): 139–158.

Harzing, Anne-Will and Van Ruysseveldt, Joris, 2004 (eds.), *International human resource management* (2nd edn.), London: Sage.

Haugen, Einar, 1966, *Language conflict and language planning: The case of Modern Norwegian*, Cambridge, MA: Harvard University Press.

1987, *Blessings of Babel: Bilingualism and language planning: Problems and pleasures*, Berlin, New York, and Amsterdam: Mouton de Gruyter.

Hayashi, Asako, 2006, Japanese English bilingual children in three different language environments. In Kimi Kondo-Brown (ed.), *Heritage language development: Focus on East Asian immigrants* (pp. 145–171), Amsterdam: John Benjamins.

Heinrich, Patrick, 2004, Language planning and language ideology in the Ryukyu Islands, *Language Policy* 3(2): 133–152.

Held, David, 2006, *Models of democracy* (3rd edn.), Oxford: Polity.

Hill, Pat and Zyl, Susan van, 2002, English and multilingualism in the South African engineering workplace, *World Englishes* 21(1): 23–35.

Hillman, Josh, 2006, *School admissions in the United States: Policy, research and practice*, London: The Institute for Public Policy Research.

Hilmarsson-Dunn, A. M., 2006, Protectionist language policies in the face of the forces of English: The case of Iceland, *Language Policy* 5(3): 293–312.

Hirataka, Fumiya, 1992, Language-spread policy of Japan. *International Journal of the Sociology of Language* 95: 93–108.

Hirvonen, Vuokko, 2008, 'Out on the fells, I feel like a Sámi': Is there linguistic and cultural equality in the Sámi school? In Nancy H. Hornberger (ed.), *Can schools save indigenous languages? Policy and practice on four continents* (pp. 15–41), Basingstoke: Palgrave Macmillan.

Hockett, Charles F., 1958, *A course in modern linguistics*, New York: Macmillan.

Hodges, Flavia, 2007, Language planning and placenaming in Australia, *Current Issues in Language Planning* 8(3): 383–403.

Hogan-Brun, Gabrielle, 2006, At the interface of language ideology and practice: The public discourse surrounding the 2004 education reform in Latvia, *Language Policy* 5(3): 313–333.

Hohepa, Pat, 2000, Towards 2030 AD: Maori language regeneration: Examining Maori language health, paper presented at the Applied Linguistics Conference, Auckland, New Zealand.

Holliday, Lloyd, 1993, The first language congress for Afrikaans. In Joshua A. Fishman (ed.), *The earliest stage of language planning: The "First Congress" phenomenon* (pp. 11–30). Berlin: Mouton de Gruyter.

Holm, Agnes and Holm, Wayne, 1995, Navajo language education: retrospect and prospects, *Bilingual Research Journal* 19: 141–167.

Holm, Wayne and Holm, Agnes, 1990, Rock Point: A Navajo way to go to school: A valediction, *Annals, AASSP* 508: 170–184.

Holt, Sally and Packer, John, 2001, OSCE developments and linguistic minorities, *MOST Journal of Multicultural Studies* 3(2): 78–98.

Hornberger, Nancy H. and King, Kendall A., 2001, Reversing language shift in South America. In Joshua A. Fishman (ed.), *Can threatened languages be saved?* (pp. 166–194), Clevedon, UK: Multilingual Matters Ltd.

Hornikx, Jos, van Meurs, Frank, and Starren, Marianne, 2007, An empirical study of readers' associations with multilingual advertising: The case of French, German and Spanish in Dutch advertising, *Journal of Multilingual and Multicultural Development* 28(3): 204–219.

Hourigan, Niamh, 2007, The roles of networks in minority language television campaigns. In Mike Cormack and Niamh Hourigan (eds.), *Minority language media: Concepts, critiques and case studies* (pp. 69–87), Clevedon, UK: Multilingual Matters Ltd.

Houwer, Annick de, 2003, Language variation and local elements in family discourse, *Language Variation and Change* 15(3): 329–349.

Hsu, William C., Cheung, Sophia, Ong, Emmelyn, *et al.* 2006, Identification of linguistic barriers to diabetes knowledge and glycemic control in Chinese Americans with diabetes, *Diabetes Care* 29: 415–416.

Hu, Yuanuan, 2007, China's foreign language policy on primary English education: What's behind it? *Language Policy* 6(3–4): 359–376.

Hudson, Alan, 2002, Outline of a theory of diglossia, *International Journal of the Sociology of Language* 157: 1–49.

Huws, Catrin Fflur, 2006, The Welsh Language Act 1993: A measure of success? *Language Policy* 5(2): 141–160.

Hyde, Barbara, 2002, Japan's emblematic English, *English Today* 18(3): 12–16.

Hymes, Dell, 1974, *Foundations in sociolinguistics: An ethnographic approach*, Philadelphia: University of Pennsylvania Press.

InterAct International, 2003a, *e-skills: IT, Telecom and contact centres*, Newcastle-upon-Tyne, UK: InterAct International for CILT.

    2003b, *SEMTA: science, engineering, and manufacturing technologies*, Newcastle-upon-Tyne, UK: InterAct International for CILT.

Isaacs, Miriam, 1999, Contentious partners: Yiddish and Hebrew in Haredi Israel, *International Journal of the Sociology of Language* 138: 101–121.

Isabelle, P. and Foster, G., 2006, Machine translation: Overview. In Keith Brown (ed.), *Encyclopedia of language and linguistics* (Vol. VII, 2nd edn., pp. 404–424), Oxford: Elsevier.

Ishtiaq, M., 2000, Spatial distribution of bilingual tribal population in India, *Man in India* 39(3–4): 371–381.

Jackendoff, Ray, 1983, *Semantics and cognition*, Cambridge, MA: MIT Press.

Jeffrey, Robin, 1997, Advertising and Indian-language newspapers: How capitalism supports (certain) cultures and (some) states, 1947–1996, *Pacific Affairs* 70(1): 57–84.

Jernudd, Björn H., 1997, The (r)evolution of sociolinguistics. In Christina Bratt Paulston and G. Richard Tucker (eds.), *The early days of sociolinguistics* (pp. 131–138), Dallas, TX: Summer Institute of Linguistics.

Jernudd, Björn and Neustupný, Jiří V., 1987, Language planning: For whom? In L. LaForge (ed.), *Proceedings of the international colloquium on language planning* (pp. 69–84), Québec, Canada: Presses de l'Université Laval.

Johnson, Sally, 2002, On the origin of linguistic norms: Orthography, ideology and the first constitutional challenge to the 1996 reform of German, *Language in Society* 31(4): 549–576.

Johnson-Weiner, Karen M., 2007, *Train up a child: Old order Amish and Mennonite schools*, Baltimore, MD: Johns Hopkins University Press.

Jones, John Paul, 2001, 2006, *Constitution finder*, from http://confinder.richmond.edu/

Jones, Paul A., 1998, Alien acts: The white Australia policy, 1901 to 1939, unpublished Ph.D. thesis, University of Melbourne, Melbourne.

Joseph, John E., 2006, The shifting role of languages in Lebanese Christian and Muslim identities. In Tope Omoniyi and Joshua A. Fishman (eds.), *Explorations in the sociology of language and religion* (pp. 165–179), Amsterdam and Philadelphia: John Benjamins Publishing Company.

Kachru, Braj B., 1986, *The alchemy of English: The spread, functions and models of non-native Englishes*, Oxford: Pergamon Institute of English.

Kaplan, Robert B. and Baldauf, Richard B., 1997, *Language planning from practice to theory*, Clevedon, UK: Multilingual Matters Ltd.

2003, *Language and language-in-education planning in the Pacific basin*, Dordrecht: Kluwer Academic Publishers.

Katz, Mira-Lisa, 2001, Engineering a hotel family: Language ideology, discourse, and workplace culture, *Linguistics and Education* 12(3): 309–343.

Keefers, L. E., 1988, *Scholars in foxholes: The story of the Army Specialized Training Program in World War II*, Jefferson, NC: McFarland Company.

Kelly-Holmes, Helen, 2000, Bier, parfum, kaas: Language fetish in European advertising, *European Journal of Cultural Studies* 3(1): 67–82.

Kelly-Jones, Helen and Atkinson, David, 2007, Minority language advertising: A profile of two Irish-language newspapers, *Journal of Multilingual and Multicultural Development* 28(1): 34–50.

Kheimets, Nina G. and Epstein, Alek D., 2005, Languages of science in the era of nation-state formation: The Israeli universities and their (non)participation in the revival of Hebrew, *Journal of Multilingual and Multicultural Development* 26(1): 12–36.

Khubchandani, Lachman M., 1997, Language policy and education in the Indian subcontinent. In Ruth Wodak and David Corson (eds.), *Encyclopedia of language and education (Vol. I: Language policy and political issues in education*, pp. 179–187), Dordrecht: Kluwer Academic Publishers.

Killingley, D. D., 2001, Hinduism. In John F. A. Sawyer and J. M. Y. Simpson (eds.), *Concise encyclopedia of language and religion* (pp. 52–54), Amsterdam, New York, Oxford, Shannon, Singapore, and Tokyo: Elsevier.

King, Jeanette, 2001, Te Kohanga Reo: Maori language revitalization. In Leanne Hinton and Ken Hale (eds.), *The green book of language revitalization in practice* (pp. 129–132), New York: Academic Press.

King, Kendall A. and Fogle, Lyn, 2006, Bilingual parenting as good parenting: Parents' perspective on family language policy for additive bilingualism, *International Journal of Bilingual Education and Bilingualism* 9(6): 695–712.

King, Robert, 1999, Orientalism and the modern myth of "Hinduism," *Numen* 46(2): 146–185.

Kleineidam, Hartmut, 1992, Politique de diffusion linguistique et francophonie: l'action linguistique menée par la France, *International Journal of the Sociology of Language* 95: 11–31.

Kloss, Heinz, 1966, German-American language maintenance efforts. In Joshua Fishman (ed.), *Language loyalty in the United States* (pp. 206–252), The Hague: Mouton.

1967, Abstand-languages and Ausbau-languages, *Anthropological Linguistics* 9: 29–41.

1969, *Research possibilities on group bilingualism: A report*, Québec: International Center for Research on Bilingualism.

Koester, Almut, 2004, *The language of work*, London: Routledge (Taylor & Francis).

Kondo-Brown, Kimi, 2006 (ed.), *Heritage language development: Focus on East Asian immigrants*, Amsterdam: John Benjamins Publishing Company.

Kopeliovich, Shulamit, 2006, Reversing language shift in the immigrant family: Case study of a Russian-speaking community in Israel, unpublished Ph.D. dissertation, Bar-Ilan University, Ramat-Gan.

Kouega, Jean-Paul, 2007, The language situation in Cameroon, *Current Issues in Language planning* 8(1): 3–92.

Kratz, E. E., 2001, Islam in Southeast Asia. In John F. A. Sawyer and J. M. Y. Simpson (eds.), *Concise encyclopedia of language and religion* (pp. 65–66), Amsterdam, New York, Oxford, Shannon, Singapore, and Tokyo: Elsevier.

Krauss, Michael, 1991, The world's languages in crisis, *Language* 68(1): 4–10.

Kulick, Don, 1992, *Language shift and cultural reproduction: Socialization, self and syncretism in a Papua New Guinean village*, Cambridge and New York: Cambridge University Press.

Kymlicka, Will and Patten, Alan, 2003, Introduction: Language rights and political theory: Context, issues and approaches. In Will Kymlicka and Alan Patten (eds.), *Language rights and political theory* (pp. 1–51), Oxford: Oxford University Press.

Labov, William, 1966, *The social stratification of English in New York City*, Washington DC: Center for Applied Linguistics.

1972, Some principles of linguistic methodology, *Language in Society* 1(1): 97–120.

1973, The linguistic consequence of being a lame, *Language in Society* 2(1): 81–115.

Ladousa, Chaise, 2002, Advertising in the periphery: Languages and schools in a north Indian city, *Language in Society* 31(2): 213–242.

Laitin, David D., 2000, Language conflict and violence: The straw that strengthens the camel's back. In Paul C. Stern and Daniel Druckman (eds.), *International conflict resolution after the Cold War* (pp. 531–560). Washington DC: National Research Council, Committee on International Conflict Resolution.

Lakoff, Robin, 1973, Language and woman's place, *Language in Society* 2(1): 45–80.

Lakoff, Robin and Bucholtz, Mary, 2004 (eds.), *Language and women's place: Text and commentaries* (revised and expanded edn.), New York: Oxford University Press.

Lam, Eva, 2007, Digital networks and multiliteracies in negotiating local and trans-local affiliations among migrant youth, *Language Education and Diversity*, University of Waikato.

Lambert, Richard D., 1994, Problems and processes in US foreign language planning, *Annals of the American Academy of Political and Social Sciences* 532: 47–58.

1999, A scaffolding for language policy, *International Journal of the Sociology of Language* 137: 3–25.

Lambert, Wallace E. and Tucker, G. Richard, 1972, *Bilingual education of children: The St. Lambert experiment*, Rowley, MA: Newbury House Publishers.

Landau, Jacob and Kellner-Heinkele, Barbara, 2001, *Politics of language in the ex-Soviet Muslim states: Azerbaijan, Uzbekistan, Kazakhstan, Kyrgyzstan,*

Turkmenistan and Tajikistan, London and Ann Arbor, MI: C. Hurst & Co. and University of Michigan Press.

Landry, Rodrigue and Bourhis, Richard Y, 1997, Linguistic landscape and ethnolinguistic vitality: An empirical study, *Journal of Language and Social Psychology* 16: 23–49.

Language and National Origin Group, 2004, Guidelines for the use of language and analysis in relation to questions of national origin in refugee cases, *The International Journal of Speech, Language and the Law* 11(2): 261–266.

LaRocque, Norman, 2005, Contracting for the delivery of education services: A typology and international examples, *Mobilizing the Private Sector for Public Education*: The Program on Education Policy and Governance at Harvard University.

Larrivée, Pierre, 2002 (ed.), *Linguistic conflict and language laws: Understanding the Quebec question*, Basingstoke: Palgrave Macmillan.

Latukefu, S., 1974, *Church and state in Tonga* (1980 ed.), Canberra, Australia: Australian National University Press.

Lautomaa, Sirkku and Nuolijärvi, Pirkko, 2002, The language situation in Finland, *Current Issues in Language planning* 3(2): 95–202.

Le Page, Robert, 1968, Problems to be faced in the use of English as the medium of education in four West Indian territories. In Joshua A. Fishman, Charles A. Ferguson, and Jyotirindra Das Gupta (eds.), *Language problems of developing nations* (pp. 431–442), New York: Wiley.

Leclerc, Jacques, 1994, *Recueil des législations linguistiques dans le monde*, Québec, Canada: Centre internationale de recherche en aménagement linguistique.

1994–2007, *L'aménagement linguistique dans le monde*, 2007, from http://www.tlfq.ulaval.ca/axl/

Lester, T., 1994, Pulling down the language barrier, *International Management* (July–August): 16–23.

Letelier, Armand, 1987, *DND language reform: Staffing the bilingualism programs 1967–1977*, Ottawa: Minister of Supply and Services.

Lewis, E. Glyn, 1972, *Multilingualism in the Soviet Union*, The Hague: Mouton.

1980, *Bilingualism and bilingual education: A comparative study*, Albuquerque and Oxford: University of New Mexico Press and Pergamon Publishers.

Lewis, Geoffrey, 1999, *The Turkish language reform: A catastrophic success*, Oxford: Oxford University Press.

Li, Guofang, 2006, The role of parents in heritage language maintenance and development: Case studies of Chinese immigrant children's home practices. In Kimi Kondo-Brown (ed.), *Heritage language development: Focus on East Asian immigrants* (pp. 15–32), Amsterdam: John Benjamins Publishing Company.

Lilla, Mark, 2007, Mr Casaubon in America: The collected works of Eric Voegelin, *The New York Review of Books*, 54: 29–31.

Lim, Young-Hee, 1996, Research in Korean and Japanese multilingual writing, unpublished graduation thesis, Tokyo University of Foreign Studies, Tokyo.

Lind, Melva, 1948, *Modern language learning: The intensive course as sponsored by the United States Army, and implications for the undergraduate course of study*, Provincetown, MA: The Journal Press.

Lipner, Julius J., 2001, Hindu views on language. In J. F. A. Sawyer, J. M. Y. Simpson, and R. E. Asher (eds.), *Concise encyclopedia of language and religion* (pp. 295–298), Amsterdam: Elsevier.

Lo Bianco, Joseph, 1987, *National policy on languages*, Canberra: Australian Government Publishing Service.

Lo Bianco, Joseph and Wickert, Rosie, 2001 (eds.), *Australian policy activism in language and literacy*, Canberra, Australia: Language Australia.

López, Luis Enrique, 2006, Cultural diversity, multilingualism and indigenous education in Latin America. In Ofelia García, Tove Skutnabb-Kangas, and Maria E. Torres-Guzmán (eds.), *Imagining multilingual schools* (pp. 238–261), Clevedon, UK, Buffalo, and Toronto: Multilingual Matters Limited.

 2008, Top-down and bottom-up: Counterpoised visions of bilingual intercultural education in Latin America. In Nancy H. Hornberger (ed.), *Can schools save indigenous languages? Policy and practice on four continents* (pp. 42–65), Basingstoke: Palgrave Macmillan.

Lüdi, Georges, 2007, The Swiss model of plurilingual communication. In Jan D. ten Thije and Ludger Zeevaert (eds.), *Receptive multilingualism: Linguistic analyses, language policies and didactic concepts* (pp. 159–178), Amsterdam and Philadephia: John Benjamins Publishing Company.

Lutz, Ellen, 2007, Recognizing indigenous peoples' human rights, *Cultural Survival Voices*, 5 (http://www.culturalsurvival.org/publications/csv/csv-article.cfm?id=109).

Maamouri, Mohamed, 1998, *Language education and human development: Arabic diglossia and its impact on the quality of education in the Arabic region*, Paper presented at the World Bank: The Mediterranean Development Forum, Marrakech.

Mac Giolla Chríost, Diarmait, 2006, Micro-level language planning in Ireland, *Current Issues in Language Planning* 7(2 & 3): 230–250.

Mackey, William, 1970, A typology of bilingual education, *Foreign Language Annals* 3(4): 596–608.

MacNamara, John, 1966, *Bilingualism and primary education*, Edinburgh: Edinburgh University Press.

 1971, Successes and failures in the movement for the restoration of Irish. In Joan Rubin and Björn Jernudd (eds.), *Can language be planned?* Honolulu: University Press of Hawaii.

MacNaughton, James C., 1994, Nisei linguists and new perspectives on the Pacific War: Intelligence, race, and continuity, *Conference of Army Historians* (http://www.army.mil/cmh-pg/topics/apam/Nisei.htm).

Malinowski, David, 2008, Authorship in the linguistic landscape: A performative-multimodal view. In Elana Shohamy and Durk Gorter (eds.), *The linguistic landscape: Expanding the scenery*, London: Routledge.

Mandel, George, 1993, Why did Ben-Yehuda suggest the revival of spoken Hebrew? In Lewis Glinert (ed.), *Hebrew in Ashkenaz* (pp. 193–207), New York and Oxford: Oxford University Press.

Marongiu, Maria Antonietta, 2007, Language maintenance and shift in Sardinia: A case study of Sardinian and Italian in Cagliari, unpublished Ph.D. dissertation, University of Illinois at Urbana–Champaign, Urbana–Champaign.

Marriott, Helen, 2006, Micro language planning for student support in a pharmacy faculty, *Current issues in language planning* 7(2 & 3): 328–340.

Martin, Elizabeth, 2002a, Cultural images and different varieties of English in French television commercials, *English Today* 18(4): 8–20.

2002b, Mixing English in French advertising, *World Englishes* 21(3): 375–411.

Martin, Terry, 2002, *The affirmative action empire: Nations and nationalism in the Soviet Union 1923–1939*, Ithaca, NY: Cornell University Press.

Masai, Yasuo, 1972, *Living map of Tokyo*, Tokyo: Jiji Tsushinsha.

Mataira, Katarina, 1980, The effectiveness of the Silent Way in the teaching of Maori as a second language, unpublished M.Ed. thesis, University of Waikato, Hamilton, New Zealand.

Mateo, Miren, 2005, Language policy and planning of the status of Basque, I: The Basque Autonomous Community (BAC), *International Journal of the Sociology of language* 174: 9–23.

Mattock, J. N., 2001, Islam in the Near East. In John F. A. Sawyer and J. M. Y. Simpson (eds.), *Concise encyclopedia of language and religion* (pp. 60–62), Amsterdam, New York, Oxford, Shannon, Singapore, and Tokyo: Elsevier.

May, Robert M., Levin, Simon A., and Sugihara, George, 2008, Ecology for bankers. *Nature* 451: 893–895.

McCarty, Teresa L., 2002, *A place to be Navajo: Rough Rock and the struggle for self-determination in indigenous schooling*, Mahwah, NJ: Lawrence Erlbaum Associates.

McClure, James A., 1983, National Defense Education Act: Interview with Senator McClure. In Senate Historical Oral History Project (ed.) (p. 118) (http://www.senate.gov/artandhistory/history/resources/pdf/McClure4.pdf).

McNamara, Tim, 2005, 21st century shibboleth: Language tests, identity and inter-group conflict, *Language Policy* 4(4): 351–370.

McRae, Kenneth D., 1975, The principle of territoriality and the principle of personality in multilingual states, *International Journal of the Sociology of Language* 4: 33–54.

2007, Towards language equality: Four democracies compared, *International Journal of the Sociology of language* 187–188: 13–54.

Mehrotra, Raja Ran, 1993, The first congress of Hindi. In Joshua A. Fishman (ed.), *The earliest stage of language planning: The "First Congress" phenomenon* (pp. 117–126). Berlin: Mouton de Gruyter.

Milroy, Lesley, 1980, *Languages and social networks*, Oxford: Basil Blackwell.

Moeliono, Anton M., 1993, The first efforts to promote and develop Indonesia. In Joshua A. Fishman (ed.), *The earliest stage of language planning: The "First Congress" phenomenon* (pp. 129–142), Berlin: Mouton de Gruyter.

Mohanty, Panchanan, 2002, British language policies in 19th century India and the Oriya language movement, *Language Policy* 1(1): 57–73.

Monnier, Daniel, 1989, *Langue d'accueil et langue de service dans les commerces*, Montreal, Québec: Conseil de la langue française.

Montolalu, Lucy Ruth and Suryadinata, Leo, 2007, National language and nation-building: The case of Bahasa Indonesia. In Lee Hock Guan and Leo Suryadinata (eds.), *Language, nation and development in Southeast Asia* (pp. 39–50), Singapore: Institute of South-East Asian Studies.

Moser, Claus, 1999, *Improving literacy and numeracy: A fresh start*, London: Department of Education and Employment.

Mugglestone, L. C., 2006, Academies: Dictionaries and standards. In Keith Brown (ed.), *Encyclopedia of language and linguistics* (Vol. I, 2nd edn., pp. 12–14), Oxford: Elsevier.

Myers-Scotton, Carol, 2002, *Contact linguistics: Bilingual encounters and grammatical outcomes*, Oxford: Oxford University Press.

Myron, Herbert B., 1944, Teaching French in the army. *French Review* 17(6): 345–352.

Nair-Venugopalk, Shanta, 2001, The sociolinguistics of choice in a Malaysian business setting, *International Journal of Sociology of Language* 152: 21–52.

Nairn, Raymond G. and McCreanor, Timothy N., 1991, Race talk and common sense: Patterns in Pakeha discourse on Maori/Pakeha relations in New Zealand, *Journal of Language and Social Psychology* 10(4): 242–262.

Nekvapil, Jiří, 2006, From language planning to language management, *Sociolinguistica* 20: 92–104.

2007, On the relationship between small and large Slavic languages, *International Journal of the Sociology of Language* 183: 141–160.

2008, Language cultivation in developed contexts. In Bernard Spolsky and Francis M. Hult (eds.), *Handbook of educational linguistics* (pp. 251–265), Oxford: Blackwell.

Nekvapil, Jiří and Nekula, Marek, 2006, On language management in multinational companies in the Czech Republic, *Current Issues in Language Planning* 7(2 & 3): 307–327.

Nelde, Peter H., Labrie, Normand, and Williams, C. H., 1992, The principles of territoriality and personality in the solution of linguistic conflicts, *Journal of Multilingual and Multicultural Development* 13: 387–406.

Neustupný, Jiří V., 1970, Basic types of treatment of language problems, *Linguistic Communications* 1: 77–98.

Neustupný, Jiří V. and Nekvapil, Jiří, 2003, Language management in the Czech republic, *Current Issues in Language Planning* 4(3 & 4): 181–366.

Ng, Sik Hung and He, Anping, 2004, Code-switching in trigenerational family conversations among Chinese immigrants in New Zealand, *Journal of Language and Social Psychology* 23(1): 28–48.

Nic Shuibhne, Niamh, 2001, The European Union and minority language rights, *MOST Journal of Multicultural Studies* 3(2): 61–77.

Nicholson, Rangi, 1990, Maori total immersion courses for adults in Aotearoa/New Zealand: A personal perspective. In Jon Reyhner (ed.), *Effective language education practices and native language survival* (pp. 107–120), Choctaw, OK: Native American Language Issues.

North, Brian, 1992, *Options for scales of proficiency for a European Language Framework* (Occasional Paper), National Foreign Language Center.

North, Brian, Figueras, Neus, Takala, Sali, van Avermaet, Piet, and Verhelst, Norman, 2003. *Relating language examinations to the Common European Framework of Reference for Languages: Learning, teaching, assessment (CEF)* (Preliminary pilot version), Strasbourg: Council of Europe.

Ó hlfearnain, Tadhg, 2007, Raising children to be bilingual in the Gaeltacht: Language preference and practice, *International Journal of Bilingual Education and Bilingualism* 10(4): 510–528.

Ó Laoire, Muiris, 1996, An historical perspective of the revival of Irish outside the Gaeltacht, 1880–1930, with reference to the revitalization of Hebrew. In Sue Wright (ed.), *Language and state: Revitalization and revival in Israel and Eire* (pp. 51–75), Clevedon, UK: Multilingual Matters Ltd.

Ó Riágain, Pádraig, 1997, *Language policy and social reproduction: Ireland 1893–1993*, Oxford: Clarendon Press.

2001, Irish language production and reproduction 1981–1996. In Joshua A. Fishman (ed.), *Can threatened languages be saved?* (pp. 195–214). Clevedon, UK: Multilingual Matters Ltd.

2007, Relationships between attitudes to Irish, social class, religion and national identity in the Republic of Ireland and Northern Ireland, *International Journal of Bilingual Education and Bilingualism* 10(4): 369–393.

Ochs, Elinor, 1986, Introduction. In Bambi B. Schieffelin and Elinor Ochs (eds.), *Language socialization across cultures* (pp. 2–13), Cambridge: Cambridge University Press.

Ogden, Charles Kay, 1932, *ABC of basic English*, London: Kegan Paul.

Oppenheimer, Stephen, 2006, *The origin of the British: A genetic detective story*, London: Constable.

Ormrod, W. M., 2003, The use of English: Language, law, and political culture in fourteenth-century England, *Speculum* 78(3): 750–787.

Ozolins, Uldis, 1996, Language policy and political reality, *International Journal of the Sociology of Language* 118: 181–200.

2003, The impact of European accession upon language policy in the Baltic States, *Language Policy* 2(3): 217–238.

Paffey, Darren, 2007, Policing the Spanish language debate: Verbal hygiene and the Spanish Language Academy (Real Academia Española), *Language Policy* 6(3–4): 313–332.

Pandharipande, Rajeshwari V., 2006, Ideology, authority and language choice: Language of religion in South Asia. In Tope Omoniyi and Joshua A. Fishman (eds.), *Explorations in the sociology of language and religion* (pp. 141–164), Amsterdam and Philadelphia: John Benjamins Publishing Company.

Paulston, Christina Bratt, 1997, Language policies and language rights, *Annual Review of Anthropology* 26: 73–85.

Pauwels, Anne, 1998, *Women changing languages*, New York: Addison Wesley Longman.

Pennycook, Alastair, 2008, Linguistic landscapes and the transgressive semiotics of graffiti. In Elana Shohamy and Durk Gorter (eds.), *The linguistic landscape: Expanding the scenery*, London: Routledge.

Peters, F. E., 2003, *The monotheists: Jews, Christians and Muslims in conflict and competition*, Princeton, NJ: Princeton University Press.

Phillipson, Robert, 1990, English language teaching and imperialism, unpublished doctorate, University of Amsterdam, Amsterdam.

1992, *Linguistic imperialism*, Oxford: Oxford University Press.

1994, English language spread policy, *International Journal of the Sociology of Language* 107: 7–24.

2003, *English-Only Europe? Challenging language policy*, London: Routledge.

Pickering, W. S. F., 2001, Blasphemy. In John F. A. Sawyer and J. M. Y. Simpson (eds.), *Concise encyclopedia of language and religion* (p. 240), Amsterdam, New York, Oxford, Shannon, Singapore, and Tokyo: Elsevier.

Pierce, John R., Carroll, John B., Hamp, Eric P. *et al.*, 1966, *Language and machines: Computers in translation and linguistics. ALPAC report*, Washington DC: National Academy of Sciences, National Research Council.

Piller, Ingrid, 2001, Identity constructions in multilingual advertising, *Language in Society* 30(4): 153–186.

 2003, Advertising as a site of language contact, *Annual Review of Applied Linguistics* 23: 170–183.

Piulais, Maria Corominas, 2007, Media policy and language policy in Catalonia. In Mike Cormack and Niamh Hourigan (eds.), *Minority language media: Concepts, critiques and case studies* (pp. 168–187), Clevedon, UK: Multilingual Matters Ltd.

Poggeschi, Giovanni, 2004, Language policy in Latvia, *Noves SL Revista de Sociolinguistica* (Autumn) (http://www6.gencat.net/llengcat/noves/hm04tardor/poggeschi1_3.htm).

Pope John XXIII, November 28, 1959, *Princeps Pastorum, On the missions, native clergy, and lay participation*. Retrieved 27 January 2008, from http://www.newadvent.org/library/docs_jo23pp.htm

Poulton, Hugh, 1998, Linguistic minorities in the Balkans (Albania, Greece and the successor states of former Yugoslavia). In Christina Bratt Paulston and Donald Peckham (eds.), *Linguistic minorities in Central and East Europe* (pp. 37–80), Clevedon, UK and Philadelphia, USA: Multilingual Matters Ltd.

Prague School, 1973, General principles for the cultivation of good language (trans. Paul L. Garvin). In Joan Rubin and Roger Shuy (eds.), *Language planning: Current issues and research* (pp. 102–111), Washington DC: Georgetown University Press.

Prator, Clifford H., 1968, The British heresy in TESL. In Joshua A. Fishman, Charles A. Ferguson, and Jyotirindra Das Gupta (eds.), *Language problems of developing nations* (pp. 459–466), New York: John Wiley and Sons.

Rabin, Chaim, 1981, What constitutes a Jewish language? *International Journal of the Sociology of Language* 30: 19–28.

Ragila, Ranjit Singh, Thirumalai M. S., and Mallikarjun, B., 2001, Bringing order to linguistic diversity: Language planning in the British Raj, *Language in India* 1 (available at: http://www.languageinindia.com/oct2001/punjab1.html).

Rahman, Tariq, 2006, Muslim/Islamic education in Pakistan and India. In Keith Brown (ed.), *Encyclopedia of languages and linguistics*, Cambridge: Elsevier.

Rajagopalan, Kanavillill, 2002, National languages as flags of allegiance, or the linguistics that failed us: A close look at emergent linguistic chauvinism in Brazil, *Journal of Language and Politics* 1(1): 115–147.

Rajah-Carrim, Aaliya, 2007, Mauritian Creole and language attitudes in the education system of multiethnic and multilingual Mauritius, *Journal of Multilingual and Multicultural Development* 28(1): 51–71.

Ramallo, Fernando, 2007, Sociolinguistics of Spanish in Galicia, *International Journal of the Sociology of Language* 184: 21–36.

Ranger, Terence, 1989, Missionaries, migrants and the Manyoka: The invention of ethnicity in Zimbabwe. In Leroy Vail (ed.), *The creation of tribalism in Southern Africa*, Berkeley and Los Angeles: University of California Press.

Rannut, Mart, 1995, Beyond linguistic policy: The Soviet Union versus Estonia. In Robert Phillipson, Mart Rannut, and Tove Skutnabb-Kangas (eds.), *Linguistic human rights: Overcoming linguistic discrimination* (pp. 179–208), Berlin and New York: Mouton de Gruyter.

Rappa, Antonio L. and Wee, Lionel, 2006, *Language policy and modernity in Southeast Asia: Malaysia, the Philippines, Singapore, and Thailand*, New York: Springer.

Ravitch, Diane, 2003, *The language police: How pressure groups restrict what students learn*, New York: Knopf.

Reath, Anne, 2004, Language analysis in the context of the asylum process: procedures, validity, and consequences, *Language Assessment Quarterly* 1(4): 209–233.

Recendiz, Nicanor Rebolledo, 2008, Learning with differences: Strengthening Hñähñö and bilingual teaching in an elementary school in Mexico City. In Nancy H. Hornberger (ed.), *Can schools save indigenous languages? Policy and practice on four continents* (pp. 99–124), Basingstoke: Palgrave Macmillan.

Reichard, Gladys, 1963, *Navaho religion: A study of symbolism* (2nd edn.), New York: Pantheon Books.

Revel, Jean-François, 1988, *La Connaissance inutile*, Paris: Grasset.

1991, *The flight from truth: The reign of deceit in the age of information* (trans. Curtis Cate), New York: Random House.

Riis, Jacob A., 1971, *How the other half lives: Studies among the tenements of New York* (Originally published in 1890 by Charles Scribner's Sons), New York: Dover Publications Inc.

Robinson, W. Peter and Giles, Howard, 2001 (eds.), *The new handbook of language and social psychology*, Chichester, England: John Wiley.

Rohsenow, John S., 2004, Fifty years of script and written language reform in the P.R.C.: The genesis of the language law of 2001. In Minglang Zhou (ed.), *Language policy in the People's Republic of China: Theory and practice since 1949* (pp. 21–45), Dordrecht: Kluwer Academic Publishers.

Rosen, Lawrence, 1977, The anthropologist as expert witness, *American Anthropologist* 79(3): 555–578.

Rosenbaum, Yehudit, Nadel, Elizabeth, Cooper, Robert L., and Fishman, Joshua A., 1977, English on Keren Kayemet Street. In Joshua A. Fishman, Robert L. Cooper, and Andrew W. Conrad (eds.), *The spread of English* (pp. 179–196). Rowley, MA: Newbury House Publishers.

Rosier, Paul and Holm, Wayne, 1980, *The Rock Point experience: A longitudinal study of a Navajo school program*, Washington DC: Center for Applied Linguistics.

Rubin, Joan, 1977, Indonesian language planning and education. In Joan Rubin, Björn H. Jernudd, Jyotirindra Das Gupta, Joshua A. Fishman, and Charles A. Ferguson (eds.), *Language planning processes* (pp. 111–129), The Hague: Mouton.

1979, *Directory of language planning organizations*, Honolulu: East-West Center Culture Learning Institute.

Rubin, Joan, Jernudd, Björn, Das Gupta, Jyotirindra, Fishman, Joshua A., and Ferguson, Charles A., 1977, *Language planning processes*, The Hague: Mouton.

Ruiz Vieytez, Eduardo Javier, 2001, The protection of linguistic minorities: A historical approach. *MOST Journal of Multicultural Studies* 3(1): 5–14.

Sakamoto, Mitsuyo, 2006, Balancing L1 maintenance and L2 learning: Experiential narratives of Japanese immigrant families in Canada. In Kimi Kondo-Brown (ed.), *Heritage language development: Focus on East Asian immigrants* (pp. 33–56), Amsterdam: John Benjamins Publishing Company.

Sampson, Helen and Zhao, Minghua, 2003, Multilingual crews: Communication and the operation of ships, *World Englishes* 22(1): 31–43.

Sánchez, Aquilino and Duenas, María, 2002, Language planning in the Spanish-speaking world, *Current Issues in Language Planning* 3(3): 280–305.

Sandel, Todd L., 2003, Linguistic capital in Taiwan: The KMT's Mandarin language policy and its perceived impact on language practices of bilingual Mandarin and Tai-gi speakers, *Language in Society* 32(4): 523–551.

Saravanan, Vanithamani, Lakshmi, Seetha, and Caleon, Imelda, 2007, Attitudes towards Literary Tamil and Standard Spoken Tamil in Singapore, *International Journal of Bilingual Education and Bilingualism* 10(1): 58–79.

Saulson, Scott B., 1979 (ed.), *Institutionalized language planning*, The Hague: Mouton.

Saussure, Ferdinand de, 1931, *Cours de linguistique générale*, Paris: Payot.

Sawyer, J. F. A., 2001, Christianity in Europe. In John F. A. Sawyer and J. M. Y. Simpson (eds.), *Concise encyclopedia of language and religion* (pp. 33–35), Amsterdam, New York, Oxford, Shannon, Singapore, and Tokyo: Elsevier.

2006, Literacy and religion. In Keith Brown (ed.), *Encyclopedia of languages and linguistics*, Cambridge: Elsevier.

Schaps, Richard, 2007, How I did it, *Inc. Magazine*, October: 128–130.

Scharer, Rolf and North, Brian, 1992, *Toward a common European framework for reporting language competency* (Position paper), Washington DC: National Foreign Language Center.

Schiffman, Harold E., 1996, *Linguistic culture and language policy*, London and New York: Routledge.

Schlick, Margaret, 2002, The English of shop signs in Europe, *English Today* 18(2): 3–7.

Shackle, C., 2001, Islam in South Asia. In John F. A. Sawyer and J. M. Y. Simpson (eds.), *Concise encyclopedia of language and religion*, Amsterdam, Oxford, Shannon, Singapore, and Tokyo: Elsevier.

Shohamy, Elana, 2001, *The power of tests: A critical perspective of the uses of language tests*, London: Longman.

2006, *Language policy: Hidden agendas and new approaches*, New York: Routledge.

2007, At what cost? Methods of language revival and protection: Examples from Hebrew. In Kendall A. King, Natalie Schilling-Estes, Jia Jackie Lou, Lyn Fogle, and Barbara Soukup (eds.), *Endangered and minority languages and language varieties: Defining, documenting and developing*, Washington DC: Georgetown University.

Shweder, R. A., Much, N. C., Mahapatra, M., and Park, L., 1997, The "big three" of morality (autonomy, community, and divinity), and the "big three" explanations of suffering. In A. Brandt and P. Rozin (eds.), *Morality and health* (pp. 119–169), New York: Routledge.

Shweder, Richard, 1990, In defense of moral realism: Reply to Gabennesch, *Child Development* 61: 2060–2067.

Silverstein, Michael, 1998, Contemporary transformation of local linguistic communities, *Annual Review of Anthropology* 27: 401–426.

Simon, Judith, 1998 (ed.), *Nga Kura Maori: The native schools system 1867–1967*, Auckland: Auckland University Press.

Simon, Szabolcs and Kontra, Miklos, 2000, Slovak linguists and Slovak language laws: An analysis of Slovak language policy, *Multilingua* 19(1/2): 73–94.

Skutnabb-Kangas, Tove, 1988, Multilingualism and the education of minority children. In Tove Skutnabb-Kangas and James Cummins (eds.), *Minority education: From shame to struggle* (pp. 9–44), Clevedon, UK: Multilingual Matters Ltd.

Smalley, William A., 1994, *Linguistic diversity and national unity: Language ecology in Thailand*, Chicago: University of Chicago Press.

Smith, David 2001, Mantras. In J. F. A. Sawyer, J. M. Y. Simpson, and R. E. Asher (eds.), *Concise encyclopedia of language and religion* (pp. 262–264), Amsterdam: Elsevier.

Smith, Graham Hingangaroa, 1997, The development of Kaupapa Maori: Theory and praxis, unpublished Ph.D. dissertation, University of Auckland, Auckland, New Zealand.

Someya, Hiroko, 2002, Writing on signs. In Yoshifumi Tobita and Takeyoshi Sato (eds.), *Modern Japanese course* (Vol. VI: *Letters and writing*, pp. 221–243), Tokyo: Meijishoin.

Spencer, Patricia E. and Marschak, Marc, 2003, Cochlear implants: Issues and implications. In Marc Marschak and Patricia E. Spencer (eds.), *Oxford handbook of deaf studies, language and education* (pp. 434–448). New York: Oxford University Press.

Spolsky, Bernard, 1970, Navajo language maintenance: six-year-olds in 1969, *Language Sciences* 13: 19–24.

1974, The Navajo Reading Study: An illustration of the scope and nature of educational linguistics. In J. Quistgaard, H. Schwarz, and H. Spong-Hanssen (eds.), *Applied linguistics: Problems and solutions: Proceedings of the Third Congress on Applied Linguistics, Copenhagen, 1972* (Vol. III, pp. 553–565), Heidelberg: Julius Gros Verlag.

1981, Bilingualism and biliteracy, *The Canadian Modern Language Review* 37: 475–485.

1983, Triglossia and literacy in Jewish Palestine of the first century, *International Journal of the Sociology of Language* 42: 95–110.

1989, Maori bilingual education and language revitalization, *Journal of Multilingual and Multicultural Development* 9(6): 1–18.

1991a, Control and democratization of sacred literacy. In Samuel Rodin (ed.), *Encounters with Judaism: Jewish studies in a non-Jewish world* (pp. 37–53), Hamilton: Waikato University and Colcom Press.

1991b, Hebrew language revitalization within a general theory of second language learning. In Robert L. Cooper and Bernard Spolsky (eds.), *The influence of language on culture and thought: Essays in honor of Joshua A. Fishman's sixty-fifth birthday* (pp. 137–155), Berlin: Mouton de Gruyter.

1991c, The Samoan language in the New Zealand educational context, *Vox* 5: 31–36.

1995a, Conditions for language revitalization: A comparison of the cases of Hebrew and Maori, *Current Issues in Language and Society* 2(3): 177–201.

1995b, *Measured words: The development of objective language testing*, Oxford: Oxford University Press.

1996, Hebrew and Israeli identity. In Yasir Suleiman (ed.), *Language and identity in the Middle East and North Africa* (pp. 181–191), London: Curzon Press.

2002a, Norms, native speakers and reversing language shift. In Sue Gass, Kathleen Bardovi-Harlig, Sally Sieloff Magnan, and Joel Walz (eds.), *Pedagogical norms for second and foreign language and teaching: Studies in honour of Albert Valdman* (pp. 41–58), Amsterdam and Philadelphia: John Benjamins Publishing Company.

2002b, Prospects for the survival of the Navajo language: A reconsideration, *Anthropology & Education Quarterly* 33(2): 1–24.

2003a, Reassessing Maori regeneration, *Language in Society* 32(4): 553–578.

2003b, Religion as a site of language contact, *Annual Review of Applied Linguistics* 23: 81–94.

2004, *Language policy*, Cambridge: Cambridge University Press.

2006, Does the US need a language policy, or is English enough? Language policies in the US and beyond. In Audrey Heining-Boynton (ed.), *ACTFL 2005–2015: Realizing our vision of languages for all* (pp. 15–38), Upper Saddle River, NJ: Pearson Education.

2007, Riding the tiger. In Nancy Hornberger (ed.), *Can schools save indigenous languages?* (pp. 152–160), Basingstoke: Palgrave Macmillan.

2008, Prolegomena to a sociolinguistic theory of public signage. In Elana Shohamy and Durk Gorter (eds.), *The linguistic landscape: Expanding the scenery*, London: Routledge.

Spolsky, Bernard and Amara, Muhammad Hasan, 1986, The diffusion and integration of Hebrew and English lexical items in the spoken Arabic of an Israeli village, *Anthropological Linguistics* 28: 43–54.

Spolsky, Bernard and Cooper, Robert L., 1991, *The languages of Jerusalem*, Oxford: Clarendon Press.

Spolsky, Bernard and Holm, Wayne, 1971, *Literacy in the vernacular: The case of Navajo*, Washington DC: United States Bureau of Indian Affairs.

1973, Literacy in the vernacular: The case of Navajo. In Ralph W. Jr. Ewton and Jacob Ornstein (eds.), *Studies in language and linguistics, 1972–3* (pp. 239–251), El Paso: University of Texas at El Paso Press.

Spolsky, Bernard and Shohamy, Elana, 1999, *The languages of Israel: Policy, ideology and practice*, Clevedon, UK: Multilingual Matters.

2001, Hebrew after a century of RLS efforts. In Joshua A. Fishman (ed.), *Can threatened languages be saved?* (pp. 349–362), Clevedon, UK: Multilingual Matters Ltd.

Spolsky, Bernard, Engelbrecht, Guillermina, and Ortiz, Leroy, 1983, Religious, political, and educational factors in the development of biliteracy in the Kingdom of Tonga, *Journal of Multilingual and Multicultural Development* 4(6): 459–470.

Spolsky, Ellen, 2001, *Satisfying skepticism: Embodied knowledge in the early modern world*, Aldershot, UK: Ashgate.

2007, *Word vs. image: Cognitive hunger in Shakespeare's England*, Basingstoke: Palgrave Macmillan.

Statistics New Zealand, 2001, *Provisional report on the 2001 Survey on the Health of the Maori Language*, Wellington: Statistics New Zealand for Te Puni Kokiri.

Stewart, William, 1968, A sociolinguistic typology for describing national multilingualism. In Joshua A. Fishman (ed.), *Readings in the sociology of language* (pp. 531–545), The Hague: Mouton.

Stotz, Daniel, 2006, Breaching the peace: Struggles around multilingualism in Switzerland, *Language Policy* 5(3): 247–265.

Strubell, Miquel, 2001, Catalan a decade later. In Joshua A. Fishman (ed.), *Can threatened languages be saved?* (pp. 260–283), Clevedon, UK: Multilingual Matters Ltd.

Suen, Hoi K. and Yu, Lan, 2006, Chronic consequences of high-stakes testing? Lessons from the Chinese Civil Service exam, *Comparative Education Review* 50(1): 46–65.

Sugirtharajah, Rasiah S., 2005, *The Bible and empire: Postcolonial explorations*, Cambridge: Cambridge University Press.

Suleiman, M. Y. I. H., 2001, Arabic linguistic tradition. In J. F. A. Sawyer and J. M. Y. Simpson (eds.), *Concise encyclopedia of language and religion* (pp. 326–336), Amsterdam: Elsevier.

Suleiman, Yasir, 1996, Language and identity in Egyptian nationalism. In Yasir Suleiman (ed.), *Language and identity in the Middle East and North Africa* (pp. 25–38), London: Curzon Press.

Sykes, Bryan, 2006, *Saxons, Vikings, and Celts: The genetic roots of Britain and Ireland* (1st American edn.), New York: W.W. Norton and Co.

Takashi, Kyoko, 1990, A sociolinguistic analysis of English borrowings in Japanese advertising texts, *World Englishes* 9(3): 327–341.

Taki, Tomonoro, 2005, Labour migration and the language barrier in contemporary Japan: The formation of a domestic language regime of a globalising state, *International Journal of the Sociology of Language* 175/176: 55–81.

Tannenbaum, Michal and Howie, Pauline, 2002, The association between language maintenance and family relations: Chinese immigrant children in Australia, *Journal of Multilingual and Multicultural Development* 23(5): 408–424.

Te Puni Kokiri, 1998, *Progress on Maori language policy* (Report), Wellington: Ministry of Maori Development.

2001, *The use of Maori in the family*, Wellington: Ministry of Maori Development.

2002, *Survey of the health of the Maori language in 2001*, Wellington: Ministry of Maori Development.

Tokyo Metropolitan Government, 1991, *Tokyo manual about official signs*, Information Liaison Council, Tokyo Metropolitan Government.

2003, *Guide for making city writing easy to understand also to foreigners*, Bureau of Citizens and Cultural Affairs, Tokyo Metropolitan Government.

Tsilevich, Boris, 2001, Development of the language legislation in the Baltic States, *MOST Journal of Multicultural Studies* 3(2): 137–154.

Tulp, Stella M., 1978, Reklame en tweetaligheid. Een onderzoek naar de geografische verspreiding van franstalige en nederlandstalige affiches in Brussel, *Taal en sociale integratie* 1: 261–288.

UNESCO Institute for Statistics, 2005, *Measuring linguistic diversity on the Internet*, Montreal, Canada: UNESCO.

US Department of Defense, 2005, *Defense language transformation roadmap*, Department of Defense.

van Els, Theo J. M., 1993, Foreign language teaching policy: Some planning issues. In Kari Sajavaara, Richard D. Lambert, Sauli Takala, and Christine A. Morfit (eds.), *National foreign language planning: Practices and prospects* (pp. 3–14), Jyväskylä, Finland: Institute for Educational Research, University of Jyväskylä.

Varennes, Fernand de, 1997, *To speak or not to speak: The rights of persons belonging to linguistic minorities* (working paper), UN Sub-committee on the Rights of Minorities.

2001, Language rights as an integral part of human rights, *MOST Journal of Multicultural Studies* 3(1): 15–25.

Vikor, Lars S., 2000, Northern Europe: Languages as prime markers of ethnic and national identity. In Stephen Barbour and Cathie Carmichael (eds.), *Language and nationalism in Europe* (pp. 105–129), Oxford and New York: Oxford University Press.

Waitangi Tribunal, 1986, *Findings of the Waitangi Tribunal relating to Te Reo Maori and a claim lodged by Huirangi Waikarapuru and Nga Kaiwhakapumau i te Reo Incorporated Society (The Wellington Board of Maori Language)*, Wellington: New Zealand Government, Waitangi Tribunal.

Wall, Diane, 2005, *The impact of high-stakes testing on classroom teaching: A case study using insights from testing and innovation theory*, Cambridge: Cambridge University Press.

Ward, Alan, 1995, *A show of justice: Racial "amalgamation" in nineteenth century New Zealand*, Auckland, New Zealand: Auckland University Press.

Warshauer, Mary E., 1966, Foreign language broadcasting. In Joshua A. Fishman (ed.), *Language loyalty in the United States: The maintenance and perpetuation of non-English mother tongues by American ethnic and religious groups* (pp. 74–91), The Hague: Mouton.

Watson-Gegeo, Katherine Anne and Gegeo, David W., 1986, Calling out and repeating routines in Kwara'ae children's language socialization. In Bambi B. Schieffelin and Elinor Ochs (eds.), *Language socialization across cultures* (pp. 17–50), Cambridge: Cambridge University Press.

Watts, Duncan J., 2007, A twenty-first century science, *Nature* 445(7127): 489.

Wee, Lionel, 2007, Linguistic human rights and mobility, *Journal of Multilingual and Multicultural Development* 28(4): 325–338.

Weeks, F. F. and Strevens, Peter, 1984, *Seaspeak reference manual: Essential English for international maritime use*, Oxford: Pergamon.

Weeks, Theodore R., 2002, Religion and Russification: Russian language in the Catholic churches of the "Northwest Provinces" after 1863, *Kritika: Explorations in Russian and Eurasian History* 2(1): 87–110.

Wei, Li, 2005, Starting from the right place: Introduction to the special issue on Conversational Code-Switching, *Journal of Pragmatics* 37(3): 275–279.

Weinreich, Max, 1980, *History of the Yiddish language* (trans. Joshua A. Fishman and Shlomo Noble), Chicago: University of Chicago Press.

Weinstein, Brian, 1989, Francophonie: Purism at the international level. In Björn Jernudd and Michael J. Shapiro (eds.), *The politics of language purism* (pp. 53–80), Berlin and New York: Mouton de Gruyter.

Wenzel, Veronika, 1996, Reclame en tweetaligheid in Brussel. In Vrije universiteit Brussel (ed.), *Brusselse thema's 3* (pp. 45–74), Brussels: Vrije universiteit Brussel.

Wieselter, Leon, 1998, *Kaddish*, New York: Alfred A. Knopf.

Wikipedia Foundation. *Wikipedia – The Free Encyclopedia*, from http://en.wikipedia.org/wiki.

Willemyns, Roland, 1993, Integration versus particularism: The undeclared issue at the first "Dutch Congress" in 1849. In Joshua A. Fishman (ed.), *The earliest stage of language planning: The "First Congress" phenomenon* (pp. 69–83), Berlin: Mouton de Gruyter.

Williams, Ashley M., 2005, Fighting words and challenging expectations: Language alternation and social roles in a family dispute, *Journal of Pragmatics*, 37(3): 317–328.

Williams, Colin H., 2007, When Mandarin gates yield, paper presented at Babel in Reverse: Language Ideology in the 21st Century conference, Duisburg.

2008, *Linguistic minorities in democratic context*, Basingstoke and New York: Palgrave Macmillan.

Williams, Nicholas, 1997, *Clappya Kernowek: An introduction to Unified Cornish revised*, Portreath, UK: Agan Tavas, the Society for the Promotion of the Cornish language.

Woods, Anya, 2002, June, *The role of language in some ethnic churches in Melbourne*, Paper presented at the Colloquium on The Sociology of Language and Religion, University of Surrey Roehampton.

Wright, Sue Ellen, 2001, Language and power: Background to the debate on linguistic rights. *MOST Journal of Multicultural Studies* 3(1): 44–54.

Yerendé, Eva, 2005, Ideologies of language and schooling in Guinea-Conakry: A postcolonial experience. In Birgit Brock-Utne and Rodney Kofu Hopson (eds.), *Languages of instruction for African emancipation: Focus on postcolonial contexts and considerations* (pp. 199–230), Cape Town, South Africa and Dar es Salaam, Tanzania: The Centre for Advanced Studies of African Society and Mkuki na Nyota Publishers.

Young, Robert W., 1977, Written Navajo: A brief history. In Joshua A. Fishman (ed.), *Advances in the creation and revision of writing systems* (pp. 459–470), The Hague and Paris: Mouton.

1978, *A political history of the Navajo Tribe*, Tsaile, Navajo Nation: Navajo Community College Press.

Zondag, Koen, 1987, "This morning the church presents comedy": Some aspects of Frisian in the religious domain, *International Journal of the Sociology of Language* 64: 71–80.

Index

Aasen, Ivar, 190
Abbasid caliphs, 45
Acadèmia Valenciana de la Llengua, 237
Académie française, 235, 236
Accademia del Crusca, 235
accommodation, speech, 11, 250
Act of Union, 215
Adalah, 190
admission criteria, 111, 112
  language proficiency, 112
  Québec, 113
  Sweden, 113
advertising
  language choice, 63, 72
Afghanistan, 141, 143
Africa
  bilingual nations, 152
African languages, 41, 57, 84, 103, 177
Afrikaans, 8, 57, 84, 117, 194, 195, 256
agencies
  summary, 259
agency, 70
  manager, 13
air–ground radio telephony, 63
airliner crash, 54
Akademio de Esperanto, 238
Åland
  linguistic autonomy, 155
Albania
  language laws, 166
Algeria
  language laws, 166
Alliance française, 107
American Bible Society, 42
American Council of Learned Societies, 138
American Samoa, 111
Americanization, 197
Amish, 52
  language loyalty, 37, 197
  local schools, 96
Anderson, Chris
  The long tail concept, 66

Andorra
  language law, 166
answering services, 85
Arabic
  Algeria, 166
  in Asia, 46
  colloquial used for chat, 87
  colloquial varieties and vernacular, 100
  diglossia, 47
  and Islam, 31, 45, 46
  in Israel, 77, 106, 148, 190, 226; medium
    of instruction, 218; newspapers, 77;
    signs, 68
  Judeo-Arabic, 23
  lingua franca, 45
  linguistic tradition, 45
  Modern Standard, 100
  national, 32
  North African, 38
  official, 45, 149; official in
    Palestine, 187
  Pakistan education, 46
  Palestinian, 27
  purism, 45
  Qur'anic, 47
  sacred, 45
  signs in Israel, 173
  spread, 45, 177, 183
  teaching, 47, 90, 106, 143, 196
  Tunisian, 18
  United Nations, 210
  vernaculars, 47
Arabic Language Academy
  Israel, 167
Arabicization, 152, 177
  in North Africa, 104
Aragón, 237
Aramaic
  imperial language, 33
  in Jewish law, 34
  New Testament, 38
  translation of sacred text, 35

291